# THE NEIGHBORS OF
# CASAS GRANDES

# THE NEIGHBORS OF CASAS GRANDES

## Excavating Medio Period Communities of Northwest Chihuahua, Mexico

**Michael E. Whalen and Paul E. Minnis**

The University of Arizona Press
Tucson

The University of Arizona Press
© 2009 The Arizona Board of Regents
All rights reserved

www.uapress.arizona.edu

Library of Congress Cataloging-in-Publication Data
Whalen, Michael E.
The neighbors of Casas Grandes : excavating medio period communities of northwest
Chihuahua, Mexico / by Michael E. Whalen and Paul E. Minnis.
p.  cm.
Includes bibliographical references and index.
ISBN 978-0-8165-2760-1 (hardcover : alk. paper)
1. Casas Grandes Region (Mexico)—Antiquities.  2. Indians of Mexico—Mexico—Casas
Grandes Region—Antiquities.  3. Excavations (Archaeology)—Mexico—Casas Grandes
Region.  4. Indian pottery—Mexico—Casas Grandes Region.  5. Pottery, Prehistoric—Mexico—
Casas Grandes Region.  I. Minnis, Paul E.  II. Title.
F1219.1.C3W533 2009
972′.16—dc22          2008053298

♻

Manufactured in the United States of America on acid-free, archival-quality paper containing a
minimum of 30 percent post-consumer waste and processed chlorine free.

14   13   12   11   10   09      6   5   4   3   2   1

*Dedicado a Profesor Julián Alejandro Hernández Chávez,
nuestro amigo y estimado colega.*

# CONTENTS

# FIGURES

# TABLES

# ACKNOWLEDGMENTS

The work reported upon in this volume began in 1996, ultimately extending over five field seasons and one summer of laboratory work. Like every large project, this one resulted from the support, cooperation, and hard work of many institutions and people. Support for the 1996 excavations at sites 231 and 317 was provided by two grants, one from the J. M. Kaplan Fund for Latin American Research and one from the National Geographic Society. Both grants were made to Minnis at the University of Oklahoma. The 1998 dig at site 242 was funded by a second grant from the National Geographic Society, made to Whalen at the University of Tulsa. The three-season (2000–2002) dig at site 204 was supported by National Science Foundation Grant SBR-0001306, made jointly to the authors at the Universities of Tulsa and Oklahoma. The 2004 analytical season was supported by grants from the University of Tulsa Office of Research and from the James W. Whalen Memorial Fund. Our thanks go to all of these institutions for their generosity.

In Mexico, authorizations to conduct the work were issued by the Instituto Nacional de Antropología e Historia. The Consejo de Arqueología reviewed our proposals and reports at the beginning and end of each field season. At the state level, the Centro INAH Chihuahua monitored the projects, gave us official letters of introduction to local officials, and facilitated the work in many other ways. Two successive directors of the Chihuahua center, Antrop. José Luis Perrea González and Antrop. Elsa Rodríguez García, deserve special thanks for their unfailingly generous assistance with all of the official aspects of the projects. In Casas Grandes, two successive directors of the INAH Museo de las Culturas del Norte, Arq. José Luis Punzo Díaz and Arq. Mercedes Jiménez del Arco, most generously opened their institution to us, providing work areas, storage, fax machine access, and a setting for a series of pleasant and productive research conferences. In Casas Grandes Mtro. Eduardo Gamboa Carrera, archaeologist in charge of the site of Paquimé, always found space for us to store our equipment and artifacts. We enjoyed many stimulating discussions with the archaeologists of the Chihuahua INAH Center, including Eduardo Gamboa, Rafael Cruz, Francisco Mendiola and Arturo Guevara. We are greatly indebted to all of our Mexican colleagues for their friendship, collegiality, and unstinting efforts on our behalf.

At home, the Universities of Tulsa and Oklahoma provided us with the many facilities needed for proposal and report writing, data analysis, and manuscript preparation. A field vehicle was provided free of charge for all six seasons by the University of Tulsa. Two small grants from the University of Tulsa Office of Research helped to pay for part of the shell and bone analyses, as well as a few extra radiocarbon dates. The Dean's Office of the Henry Kendall College of Arts and Sciences assisted the project by paying the Mexican government's 15 percent curation fee for the 1998 field season.

The U.S. base for our work was El Paso, Texas, where we assembled crews, organized equipment, and transacted all kinds of business before and after each field season. As they have done since the beginning of our work in Chihuahua in 1989, Bonnie and Bill Whalen and Nancy and Rudy Barreda provided an invaluable local support network.

The Whalen guest house was always available for transient archaeologists, and heavy use was made of it. The constant availability of this base of operations enormously facilitated the projects.

No analysis can be better than the field and laboratory work that underlies it, and the highest standards of professional performance were maintained by our crews. More than 60 archaeology students from the United States, Canada, Mexico, and Europe worked in the field and laboratories, and each is listed here with the year(s) of participation: Jesús Antono (1998), Jamie Arbolino (1996), Elizabeth Bagwell (2000), Rudi Benskin (1996), Sean Bergin (2004), Michael Boyd (2001), Matthew Brady (1998), Chris Brooks (1998), Jessica Burgett (2000–02), Cassandra Burns (2001), Michael Cannon (1996), Casey Carmichael (2001), Hillary Chester (1996), Carla Córdova (2000), Tom Cowan (2001), Susan Curtiss (2000), Cristina Dawson (1996), Margaret Dew (2002), Reza Diamond (1996), Amber Earley (2000–02), Jason Earls (2002), Travis Ellison (2002), Michael Etnier (1996), Deborah Ferguson (1996), John Fogg (1998), Sarah Ford (2001–02), Dawn Frost (1996), Emiliano Gallaga (1998), Natalie Godwin (1996), Nicole Hamm (2004), Abby Holeman (2000–01, 2004), Ryan Howell (2000–04), Jeanna Jones (2000–02), Karen Kueteman (1998), M. Patricia Lee (1998–2001), Arthur MacWilliams (1998), Carmen Magareños (1998), Arturo Marquez-Alameda (1996), Michael McKay (2001–02), Eric Menzel (1998), Aaron Minnis (1996), Nancy Morán (2001), Isabella Muntz (2000), Constance Murry (1998), Jillian Newell (1998), Jennifer Nisengard (1998), Brandy Orr (1998), Todd Pitezel (1998–2004), Henrike Prinz (2000), Susan de Quevedo (2002), Karen Rebnegger (1998, 2000), Juan Cristián Rodríguez (2001–02), Ryan Rowles (2001–02), Jay Smith (2001), Iris Spaargaren (2000), Heather Szarka (2000–02), Yanina Valdos (2002), Paulina Van Hout (2000), Victoria Vargas (1996, 2000), César Vásquez (2002), Lorena Vásquez (2002), and Alice Yao (2002).

The four sites reported upon in this volume lay on lands with diverse ownership patterns. Sites 231 and 242 were, respectively, on the lands of the Ejidos of San Diego and Mata Ortiz, and both are parts of the Municipio of Casas Grandes. We are most appreciative of the cooperation of municipal and ejido officials and of the citizens of these localities. In contrast, sites 231 and 204 lay on privately owned land. Mr. Ray Whetten of Colonia Juárez allowed us to work on site 317. Site 204 is part of the Rancho El Quemado, and its owner, Sr. Alberto Varrela Q., also of Colonia Juárez, authorized our three-season dig there. The Whetten and Varrela families frequently visited the excavations, and they always made us feel most welcome on their properties. The research could not have been conducted without these generous permissions, and we owe these landowners a great debt of gratitude.

Prof. Julián Hernández Chávez, director of the Escuela Preparatoria Francisco Villa in the city of Nuevo Casas Grandes, has been the bedrock of our local support since the inception of our work in 1989. He was instrumental in securing ejido permission for us to work on site 242, he provided secure storage at his home for a mountain of project equipment, and he assisted us in many other ways too numerous to list here. It would be impossible to overstate the value of Prof. Hernández's contributions to all our work in Chihuahua.

Finally, we most respectfully acknowledge the work of the late Dr. Charles C. Di Peso, the late Mtro. Eduardo Contreras, and all of their Mexican and North American colleagues of the Joint Casas Grandes Project. Their extensive and detailed analyses and typologies of the vast body of excavation data from Casas Grandes and neighboring sites form the essential base from which our work began.

# THE NEIGHBORS OF
# CASAS GRANDES

# 1

## Investigating the Casas Grandes Regional System

Existing literature contains a good deal of discussion of middle-range, mid-level, or intermediate societies, also known as chiefdoms (e.g., R. Beck 2003; Curet 2003; Drennan 1995; Earle 1997; Feinman and Neitzel 1984; Johnson and Earle 2000; Lesure and Blake 2002). These are medium-sized entities that have left behind acephalousness, egalitarianism, and consensus-based decision making while still lacking the most elaborate refinements of social and political structure. Nevertheless, they characteristically organize regional populations in the thousands, and they contain some degree of heritable social ranking and economic stratification. The power of their leaders is highly variable, however, as is the extent of the control that these leaders are able to exert over regional populations.

In the simplest case, chiefs are not able to control many aspects of social and economic life. Instead, they operate by manipulating the symbols of power and by negotiating their social positions through use of these symbols. The regional systems associated with these emergent mid-level societies, predictably, have relatively low levels of structure and centralization. At the other end of the spectrum, chiefly authority and power are extensive, resting on firm control of a society's economy, ideology, and military force. Regional systems in these developed chiefdoms are likely to show high levels of centralization and organization. Earle (1997) illustrates the variability in chiefdoms, using archaeological and ethnohistoric data to present three cases of increasingly extensive and solidly grounded chiefly authority in prehistoric Denmark, prehistoric Peru, and aboriginal Hawaii. This study underscores the validity of Drennan's (1995) contention that to classify a society as a chiefdom does not conclude the investigative process, but merely begins it. All of the highly variable details of its operation remain to be specified.

Archaeologists have long been aware that some late prehistoric societies in North America developed significant levels of sociopolitical complexity and regional organization. Nevertheless, such systems in prehistoric North America clearly were not of the scale found among the complex societies of neighboring Mesoamerica, nor were there as many. Often-discussed examples are the Chaco and Hohokam cultures of the southwestern United States and the Mississippian societies of the U.S. Southeast. There is, however, another complex late prehistoric polity that developed in the same region as the Chacoan and Hohokam cultures but has been much less intensively studied than its neighbors. Casas Grandes, also known as Paquimé, is located in northwestern Chihuahua, Mexico (fig. 1.1).

**Figure 1.1** Northwestern Mexico and the U.S. Southwest. The prehistoric cultures discussed in this volume are shown in italics. The mountain symbols mark the Sierra Madre Occidental.

Casas Grandes is recognized as the center of one of the major regional systems of the U.S. Southwest and northern Mexico (e.g., Lekson 1999, 2002; Riley 2005; Schaafsma and Riley 1999; Whalen and Minnis 2001a, 2003; Wilcox 1999). The community is best known through the excavations of the Joint Casas Grandes Project between 1958 and 1961 (Di Peso 1974: vols. 1–3; Di Peso, Rinaldo, and Fenner: vols. 4–8). Despite its acknowledged status, Casas Grandes continues to play a small role in current discussions of sociopolitical development north of Mesoamerica. The problem is that Casas Grandes has to date been studied at a level so far below what has been achieved among its northern neighbors that it scarcely can be discussed in the same terms. Fortunately, work by a number of archaeologists in recent years has begun to remedy this situation. The present volume presents our latest efforts.

The plan of the volume is as follows. The first part of the present chapter will pose some still-unanswered questions about the history and structure of the Casas Grandes regional system, while the second part will introduce the sites to be analyzed in consideration of these questions. The sites studied here represent a range of types, including one of the largest communities in the region, two small villages of the sort in which most of the region's population lived, and a small administrative center. Succeeding chapters consider the chronologies, architecture, and artifacts of these communities. The analytical results provide the data for an examination of the structure and dynamics of this part of the Casas Grandes polity in the final chapter.

## Previous Settlement Pattern Research

Our work in Chihuahua began with a reconnaissance survey in 1989. Building on this, we conducted an intensive settlement pattern survey in 1994 and 1995 at a range of distances around Casas Grandes. The object of this work was to study the regional system that formed there during the Medio period (now dated to ca. A.D. 1200–1450). Di Peso defined the Medio period as the apogee of the center's development, and also as the time of its decline. Relying largely on the intensive survey data, we presented a model of the structure and organization of the Casas Grandes regional system (Whalen and Minnis 2001a). The discussion that follows is summarized from this source. The survey recorded more than 300 Medio period sites. Most were small or medium-sized communities, although a few were large. Casas Grandes is many times the size of the next largest community, making it indisputably the primate center of the region. Analyses of these settlement pattern data permitted definition of several interaction zones at increasing distances around the primate center of Casas Grandes.

An inner zone, containing about half of the recorded sites, lies within ca. 30 km from the primate center. It will be referred to as the Core Zone in the present study. The region's largest average site size was found here, although all of our Core Zone survey units contained a range of small to large communities. The average distance of small or medium-sized sites from a large one was 2.5 km, so that large Medio settlements were close to their smaller neighbors all over the Core Zone. This is suggestive of some degree of settlement system organization under the assumption that the sites were contemporaneous and that large settlements discharged more administrative functions than did smaller ones. Present on and around Core Zone sites were large ovens, agricultural terraces, ball courts, and the stone doors of birdcages, where macaws and other parrots presumably were kept for their plumes. Some of these facilities, namely ball courts, birdcages, and large ovens were arguably used in such social-integrative activities as ritual contests, public feasting, and prestige goods production. Numerous agricultural terraces showed intensification of agricultural production in the Core Zone. Long-distance trade in exotic materials and items was evident here, as was the production of exotica using items and materials procured from afar. Figure 1.2 shows an aerial view of the part of the Core Zone that contains all of the sites and areas discussed in this volume.

Beyond the Core Zone, ca. 30–90 km from Casas Grandes is a near-periphery that we termed the Middle Zone. About half of the survey sites were recorded here. The

**Figure 1.2** Locations of the sites and areas discussed in this volume. Site 204 is 17 km in a straight line from Casas Grandes.

domestic architecture and the ceramic assemblage were similar to those of the Core Zone. Nevertheless, a number of conspicuous Core Zone features were rare or absent. Although large sites were present in the Middle Zone, all of them clustered on the eastern edge of the survey area, in the upper Casas Grandes River valley and away from most of the area's small and medium-sized settlements. Average distance of a small or medium-sized community to a large one in the Middle Zone was 15 km, or about six times the Core Zone average of 2.5 km, and many small and medium Middle Zone settlements lay 25–35 km from the nearest large settlement. Middle Zone settlements appear to have been simpler than their Core Zone counterparts. Utilitarian facilities like small ovens were common in the Middle Zone, but ball courts, birdcages, extensive upland agricultural terrace systems, and large ovens were all rare or absent. Finally, relative to the Core Zone, the diversity of imported ceramics was small in the Middle Zone.

Our premise is that the Core Zone was the most organized part of the Casas Grandes regional system. Some of the control strategies that existed here can be posited in general terms from the strongly primate nature of the settlement system. We expect, for instance, that wealth, authority, and many of the society's elite people would have been concentrated in the primate center of Casas Grandes and, perhaps, in a few other large communities. The elite of the primate center are also expected to have exerted a substantial degree of control over the regional economy and over long-distance trade. The presence of public architecture in a community is another widely recognized indication that local leaders were able to recruit labor and gather resources for communal activities. The fact that Casas Grandes has the greatest diversity and amount of public architecture of any known prehistoric community in northern Mexico and the U.S. Southwest certainly implies a significant degree of centralization of authority and control over labor and resources.

Beyond these generalizations, we must inquire further into the specific processes by which elite political entrepreneurs at Casas Grandes established and perpetuated their authority. Timothy Earle (1997) recognizes several sources of power in mid-level societies that can be summed up under economic, ideological, and military headings. The highly variable ways of combining these power sources he terms "power strategies." Earle expects these to be variable in different environments and under diverse historical circumstances, thereby producing many evolutionary trajectories. Earle further asserts that all three power sources are unlikely to be used with equal effectiveness in mid-level societies, as they are diffuse and thus hard to monopolize with uniform efficiency. In the Casas Grandes case, we argue that elite authority was derived and perpetuated by control of two of the three power sources just mentioned: a political economy and a regional ideology. Conflict is believed to have existed in the Casas Grandes regional system, and Riley (2005:146–48) provides a summary of the evidence for this. Nevertheless, military force does not seem to us to have played a major role in the organization and integration of the polity.

We see several components to the political economy. The first of these is distribution of prestige goods of a range of qualities, from parrots and their plumes to simply finished ornaments of common (and therefore relatively cheap) marine shells. Procurement of exotica requires long-distance trade, for which there is ample evidence at Casas Grandes. In the manner of primate centers, we presume that Casas Grandes either monopolized or at least dominated this trade and the craft activities that were based upon it. In either case, the elite of the primate center would have been able to exert significant control over the quantities of prestige goods in circulation. Specialized production of a range of nonexotic items is also seen at Casas Grandes. Minnis (1988) argued for specialization in the production of turkeys and in agave processing. VanPool and Leonard (2002) see the Type IA basalt metates as the products of specialists, and Sphren (2003) considers the most elaborate and finely made of the polychrome ceramics to be of specialist manufacture. We still do not understand how these productive activities were organized or to what extent their control was centralized. Even so, Casas Grandes seems to have been the major economic powerhouse of its region.

A second evident control strategy is mobilization of Core Zone agricultural productivity through construction of large systems of terraces and canals. Some of this productive intensification seems to have been accomplished through the establishment of Casas Grandes–type settlements in upland areas, as exemplified by site 242 (Whalen and Minnis 2001b; Minnis, Whalen, and Howell 2006). Refer to figure 1.2 for the site's location. In this volume, we argue that communities like site 242 were administrative satellites under the direct control of Casas Grandes. Other productive intensification was apparently done within local Core Zone settlement clusters, which are likely to have been subordinate to Casas Grandes. This productive intensification all over the Core Zone likely is an indication of the ability of the primate center to mobilize surplus agricultural productivity over a wide area. This mobilization, in turn, would have provided the primate center with significant resources to invest in a variety of integrative activities.

A regional ideology, or a construct of symbols and meanings that was critical to the formation and perpetuation of a social order at a supra-local scale, is reflected in the wide use of ritual architecture and, presumably, performance of the associated ceremonial activities. Ball courts are widespread over the Core Zone, and every settlement lay within a few kilometers of a court. Some courts were attached to settlements, but there were also isolated courts that apparently served a number of smaller, scattered settlements. The Core Zone's ball courts, then, are seen as adding powerful ritual overtones to a wide range of social, economic, and ceremonial activities. Finally, many authors (e.g., Moulard 2005; Rakita 2001; Townsend 2005; VanPool and VanPool 2007; Whalen and Minnis 2001a) have noted the likely existence of some type of regional cult reflected in the symbols used on Ramos Polychrome pottery, a ware closely associated with Casas Grandes. Mesoamerican motifs frequently appear here, and they seem to be components of an elite-dominated political ideology.

Our contention is that there existed within the Core Zone a set of economic, political, and ritual structures by which the primate center both supported itself and maintained authority over its neighbors. Nevertheless, a simple, uniform hegemony does not appear to have existed. For example, ball courts, macaw cages, and large ovens were not uniformly distributed within the Core Zone. None of these were recorded among Casas Grandes' near neighbors, that is, those within 10–15 km of the primate center. The center itself, however, had the region's largest and most elaborate set of courts, cages, and large ovens. It appears, then, that Casas Grandes absorbed from its nearest neighbors many of the social, political, and economic functions that were linked to ball courts and the production of exotica.

Between 15 and 30 km from the primate center but still within the Core Zone, ball courts, birdcages, and large ovens are found at a range of small to very large Medio settlements. In this area an organizational structure involving the ball game ritual and prestige goods is clearly present, but it appears to depart from the pattern of monopoly postulated in the immediate vicinity of Casas Grandes. The distribution of ball courts provides a hint of incomplete control of the Core Zone. Extant literature shows that Late Postclassic Mesoamerican ball courts were most common in regional systems that lacked strong, centralized political control and were fragmented into competing units where there was much factional competition for power, prestige, and resources among elites of near-equal status (Santley, Berman, and Alexander 1991). Ball courts, it is argued, were stages where rivalries were played out in a ritualized context. If the

Chihuahuan courts functioned even partially as stages for personal or factional competitions, then their relative abundance among communities within about a day's walk of the primate center may indicate a high level of factional rivalry among the elites of the outer part of the Core Zone, which in turn hints at a relatively low level of political centralization within that area during at least part of the Medio period.

Another hint of incomplete control over the Core Zone was the presence of local settlement clusters that might have had some degree of autonomy from the primate center. The first of these lies in and around the Arroyo el Alamito (refer to fig. 1.2). The Alamito cluster lies on the broad piedmont slope at the foot of the Sierra Madre Occidental, some 20 km southwest of Casas Grandes. There are almost no visible room-block mounds on the piedmont slope that extends for about 5 km north of the Alamito cluster. To the south of the Alamito cluster, Medio settlements are few and far between for a distance of about 6 km. In other words, the cluster is spatially distinct. Present here is the full range of Medio settlement sizes, from small to very large. Moreover, the cluster's large and very large settlements are located in its center, and small and medium-sized settlements are scattered around them. The Alamito cluster contains all the features and facilities previously identified as likely having had organizational or integrative functions. For instance, there are four ball courts in the cluster. Macaw cage-door stones were found in three Alamito cluster settlements, attesting to a significant presence of aviculture there. Associated with a number of settlements in the Alamito cluster are the vast ovens that we have argued were large-scale food processing facilities associated with public feasting (Minnis and Whalen 2005).

Using the well-defined Alamito cluster as a model, we believe that another Core Zone settlement cluster can be defined in the Arroyo la Tinaja drainage, located about 20 km to the west of Casas Grandes (refer to fig. 1.2). The Arroyo la Tinaja is the major drainage leading from the highlands of the Sierra Madre into the lowlands around Casas Grandes. The Tinaja valley is relatively well watered, and it was clearly an area of population concentration in Medio times. The Tinaja drainage is bounded by a narrow valley, making it a well-defined spatial entity. It was found to have the same characteristics as the Alamito cluster. There was a site hierarchy headed by a single, large community, plus multiple examples of ball courts, birdcages, and large ovens.

In sum, we can recognize two spatially discrete sets of Medio settlements in the Core Zone. Each of these local settlement clusters is characterized by a wide range of settlement sizes, multiple ball courts, macaw cage-door stones that indicate the production of at least one category of exotica (plumes), large ovens which we take to be large-scale food processing facilities, and a number of *trincheras,* or low terrace systems for soil and water control. Furthermore, the Alamito and Tinaja clusters each lie about 20 km from the primate center of Casas Grandes, and the two clusters are separated from each other by about the same distance. We thus have several hints that the primate center of Casas Grandes did not exercise uniform, comprehensive control over its neighbors, even in the small Core Zone where interaction and integration were at their highest levels. This, in turn, suggests a significantly simpler kind and extent of regional organization and control than was originally proposed (e.g., Di Peso 1974: vol. 2). When we first made this interpretation, however, we regarded it as a working model, rather than as a

definitive pronouncement, and the need for more intensive investigation of a number
of specific problems was clear.

## Unresolved Issues

After the survey-based study, several questions stood out as needing further investigation. The first of these concerns the developmental histories of the primate center and
its neighbors. Resolution of this question clearly is critical to any attempt to evaluate
models of regional polity formation. We envision two rather different possible scenarios.
In the first, the large settlements of the Core Zone are all contemporaneous, reaching
their peaks in the fourteenth century, along with Casas Grandes. In this case the primate
center, which grew much larger than any of its fellows, monopolized the ceremonial,
political, and economic functions reflected, for instance, in the ball-court ritual, only
within the limit of daily interaction, or within a radius of about 15 km. Contemporaneous outliers beyond 15 km, although still influenced by the primate center, showed a
somewhat higher level of autonomy, implying a lack of centralized control.

In an alternative scenario, the largest settlements of the Core Zone were not fully
contemporaneous with the fourteenth-century peak of Casas Grandes. Instead, a group
of early Medio peer polities of the late twelfth and the thirteenth centuries—Casas
Grandes among them—all used integrative strategies that included ball courts and
such valued goods as seashell ornaments and exotic bird plumes. By the middle or late
thirteenth century, Casas Grandes gained ascendancy over its neighbors. Whether this
resulted from internal or external forces remains unclear (see Whalen and Minnis 2003
for an opinion), but in either case the community rapidly expanded to its fourteenth-
century apogee. Much of this growth was by absorption of population from the surrounding area, resulting in reduction of outlying communities. If this scenario is even
partially correct, there should have been significant changes in regional organization
and power structures between the early and late parts of the Medio period. This scenario also implies a higher level of regional control than under the former alternative.

Evaluation of these two alternatives requires that we be able to distinguish early
from late Medio occupations. Unfortunately, this cannot be done from ceramics, as
the original three phases into which Di Peso divided the Medio at Casas Grandes do
not have useable ceramic definitions (e.g., Whalen and Minnis 1996b:737). Briefly, our
tabulations from the Casas Grandes report show that the same 22 local pottery types
occur in almost the same proportions in all three phases. The primate center's ceramic
assemblage, then, appears to have limited utility for the kind of intensive seriation that
we require. Neither has our surface survey allowed us to isolate markers for any division of the Medio period. As a result, we have been unable to evaluate the two developmental models just summarized. Accordingly, succeeding chapters of this volume
devote a good deal of space to the question of a division of the Medio period into finer
chronological units. This is the essential first step in reconstructing the histories of the
primate center and its neighbors.

The second issue in urgent need of further consideration is the nature, extent, and
timing of the control that Casas Grandes was able to exert over its neighbors in the Core

Zone, where integration was evidently highest. This seems to have been a complex and multifaceted situation rather than a simple, uniform hegemony, as we have indications both of direct linkages with individual communities (like site 242) and of the existence of local polities (like the Alamito and Tinaja areas) that may have been less closely tied to the primate center. Such a situation is consistent with current thinking on the regional structures of intermediate-level societies, where negotiation, competition, and fragmented political landscapes are the norm (e.g., Blanton et al. 1996). Obviously, this situation can exist at many levels, and the task before us is specification of the extent of centralization that existed in the Core Zone, or the Casas Grandes core area.

We contend that the influence that any central place exerted over its neighbors can best be monitored by study of (a) the level of organizational complexity of the central place itself; (b) the levels of complexity maintained by neighboring settlements, especially the large ones; and (c) the extent to which the power and authority of the central place were projected into its hinterland. The work of Di Peso and his colleagues at Casas Grandes provides an extensive characterization of the central place. Our task, then, is to examine diachronically the levels of complexity maintained by the center's neighbors and to monitor the appearance among them of the signifiers of centralized power. We now turn to consideration of the methods by which these questions are to be pursued at the community level.

## Community Complexity and the Spread of Power

What continues to be an effective way to monitor community complexity was outlined and applied to prehistoric Southwest U.S. data by Lightfoot (1984). The major assumption of his study is that there should be a strong, positive association between major demographic, economic, social, and political change and the increasing complexity of decision-making hierarchies. In other words, it is the concepts of power, authority, and their distribution that are seen as critical to understanding the structures of hierarchical societies. Specifically, Lightfoot (1984:42–49) theorizes that if larger, centrally located settlements were the seats of important decision makers, then these settlements should contain a number of specific, measurable elements. First, there should be indication of "funds of power." The political activities of decision makers are characteristically financed through accumulation of both food and valued goods, and Lightfoot cites a number of studies recognizing the high positive correlation between the presence of decision-making activists and large storage space.

Second, intensification of subsistence production to fuel the funds of power should be in evidence. Archaeological indicators include shifts in cultivation patterns (as reflected in preserved plant remains), and changes in distribution and density of processing implements such as grinding stones or large jars. Similarly, processing or productive features such as large ovens or grinding facilities may also show distributional or frequency changes.

Third, important decision makers should have easier or fuller access to valued commodities in the context of prestige goods economies. This should be reflected in the archaeological record by differential distribution of such materials. Likewise, there should be differential distribution of the facilities for producing valued goods or for keeping the component raw materials.

Fourth, symbols of authority or power lie in architecture and in what has been termed the "built environment," both domestic and public. Great kivas, platform mounds, and ball courts likely were all loci for public assemblies as well as arenas for the exercise of authority in integrative and administrative activities. Domestic architecture, too, is widely recognized as an indicator of the roles and statuses of its occupants. These may be reflected in relative size and elaboration of domestic spaces, or, in some cases, in a perceptibly different technique of construction. Differences in type, size, or elaboration of residential architecture also may be apparent.

Fifth, the presence of important people in a community should be reflected and symbolized in differential mortuary treatment. Both grave goods and grave placement are significant. In short, Lightfoot (1984) advocates using the perceived level of elaboration of communities and their special facilities to gauge the power bases of local leaders who manipulate labor, goods, services, kinship, and ceremonies to serve their own ends. The evidences of this manipulation, it is plausibly argued, should take a number of specific forms and should be readily perceptible in the archaeological record.

There have been several analyses of the manifestations of power and authority in rural settlements around the great Mississippian center of Cahokia (e.g., Anderson 1994; Emerson 1997; Pauketat 2003). One of these studies (Emerson 1997:37–38) explicitly takes Lightfoot's (1984) manifestations of power and authority in individual communities as the basis of an investigation of the extent and distribution of power among Cahokia's neighbors. Despite its specific focus, Emerson's method is applicable to any mid-level society. His basic assumption is that patterns of architecture, activities, and artifacts in rural settlements should covary perceptibly with patterns and periods of elite dominance of hinterland settlements from a central place.

Emerson (1997:4) begins his inquiry by defining the "archaeology of power," or a set of visible manifestations of authority and power in a chiefdom-level settlement system. Briefly, he contends that certain forms of architecture and artifacts are signifiers of sacred and secular power. The appearance, ubiquity, and disappearance of these signifiers in a center's rural hinterland thus serve as sensitive monitors of the rise, spread, and decline of centralized power in a region. In addition, these indicators allow identification of the levels of power and authority that existed at different levels in the settlement system. A number of specific signifiers of power are identified in chiefly societies, and the ensuing discussion is summarized from Emerson (1997:37–39). First, increased political control of a rural hinterland should be marked by the appearance of specialized architecture associated with domination and control. This is termed the "architecture of power," and it can take many forms, from elaborate residences for rural elites to road systems or fortifications. To this list, we would add large-scale productive facilities: field systems, canals, or other productive enhancements built at a supra-community level and under the patronage of the elite of society. Johnson and Earle (2000) recognize control of major parts of the means of agricultural productivity as a critical aspect of chiefly power. Exotic and prestige goods form the artifactual component of the signifiers of political power. These characteristically are nonlocal, imported items, and their procurement and distribution are presumed to have been controlled by elites. Exotica and prestige goods signify the status and authority of their possessors, and they also can be distributed among followers or peers to form or reinforce the factions and alliances that are critical to chiefly power. Political power thus is signified by the spread of the architecture of power, supracommunity productive facilities, and prestige goods in a hinterland.

Leaders must rely on more than political and economic power to dominate their regions, however, and Emerson identifies the "architecture of ideology" as the second component of an expanding system of regional control. Like the architecture of power, that of ideology can take many specific forms. In general, however, it is a set of constructions associated with the ritual system of the region's main center or centers. Artifacts and architecture are signifiers of the spread of ideological power. Especially important here is what Emerson terms *sacra,* or ideologically empowered items that symbolize the precepts of the center-dominated religious system. Exotica and prestige goods may play a dual role here, as they can also function as sacred items or be the carriers of sacred symbols.

Lastly, Emerson asserts that the creation of sacred landscapes in a region can be a component of expanding centralized control. These sacred landscapes often consist of architectural forms that mirror the cosmic order in the elite-controlled religious system. Such cosmic reconstructions are assumed to exist in their largest and most elaborate forms in a region's major center or centers. For example, the Mississippian temple mound and plaza complex are seen as reconstructions of a cosmic pattern (Knight 1989). The spread of an architecture of ideology and of sacred items, and the creation of sacred landscapes in a rural countryside are taken as signifiers of the elite-controlled ideology that is one of the characteristic bases of power.

Similar arguments have been made for Chaco Canyon in the U.S. Southwest. Many scholars (e.g., papers collected by Kantner and Mahoney 2000 and by Lekson 2006) see a package of architectural and ritual elements that was projected from Chaco Canyon across the surrounding landscape. Great houses and great kivas are two of the components of this package, and both served a range of political and ritual functions. Going further, Van Dyke (2004) contends that the great houses were fundamental elements of the Chacoan symbolic landscape, reflecting and maintaining social memory, group cohesion, and cosmological order. This Chacoan effect was especially strong in the San Juan Basin, although it was projected in varying degrees to more distant outliers.

We readily concede that the extant Mississippian and Chacoan archaeological and chronometric records are far better than those of Casas Grandes, so that interpretations can be pursued at finer levels. Nevertheless, we are intrigued by the potential application of many of these concepts and methods to the Casas Grandes case, where critical issues also center on the relationships among elites, power, and ideology in a hierarchical social context. To begin thinking about the spread of power from Casas Grandes, we must first define its signifiers and then monitor their distribution over time and space. Clearly needed to pursue these goals are excavation data from a range of Medio period communities of different sizes and kinds. These data should come from the Core Zone, as our most pressing questions are focused there. Di Peso's excavations extensively described the primate center, but in the mid-1990s, little was known about its neighbors. This is the intellectual climate within which we began the excavation program that is the focus of this volume.

## The Excavation Program

Motivated by the concerns expressed in the preceding section, we began excavations in 1996 on some of the Core Zone neighbors of Casas Grandes. By 2002, four Medio period communities had been investigated in five seasons of excavation. These included one of the largest neighbors of the primate center (site 204), two small, ordinary villages (sites 231 and 317), and a small administrative center (site 242). Two of these sites (204 and 242) are ball-court communities (refer to figure 1.2 for site locations). Succeeding pages describe each site, its environmental setting, the rationale for its selection, and the work carried out there.

## The Large Community

Site 204, or the Tinaja site, is one of the two largest Core Zone neighbors of Casas Grandes. It is located in the Arroyo la Tinaja valley, some 17 km west of Casas Grandes at an elevation of about 1,640 m. The Tinaja valley (refer to fig. 1.2) is an east-west oriented river valley and is one of the major tributaries of the Piedras Verdes River, which joins the Palanganas River to form the Casas Grandes River. Explorers and archaeologists early recognized the large number of ruins in the Tinaja valley. Black-iston (1906) suggested that this valley (which he spelled "Tenaja") was a frontier pro-tecting the Casas Grandes core from marauders from the west. Later, Brand (1943:143) plausibly argued that the Tinaja valley and the adjacent Tapicitas valley were cor-ridors for communication between the Sierra Madre and the Casas Grandes region. More recently, our intensive survey in both valleys recorded a number of Medio period sites. Most of these were small to medium-sized communities, but one of the region's largest settlements is located there. It was referred to by Brand (1943) as the Upper Tinaja site, and it is identified in the present study by our survey number, 204. In addition, four ball courts were found (Whalen and Minnis 1996b, 2001a). Together, these sites and facilities form the Tinaja settlement cluster described in the preceding section of this chapter, which appears to have been an important part of the Paquimé polity.

The Arroyo la Tinaja valley is narrow and contains a seasonally flowing stream that likely carried more water in prehistoric times than it does now. The site 204 community was located at a slight narrowing of the valley, where bedrock appears to be closer to the surface than in the rest of the drainage. This may have caused a higher water table at this location, facilitating access to domestic and irrigation water. In addition, site 204 is located directly across from the pass that connects the Arroyo la Tinaja with the Pie-dras Verdes River valley, placing the community in a location suitable for controlling transit and communication between the two adjacent valleys, both of which were densely populated during the Medio period. Also significant is the presence of an *ata-laya,* a possible shrine or communication feature, on a high point across the valley from 204. This point offers a direct line of sight to Cerro Moctezuma, some 5 km distant. This is one of the region's major topographic features, near the eastern foot of which sits Casas Grandes. Figure 1.3 is an aerial view of the setting. Swanson (2003) provides

**Figure 1.3** Site 204 and its environs. The center of Casas Grandes lies just on the other side of Cerro Moctezuma. (Photo © Adriel Heisey; used by permission)

a discussion of the atalaya system in the Casas Grandes region, and Pitezel (2003, 2007) discusses Cerro Moctezuma.

Figure 1.4 shows the components of site 204. The site is dominated by a large mound that covers about 7,500 sq m and is hereafter referred to as Mound A. Construction on the west end of the mound was noticeably different than that of the central and eastern parts. Visible on the west end were rock alignments that were not so numerous or conspicuous on other parts of Mound A. These architectural remains were placed on lower ground adjoining the west end of the mound and may have been the foundations of mud-and-stick constructions that would have contrasted sharply with the substantial adobe walls of the rooms of Mound A. Two small room-block mounds are located east and west of Mound A. These are termed, respectively, Mounds B and C. We originally estimated that all three mounds together contained approximately 220 rooms, with most of these in Mound A. In addition to the room-block mounds, there is a diversity of other sorts of features at site 204. A small midden lay just north of the central portion of the main mound. A ball court of the formal I shape and a large earthen oven are prominently located west of the main mound. An additional large oven is located at the base of the hill that runs all along the north side of the main mound. Also along the hill base is a series of one-room, stone-walled structures and a long single-course stone

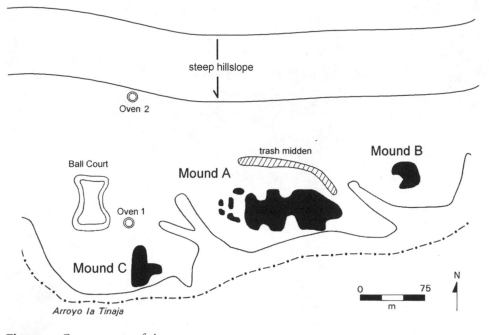

**Figure 1.4** Components of site 204.

wall. Various amorphous stone features are also present on the hillslope, as is a dense scatter of the coarse, heavy stone tools often associated with agave farming in southern Arizona (Fish, Fish, and Madsen 1992). Finally, trincheras, or low stone alignments used to retain soil and moisture for agricultural production, are ubiquitous around site 204 (Minnis, Whalen, and Howell 2006).

One of the issues that could be investigated only at a large, prominent neighbor of Casas Grandes was the question of the relative status of the head people of the outlying communities, as compared to those of the primate center. At site 204, status was expected to be reflected in architecture, features, burials, and artifacts. We planned to use these observations as a measure of the nature and extent of the control exerted by Casas Grandes over its neighbors in the outer part of the Core Zone. Based on our survey data, site 204 appeared to be an excellent choice for such an investigation. Whereas the surface assemblage at the typical Medio settlement was fairly sparse, at site 204 the surface artifact density was unusually high and diverse, including a remarkable number of fragments of vesicular basalt metates. A large fragment of the stone door of a macaw cage (see Di Peso 1974:2:427, fig. 139-2) also lay on the surface of the main mound. The site's formal, I-shaped ball court and the large oven beside it suggested a ritual and public feasting complex. In short, if there were elites anywhere in the region besides at the primate center, site 204 seemed to be a good place to seek evidence of them and to gauge their relative status. In addition, site 204 was one of the major communities whose occupational histories were expected to be of particular significance for evaluating the growth models of the Casas Grandes polity discussed in the

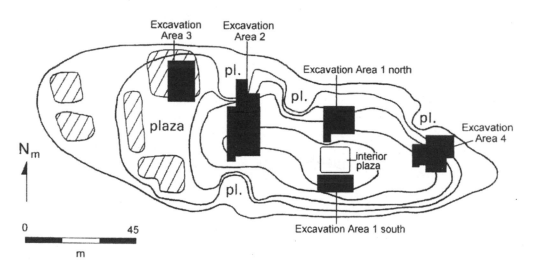

**Figure 1.5** Excavation areas on Mound A, site 204 (pl. = plaza).

preceding section of this chapter. The site had been heavily looted, as is characteristic of all the sites of northwestern Chihuahua. The vandalism was entirely hand-digging, however, so that large portions of the prehistoric deposits were expected to remain intact. Room clusters were excavated on each of the site's three mounds, although the large Mound A was the scene of the most intensive effort. Figure 1.5 shows the excavation areas.

The oldest occupation on the site is represented by two pit structures that underlay the pueblo rooms of Excavation Area 4. Pit Structure 204-1, shown in figure 1.6a, lay close beneath the overlying Medio rooms and was moderately damaged by intrusive features and by looting. The round-cornered, quadrilateral shape of the structure is unusual, and no similar examples were found among the 33 pit structures dug by Di Peso and colleagues (1974) at sites in the area. The floor area of Pit Structure 204-1 was about 7.6 sq m, and its floor was smoothly covered with several coats of fine plaster. Two small, hemispherical fire pits were placed near the center of the floor. No other features or post holes were observed. A few pieces of chipped stone were the only artifacts recovered from the fill of the structure and its features. A charcoal sample from one of the fire pits gave a date of 905 ± 35 B.P. As discussed in chapter 2, this equates to A.D. 1030–1120 (cal, 2σ).

Pit Structure 204-2 (fig. 1.6b) lay only a few meters from Structure 204-1, and it was damaged in the same way by looters' holes dug into the overlying pueblo rooms. Even so, some of the perimeter and much of the floor had survived. This clearly was a different kind of structure than the one just described. The perimeter of the 204-2 structure was formed of a solid adobe curb about 12 cm high. Its original height is unknown. The floor of the structure covered about 11 sq m, and it consisted of several layers of hard, fine plaster. This was noticeably finer material than was used on the floors and walls of the succeeding pueblo rooms. Only one floor feature was observed

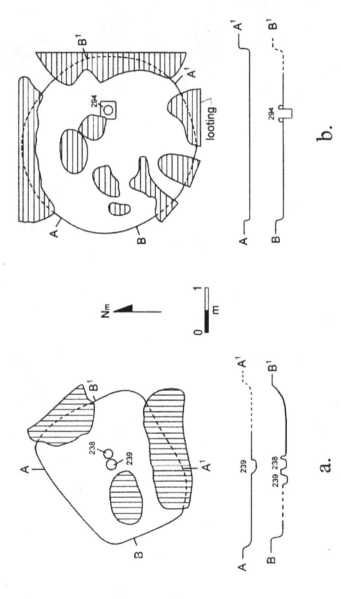

**Figure 1.6** Two pit structures underlying Mound A, site 204.

in this structure. This was a small, deep, cylindrical fire pit surrounded by a low, quadrilateral, adobe platform. It was not like the platform hearths found in the succeeding pueblo architecture, as it had no air vent or ash pit. Rather, the platform simply enclosed the fire pit and raised its mouth some 6 cm above the floor level. It is a very different feature than the simple, hemispherical fire pits present in Pit Structure 204-1 and those excavated in pit houses by the Joint Casas Grandes Project. In fact, the very fine floor and the relatively elaborate, enclosed hearth suggest a special-purpose use of Pit Structure 204-2.

Unfortunately, there were almost no artifacts in contexts clearly associated with the structure, and none of those present were temporally diagnostic. A good charcoal sample was secured from the bottom of the enclosed hearth, however. This dated to 990 ± 30 B.P., or A.D. 980–1160 (cal., 2σ). This is very close to the date of the nearby Pit Structure 204-1, and analysis presented in chapter 2 shows that the two dates are statistically indistinguishable. They were therefore averaged to A.D. 1030–1160 (cal., 2σ). Both of the 204 pit structures fall into the late part of the Viejo period, and they closely predate the site's early Medio period occupation (which we believe began in the mid- to late 1100s rather than at the commonly accepted date of 1200).

The pueblo rooms of site 204 were the focus of excavation. A set of 10 rooms (Area 1) and another group of 9 (Area 2) were dug in a major effort in the central part of Mound A (figs. 1.7 and 1.8). On the west end of Mound A (Area 3), four rooms and a portion of a plaza were investigated among the low mounds that had been thought to be the remains of insubstantial mud-and-stick structures. Instead, we found adobe-walled rooms of the standard type, which are shown in figure 1.9. On the east end of the mound (Area 4), we dug eight rooms that had the poorest construction seen at the site (fig. 1.10). Wall footings were shallow and insubstantial, and large cracks had formed in some of the poorly supported walls. These rooms yielded late dates, suggesting that they represent the end of the site's occupation. Smaller excavations were done on Mounds B and C, each of which had three rooms dug (figs. 1.11 and 1.12).

There were two large ovens at site 204, both of which were investigated. Our intensive survey found ovens of this sort on 25 Medio period sites and an additional 18 were recorded at isolated localities. All are in the Core Zone. The excavated sample of 11 ovens includes five from Casas Grandes (Di Peso, Rinaldo, and Fenner 1974:4:274–76), one from site 236 (Sayles 1936b:36), one each from sites 239, 257, and 317 (Whalen and Minnis 1997), and two reported here from site 204. The Casas Grandes report termed them "conical pit-ovens" (Di Peso, Rinaldo, and Fenner 1974:4:274). The term is appropriate, as all of the excavated ovens were shaped like inverted, truncated cones. The mouths of these ovens usually were surrounded by a ring of scattered, fire-cracked rock, and this ring often was their most conspicuous surface characteristic. This rock debris is presumed to be material removed from the oven to ready it for its next use. At Casas Grandes, debris removed from four of the ovens in Medio times was piled into a mound 2 m high and 16 m in diameter. Their walls were lined with stones set in adobe mortar. In some cases, the mortar was spread to form a plaster over the stones, whereas in others it was not. The stone linings did not extend to the lowest parts of the ovens, where the unlined walls sometimes were plastered and at other times were bare earth.

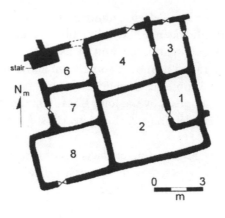

**a.**

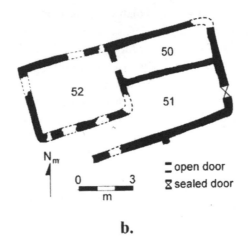

**b.**

**Figure 1.7** Rooms in Excavation Area 1, Mound A, site 204. The rooms labeled *a* are from Excavation Unit 1 north, and the *b* rooms are from Excavation Unit 1 south.

Every excavated oven was filled with a large quantity of fire-cracked rock and charcoal-laden soil. High temperatures obviously were generated in these ovens, as the rocks lining the walls were severely fire-cracked, and some of the adobe mortar was nearly vitrified. Drawings of some of the Casas Grandes ovens are provided in the site report (Di Peso, Rinaldo, and Fenner 1974:4:276, 468). The oven from site 239 is illustrated elsewhere (Whalen and Minnis 2001a:127). Figure 1.13 shows the two conical pit-ovens from site 204 and one from site 317.

Table 1.1 gives the dimensions and volumes of 10 of the excavated conical pit-ovens. The eleventh, dug long ago by Sayles (1936b:36) could not be included here, as its dimensions were not provided. It is clear from the table that the conical pit-ovens at

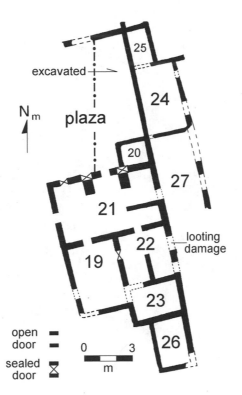

**Figure 1.8** Rooms in Excavation Area 2, Mound A, site 204.

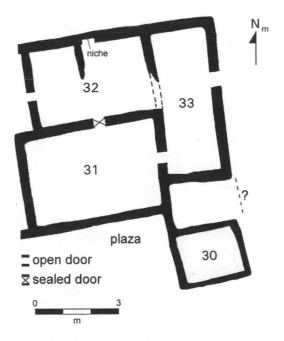

**Figure 1.9** Rooms in Excavation Area 3, Mound A, site 204.

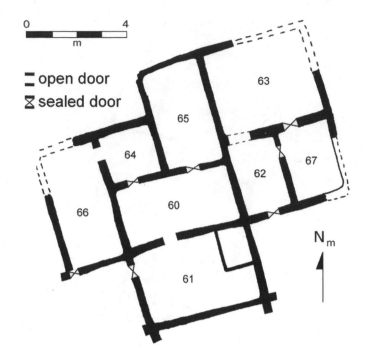

**Figure 1.10** Rooms in Excavation Area 4, Mound A, site 204.

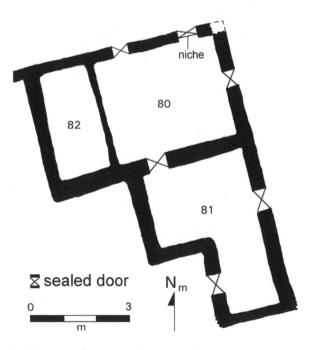

**Figure 1.11** Rooms in the Mound B excavation area, site 204.

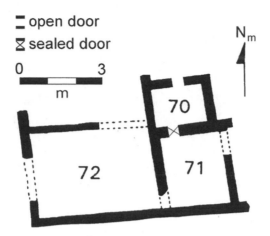

**Figure 1.12** Rooms in the Mound C excavation area, site 204.

Casas Grandes were by far the largest in the present sample. One of them (CG 1-9) is extremely large. It lies beside the Mound of the Heroes and is the only one at the primate center to be associated with a platform mound. All of the conical pit-ovens from the neighboring sites were much smaller than those at Casas Grandes. Although the ovens in this sample differ in size and in some construction details, they are alike enough to form a well-defined class. We have interpreted them as facilities for baking agave (Minnis and Whalen 2005), and chapter 7 continues this discussion. In this view, the conical pit-ovens are very large-scale facilities that likely provided food for public feasting (Whalen and Minnis 2001a; Minnis and Whalen 2005).

The final major feature of site 204 is the ball court (fig. 1.14). It is I-shaped, with 668 sq m of field area. We have data on 13 ball courts from Chihuahua. Twelve of them were reported in our earlier study (Whalen and Minnis 1996b), while the thirteenth recently was described at the Casa de Fuego site (Harmon 2005). The areas of these courts range from 244 to 1,194 sq m, with a mean area of 642 sq m (SD = 257). Only the I-shaped Court Number 1 from Casas Grandes exceeds 1,000 sq m. The court at site 204 thus is about average in size. It stands out, however, for being completely enclosed by earthen embankments that presently are more than a meter high.

A test trench was dug across part of the court, as shown in figure 1.14. Figure 1.15 illustrates the trench profile. A gray upper layer (1) was recent alluvial deposition. Red-brown, gravelly soil (2) was dug from the playing field and heaped up to form at least part of the surrounding embankments. A gray-brown level (3) was fill accumulated inside the court since its abandonment. The floor of the court consisted of a fine, red, clayey soil (5) that was laid down in a layer 15 to 20 cm thick, and its surface was eroded and uneven. Finally, the sterile soil (4) was a red, gravelly mixture that underlay the entire site. The upper levels of ball-court fill contained a few sherds of Plain, Scored, Indented Corrugated, and Playas Red, but only four Plain sherds came from the lower levels. These sherds suggest only that the court belongs to the Medio period, as has been assumed for all of the region's ball courts.

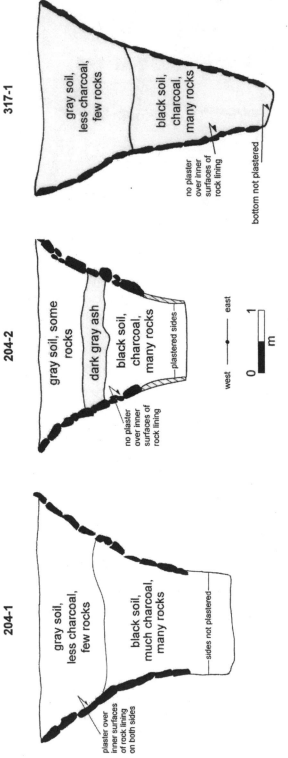

**Figure 1.13** Profiles of three conical pit-ovens. The first two are from site 204, and the third is from site 317.

**Table 1.1** Metric Data on Conical Pit-Ovens from Casas Grandes and Neighboring Sites

| Oven # | Mouth diameter (m) | Base diameter (m) | Depth (m) | Volume (cu m) |
|---|---|---|---|---|
| CG 2-1[a] | 4.0 | 1.7 | 2.5 | 16.8 |
| CG 4-1[a] | 4.0 | 1.8 | 2.7 | 19.2 |
| CG 5-1[a] | 3.7 | 1.6 | 2.8 | 16.3 |
| CG 6-1[a] | 3.4 | 1.8 | 2.3 | 12.6 |
| CG 1-9[a] | 5.7 | 1.8 | 3.5 | 42.4 |
| 204-1 | 3.5 | 1.5 | 2.2 | 9.1 |
| 204-2 | 2.6 | 1.1 | 2.2 | 6.2 |
| 239 | 3.1 | 1.5 | 2.1 | 8.6 |
| 257 | 3.4 | (1.5)[b] | (1.6)[b] | (7.9)[b] |
| 317 | 3.6 | 1.1 | 2.2 | 10.4 |

a. Data from Di Peso, Rinaldo, and Fenner (1974:4:276 and 4:468).
b. This oven was not excavated to the bottom, so that dimensions are approximate.

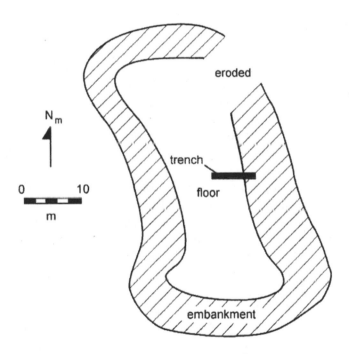

**Figure 1.14** Ball court at site 204.

Perhaps the most productive part of the site 204 work, however, was done in the large trash midden discovered to the north of Mound A. The midden was noted in the original site reconnaissance, but it appeared to be small, and it was presumed to be shallow like the few other Medio period middens found on our regional survey. Besides our observation, the extant literature contains a number of comments on the

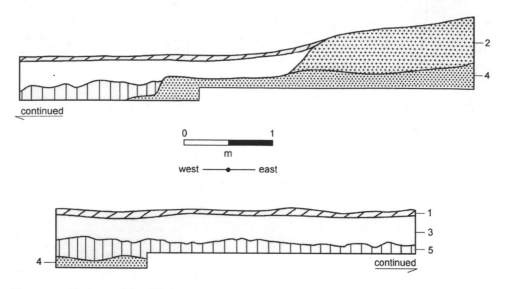

**Figure 1.15** Test trench profile from the ball court at site 204.

sparseness of midden deposits in northwestern Chihuahua (e.g., Brand 1933:91; Carey 1931:328; Lister 1946:433). Testing of the site 204 midden and environs with a hand-operated soil auger yielded surprising results. Instead of being small, the 204 midden was found to be large, much of its surface being hidden by soil washed over it from the nearby hillslope. A hand-operated soil corer showed that the midden covered some 200 sq m, with a depth that varied between 80 and 120 cm. Accordingly, a series of six 1 × 2 m test pits was placed across the midden. Each pit was excavated in 5 cm levels. The work was laborious, but it provided an unprecedented opportunity to study and date artifacts, especially ceramics, in a good stratigraphic sequence. A search was made for other midden deposits on the site, and a very deep deposit of ca. 180 cm was found and tested near Area 4, on the east end of Mound A. Two smaller and shallower middens were located on the western end of Mound A and adjacent to Mound C, respectively. Unfortunately, we could not find midden deposits associated with Mound B. In all, nine midden test pits were dug (fig. 1.16) and, as subsequent chapters will show, they played a major role in this volume's analyses.

In sum, we excavated 37 rooms at site 204, plus the midden and several other extramural contexts. This is the largest systematically excavated Medio period data set collected since the original work at Casas Grandes. Despite the extensive looting, 50–90 percent of each of the excavated rooms was found to be intact. As a result, we were able to acquire material from undisturbed contexts, although care was required to determine the depositional histories of the excavated areas. The one completely negative effect of the looting, however, was the entire absence of human burials. Three seasons of excavation at this large community did not recover a single intact Medio period burial. These often were seated in small, cylindrical pits in room corners. Looters proved especially adept at locating these corners and digging down to remove the burial and its associ-

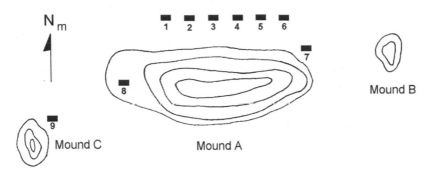

**Figure 1.16** Midden test pits dug at site 204. No midden was located in association with Mound B.

ated offerings. This is an unfortunate gap in the data set, not only at 204, but at every other site we have excavated in the Casas Grandes area.

## The Small Villages

Sites 231 and 317 both lie in the middle of the broad piedmont slope above the confluence of the Piedras Verdes and Palanganas rivers and at elevations of 1,600 to 1,700 m (refer to fig. 1.2). Figures 1.17 and 1.18 show the sites and their environs. This area slopes up to the foothills of the Sierra Madre, and we refer to the sites located here as *upland* communities in contrast to those in the river valleys. Except for a published description of a large oven (Sayles 1936b:36), there had been little recognition in print of the many Medio period sites scattered over this portion of the piedmont slope until they were recorded by our regional survey (Whalen and Minnis 2001a). We did not expect such a high site density in this upland location, as it is not close to the best farmland of the major river valleys. It is likely that the settlement of the uplands was an attempt to increase the agricultural productivity of the area after the prime river valley niches were all occupied. Today, the area is very dry, and its drainages carry water only after significant rainfall. There are a few springs flowing from the base of the nearby mountains. The dominant vegetation is grass with occasional forbs, and walnuts, oaks, junipers, piñon pines, and various shrubs are found along the drainages. The land presently is used mostly for livestock grazing, although a little rainfall farming still is practiced there.

There are several indications that this upland area was much more inviting in the past. The first is the large number of Medio period communities found in this part of the piedmont. The second is the extensive system of prehistoric agricultural features still visible here. These include dams, small canals, fields marked by linear alignments of stones that are known locally as trincheras, and "rock mulch" features. The last are piles of small stones that probably were used for the cultivation of agave. The stones would have been heaped around the plant bases to conserve moisture and lower the soil temperature. The term "rock pile fields" has been used to describe similar remains in a similar upland setting in the Hohokam area (Fish, Fish, and Madsen 1992). Taken

**Figure 1.17** Site 231 and its environs. The mound excavations are visible in the bottom center of the photograph. (Photo © Adriel Heisey; used by permission)

together, all of these facilities demonstrate that a great deal of energy was put into construction and maintenance of upland agricultural systems in the Medio period. This, in turn, argues that water was more abundant and dependable at that time (Minnis, Whalen, and Howell 2006). In addition, local informants say that springs were more common in historic times than today. There is every indication, then, that the piedmont slope was an important part of Medio period agricultural strategies.

This area is about 20 km from Casas Grandes, on the periphery of the Core Zone. Site 317 sits alone in its locality, without near neighbors. Site 231 is found in about the same topographic situation as 317, but its social setting is considerably different, as it lies in the Alamito settlement cluster described earlier in this chapter. Sites 231 and 317 both are small villages, neither having much to distinguish it from the other members of this most common class of Medio settlement. The two sites were selected for excavation in 1996 in hopes of locating Medio period ceramics useful for establishing a chronology. As this was our first attempt at seriation within the Medio period, we used the published ceramic type frequency data in a discriminant analysis, the object of which was to construct a function that could be used to seriate the survey sites based on observed type frequencies of their surface ceramics. Discriminant analysis classifies cases into mutually exclusive groups based on a set of selected characteristics, and the analysis provides several statistical measures of how reliable the classification is. The theoretical bases of the analysis are discussed elsewhere (e.g., Hair, Anderson, and Tatham 1987).

In the present analysis, we formed two classificatory groups: early Medio period (Di Peso's Buena Fe phase) and late Medio (Di Peso's Paquimé and Diablo phases). Two groups were used instead of three, as most of the ceramic data tabulated by Di Peso and his coworkers are grouped either as Buena Fe phase or as combined Paquimé-Diablo phases. The classificatory variables were the frequencies of 19 ceramic types in reported proveniences (Di Peso, Rinaldo and Fenner 1974: vols. 4 and 5). As noted, almost all types occur in almost all proveniences at Paquimé, but their frequencies fluctuate subtly over time. From the Paquimé site report, we selected a set of 42 proveniences that were clearly either early or late Medio period based on their stratigraphic positions. These data were used to construct a discriminant function for chronological classification based on ceramic type frequencies. The function achieved good discrimination of the two time periods (canonical correlation coefficient: 0.895; significance of group means difference: .0002). The function was then applied to some of the 1994 survey sites. We used only sites that yielded at least 75 sherds from systematic surface collections; i.e., where every sherd within a designated area was collected and classified. The discriminant analysis classified some sites as early Medio and others as late. These analytical results, however, could never be stronger than the data upon which they were based, and we had strong reservations about the validity of the Buena Fe and Paquimé-Diablo ceramic distinction that underlay the discriminant analysis.

The next step, then, was to test the validity of the analytical results by radiocarbon dating of some of the sites classed as early and late Medio. Several criteria were used to select two sites for testing. The first criterion was site size. The extreme complexity of the deposits at Casas Grandes led us to expect similar situations at other large Medio period sites, none of which had then been excavated. We presumed that deposits on small sites would be shallower and simpler than those of their larger neighbors. Representative sampling also is easier at small sites than at large ones. The aim of our seriation work, then, seemed best served by selection of small sites that we hoped would represent discrete time intervals. The second site selection criterion was apparent site condition. Looting characteristically is severe on Medio period mounds, and our object was to select sites where this disturbance was minimal, or at least no worse than average. In addition to obtaining material for radiocarbon dating, we also sought to recover the largest possible ceramic samples to assist in the seriation work. Small Medio sites often have sparse surface ceramics, however, and we did not know to what extent this would reflect a paucity of subsurface artifacts. Accordingly, a third site selection criterion was the presence of at least moderate numbers of sherds on the site surface. Together, these three site selection criteria eliminated many of the sites classed by the discriminant analysis as early and late Medio. Sites 231 and 317, however, had all of the desired characteristics. They lay about 3 km apart, and both were relatively easy of access. Site 231 was classed as early Medio, while 317 appeared to belong to the

**Figure 1.18** Site 317 and its surroundings. The main mound is visible in the bottom center of the photograph. It is bisected by a machine-made cut. (Photo © Adriel Heisey; used by permission)

late part of the period. Each site is characterized following, and the work done there is described.

*Site 317.* Site 317 is a cluster of three small room-block mounds, plus two large ovens, as shown in figure 1.19. Mound A covers about 320 sq m, Mound B measures 417 sq m, and Mound C is 105 sq m. The site falls into the "small" settlement category defined in our regional survey (Whalen and Minnis 2001a:124–25). We also note that the median mound area for the survey sites was 500 sq m, so that the site 317 mounds fall into the center and the lower end of the size distribution. Site 317 lies some 19 km from the primate center.

One additional characteristic of site 317 played a part in its selection. Some 12 years earlier, according to a local informant, a bulldozer had been used to cut a three-meter-wide trench through the center of Mound A with the object of making a silage pit for storing cattle fodder. (The trench was no longer used for this purpose when we recorded the site in 1994.) The mound thus was completely bisected by a cut that extended down to sterile soil. Although some rooms were destroyed by the cut, its sides provided the first two profiles of a Medio period mound that we had ever seen. Sectioned walls and floors were clearly visible, as was a pit-house-like feature that lay beneath the pueblo

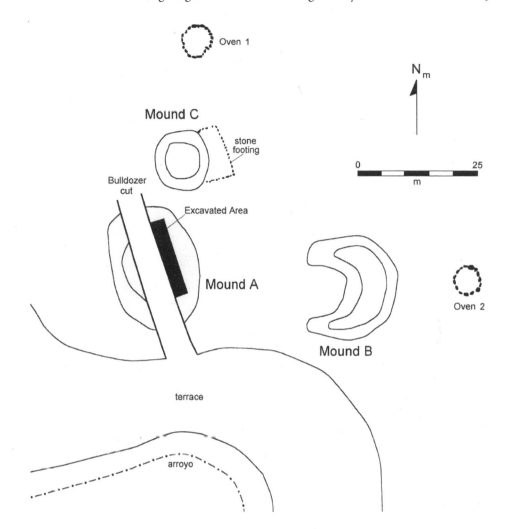

**Figure 1.19** Components of site 317.

rooms. Figure 1.20 shows these profiles. This was the first Medio site that we had dug on, and the exposed architectural elements greatly expedited the work of finding and delineating rooms. Apart from the trench, Mound A showed an unusually light level of looting damage. Excavation at site 317 proceeded outward from the east profile. Four large rooms and a small one were completely excavated, as was the underlying pit house. A sixth room was delineated on the surface, but it was not excavated. Figure 1.21 shows the pueblo rooms.

The pit structure that underlay the Medio period rooms is shown in figure 1.22. Because overlying walls were not removed, the entire floor of the pit structure was not exposed. In addition, part of the structure's perimeter was destroyed by the large cut that bisected Mound A (refer to fig. 1.19). Nevertheless, the pit structure clearly was round. It was about 3 m in diameter, and its floor area was about 7 sq m. Like the 204

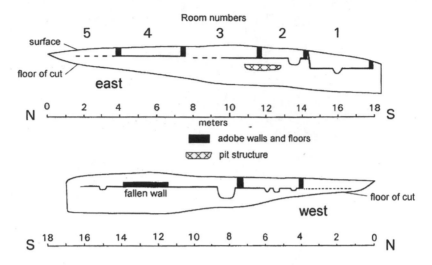

**Figure 1.20** Profiles of the Mound A trench, site 317.

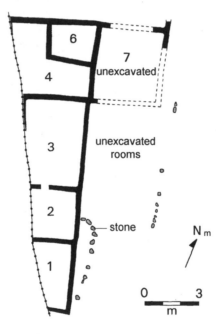

**Figure 1.21** Excavated rooms at site 317.

pit structures, the floor of Pit Structure 317-1 was covered with a smooth layer of fine plaster. No diagnostic artifacts were recovered from the fill, and chapter 2 discusses the problematic radiocarbon dates from the structure. As argued there, radiocarbon dates on overlying and intrusive rooms and features indicate that the pit structure was of pre-Medio age. Its construction and size resemble the region's dated late Viejo pit structures, and it likely was their contemporary.

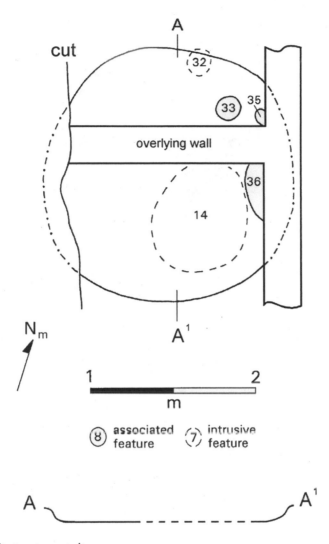

**Figure 1.22** Pit structure at site 317.

Two features on the site appeared from the surface to be conical pit-ovens. Their locations are shown in figure 1.19. Oven 1 was excavated and was illustrated earlier in this chapter (fig. 1.13). Its volume of about 10 cu m was the largest in the excavated sample from neighboring sites (refer to table 1.1). Its shape is less regular and its construction is a little rougher than is true of the ovens dug at site 204. Nevertheless, we presume that all conical pit-ovens were used for large-scale baking of agave. This question is discussed further in chapter 7.

*Site 231.* A single room-block mound covers 1,270 sq m (fig. 1.23). Like 317, site 231 falls into the "small" settlement class. Site 231 lies about 3 km SSE of site 317, and it is part of

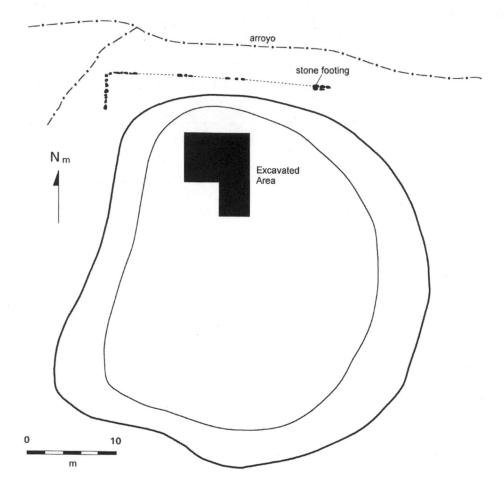

**Figure 1.23** Map of the site 231 mound. The contour interval is 50 cm.

a cluster of Medio settlements located around the large Alamito arroyo. Site 231 is about 20 km from Casas Grandes, near the periphery of the Core Zone.

Site 231 was investigated in 1996, in the same field season as the 317 work. The excavation problem at site 231 was quite different than at 317. As there was no deep profile to reveal rooms, they had to be discovered from the surface. The room-block mound was covered by an amorphous cap of hard soil and disaggregated adobe. Ranging from 5 cm to 15 cm thick, it completely obscured wall tops. We have since found this to be a common situation. As a further complication, the adobe walls of the rooms were very thin (ca. 15–20 cm), and they were of the same color and nearly the same texture as the upper room fill. Lastly, we found that site 231 was much more heavily looted than had been evident from a surface inspection. Many of the looters' holes had been filled, which is most unusual for the region. The result of all these complications was that work at site 231 went much more slowly than it had at site 317. Eventually, walls were

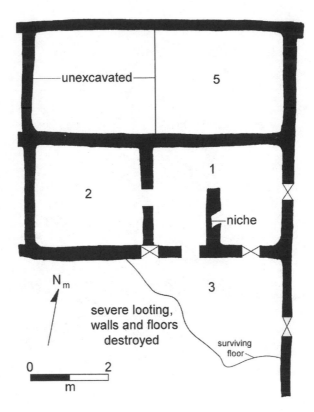

**Figure 1.24** Excavated rooms at site 231.

located, two small rooms were completely cleared, and major portions of two large ones were dug (fig. 1.24).

## The Small Ritual and Administrative Center

Site 242 occupies the same broad piedmont slope as sites 231 and 317, although it lies between the valley of the Palanganas River and the foothills of the Sierra Madre. It is located about 10 km south of sites 231 and 317 (refer to fig. 1.2). This is about 27 km from Casas Grandes, in the most distant part of the Core Zone. The site's 1,700 m elevation is about the same as that of the two sites just discussed. Site 242 lies beside one of the large arroyos descending from the Sierra Madre to the Palanganas River. Figure 1.25 shows the site and its surroundings. This arroyo may have been the determining factor in the location of the community, as will be evident in succeeding discussion. Perhaps also significant is the site's location just below one of the major routes leading up into the Sierra Madre. The site consists of a single adobe room-block mound that covers about 700 sq m, making it a small site in the survey classification (fig. 1.26). There are several small Medio period sites within 2 km of 242, but we know of no major settlement or settlement cluster in this part of the uplands. This pattern suggests a scattered, rural population on the periphery of the Core Zone.

**Figure 1.25** Site 242 and its piedmont-slope location. (Photo © Adriel Heisey; used by permission)

Site 242 has a number of unusual characteristics, suggesting that it served functions beyond those normal for small Medio villages. First, the room-block mound at 242 was remarkably tall. Fewer than 10 percent of the mounds recorded on the Core Zone survey exceeded 1.5 m in height. The 242 mound was nearly 3 m high, making it unique among small Medio settlements. The mound seems to have suffered relatively little looting, likely as a result of its height and the consequent depth of its floor deposits. Second, site 242 has one of the largest and most elaborate I-shaped ball courts presently known outside of the primate center. Earth embankments define three sides, and the fourth is formed by a small, low platform mound that measures ca. 250 sq m in area. Platform mounds, although present at the primate center, are almost unknown among neighboring communities. In fact, the 242 mound was the only apparent platform mound recorded among more than 300 Medio period sites in our regional survey. Site 242 is further distinguished by the presence of at least 11 large, C-shaped stone features that cluster about the room-block mound. These features clearly are not remains of large ovens like those described at site 317. Instead, they may be open-sided residences of some sort. This supposition is reinforced by the presence beside one arc of a small, shallow midden deposit. We recorded a few similar features on other Medio period sites, but never more than one or two were found in the same place.

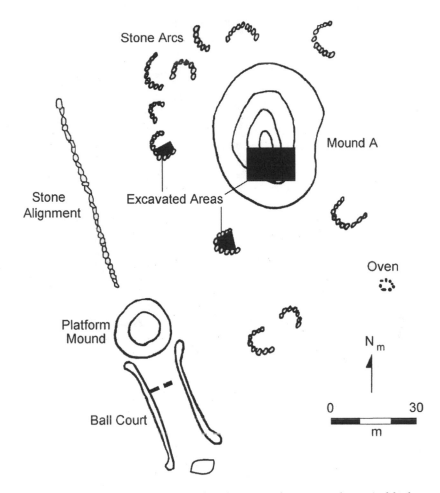

**Figure 1.26** Components of site 242. Tested and excavated areas are shown in black.

Finally, just south of site 242 lies a vast system of trincheras, or low stone terraces used to support upland agriculture in the Medio period (Minnis, Whalen, and Howell 2006). This terrace system extends some 1.4 km along a large arroyo and covers nearly 100,000 sq m. A second system of comparable size lies a short distance to the north of the site. Each system is many times larger than those found around other Medio settlements, and the productive capacity of either one would have exceeded the requirements of the small 242 settlement. Moreover, the building and use of terrace systems of this size would have required far more labor than was available in a small community like 242. In sum, site 242 is a small Medio period community with an extraordinary amount of public, ritual architecture and productive capacity. The community also contained a number of what may be temporary housing units. In these instances, large stones formed arcs that ranged from 4 m to nearly 8 m in diameter. The lowest course of each arc was formed of large (ca. 50 kg), elongated stones that were set upright into the ground, defining the arc. Tumbled around the uprights were other large, loose stones that we presume to have

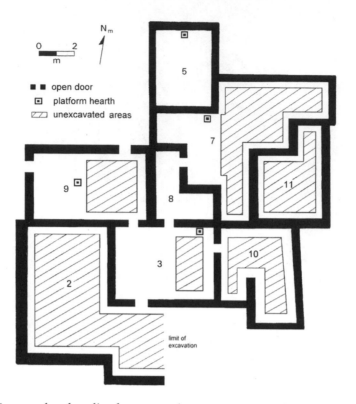

**Figure 1.27** Excavated and outlined rooms at site 242.

been piled atop the uprights to form low, dry-laid walls. There are not enough stones in or around any arc for the walls to have reached more than about 1.5 m in height. These characteristics call to mind an administrative center that drew in a scattered rural population for labor and ritual. Excavation clearly was needed to investigate this idea further, and this effort was expected to be an important part of our ongoing attempt to understand the set of organizational strategies in use in the Core Zone.

We began work at site 242 in the summer of 1998. Excavation of a shallow trench across the mound removed the cap of hardened soil and rapidly exposed wall tops. Room clearing proceeded from there. Figure 1.27 shows the rooms dug or outlined there. Rooms 3, 5, 7, 8, and 9 were wholly or partially excavated, whereas Rooms 2, 10, and 11 were only defined by wall trenching. This incomplete excavation was made necessary by the 2 m depth of fill in the large rooms. Figure 1.28 illustrates one of the two stone arcs (the postulated temporary housing units) that were partially excavated. Neither arc had a prepared floor surface, and no interior features were found. There were, however, plentiful artifacts in a layer about 20 cm thick. In fact, about half of the sherds and lithics recovered from the site came from these two arcs.

The ball court at site 242 is shown in figure 1.29. It has an I-shaped playing field with an area of 896 sq m, and it is one of the largest courts known outside of the primate center. The long axis of the 242 court is oriented to true north, as is Court 1 at

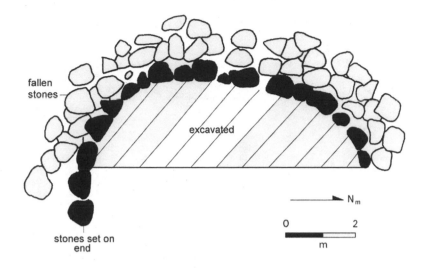

fallen
stones

excavated

stones set on
end

N<sub>m</sub>

0        2

m

a.

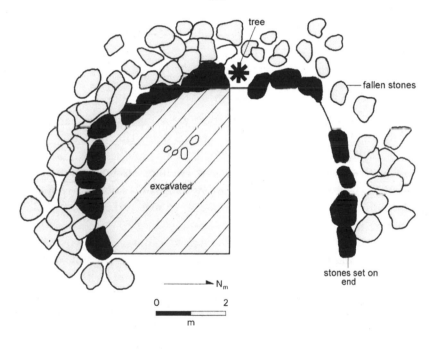

tree

fallen stones

excavated

stones set on
end

N<sub>m</sub>

0        2

m

b.

**Figure 1.28** Excavated stone arcs at site 242.

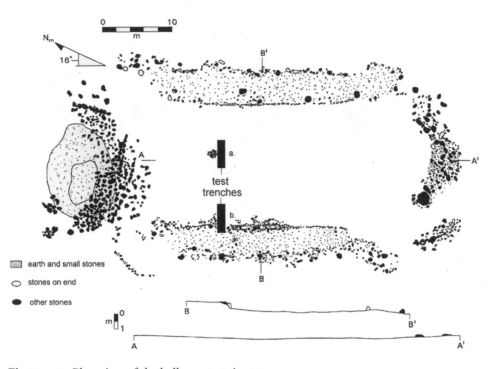

**Figure 1.29** Plan view of the ball court at site 242.

Casas Grandes. The side walls of the 242 court are formed by low, earthen mounds that presently stand about 30 cm above the central floor. The long edges of the playing field also are delimited by flat stones set on end. The southern field boundary is an earthen embankment that presently is about 30 cm high. Stones are scattered around this bank, but few were observed to be set on end. The court's northern field boundary was formed by the only non–room-block mound known in the region outside of the primate center.

Two short test trenches were dug in the 242 ball court, as shown in figure 1.29. The central trench was positioned around a small pile of stones visible on the surface but of uncertain association with the playing field. The second trench investigated the field's edge structure. Both trenches were dug to sterile soil. Excavation of the central trench (fig. 1.30a) removed about 7 cm of alluvial fill (stratum 1 in the figure) before encountering a clayey surface (stratum 2) that ranged from 3 cm to 6 cm thick. This seems to have been the court's field surface. A brown, gravelly fill (stratum 3) was laid down to form a level surface beneath the clayey surface. The fill layer ranged between 5 cm and 15 cm thick, overlying sterile soil (stratum 4). The stone pile near the center of the court penetrated the presumed floor surface, although its association with the court remains unclear. The western trench found fragments of the same clayey surface just below a thin, alluvial layer, as shown in figure 1.30b. The floor surface sloped up and over the lower part of the earthen side embankment, into which was set one of the upright, side-marker stones. These excavations demonstrate that the court was

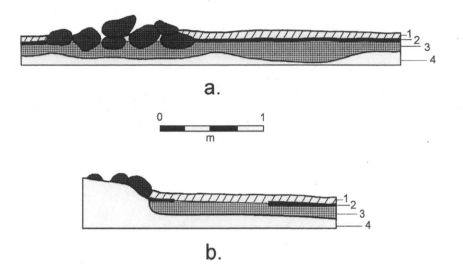

**Figure 1.30** Test trench profiles in the ball court at site 242: *a.* central floor trench; *b.* side-wall trench.

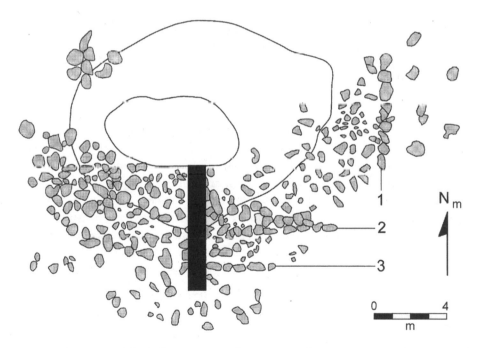

**Figure 1.31** Plan view of the ball-court mound at site 242. The contour interval is 75 cm. The heavy black line is a test trench.

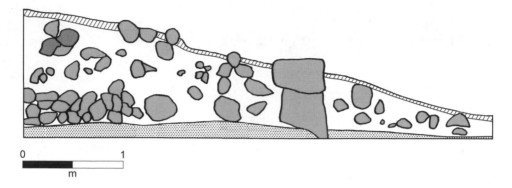

**Figure 1.32** Profile of the ball-court mound test trench at site 242. The stones sit on sterile soil. The mound fill is a matrix of earth and stones, only the larger of which are shown here. A thin layer of windblown soil covers the mound.

shallow, with a simply prepared floor. No artifacts or dateable material were found in either trench.

The small mound at the court's north end is illustrated in figure 1.31. It was about 1.5 m high, and it covered about 80 sq m. A good number of stones lay scattered around the ball-court side of the mound. Three alignments were visible in these stones (refer to fig. 1.31). Alignments 1 and 2 paralleled the mound's south side. They may represent steps or low terraces leading from the playing field to the mound. The third alignment on the east side of the mound could have connected with either alignment 1 or 2, and may be an eastward extension of the mound's terracing. We note that none of these stones is cut or faced. Instead, all are flat-sided field stones. A trench was dug into the south side of the mound; the profile of this trench is illustrated in figure 1.32. The fill of the mound was solid earth and rock rubble piled atop a foundation of large stones. The trench emphasized the presence of the stone foundations previously identified as alignments 1 and 2. No artifacts or dateable material were recovered from the mound. Nevertheless, we consider the mound and the ball court at site 242 to be contemporaneous with the rest of the site's Casas Grandes–like architecture. We make this assumption because the site 242 pattern of an I-shaped ball court with a stone-faced end mound is repeated at only one other known site in the region: Casas Grandes.

# 2

## Dating the Medio Period

The chronology of Casas Grandes and the Medio period has a long and controversial history. Briefly, by the middle 1920s the Casas Grandes culture was correctly dated, and the new chronology proposed by Di Peso in the 1970s was an erroneous deviation from the course established nearly 50 years before. Today, the deviation has been corrected, and archaeologists have returned to the original dating of the primate center. The ensuing discussion briefly summarizes this process and proposes some new perspectives.

### Early Chronometric Work

The original chronology of Casas Grandes was based primarily on the dendrochronology, or tree-ring dating, that had been so effective in the adjacent U.S. Southwest. The site of Casas Grandes yielded 386 tree-ring samples, of which 78 were dated and 54 were classified as "significant dates and not mere multiples of the same tree" (Di Peso, Rinaldo, and Fenner 1974:4:9). A problem with the Casas Grandes samples was apparent during excavation, however. The beams that were to be dated had been trimmed to a uniform diameter, resulting in the loss of unknown numbers of outer rings. Therefore, cutting dates could not be derived. The Casas Grandes report describes an unsuccessful attempt to extrapolate the derived dates to cutting dates (Di Peso, Rinaldo, and Fenner 1974:4:9–11).

The Joint Casas Grandes Project also processed 10 radiocarbon samples from several sites (Di Peso, Rinaldo, and Fenner 1974:4:24), and there was an attempt to correlate these with the tree-ring dates. Room 21C-8, for instance gave a non-cutting tree-ring date of A.D. 1113–1234, whereas a radiocarbon sample from the same beam yielded a reading of 740 ± 100 B.P. Di Peso used the uncalibrated date of A.D. 1210 ± 100, or 1110–1310, arguing that it supported the tree-ring date just given (Di Peso, Rinaldo, and Fenner 1974:4:11). We used the OXCAL program (Bronk Ramsey 2000) to calibrate this radiocarbon date to A.D. 1110–1410 at 2σ. This longer time interval emphasizes the possibility that the non-cutting tree-ring date is too young. Di Peso chose to believe that only a few outer rings had been removed, so that the dates he had were close to cutting dates and could be used as such (e.g., Di Peso, Rinaldo, and Fenner 1974:4:11–24). Under this assumption, a chronological framework was constructed for Casas Grandes. The site's occupation was placed largely within a time unit defined as the Medio period, dating from A.D. 1060 to 1320. This was the time of adobe, pueblo-style architecture at the primate center, and the demise of the center marked the end of the period. The Medio period was subdivided into three phases: Buena Fe (A.D. 1060–1205), Paquimé (A.D. 1205–1261), and Diablo (A.D. 1205–1310) (Di Peso, Rinaldo, and Fenner 1974:2:297, 310, 316). These phase divisions were based largely on "architectural stratigraphy" (Di Peso, Rinaldo, and Fenner 1974:4:8), or perceived changes in the site's architecture. This chronology represented a radical departure from the established dating of Casas Grandes. Since the middle 1920s, archaeologists had used ceramics to date the Casas Grandes culture as roughly contemporaneous with that of the Lower Gila of the adjacent U.S. Southwest (e.g., Carey 1931:352; Kidder 1924:321). Di Peso dismissed this, however, arguing that Gila Polychrome, one of the most numerous of the fourteenth-century imports at Casas Grandes, dated earlier in northwestern Chihuahua than in the U.S. Southwest (Di Peso, Rinaldo, and Fenner 1974:4:29).

This was a proposition that few were willing to accept, and controversy began to arise shortly after the new chronology was published. To briefly recapitulate these arguments, Doyel (1976:32) observed "a serious anomaly" in the lack of fit between Di Peso's proposed chronology and the known times of occurrence of Gila Polychrome in southeastern Arizona. Wilcox and Shenk (1977) stressed the point that none of the tree-ring samples from Casas Grandes, upon which the chronology was heavily based, yielded cutting dates. LeBlanc (1980) reviewed all of the dates from Casas Grandes to assert that they do not support the time interval proposed by Di Peso but point instead to an occupation of ca. A.D. 1150–1300 for the site. Carlson (1982) used dated southwestern ceramics to place the Medio period at ca. A.D. 1275 to 1400, explicitly rejecting Di Peso's chronology. Lekson (1984) carried on the critique, reviewing the Casas Grandes tree-ring dates, the few radiocarbon samples obtained there, and the established histories of intrusive ceramics from the U.S. Southwest. His conclusion was that Casas Grandes dated from about A.D. 1130 to the early 1400s. A similar conclusion was reached by Wilcox (1986:28–29), and Braniff (1986:79) used data on the occurrence of Casas Grandes ceramics together with intrusive pottery from the southwestern United States at the Ojo de Agua site in northeastern Sonora to argue that Casas Grandes intrusion into that area did not take place until about A.D. 1200 to 1500. This, in turn, suggested a later date for Casas Grandes itself.

The most widely accepted reinterpretation of Casas Grandes' chronology is a study by Dean and Ravesloot (1993) of the primate center's original tree-ring specimens. The problem with the Casas Grandes tree-ring samples is that all but one consisted entirely of heartwood rings, all of the sapwood rings having been removed by shaping of the beams or by decay (Ravesloot, Dean, and Foster 1995), so that cutting dates cannot be determined. To overcome this obstacle, Dean and Ravesloot (1993) used a regression analysis based on living trees to estimate the original number of sapwood rings based on the observed number of heartwood rings in the prehistoric specimens. Based upon this estimate is a further estimate of the cutting date of the beam in question. These cutting-date estimates are not single figures but ranges within which the true date likely falls. Like radiocarbon dates, these ranges are expressed at levels of one or two standard deviations (Ravesloot, Dean, and Foster 1995:245). Ravesloot, Dean, and Foster mention several complicating factors in this process. First the regression equation that estimates sapwood ring counts was developed on Ponderosa pines growing in the vicinity of

Santa Fe, New Mexico. The Casas Grandes study assumed that the northern New Mexican heartwood-to-sapwood ratios also characterized the Chihuahuan trees. Second, the authors note that the regression equation employed in the analysis is used with maximum precision only when the exact number of heartwood rings can be determined for a sample. This requires presence on the sample of the heartwood-to-sapwood contact, which was absent in nearly all of the Casas Grandes samples. As a result, the analysts expect the Casas Grandes cutting dates that they derived to be underestimates of the true situation (Dean and Ravesloot 1993:93; Ravesloot, Dean, and Foster 1995:246). This means that the excavated parts of Casas Grandes very likely are somewhat younger than the estimated cutting dates suggest. With this caution, the analysts contend that major episodes of construction occurred at Casas Grandes during the 1200s, 1300s, and early 1400s, with some occupation lasting until the late 1400s (Dean and Ravesloot 1993:93; Ravesloot, Dean, and Foster 1995:247). As Dean and Ravesloot point out, their reassessment of the Medio period is based on only 45 tree-ring specimens from a large site. Still, their results demonstrate that Di Peso's chronological placement of the Medio period is inaccurate, and they proposed the dates of A.D. 1200 to 1450 to enclose much of the occupation of the center of Casas Grandes during the Medio period.

Dean and Ravesloot make an important point about Di Peso's definition of the three phases of the Medio period. They contend that there is so much overlap in the estimated cutting dates of beams from rooms assigned to these phases by Di Peso and his colleagues that it may be impossible to define a series of discrete time intervals within the Medio (Dean and Ravesloot 1993:96). Other studies have found that Di Peso's definition of three phases of the Medio period cannot be supported on the grounds of ceramics (Whalen and Minnis 2001a) or architecture (Frost 2000). In fact, our position is that the three phases should be abandoned. This unfortunate necessity leaves us with no internal subdivisions of the Medio period. To remedy this situation is one of the major goals that we pursue throughout the present volume.

Finally, we note that chronometric dates have been secured from Medio or Medio affiliated sites other than the primate center, most of which are located on the peripheries of the Casas Grandes world. Some two dozen chronometric dates have been summarized for northern Sonora and southwestern New Mexico (Fish and Fish 1999:31). They range from the mid-1200s to the mid-1600s, with most in the 1300s and 1400s. Within the Casas Grandes Core Zone, Harmon (2005:161) described five unpublished radiocarbon, archaeomagnetic and tree-ring dates extending from the early 1200s to the early 1500s at the Casa de Fuego site. Additional archaeomagnetic dating has been done on a small scale at two of the sites discussed in this volume. The archaeomagnetic sample group for site 317 was dated to the early 1300s, while that of site 231 was placed in the late 1300s or early 1400s (Deaver and Heckman 2005). There are about 30 radiocarbon dates from Medio contexts at the southern limit of Casas Grandes' interaction (Kelley et al. 1999:69–71; Stewart, MacWilliams, and Kelley 2004:207–28). Many of these fall into the A.D. 1200–1450 interval. Some extend back into the mid-1100s, and a few reach as far forward as the early 1600s.

It is clear from these studies that most extant Medio period dates cluster between the early 1200s and the mid- to late 1400s. There are tantalizing hints, however, that the

Medio period may extend beyond the traditionally cited interval of A.D. 1200 to 1450. Dean and Ravesloot (1993) left this possibility open in their dendrochronology reanalysis, as they sought only to define the central tendency of the site's occupation. The other studies just cited contain a number of Medio dates before A.D. 1200 and after A.D. 1475. There are two possible explanations for this situation. The first is the predictable dispersal of any date series. Radiocarbon dating is a probabilistic method, so that any series of dates, even if actually contemporaneous, will be distributed over a broad interval of radiocarbon years. Furthermore, the time range over which the dates are spread may be expected to increase as the number of dated samples increases. This means that the maximum spread of a series of radiocarbon dates should not be taken as an accurate indicator of the duration of the event or interval being dated, a fact that should be kept in mind when interpreting any date distribution (this discussion is abstracted from Shott (1992:210–11)).

The other possible explanation, of course, is that the Medio period extends in one or both directions beyond the A.D. 1200–1450 range. There is some published expression of this idea. One recent article observes that "the span of the Medio period is now widely understood to approximate A.D. 1130–1200 to the early to late 1400s" (Stewart, MacWilliams, and Kelley 2004:235). Elsewhere it is stated that the Medio "is currently thought to begin ca. A.D. 1130/1150 to 1250" (Stewart et al. 2005:188). The data currently in hand can be interpreted no further, but they at least raise the possibility of a pre–A.D. 1200 beginning for the Medio period. The issue will be resolved only by more excavation and dating at Viejo-to-Medio transitional sites. Exactly when the Medio period ended also remains unclear, and the resolution of this problem also must await the collection of more chronometric data. Recall that the Dean and Ravesloot (1993) reevaluation of Di Peso's tree-ring samples dates much of the building at Casas Grandes from the mid- to late 1200s through the 1300s, with some construction or rebuilding continuing into (and possibly through) the 1400s. These authors also argue that the Medio period at Casas Grandes could have lasted into the late 1400s or early 1500s (Dean and Ravesloot 1993:98). There are enough post-1450 dates in the sources summarized in the preceding pages to make this a very real possibility.

Lastly, there is the problem of defining internal subdivisions of the Medio period. Preceding discussion showed that Di Peso's three phases of the Medio have been criticized extensively and should no longer be used. The problem is what to replace them with. Based on their reevaluation of the Casas Grandes tree-ring dates, Dean and Ravesloot (1993) suggested that a simple division of the Medio period into early and late parts is all that the available data will support, although they did not provide any precise chronological definition of early versus late Medio. A quarter-century ago, Lekson (1984) established what we consider a good basis for defining the early/late Medio division. His argument was phrased in terms of Di Peso's original and now-defunct phases, but his approach remains a useful one. He proposes division of the Medio period according to the presence or absence of a common trade ware from the U.S. Southwest: Gila Polychrome. This ceramic type has been well dated from ca. A.D. 1300 into the early 1400s, a chronological placement which remains valid today (Crown 1994; Lekson 2002). More recently, we have used the term *early Medio* to cover thirteenth-century deposits in

**Table 2.1**    Radiocarbon Date Count and Processing Method

| Site | Number of dated samples | Type of counting |
| --- | --- | --- |
| 204 | 50 | all extended |
| 231 | 11 | 5 extended, 6 standard |
| 242 | 12 | all standard |
| 317 | 11 | all standard |

the Casas Grandes area (Whalen and Minnis 2003:323), although we did not then provide precise chronological boundaries. If we combine Lekson's idea with the early/late Medio division just cited, then the early part of the Medio period would extend from its beginning to 1300 (or pre–Gila Polychrome times), while the late Medio, with its Gila Polychrome, would begin after A.D. 1300. We note that the early and late Medio terminology and dividing date of A.D. 1300 also are being used on the southern edge of the Casas Grandes culture area (Burd, Kelley, and Hendrickson 2004:179).

### New Chronological Data

As preceding discussion showed, the dating of Casas Grandes was based almost entirely on dendrochronology. We have collected more than 50 dendrochronology samples from the sites described in this volume. These were submitted to the Laboratory of Tree Ring Research at the University of Arizona. All samples lacked sapwood rings, and none yielded a date. Archaeomagnetic dating has been done on a small scale in the Casas Grandes area, as noted in the preceding section, although appropriate contexts are not ubiquitous. Because of its reliability and the ubiquity of usable samples, we chose to rely on radiocarbon dating. We accumulated from the four sites discussed here 84 radiocarbon dates, nearly all of which come from Medio period contexts. These dates represent the largest body of chronometric information ever accumulated in northwestern Chihuahua. Of the 84 dates, 55 (66 percent) were processed with extended counting. Normal counting time is about 2,000 minutes, while extended counts are done for 4,000 minutes. The practical result of extended counting is reduction of the standard deviation of each date. Table 2.1 shows the number of samples dated and the type of processing done at each site. All dates were corrected for isotopic fractionation.

Before we analyze the periods of occupation of the four sites discussed in this volume, some methodological issues must be considered. Each of our four sites has a series of radiocarbon dates. Each series covers a time range that is determined by the distribution of the midpoints of the measurements and by the precision of their age determinations, as reflected by the standard deviation of each date, or the ± factor. A radiocarbon "date" thus is actually a probability statement about where the true sample age actually falls. By definition, a radiocarbon date does not indicate a specific point in time (Taylor 1987:125). Rather, it indicates a time interval which, at a given probability, contains the sample's true age. Accordingly, a group of radiocarbon dates should also be seen as a group of probability statements that contains somewhere within it the occupation span of the dated context. This assumes, of course, that the set of radiocarbon samples encompasses the entire chronological range of the context in question.

A constant problem is how to determine which part or parts of a date series' range most likely reflects the true occupation span. The first step in this process often is "trimming," or elimination of outlying dates that strongly diverge from the rest. Outliers have been termed "one of the most serious sources of bias" in the analysis of radiocarbon date series (Shott 1992:212), and many others echo the same concern (e.g., Aitken 1990; Long and Rippeteau 1974; Ward and Wilson 1978; Wilson and Ward 1981). Elimination of outliers can significantly reduce the dispersion of a radiocarbon date series, thus narrowing its time span. Logically, sample series with low dispersion should give better estimates of dates of occupation than do series with higher dispersion (Ash and Brown 1990:181).

Nevertheless, there is also the caution that "rejection of outliers is a thorny subject likely to stimulate accusations that the data are being manipulated to fit preconceived ideas" (Aitken 1990:97). It is essential, therefore, to use an explicit and consistent methodology for identification of outliers. Once outliers are identified, which is a statistical task, we should turn to the question of whether or not they should be eliminated from the date series, which is an archaeological problem. Anscombe (1960:123–24) emphasizes this point by observing that variability or dispersion in a set of observations arises from two sources. The first is inherent variability, which is a population characteristic that cannot be reduced without changing the nature of the population. Errors of sampling, measurement, or execution comprise the second source of variability, and they are reducible. In a radiocarbon date series, outliers exist because either (1) they are accurate dates that simply are not coeval with the rest of the series, perhaps reflecting an undiscovered component of the site's history, or (2) they are inaccurate dates produced by a range of problems (e.g., reuse of old wood). The problem is to decide which source of variability is most likely producing the dispersion of the set of dates.

There are several statistical approaches to the identification of outliers in radiocarbon date series. The one employed here was provided by Ward and Wilson (1978). It relies on standard procedures of statistical hypothesis testing and decision making. The first step is to use the date series and its weighted mean to test the null hypothesis ($H_0$) that the individual dates are coeval or are all dating the "same" event, within the limits of radiocarbon precision. In statistical terms, the null hypothesis says that the individual dates do not differ from each other at a significant level. That is, they do not differ at a level greater than would be expected by chance alone, assuming that all are measuring the same event. The alternative hypothesis ($H_1$) is that the dates are not coeval, do not all measure the same event, and are significantly different. That is, they differ at a level greater than would be expected by chance alone, assuming that all are measuring the same event. The statistic that Ward and Wilson used for this test is T′, calculated as

$$T' = \sum_{i=1}^{n} (A_i - A_p)^2 / s_i^2$$

Here, $A_i$ is a radiocarbon date in years B.P., $A_p$ is the weighted or pooled average of the entire series of dates, and $S_i$ is the sum of several error terms. Refer to Shott (1992) or Ward and Wilson (1978) for a fuller explanation. The T′ statistic has a chi-squared distribution with $n - 1$ degrees of freedom, so the table of critical values of chi-squared provides the associated probabilities to use in deciding whether to accept the null hypothesis or to reject it in favor of the alternate hypothesis. Acceptance of the null hypothesis means that no dates are identified as outliers and that no date rejection is required. In addition, because all dates have been shown to be measuring the same event, they can meaningfully be averaged into a single figure (Ward and Wilson 1978). This is the weighted mean and its standard deviation, which can then be calibrated to produce a calendar date (Ottaway 1987). If the null hypothesis is rejected, Ward and Wilson (1978:27–29) return to their calculations on the original date series and remove the date which contributed the most to the value of the $T'$ statistic that led to rejection of the null hypothesis. They then recalculate the weighted mean and retest the null hypothesis for the newly reduced data set. If the null hypothesis is accepted this time, no further rejection is required. This is an iterative process in which the hypothesis testing and date rejection continues until what Aitken (1990:97) terms "an acceptable group" (i.e., an acceptably homogeneous one) has been formed. This method has been used by Burd, Kelley, and Hendrickson (2004), Hassan and Robinson (1987), and Shott (1992).

It should be evident that there are some dangers in automatic or uncritical application to a radiocarbon date series of this or any other method of outlier reduction. A heterogeneous series of dates, or one with high dispersion, could contain a number of aberrant dates that may safely be rejected. Alternatively, however, the series may be heterogeneous because it is accurately measuring a sequence of several occupation episodes. In the former case, we would be trimming aberrant dates to reflect the true homogeneity of the series. In the latter case, however, we would be forcing the data into homogeneity by removing much of its meaningful variability. In this case, we have obviously distorted the data, turning a long occupation into a short one. This example strongly emphasizes the need to think carefully about *why* a date series is heterogeneous before eliminating any outliers. We now turn to consideration of individual site chronologies.

## Site-Specific Chronologies

In this section we discuss the probable chronologies of our four sites and their major features.

### Site 204

Site 204 is by far the largest and most complex of the four sites. Six groups of contiguous rooms were excavated on three different mounds. Also dated were sub-room deposits and extramural areas. Table 2.2 shows the contexts of the site's dates.

*Mound A.* Mound A contains by far the largest room block on the site, with most of the site's excavated rooms and half of the site's radiocarbon dates. The preceding chapter described excavations on four parts of the large mound, designated Areas 1–4 in the order of their exploration. Each area produced a date series, and each series is analyzed following.

**Table 2.2**    Contexts of Radiocarbon Dates from Site 204

| Context | Number of dates |
| --- | --- |
| Mound A | 25 |
| Mound B | 3 |
| Mound C | 4 |
| Sub-room | 3 |
| Extramural areas | 15 |
| **Site total** | 50 |

**Table 2.3**    Radiocarbon Dates from Area 1, Site 204

| Sample[a] | Context | Material | Years B.P. | Years A.D., calibrated, 2σ |
| --- | --- | --- | --- | --- |
| B-150361 | Room 50, wall post | unburned wood | 920 ± 40 | 1020–1220 |
| B-148558 | Room 2, floor contact | wood charcoal | 800 ± 60 | 1110–1300 |
| B-150364 | Room 6, floor Feature 33 | wood charcoal | 800 ± 40 | 1160–1290 |
| B-150365 | Room 8, sub-floor Feature 69 | wood charcoal | 800 ± 40 | 1160–1290 |
| B-147579 | Room 50, sub-floor Feature 52 | wood charcoal | 780 ± 40 | 1180–1300 |
| B-150359 | Room 4, floor Feature 17 | wood charcoal | 770 ± 40 | 1190–1300 |
| B-150358 | Room 1, floor contact | wood charcoal | 760 ± 40 | 1190–1300 |
| B-150363 | Room 7, floor Feature 49 | wood charcoal | 760 ± 40 | 1190–1300 |
| B-147577 | Room 8, floor level | wood charcoal | 750 ± 40 | 1210–1310 |
| B-150362 | Room 8, floor contact | wood charcoal | 750 ± 50 | 1160–1310 |
| B-147578 | Room 51, sub-floor Feature 38 | wood charcoal | 720 ± 40 | 1220–1320 (81.2%) 1350–1390 (14.2%) |
| B-150366 | Room 51 intrusive Feature 60 | wood charcoal | 670 ± 40 | 1270–1400 |
| B-150360 | Room 6, middle fill | wood charcoal | 560 ± 40 | 1300–1370 (50.5%) 1380–1440 (44.9%) |

a. B is Beta Analytic.

Area 1 lies in the east-central part of Mound A, and it contains the only interior plaza on the site. Ten rooms were dug here, seven to the north of the plaza and three on its south side. These rooms yielded the 13 radiocarbon dates listed in table 2.3. The features are all hearths, ovens, or other fire pits. There is a complication in the conversion of some of these dates (e.g., Beta 147578, 720 ± 40 radiocarbon years B.P.) to calendar years, a problem that arises at a number of points throughout this study. The radiocarbon date just given falls on a major "wiggle," or what Taylor (1997) terms a short-term variation, in the radiocarbon calibration curve. The result is that a single radiocarbon date may correspond to several calendar dates. The probability distribution of the calibrated date

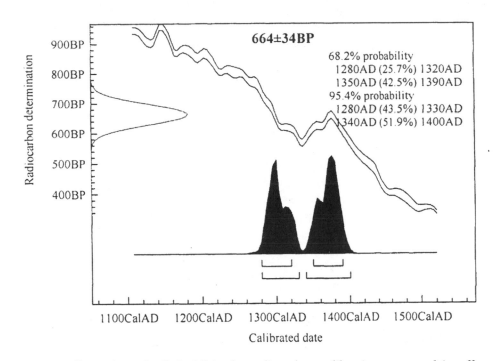

**664±34BP**

68.2% probability
1280AD (25.7%) 1320AD
1350AD (42.5%) 1390AD
95.4% probability
1280AD (43.5%) 1330AD
1340AD (51.9%) 1400AD

**Figure 2.1** Illustration of a "wiggle" in the radiocarbon calibration curve and its effect on calendar date determination. Figure generated by OXCAL v3.5 (Bronk Ramsey 2000). Atmospheric data from Stuiver et al. 1998.

may, therefore, have several peaks. Figure 2.1 illustrates this situation. The calibration curve "wiggle" produces two time ranges, each with a probability of containing the true date. At 2σ, the interval of A.D. 1220–1320 has an 81.2 percent chance of containing the true date, whereas the A.D. 1350–1390 interval has a 14.2 percent chance. The true date most likely lies in the first interval, but in accordance with standard practice, both intervals and their associated probabilities are listed in the following table. We will do this throughout the chapter whenever there is more than one calibrated date at 2σ. Only one time interval appears when dates do not fall on the "wiggle."

The two most recent dates (670 ± 40 and 560 ± 40) can be removed on stratigraphic grounds. The first is from the fill of an intrusive oven (Feature 60) that cut through the wall and floor of Room 51. Feature 60 is clearly a late Medio construction that extends into the older room below. The second excluded date comes from the middle level of the fill of Room 6. This is another late Medio date, and the preceding table shows that it fits well with the early Medio floor date from beneath it. Finally, the third suspect date is the oldest one (920 ± 40 B.P.), which comes from an unburned juniper post found in the south wall of Room 50. Fragments of another such post were found in an Area 2 room, so that the posts appear to be room construction elements. Nevertheless, the calibrated 2σ date range of the Room 50 sample was unusually wide, and most of this interval is too early for the context. Accordingly, we decided to exclude this date from the analyzed set. These three omissions leave 10 dates from room floor levels or from sub-floor contexts. It will be evident from table 2.3 that the sub-floor dates are about the same as the floor dates, indicating that the rooms were constructed over a surface that had recently been in use. In fact, the test for consistency of the combined set of floor and sub-floor dates leads to acceptance of the null hypothesis of no significant difference among the ten dates in the series (T' = 3.71, $\chi^2_{.05}$ = 18.31). The small value of T' indicates a tight group of dates, as is also evident from inspection of the table. All of the dated rooms belong to the early part of the Medio period (A.D. 1150–1300), and all of them lie north of the interior plaza. We have no floor dates for the southern Rooms 50, 51, and 52, because none of these yielded adequate charcoal samples from floor contexts. There are several indications that these three rooms are also early Medio, however. First, the late Medio Feature 60 cuts into Room 51, as just discussed. The stratigraphy of this situation is clear: the earlier room was cut by the later feature. Second, table 2.3 shows two sub-floor dates of 780 ± 40 and 720 ± 40 from Rooms 50 and 51. These are statistically indistinguishable from the sub-floor date of 800 ± 40 from early Medio Room 8.

A problem in radiocarbon date series analysis is that it can be difficult to comprehend sets of dates that have different midpoints and spreads through simple visual inspection. Fortunately, these data sets can be summarized graphically, and Kintigh (2002:99–101) provides a method for doing so, as described in the following discussion. The dates used in this analysis must be expressed as radiocarbon years before present (B.P.), since calibrated dates are not normally distributed. The analysis gives equal weight to each radiocarbon date, treating it as a normal probability distribution with a mean and a standard deviation supplied by the laboratory (e.g., 550 B.P. ± 50). Within each radiocarbon date distribution, the probability of the true date falling into a particular time interval (e.g., 500–530 B.P.) can be calculated as the area under the normal curve over that time interval. A number of date distributions plotted on the same time axis would show some degree of overlap. Any given time interval would have portions of a number of date distributions above it. Each of these date distributions is a normal curve, and the area under each curve represents that date's probability of falling into the given time interval. The analysis sums these probabilities for all dates at each time interval, presenting these data as percentages in a single histogram that shows which time intervals contain the highest probability sums for the date series. The shape of this cumulative probability histogram provides additional information about the occupation span. A compact, unimodal histogram will be produced when the date ranges have a high degree of overlap. This suggests a single, continuous occupation. A multimodal histogram indicates discrete groups of dates which, in turn, may suggest gaps in the occupation or the date sequence.

Figure 2.2 is the cumulative probability distribution for the 10 Area 1 room and sub-room dates. The arrows enclose 68 percent of the combined date distribution—820–700 B.P., for which the calendar date is cal A.D. 1150–1330 (2σ)—and the horizontal dash shows the center of the distribution. Its tall, narrow, unimodal shape indicates a concentrated period of occupation, with much overlap in the individual date ranges. Area 1 clearly contains a set of early Medio rooms that were not in use in the late part of the period.

```
Years      Cum
B.P.        %

970        0.05    |
940        0.19    |
910        0.73    | *
880        2.65    | **
850        8.39    | ******
820       21.11   >| ************
790       40.91    | *********************
760       62.49   -| ************************
730       79.43    | *****************
700       89.95   >| **********
670       95.79    | ******
640       98.64    | ***
610       99.70    | *
580       99.96    |
550      100.00    |
```

**Figure 2.2** Cumulative probability distribution for ten radiocarbon dates from Area 1, Mound A, site 204. The arrow points encompass 68 percent of the distribution, and the dash shows its center.

**Table 2.4**    Radiocarbon Dates from Area 2, Site 204

| Sample[a] | Context | Material | Years B.P. | Years A.D., calibrated, $2\sigma$ |
|---|---|---|---|---|
| B-158386 | Room 19, sub-floor Feature 131 | wood charcoal | $710 \pm 40$ | 1240–1310 (73.5%) 1350–1400 (21.9%) |
| B-158383 | Room 21, sub-floor Feature 120 | wood charcoal | $750 \pm 40$ | 1220–1300 |
| B-158385 | Room 19 floor level | wood charcoal | $660 \pm 40$ | 1280–1400 |
| B-158378 | Plaza midden | corncobs | $600 \pm 50$ | 1290–1420 |
| B-158379 | Room 21, floor contact | wood charcoal | $600 \pm 40$ | 1220–1420 |
| B-158389 | Room 26, floor Feature 161 | wood charcoal | $560 \pm 40$ | 1300–1430 |

a. B is Beta Analytic.

Area 2 lies in the west-central part of Mound A, about 25 m west of Area 1. Nine rooms and part of a plaza were excavated in Area 2. Charcoal from floor contexts was sparser here than in Area 1, so that fewer radiocarbon samples were processed. The floors of the Area 2 rooms were not as deeply buried as those of Area 1, perhaps affecting charcoal preservation. Looting was also more severe here than in Area 1. Table 2.4 shows the six Area 2 radiocarbon dates and their contexts.

Of these six samples, the first two come from sub-floor contexts, while the last four are from room floors, the plaza floor, or floor features. All of the floor features are hearths or fire pits. The table suggests that the two sets of samples are of different ages,

```
Years        Cum
B.P.          %

 800         0.02     |
 770         0.24     |
 740         1.49     |*
 710         5.72     |****
 680        15.09     |********
 650        29.94    >|**************
 620        48.88     |*******************
 590        69.07    -|********************
 560        85.60    >|*****************
 530        95.19     |*********
 500        98.92     |****
 470        99.84     |*
 440        99.98     |
 410       100.00     |
```

**Figure 2.3** Cumulative probability distribution for six radiocarbon dates from Area 2, Mound A, site 204.

and we focus first on the room and plaza floor group. It is apparent that all four of the floor dates are close in time. The test for consistency among them results in acceptance of the null hypothesis of no significant difference ($T' = 1.24$, $\chi^2_{.05} = 7.81$). The cumulative probability histogram of the four dates (fig. 2.3) is narrow, tall, and unimodal, and 68 percent of the area under the curve encloses a span of 650–550 B.P. The calendar equivalent is cal A.D. 1290–1420 ($2\sigma$), which is the late part of the Medio period. This chronology is reinforced by the two sub-floor dates shown in table 2.4. The test for continuity shows that the two dates are not significantly different and can be averaged. The weighted average and its standard deviation is 730 ± 45 radiocarbon years B.P., or cal A.D. 1210–1320 ($2\sigma$). The sub-floor contexts thus date mainly to the thirteenth century, while the rooms above them yielded mainly fourteenth-century dates. We note that the late Medio Area 2 rooms are close to their early Medio Area 1 counterparts in both distance and style. Moreover, some of the Area 2 rooms were much more extensively remodeled than were those of Area 1. We suspect that the Area 2 rooms were built sometime in the early Medio period, and they continued to be occupied and remodeled in late Medio times. The nearby Area 1 rooms were evidently abandoned at this time. If this supposition is correct, then the central part of Mound A would have been first built in the early part of the Medio period.

Area 3 is at the westernmost end of Mound A. As mentioned in the preceding chapter, Area 3 contains a set of low mounds grouped around a plaza. These mounds were only about 50 cm high, and we suspected that they contained less substantial architecture than was found in the rest of Mound A. Four rooms and a small portion of the plaza were dug in Area 3. Three of these rooms were much like those of Areas 1 and 2, while the fourth was a small, flimsy construction added over a part of the plaza. The

**Table 2.5**  Radiocarbon Dates from Area 3, Site 204

| Sample[a] | Context | Material | Years B.P. | Years A.D. calibrated, 2σ |
|---|---|---|---|---|
| B-170541 | Room 32, floor | wood charcoal | 940 ± 40 | 1010–1190 |
| A-12569 | Room 32, floor Feature 240 | wood charcoal | 740 ± 35 | 1210–1300 |
| A-12567 | Room 31, floor | wood charcoal | 865 ± 30 | 1040–1100 (14.8%) |
|  |  |  |  | 1110–1140 (8.4%) |
|  |  |  |  | 1150–1260 (72.2%) |
| B-170539 | Room 31, floor | wood charcoal | 790 ± 40 | 1160–1290 |
| A-12742 | Room 33, floor | wood charcoal | 595 ± 30 | 1300–1420 |
| B-158387 | Room 33, floor | wood charcoal | 590 ± 40 | 1300–1420 |
| B-158388 | Room 33, floor Feature 160 | wood charcoal | 470 ± 60 | 1310–1360 (6.4%) |
|  |  |  |  | 1380–1530 (79.4%) |
|  |  |  |  | 1560–1640 (9.6%) |

a. B is Beta Analytic; A is University of Arizona.

seven dates from these rooms are shown in table 2.5, and they cover both the early and late Medio intervals. The multimodal cumulative probability distribution (fig. 2.4) illustrates this situation. There are no archaeological grounds for rejecting any of these dates.

A room-by-room look at the dates is revealing. Room 31 has two dates, and the test for consistency leads to acceptance of the null hypothesis of no significant difference between them ($T' = 0.75$, $\chi^2_{.05} = 3.85$). This result permits averaging of the two dates and calculation of a pooled standard deviation, producing the date of 831 ± 14 B.P. The equivalent is cal A.D. 1185–1260 (2σ), which is in the early part of the Medio period. Room 32 also has two dates, although they are farther apart than those in the previous example. The test for continuity rejects the null hypothesis in favor of the alternative that the two dates are significantly different ($T' = 5.12$, $\chi^2_{.05} = 3.85$). Both dates are from floor contexts, although the 740 ± 35 date is the more reliable, as it comes from charcoal found within a floor hearth. It is also consistent with the room's Medio period ceramic assemblage. The other date (940 ± 40) comes from charcoal found on the floor, although its time span lies mostly in the preceding Viejo period. Its calendar age is cal A.D. 1010–1195 (2σ). This could be a manifestation of the "old wood" problem, that is, the reuse of earlier wood by later people. If we reject this date as inconsistent with the room's Medio period ceramics, we are left with a more believable date for Room 32: 740 ± 35, or cal A.D. 1200–1300 (2σ). Like the adjacent Room 31, then, Room 32 likely dates to the early part of the Medio period.

Lastly, Room 33 has three dates, all of which are fairly close together. The null hypothesis of no significant difference is accepted ($T' = 1.9$, $\chi^2_{.05} = 5.99$). Accordingly, it is proper to average all three dates to give a single range for the room. The weighted average and its standard deviation are 564 ± 38 B.P., or cal A.D. 1300–1440 (2σ). Unlike

```
Years      Cum
B.P.        %

1070       0.03    |
1040       0.24    |
1010       1.21    |*
 980       3.80    |***
 950       8.00    |****
 920      12.90    |*****
 890      19.05   >|******
 860      26.08    |*******
 830      31.90    |******
 800      37.80    |******
 770      44.89    |*******
 740      51.64   -|*******
 710      55.66    |****
 680      57.49    |**
 650      60.34    |***
 620      67.63    |*******
 590      77.64    |**********
 560      84.68   >|*******
 530      88.46    |****
 500      91.38    |***
 470      94.27    |***
 440      96.76    |**
 410      98.49    |**
 380      99.42    |*
 350      99.82    |
 320      99.96    |
```

**Figure** 2.4 Cumulative probability distribution for seven radiocarbon dates from Area 3, Mound A, site 204.

its two neighbors, then, Room 33 has a late Medio date. It thus appears that two-thirds of the dated rooms in this group are early Medio, whereas the third room falls solidly into the late part of the period. We suspect that the late date of Room 33 represents a reuse of an early Medio room. The three rooms are contiguous, and their architecture is the same. Moreover, a single, continuous adobe wall forms the north walls of both Rooms 32 and 33. This is a strong indication that both rooms were built at the same time, not a century or more apart. The Area 3 situation thus seems to be construction of rooms in the 1200s, followed by abandonment of some rooms and continued use of others in the 1300s.

Area 4 lies at the eastern extremity of Mound A, and its outer walls formed the end of the pueblo architecture. The Area 4 room floors lay only about 1 m beneath the ground surface, and they had been extensively looted. This area also yielded a smaller set of charcoal samples than did any other Mound A excavation unit. In fact, six of the

**Table 2.6** Radiocarbon Dates from Area 4, Site 204

| Sample[a] | Context | Material | Years B.P. | Years A.D. calibrated, 2σ |
|---|---|---|---|---|
| B-170540 | Room 64, floor Feature 208 | wood charcoal | 560 ± 50 | 1300–1435 |
| A-12570 | Room 64, floor Feature 256 | wood charcoal | 665 ± 35 | 1280–1330 (44.0%) |
| | | | | 1340–1400 (51.4%) |
| B-170542 | Room 60, floor Feature 199 | wood charcoal | 600 ± 40 | 1295–1420 |

a. B is Beta Analytic; A is University of Arizona.

```
Years        Cum
B.P.          %

 800        0.01    |
 770        0.17    |
 740        1.50    |*
 710        6.93    |****
 680       19.01   >|***********
 650       35.41    |****************
 620       53.02   -|******************
 590       70.36    |****************
 560       84.44   >|**************
 530       93.30    |*********
 500       97.69    |****
 470       99.40    |**
 440       99.88    |
 410       99.98    |
```

**Figure 2.5** Cumulative probability distribution for three radiocarbon dates from Area 4, Mound A, site 204.

eight rooms dug here had no adequate charcoal samples in floor contexts. From the other two rooms, three dates were obtained from charcoal in fire pits that were built into room floors. Table 2.6 shows these dates and their contexts. The three dates clearly form a tight cluster, and the test for continuity shows that there is no significant difference among them ($T' = 1.33$, $\chi^2_{.05} = 5.99$). The cumulative probability distribution (fig. 2.5) is tall, narrow, and unimodal, and its 68 percent range is 680–560 B.P. The calendar date is cal A.D. 1290–1420 (2σ), which corresponds to the late part of the Medio period.

It is clear that these Area 4 rooms are not reoccupied early Medio constructions, as we have argued to be the case in other Mound A areas. In fact, the Area 4 rooms are all built in a noticeably different way. They have the same poured adobe walls as the rest of the pueblo, but their wall footings are shallow, narrow, and unstable. In some cases, the lower portion of a wall was simply poured on a thin layer of loose rock rubble. In

**Table 2.7**    Radiocarbon Dates from Viejo Contexts, Site 204

| Sample[a] | Context | Material | Years B.P. | Years A.D., calibrated, 2σ |
|---|---|---|---|---|
| A-12570 | Pit House 1, floor contact | wood charcoal | 905 ± 35 | 1030–1220 |
| A-12571 | Pit House 2, floor Feature 294 | wood charcoal | 990 ± 30 | 980–1070 (58.6%) |
|  |  |  |  | 1080–1160 (35.8%) |

a. A is University of Arizona.

consequence of this shoddy construction, many wall cracks and much wall shifting were observed in all of the Area 4 rooms. All of the Area 4 room construction appears sloppy and unstable compared to the deeply footed and uncracked walls characterizing the rest of the pueblo. We assume, therefore, that all of the undated Area 4 rooms are approximately contemporaneous with the dated ones. That is, they all belong to the site's late Medio occupation. No early Medio deposits or features lay beneath the Area 4 rooms, but two Viejo period pit houses were found there. They are discussed following to complete consideration of the radiocarbon dates from Mound A.

Viejo contexts were found in two pit houses beneath Area 4, that is, under the easternmost part of Mound A. They produced the dates shown in table 2.7. Both dates were processed by the University of Arizona. In addition, recall that there are two additional early dates from site 204. One of these (940 ± 40) is from an unburned juniper post found in the south wall of Medio period Room 50, Area 1. The second date is identical to the first (940 ± 40), and it is from the floor of Medio period Room 31, Area 3. No Viejo period structures, features, or pottery were present in either case. The dates may, therefore, result from reuse of older wood in the succeeding Medio occupation. Whatever the case, these two dates are excluded from table 2.7 because of their lack of appropriate context. The two dates shown in that table are similar enough to accept the null hypothesis of no significant difference between them (T′ = .97, $\chi^2_{.05}$ = 3.84). They can, therefore, be averaged, giving the interval 980–890 B.P., or cal A.D. 1030–1160 (2σ). This concludes the discussion of the radiocarbon dates from Mound A. We now turn to Mounds B and C.

*Mound B.* This small group of 10 to 12 rooms lies about 100 m northeast of Mound A. Here, we excavated three rooms from the center of the mound. Charcoal was present in moderate quantity in two of the rooms, providing three radiocarbon samples from good floor contexts, including a fire pit. Table 2.8 shows these dates and their contexts, and figure 2.6 shows their cumulative probability distribution.

The two Room 81 dates are virtually identical, falling into early Medio times. The other date (500 ± 40) dates to the late Medio and appears to be an outlier. This is confirmed by the test for continuity, which requires rejection of the null hypothesis and acceptance of the alternate hypothesis of a significant difference among the dates (T′ = 7.83, $\chi^2_{.05}$ = 7.81). The source of the difference clearly is the 500 ± 40 B.P. date, which comes from a different room than the other two. Archaeological grounds,

**Table 2.8**    Radiocarbon Dates from Mound B, Site 204

| Sample[a] | Context | Material | Years B.P. | Years A.D., calibrated, 2σ |
|---|---|---|---|---|
| B-170543 | Room 80, floor contact | wood charcoal | 500 ± 40 | 1320–1350 (8.1%) |
|  |  |  |  | 1390–1480 (87.3%) |
| B-170544 | Room 81, floor level | wood charcoal | 710 ± 40 | 1240–1330 (73.5%) |
|  |  |  |  | 1350–1400 (21.9%) |
| A-12572 | Room 81, floor Feature 317 | wood charcoal | 720 ± 30 | 1240–1310 (88.4%) |
|  |  |  |  | 1360–1390 ( 7.0%) |

a. B is Beta Analytic; A is University of Arizona.

```
Years        Cum
 B.P.         %

 800        1.53    |*
 770        8.42    |*******
 740       26.22   >|******************
 710       48.15    |*********************
 680       61.19   -|*************
 650       65.58    |****
 620       66.66    |*
 590       67.67    |*
 560       71.02    |***
 530       78.44    |*******
 500       88.23   >|**********
 470       95.65    |*******
 440       98.98    |***
 410       99.86    |*
 380       99.99    |
```

**Figure 2.6** Cumulative probability distribution for three radiocarbon dates from Mound B, site 204.

therefore, suggest that it should not be rejected out-of-hand. It is noteworthy that Room 80 was heavily used, with many visible modifications in the floor and walls. Room 81, in contrast, showed less modification. It may be, therefore, that the late Medio date from Room 80 represents a later reuse of an early Medio room. This argument is strengthened by the observation that Rooms 80 and 81 share the same long, uninterrupted east wall, against which all of their north-south walls abut. This is a good indication that the two rooms were built at the same time. Note also that Rooms 80 and 81 lie in the center of Mound B, surrounded by other rooms. Therefore, Room 80 is unlikely to have been a later addition. Lastly, the architecture and wall footings are similar in both rooms, as well as in the undated Room 82. We conclude, then, that the excavated part of Mound

**Table 2.9**   Radiocarbon Dates from Mound C, Site 204

| Sample[a] | Context | Material | Years B.P. | Years A.D., calibrated, $2\sigma$ |
|---|---|---|---|---|
| B-158380 | Room 71, floor | wood charcoal | $720 \pm 40$ | 1280–1320 (81.2%) |
|  |  |  |  | 1350–1390 (14.2%) |
| B-158381 | Room 71, floor | wood charcoal | $600 \pm 40$ | 1290–1420 |
| B-158382 | Room 72, floor | wood charcoal | $790 \pm 40$ | 1180–1290 |
| B-158384 | Room 72, floor | wood charcoal | $580 \pm 40$ | 1300–1420 |

a. B is Beta Analytic.

B was built and occupied in the early part of the Medio period, and portions of it continued to be used in late Medio times.

*Mound C.* This small mound is much like Mound B in size, probably having 10 to 15 rooms. It lies about 125 m southwest of the western end of Mound A. We excavated three rooms in the center of the mound. Room floors lay as little as 75 cm beneath the ground surface, looting was heavy, and undisturbed contexts were few. Table 2.9 shows the dates, contexts, and calendar-year equivalents of the four radiocarbon samples from Mound C rooms. Note that all four samples are charcoal on or near floors; no samples were recovered from floor features. We are, therefore, dating second-quality contexts.

These dates have a wide spread. In each room, one date is early Medio, whereas the other is late. The test of continuity, however, leads to acceptance of the null hypothesis of no significant difference among the dates ($T' = 7.29, \chi^2_{.05} = 7.81$). This counterintuitive result is obtained because the data set is perfectly balanced between the early and late values, resulting in identification of no outliers. Figure 2.7 shows the cumulative probability distribution of the four dates. The figure's strong bimodality is predictable, with the two peaks representing, respectively, the two early and the two late dates. There is no archaeological basis for rejecting either group, leading to the shaky conclusion that Mound C was occupied throughout the Medio period. This concludes the discussion of the small mounds of site 204, and we now turn to the final topic of this chapter: the dating of extramural areas.

*Extramural Areas.* The last group of 16 radiocarbon dates comes from two extramural Medio period features: Oven 1 and the midden associated with Mound A (see fig. 1.4). A large amount of charcoal was found throughout the fill of the oven, and two samples were dated from the lower levels. Table 2.10 shows these dates and their contexts. The last use of the oven was in the late part of the Medio.

The preceding chapter described the large, deep Mound A midden and the test pits dug there (see fig. 1.16). Charcoal samples were taken whenever possible. Unfortunately, the upper 20–30 cm of each test pit contained little or no recoverable charcoal. This is probably due to degradation of the charcoal by heavy runoff water from the adjacent

```
Years      Cum
B.P.        %

 880      0.57    |
 860      1.69    |*
 840      4.05    |**
 820      8.01    |****
 800     13.51    |******
 780     19.95    >|******
 760     26.69    |*******
 740     33.35    |*******
 720     39.50    |******
 700     44.56    |*****
 680     48.63    |****
 660     52.64    -|****
 640     58.01    |*****
 620     65.61    |*******
 600     74.99    |********
 580     84.32    >|********
 560     91.69    |*******
 540     96.34    |*****
 520     98.69    |**
 500     99.62    |*
```

**Figure 2.7** Cumulative probability distribution for four radiocarbon dates from Mound C, site 204.

**Table 2.10**   Radiocarbon Dates from the Southern Oven, Site 204

| Sample[a] | Context | Material | Years B.P. | Years A.D., calibrated, 2σ |
|---|---|---|---|---|
| B-158376 | lower fill | wood charcoal | 510 ± 40 | 1310–1360 (13.2%) 1380–1470 (82.2%) |
| B-158377 | lower fill | wood charcoal | 510 ± 40 | 1310–1360 (13.2%) 1380–1470 (82.2%) |

a. B is Beta Analytic.

hillslope. The middle and lower test pit levels contained highly variable quantities of charcoal. The midden charcoal samples were usually smaller than those from the rooms, and material from between two and four adjacent 5 cm levels was combined to make up the charcoal samples that were dated. In this sense, the sample contexts are not as precise as those from room floor features. On the other hand, the midden samples all have a stratigraphic order that is lacking in the room dates. Thirteen charcoal samples from five test pits were dated. Table 2.11 shows these dates and their contexts.

We begin by looking at dates from the lowest levels of the pits, or the beginnings of their depositional sequences. There are six dates, two each from the lower levels of pits

**Table 2.11**   Radiocarbon Dates from Five Mound A Midden Test Pits, Site 204

| Sample[a] | Context | Material | Years B.P. | Years A.D., calibrated, 2σ |
|---|---|---|---|---|
| A-12748 | pit 1, upper levels | wood charcoal | 750 ± 30 | 1220–1300 |
| A-12749 | pit 1, lower levels | wood charcoal | 780 ± 40 | 1190–1270 |
| A-12751 | pit 1, lower levels | wood charcoal | 865 ± 40 | 1030–1270 |
| A-13599 | pit 2, upper levels | wood charcoal | 675 ± 35 | 1270–1330 (48.6%) |
|  |  |  |  | 1340–1400 (46.8%) |
| A-13598 | pit 2, lower levels | wood charcoal | 810 ± 30 | 1160–1290 |
| A-12745 | pit 4, upper levels | wood charcoal | 700 ± 30 | 1260–1320 (71.6%) |
|  |  |  |  | 1350–1390 (23.8%) |
| A-12744 | pit 4, upper levels | wood charcoal | 650 ± 40 | 1280–1400 |
| A-12746 | pit 4, upper levels | wood charcoal | 635 ± 30 | 1290–1400 |
| A-12747 | pit 6, lower levels | wood charcoal | 810 ± 35 | 1160–1290 |
| A-12750 | pit 6, lower levels | wood charcoal | 865 ± 30 | 1040–1100 (14.8%) |
|  |  |  |  | 1110–1140 (8.4%) |
|  |  |  |  | 1150–1260 (72.2%) |
| A-13601 | pit 7, upper levels | wood charcoal | 670 ± 30 | 1280–1330 (45.9%) |
|  |  |  |  | 1340–1400 (49.5%) |
| A-13600 | pit 7, upper levels | wood charcoal | 645 ± 30 | 1280–1400 |
| A-12743 | pit 7, lower levels | wood charcoal | 800 ± 40 | 1160–1290 |

a. A is University of Arizona.

1 and 6, and one each from pits 2 and 7 (refer to table 2.11). These pits lie along the long axis of Mound A, so that they presumably received trash from many parts of the room block. The six dates do not differ significantly (T' = 1.63, $\chi^2_{.05}$ = 11.07). They can, therefore, be averaged to produce a single date of 823 ± 25 B.P., which is cal A.D. 1160–1280 (2σ). Figure 2.8 shows the cumulative probability distribution for the six dates. It is tall and unimodal, reflecting the averaged date just given. Accumulation of the Mound A midden clearly started in the early part of the Medio period.

Seven dates come from the upper parts of test pits 1, 2, 4, and 7. The null hypothesis of no significant difference among them is accepted (T' = 2.64, $\chi^2_{.05}$ = 12.59). Figure 2.9 illustrates this situation. As the dates in the group do not differ significantly, they can be averaged to give the figure 676 ± 23 B.P., which in calendar years is cal A.D. 1280–1390 (2σ). This date range is mostly in the 1300s, or the late part of the Medio period. This group of late Medio dates thus articulates well with the early Medio lower group, which dated to cal A.D. 1160–1280 (2σ). Together, these two sets of dates argue that much of the accumulation of the midden had taken place by the mid- to late 1300s. Recall, however, that the top few levels of the midden remain undated.

## Site 231

Table 2.12 shows the 10 radiocarbon dates from the site 231 community. The site's initial dates were done by the Desert Research Institute, Las Vegas, Nevada, and others

```
Years      Cum
 B.P.       %

 960       0.32   |
 940       1.14   |*
 920       3.40   |**
 900       8.30   |*****
 880      16.70  >|********
 860      28.39   |***********
 840      42.59   |*************
 820      58.48  -|****************
 800      73.79   |**************
 780      85.75  >|************
 760      93.32   |********
 740      97.31   |****
 720      99.08   |**
 700      99.74   |*
```

**Figure 2.8** Cumulative probability distribution for six radiocarbon dates from the lower levels of the midden test pits, site 204.

```
Years      Cum
 B.P.       %

 840       0.06   |
 820       0.37   |
 800       1.50   |*
 780       4.26   |***
 760       9.06   |*****
 740      15.56   |*******
 720      23.89  >|********
 700      35.33   |**********
 680      50.40  -|****************
 660      67.01   |******************
 640      81.46   |**************
 620      91.24  >|**********
 600      96.49   |*****
 580      98.80   |**
 560      99.66   |*
 540      99.92   |
 520      99.98   |
```

**Figure 2.9** Cumulative probability distribution for seven radiocarbon dates from upper levels of the midden test pits, site 204.

were recently added by the University of Arizona Radiocarbon Laboratory. The Desert Research Institute (DRI) samples were not processed with extended counting, whereas those from Arizona were. It is notable that the DRI measurements generally have lower precision than those from Arizona, as reflected by the relative sizes of their standard deviations. Nevertheless, for the combined set of 10 dates, $T' = 4.244$ and $\chi^2_{.05} = 18.31$.

**Table 2.12**   Radiocarbon Dates from Site 231

| Sample[a] | Context | Material | Years B.P. | Years A.D., calibrated, 2σ |
|---|---|---|---|---|
| DRI-3280 | Room 2, lower fill | charred corncobs | 546 ± 106 | 1260–1530 |
| DRI-3262 | Room 5, floor Feature 27 | wood charcoal | 559 ± 62 | 1290–1450 |
| DRI-3263 | Room 5, floor Feature 26 | wood charcoal | 568 ± 132 | 1210–1650 |
| DRI-3227 | Room 1, floor Feature 13 | wood charcoal | 607 ± 58 | 1280–1430 |
| A-12576 | Room 5, floor Feature 23 | wood charcoal | 650 ± 50 | 1280–1410 |
| DRI-3228 | Room 5, floor Feature 16 | wood charcoal | 658 ± 115 | 1150–1480 |
| A-12575 | Room 2, floor Feature 2 | wood charcoal | 675 ± 60 | 1240–1410 |
| DRI-3229 | Room 2, floor Feature 9 | wood charcoal | 680 ± 66 | 1220–1410 |
| A-12573 | Room 1, floor Feature 11 | wood charcoal | 695 ± 45 | 1240–1330 (60.0%) |
|  |  |  |  | 1340–1400 (35.4%) |
| A-12577 | Room 5, floor Feature 24 | wood charcoal | 740 ± 40 | 1210–1310 |

a. DRI is Desert Research Institute; A is University of Arizona.

Because T′ is less than chi-squared, we accept the null hypothesis of coeval dates, and no rejection of outliers is required. The floor features identified in the table all are fire pits.

Figure 2.10 shows the cumulative probability histogram for the ten dates from site 231. The 68 percent spread is 720–540 radiocarbon years B.P., or A.D. 1220–1450 (cal, 2σ). This site occupation estimate spans much of the Medio period. We note that this time range is consistent with the archaeomagnetic placement of the site's dated contexts from the late 1300s to the early 1400s (Deaver and Heckman 2005) that was discussed earlier in this chapter.

## Site 242

Table 2.13 shows the dates and contexts of 12 radiocarbon samples from site 242. These dates are widely distributed, their 2σ spreads spanning more than 500 years, or nearly double the length of the Medio period. The table also reveals the probable reason for this situation. At site 231, nearly all of the radiocarbon dates were derived from charcoal found inside floor features in the pueblo rooms. This is a very good context from which to estimate the occupation span of a group of rooms. At site 242, however, only one of the dates came from such a secure context. Instead, nearly all of the site's dates are from charcoal that came out of the 10 cm thick floor level of each room.

The reason for this is that site 242 had almost none of the small, hemispherical hearths that were the most common kind of intramural feature at the other small sites. Instead of the small, hemispherical fire pits that were easily sealed over with contents intact when laying new floors, site 242 used a different kind of hearth that was elevated ca. 10 cm on a platform of adobe. These platform hearths are well known from the primate center of Casas Grandes, although they seem to have been much less common

```
Years        Cum
 B.P.         %
 900         0.37    |
 870         0.71    |
 840         1.43    |*
 810         3.26    |**
 780         7.46    |****
 750        14.99    |*******
 720        25.31   >|*********
 690        37.13    |************
 660        49.21    |***********
 630        60.58   -|**********
 600        70.62    |*********
 570        78.98    |********
 540        85.56   >|*******
 510        90.41    |*****
 480        93.79    |***
 450        96.05    |**
 420        97.54    |*
 390        98.51    |*
 360        99.13    |*
 330        99.51    |
 300        99.74    |
```

**Figure 2.10** Cumulative probability distribution for ten radiocarbon dates from site 231.

among the neighbors of the center. Site 242, however, is an exception in this and in most other aspects of its architecture. Elsewhere (Whalen and Minnis 2001b) we have argued that site 242 was a replica of Casas Grandes, using much of the architectural elaboration of the primate center, although on a smaller scale. Platform hearths were part of this elaboration, and one was present in nearly every room at site 242. Such hearths clearly were not abandoned and replaced as casually as the simpler, hemispherical hearths at such sites as 317 and 231. Instead, they appeared to have been cleaned out and repaired repeatedly. They were clearly cleaned out before abandonment of site 242, as almost no dateable material came from them. As a result, we were forced to take radiocarbon samples from the floor levels. Charcoal was abundant there, but its context was much less secure than hearth fill would have been. One can imagine many ways that charcoal could have come to be near the floors of the abandoned rooms, so that the spread of the resultant dates is predictable.

The high level of dispersion of this set produces a predictable result in the test for coeval dates. For site 242, T' is 31.66, and $\chi^2_{.05}$ is 19.68. This result permits rejection of the null hypothesis and acceptance of the alternate hypothesis that the radiocarbon dates from site 242 differ significantly, and cannot be considered to be coeval. Previously we observed that this level of heterogeneity in a radiocarbon date series can be the result of either an inherent variability in the set of dates or of some problem with the samples (e.g., contamination or mixing of material). Before we take steps to trim

**Table 2.13**    Radiocarbon Dates from Site 242

| Sample[a] | Context | Material | Years B.P. | Years A.D., calibrated, $2\sigma$ |
|---|---|---|---|---|
| B-122246 | Room 3, floor contact | wood charcoal | 410 ± 60 | 1410–1640 |
| B-122252 | Room 7, floor contact | wood charcoal | 510 ± 50 | 1300–1370 (21.2%) |
| | | | | 1380–1480 (74.2%) |
| B-122247 | Room 3, floor Feature 7 | wood charcoal | 540 ± 60 | 1290–1450 |
| B-122250 | Room 7, floor contact | wood charcoal | 570 ± 50 | 1300–1440 |
| B-122245 | Room 3, floor level | wood charcoal | 630 ± 50 | 1280–1410 |
| B-122251 | Room 7, floor level | wood charcoal | 640 ± 50 | 1280–1410 |
| B-122253 | Room 8, floor level | wood charcoal | 650 ± 50 | 1280–1410 |
| B-122248 | Room 5, floor contact | wood charcoal | 680 ± 60 | 1240–1410 |
| B-122255 | Room 9, floor level | wood charcoal | 720 ± 50 | 1210–1330 (76.4%) |
| | | | | 1340–1400 (19.0%) |
| B-122256 | Room 9, floor contact | wood charcoal | 720 ± 50 | 1210–1330 (76.4%) |
| | | | | 1340–1400 (19.0%) |
| B-122249 | Room 5, floor level | wood charcoal | 830 ± 50 | 1040–1100 (10.1%) |
| | | | | 1110–1290 (85.3%) |
| B-122254 | Room 8, floor contact | wood charcoal | 830 ± 50 | 1040–1100 (10.1%) |
| | | | | 1110–1290 (85.3%) |

a. B is Beta Analytic.

outliers, it is imperative to consider these two alternatives. Available data argue that the site's occupation was not an exceptionally long one, as reflected by the extreme paucity of surface artifacts. Moreover, if site 242 was the sort of administrative node that we have suggested it to be, then its main period of use should be closely contemporaneous with that of the primate center of Casas Grandes. Lastly, our excavation at site 242 failed to find either features or ceramics from any period except the Medio. Accordingly, we supplemented the statistical process with an archaeological decision; rejecting the idea of a very long use of site 242 we proceeded to trim some of the outliers.

To do this, we returned to our calculations of the T′ statistic. As noted in preceding pages, each individual date contributes to the final value of T′, and the more out-of-line the date is, the larger its contribution to T′. Accordingly, to produce a trimmed value of T′ we looked back at the values summed to form T′ and removed the date that contributed the most to this sum. We then repeated the series of calculations and retested the null hypothesis of coeval dates. We reached an acceptable grouping that conforms to the null hypothesis of coeval dates by removing two outlying values. These are the first value and last two values shown in table 2.13. Because the last two values are identical, both represent a single outlying spread for trimming purposes.

Figure 2.11 shows the cumulative probability distribution of the remaining nine dates. As before, we use the range determined by 68 percent of the area under the curve as an estimate of the period of most intense occupation of the dated portions of the site. In the present case, this is 550–760 radiocarbon years B.P. The calendar age of this

```
Years       Cum
B.P.         %

1000        0.01    |
 970        0.06    |
 940        0.29    |
 910        0.98    |*
 880        2.46    |*
 850        4.86    |**
 820        8.02    |***
 790       12.05    |****
 760       17.69   >|******
 730       25.62    |*******
 700       35.62    |*********
 670       46.91    |***********
 640       58.39   -|***********
 610       68.80    |**********
 580       77.75    |*********
 550       85.34   >|********
 520       91.50    |******
 490       95.88    |****
 460       98.39    |***
 430       99.51    |*
 400       99.89    |
```

**Figure 2.11** Cumulative probability distribution for nine radiocarbon dates from site 242.

range is cal A.D. 1270–1410 (2σ). This is congruent with the peak of occupation at Casas Grandes, and it fulfills the expectations of our earlier interpretation of site 242 (Whalen and Minnis 2001b).

## Site 317

This small settlement yielded the 11 radiocarbon dates shown in table 2.14. All of the dates come from a set of contiguous rooms in Mound A. These dates can be divided into two groups based on stratigraphy. The first group consists of seven dates from floor levels or floor features in the pueblo rooms. All of these floor features are hemispherical fire pits. The second group is four dates from features found underneath the rooms. These are the pit house and the large oven discussed in the preceding chapter, and their dates are the last four in the table. The two groups are treated separately in this analysis, as they clearly represent noncontemporaneous contexts.

For the combined set of seven pueblo dates, T′ is 6.55, and $\chi^2_{.05}$ is 14.07, permitting acceptance of the null hypothesis of no significant difference in the radiocarbon dates from the two laboratories. This means that none of the dates is deviant enough to be rejected as an outlier. Figure 2.12 shows the cumulative probability distribution for the seven dates. The histogram for site 317 is compact and unimodal, indicating a single continuous occupation of this part of the site. The figure's 68 percent range is 630–420

**Table 2.14**   Radiocarbon Dates from Site 317

| Sample[a] | Context | Material | Years B.P. | Years A.D., calibrated, 2σ |
|---|---|---|---|---|
| B-106833 | Room 2, floor Feature 13 | wood charcoal | 410 ± 50 | 1420–1530 (66.0%) 1540–1640 (29.4%) |
| DRI-3278 | Room 3, floor Feature 32 | charred corncobs | 478 ± 73 | 1300–1370 (14.1%) 1380–1530 (69.5%) 1560–1640 (11.8%) |
| B-106831 | Room 1, floor level | wood charcoal | 500 ± 60 | 1300–1520 |
| B-106835 | Room 4, floor Feature 27 | wood charcoal | 560 ± 60 | 1290–1440 |
| DRI-3277 | Room 3, floor Feature 17 | charred corncobs | 576 ± 139 | 1160–1650 |
| DRI-3279 | Room 4, floor Feature 31 | charred corncobs | 606 ± 79 | 1270–1450 |
| B-106832 | Room 2, floor Feature 11 | wood charcoal | 650 ± 60 | 1270–1420 |
| B-106834 | Pit House, floor level | wood charcoal | 520 ± 50 | 1300–1370 (28.0%) 1380–1460 (67.4%) |
| DRI-3230 | Pit House, floor Feature 36 | wood charcoal | 682 ± 64 | 1220–1410 |
| DRI-3276 | Sub-room oven, Feature 14 | charred corncobs | 760 ± 35 | 1010–1430 |
| B-106836 | Sub-room oven, Feature 14 | wood charcoal | 790 ± 50 | 1150–1300 |

a. B is Beta Analytic; DRI is Desert Research Institute.

radiocarbon years B.P. In calendar years, this is cal A.D. 1280–1530 (2σ). Archaeomagnetic dates from hearths in three rooms at this site suggest an occupation in the early 1300s (Deaver and Heckman 2005), covering only the early end of the radiocarbon date range. In any case, the site's occupation is in the late part of the Medio period. It is also possible that site 317 could have been occupied in the late fifteenth or early sixteenth centuries. Reference to table 2.14 shows that four of the seven date ranges extend beyond 1475. Several of the dates have large standard deviations, however, which affects the weighted mean and widens its standard deviation. We are thus left with only the hint that occupation at site 317 may have extended beyond those of the other sites discussed here.

Still to be considered are the sub-pueblo dates from site 317. Under some of the rooms is a large oven that overlies and partially intrudes into a circular, pit-house-like structure. The radiocarbon dates from this context are less clear, however. Two statistically identical dates come from the oven: 760 ± 35 B.P. (DRI-3276) and 790 ± 50 B.P. (B-106836). These dates have a weighted mean and standard deviation of 779 ± 56, or cal A.D. 1150–1310 (2σ). The oven clearly dates to the early part of the Medio period, and it is logical that it should be overlain by the late Medio period rooms just discussed. In contrast, the pit house presents a murkier picture. Almost no artifacts were recovered from it, and there was little dateable material. A small charcoal sample from its floor level dated to 520 ± 50 B.P., and another date of 682 ± 64 B.P. came from a fire pit in the structure's floor. The context of the latter sample is clearly the better of the two. In addition, the 520 ± 50 B.P. date falls into the late part of the Medio period, or later than

```
Years        Cum
B.P.          %

840         0.52        |
810         0.93        |
780         1.72        | *
750         3.24    +   | **
720         5.89        | ***
690        10.01        | ****
660        15.71        | ******
630        22.88    >   | *******
600        31.57        | ********
570        41.84        | *********
540        53.26    -   | ***********
510        64.66        | ***********
480        74.80        | **********
450        83.21        | ********
420        89.92    >   | *******
390        94.76        | *****
360        97.68    +   | ***
330        99.08        | *
300        99.64        | *
270        99.84        |
240        99.92        |
```

**Figure 2.12** Cumulative probability distribution for seven floor-level radiocarbon dates from site 317.

the early Medio oven that overlies the pit house. We therefore reject this date on stratigraphic grounds. The remaining date is problematic for the same reason, although it is closer in time to the date of the overlying oven. Still, there is only about a 20 percent overlap in the 1σ ranges of the 779 ± 56 B.P. date of the oven and the 682 ± 64 B.P. date from the pit house fire pit. In sum, we must consider the pit house to be inadequately dated. Its position beneath the early Medio oven suggests a pre-Medio date, but this cannot be verified with the data in hand. Site 317 thus appears to have a complex occupational history, although the rooms that we excavated there clearly fall into late Medio times.

## A Medio Period Chronology

The aim of this chapter was to establish the chronological foundation upon which the rest of our analyses would be based. The chapter began with a discussion of the chronology of the Medio period, proceeding from there to consideration of the specific chronologies of the four sites that are the subject of this volume. Di Peso's original chronology for Medio period Casas Grandes has been discarded based on a revised dating of the site's tree-ring samples. Likewise, the three phases into which he divided

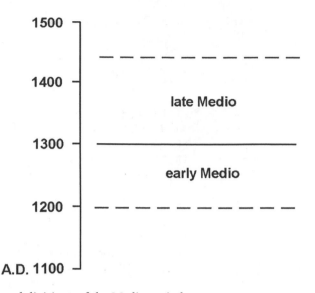

**Figure 2.13** Proposed divisions of the Medio period.

the Medio period should no longer be used, as they have not chronometric nor ceramic nor architectural definition, either within or outside of the primate center. A number of useful revisions to the Di Peso chronology have been suggested over the past 20 years. These ideas, plus the proposed revision based on our new radiocarbon dates, provide the Medio period chronology and subdivisions shown in figure 2.13.

The Medio period clearly is underway by A.D. 1200, although there are hints in the Casas Grandes area and elsewhere that it may begin a little before this date. On ceramic grounds, the early/late Medio split at about A.D. 1300 reflects the presence or absence of imported Gila Polychrome and its local variant, Escondida Polychrome. These two types are absent in early Medio deposits, but present in late Medio contexts. Chapter 3 will discuss other ceramic correlates of the early and late divisions of the Medio period. We are able to add little to an understanding of the end of the Medio. We take the end of Medio times to be marked on a regional basis by the disappearance of the ceramic assemblage and architecture that characterize the period, which at present is not well dated. Based on the Casas Grandes tree-ring samples, Dean and Ravesloot (1993) suggested that the end of the Medio might have been as late as the sixteenth century. One of our excavated sites (317) supports this idea, as the span of its radiocarbon dates reaches into the early 1500s. Earlier discussion in this chapter showed that similar late Medio dates have been reported from southern Chihuahua (Kelley et al. 1999; Stewart, MacWilliams, and Kelley 2004). Even with this information, however, we clearly need a good deal more work in late contexts before reaching an understanding of when the Medio period ended. We cannot simply assume that the demise of Casas Grandes coincided with the end of the Medio everywhere.

The second question dealt with in this chapter is the chronological placement of our four excavated sites. The chronometric data from each site are summarized here.

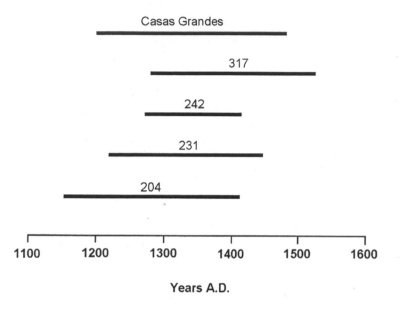

Figure 2.14 Estimated occupation spans of five Medio period sites.

Site 317 provided seven radiocarbon dates from the pueblo architecture. None of the seven dates was rejected on statistical or archaeological grounds. The weighted mean of the seven dates was 630–420 radiocarbon years B.P., or cal A.D. 1280–1530 (2σ). The excavated rooms were all in use in the late Medio. Beneath the rooms lay an early Medio oven and a pit house of uncertain date. Site 231 had 10 radiocarbon dates, none of which was rejected. The site's estimated period of occupation is 720–540 radiocarbon years B.P., or cal A.D. 1220–1450 (2σ). This interval spans the last part of the early Medio and most of the late Medio. Site 242 had 12 radiocarbon dates, almost all from second-quality contexts (i.e., floor levels rather than floor features). This series of dates showed high dispersion, and three of the most extreme values were rejected by statistical testing. The weighted mean of the remaining nine dates was within the occupation range of site 231: 760–550 B.P., or cal A.D. 1270–1410 (2σ). The excavated parts of site 242 begins at the end of the early Medio and spans much of the late Medio. In addition, the occupation of both sites was highly congruent with that of the primate center of Casas Grandes.

Site 204 represents a much larger and more complex community. Here, we processed 41 radiocarbon dates, making it by far the best-dated prehistoric site in Chihuahua. There appears to be a small Viejo component beneath the pueblo architecture. Medio period occupation of the site began by at least A.D. 1200 and lasted into the early 1400s. A single, meaningful weighted average could not be calculated for the whole site, due to the wide span of its occupation. Instead, date series were analyzed separately for the site's different excavation areas. These analyses showed that occupation was not spread evenly across the entire time interval. Instead, it is clear that the site's peak of occupation came between the late 1200s and the early to mid-1300s. Thereafter, occupation seems to have declined considerably, although vestiges persisted into the early to mid-1400s. Much of Site 204, then, is early Medio, although a smaller late Medio component also is present. Figure 2.14 summarizes the perceived occupation spans of the four Medio period sites discussed here, shown in relation to the probable occupation span of Casas Grandes.

This chapter has introduced a division of the Medio period into early and late parts and has sorted our excavated contexts into these categories. The discussion has been heavily chronometric; in chapter 4 we use ceramic data to further refine the early/late Medio division proposed here. First, however, we compare the domestic architecture of our four sites with that of Casas Grandes and consider the probable room chronology.

# 3

## The Architecture of the Medio Period

The architecture at Casas Grandes was described extensively (Di Peso, Rinaldo, and Fenner 1974: vols. 4 and 5). For many years, these descriptions were the major ones extant, and they necessarily have been taken as the norm. There were hints, however, that the elaborate building style of the primate center was not matched by its neighbors. For instance, Di Peso's brief excavations at the Reyes 1 and 2 sites in the Casas Grandes Valley (Di Peso, Rinaldo, and Fenner 1974:5:854–67) revealed four Medio period rooms with thin adobe walls and simple quadrilateral shapes. Our regional survey (Whalen and Minnis 2001a) recorded many wall segments exposed by erosion or looting on Medio sites. These bits of domestic architecture more closely resembled the buildings at the Reyes sites than those at the primate center, strengthening the impression that the famous architecture of Casas Grandes was not typical of its region. The work described in the present volume confirms this idea. Here we compare and contrast the domestic architecture of the primate center and the four neighboring settlements at which we conducted excavations.

First, however, we should note the problem of room chronology in the Casas Grandes region. Archaeologists working in parts of the U.S. Southwest have been able to use dendrochronology for precise dating of the building or remodeling of pueblo rooms. Unfortunately, this has not been the case in Chihuahua. Some tree-ring dates have come from the enormous posts and beams used at Casas Grandes, but such massive construction was not characteristic of the center's neighbors, and only small samples have been recovered there. More than 50 samples from the sites discussed in this volume have been examined by the Laboratory of Tree-Ring Research at the University of Arizona, but none has yielded a cutting date. Accordingly, the most effective indicator of room construction and remodeling sequences is unavailable for the pueblo architecture discussed here.

Chapter 2 discussed radiocarbon dates from sites analyzed here. The samples from floor contexts date the last episodes of room use. A few rooms from site 204 have final episodes that date to the early Medio, or before A.D. 1300 in our chronology. No other site in the present sample yielded such deposits. Instead, most rooms at 204 and 231, and all of those at sites 242 and 317 have floor-context dates that fall into the late Medio, or after A.D. 1300. As discussed in chapter 2, we suspect that some of these late-dated rooms were built in the early Medio and were used and remodeled in the late part of the period. Even so, the late Medio architectural data set is substantially larger than its early predecessor in the present data set.

Also to be considered here is the architectural chronology of the primate center. Architecture was the basis of Di Peso's initial tripartite division of the Medio period (Di Peso, Rinaldo, and Fenner 1974:6:80). That is, single-story, "ranch-style" compounds like Unit 11 were assigned to the initial, or Buena Fe, phase, whereas the multistory, "high-rise" structures were placed in the mid-Medio Paquimé phase. The degenerate architecture marking the demise of the center was assigned to the terminal-Medio Diablo phase. Subsequent analyses have shown this sequence to be invalid on chronometric, ceramic, and architectural grounds.

An architectural study by Frost (2000) carried out statistical analyses of the metric attributes of Casas Grandes rooms that Di Peso had assigned to the phases just mentioned. Frost's study shows that the architectural attributes of the three phases originally proposed for the Medio period are indistinguishable on statistical grounds, thereby removing the underpinning of Di Peso's phase divisions. Because they no longer have chronometric, ceramic, or architectural definition, we contend that the Buena Fe, Paquimé, and Diablo phases should no longer be used. Accordingly, we will analyze all of the primate center's architecture together. Later in this volume, we argue that all of the excavated portions of Casas Grandes belong to the late Medio period, after A.D. 1300. First, however, we contrast architectural characteristics and intramural features for the Medio period rooms at Casas Grandes and at neighboring sites 204, 231, 242, and 317.

## The Domestic Architecture of the Casas Grandes Region

We computerized the data from Di Peso, Rinaldo, and Fenner (1974: vols. 4 and 5) to enable statistical analyses. Di Peso and colleagues (1974:4:203) record 282 excavated Medio period rooms. The attributes of some of these rooms were so extensively obscured by erosion or later construction that we omitted them from our data set, which contains a total of 235 rooms. Added to this data set were the 48 rooms we excavated at neighboring sites 204, 231, 242, and 317. The ensuing discussion compares and contrasts room characteristics and intramural feature assemblages among the primate center and its neighbors.

### Construction Technique

The most common load-bearing wall construction technique at Casas Grandes is poured, or "puddle," adobe (Di Peso, Rinaldo, and Fenner 1974:4:217). Here, a stiff adobe mix is poured between forms to make horizontal wall sections a few meters long. These rise to full wall height in successive courses. This puddle adobe construction is the signature building technique of the primate center. The technique also is evident at the neighbors of the primate center. Here, we observed amorphous, horizontal wall sections with widely spaced joints; texture and color variations distributed in long, horizontal bands along the walls; and horizontal wall sections that had slipped a few centimeters out of alignment with their underlying segments. Figure 3.1a shows horizontal wall joints in Room 22 at site 204. All floors and walls originally were covered with a medium-textured adobe plaster, as shown in figure 3.1b. Succeeding discussion will show that the adobe

**Figure 3.1** Construction techniques in Chihuahuan pueblos, as evident at site 204: *a.* the horizontal sections in which the walls were poured; *b.* the medium-textured adobe plaster that covered floors and walls.

**Table 3.1**    Room Floor Area Statistics for Five Medio Period Sites

| Site | No. of Rooms | Mean (sq m) | SD | Range (sq m) |
|------|---|---|---|---|
| Casas Grandes[a] | 235 | 25.0 | 19.1 | 1.4–120.0 |
| 242 | 5 | 20.4 | 7.9 | 9.9–28.8 |
| 231 | 3 | 10.5 | 5.2 | 6.7–16.0 |
| 204 | 35 | 9.0 | 5.3 | 2.4–24.1 |
| 317 | 5 | 8.9 | 3.0 | 5.1–12.0 |

a. Data from Di Peso, Rinaldo, and Fenner (1974:4:197–475 and 5:475–822).

walls of Casas Grandes differed greatly in thickness from those of its neighbors, but the same construction technique appears to have been used on all of them.

## Room Size

We use floor area as the measure of room size. Original wall height is unknown in nearly every case, due to extensive erosion of middle and upper wall segments at all of the excavated sites. Table 3.1 shows room-area statistics for Casas Grandes and the four neighboring sites. There are two groups of mean room sizes in this sample. The sites in the first group have mean floor areas of 20 to 25 sq m, whereas the sites in the second group have mean floor areas of 9 to 11 sq m, only about half the size of the first group of rooms. The two sites in the large-room group are Casas Grandes and site 242, whereas sites 204, 231, and 317 make up the small-room group.

We observe that the small-room group includes site 204, even though it was a much larger and more elaborate community than the other two small-room sites 231 and 317. The 204 room-size range, however, shows that this site contains the largest rooms in the small-room group. In fact, three of the site's rooms exceed 16 sq m, and rooms of this size have no known counterparts at sites 231 or 317.

It is interesting to compare these figures to those from prehistoric pueblos in the U.S. Southwest. Cameron (1999:227) provides data on room sizes from a 1,733-room sample from 24 eastern and western pueblos. To this, we add 1,133 rooms from Chaco Canyon (Lekson 1984:40), 64 rooms from the NAN Ranch pueblo (Shafer 2003), and 46 rooms from the Joyce Well site (McCluney 2002). The grand total is 2,975 rooms from 27 prehistoric pueblos. Figure 3.2 shows a histogram of the mean room sizes in this sample. The mean of this distribution is 8.1 sq m (SD = 2.6). The two largest figures of around 15 sq m come from the Grasshopper pueblo of east-central Arizona and the NAN Ranch pueblo of southwestern New Mexico. In addition, Cameron (1999) reports that the mean size of 1,001 rooms at the historic Oraybi pueblo to be about 16 sq m. Despite a few pueblos with large mean room sizes, then, it is apparent from figure 3.2 that most of the present sample had small rooms. Similar data come from a study by James (1995:448), who suggested an average room size of about 10 sq m in western pueblos at European contact.

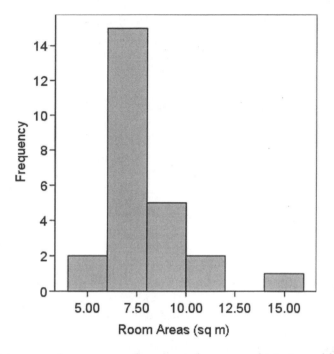

Room Areas (sq m)

**Figure 3.2** Histogram of mean room floor areas from 27 prehistoric pueblos in the U.S. Southwest (data sources: Cameron 1999; Lekson 1984:40; Schafer 2003; McCluney 2002).

These southwestern data permit two observations about Chihuahuan pueblos. First, they emphasize how large were the rooms at Casas Grandes (mean − 25 sq m) and its satellite community 242 (mean − 20 sq m). Second, the data show that the mean room sizes from the other three neighbors of Casas Grandes, sites 204, 231, and 317, fit about in the middle of the distribution shown in figure 3.2. That is, the ordinary neighbors of Casas Grandes seem to have had rooms of about the same size as other southwestern pueblos.

### Room Shape

Casas Grandes has long been known for its irregularly shaped rooms, some of which have 16, 18, and even 20 walls. For the present discussion, rooms with four and six walls (i.e., quadrilateral and L-shaped rooms) are considered to be simple shapes, whereas rooms with eight or more walls are referred to as compound shapes. These include cruciform rooms and other irregular shapes formed by room segments jutting out in many directions. It is clear from the analysis that simple room shapes overwhelmingly dominate the Casas Grandes sample, contributing 83 percent of the total. Rooms with compound shapes are conspicuous but rare at the primate center.

The size ranges of simple versus compound rooms are comparable, the former being 3.4 to 105.7 sq m, while the latter's range is 16.2 to 120 sq m. The mean sizes tell another story, however. Rooms with simple shapes have a mean area of 22.2 sq m (SD = 17.0,

$n = 195$), whereas compound rooms show a mean area of 40 sq m (SD $= 22.5$, $n = 40$). This mean difference is statistically significant ($t = -5.338$, df $= 233$, $p < .0001$). Compound-shaped rooms are larger, on average, than simple-shaped rooms in the Casas Grandes sample. Among the neighboring communities, only site 242 has an excavated compound-shaped room. Room 7 has 14 walls and, at 28.8 sq m, it is the largest room in the site's sample. The rest of the rooms at 242, as well as all of those from 204, 231, and 317 are simple quadrilateral or L shapes. We emphasize the absence of compound rooms at site 204. Even though this was a much larger and more elaborate community than 231 or 317, its room architecture resembles theirs more closely than it does that of Casas Grandes or site 242.

## Wall Thickness

The thickness of its adobe walls is another prominent feature of the primate center. The mean wall thickness in our sample of 230 rooms is a massive 73.7 cm (SD $= 15.2$). Some of the site's walls exceed 100 cm thick. There are two modes in the wall thickness distribution. One peak centers on 50–60 cm, and we term these thick walls. The second and larger mode has its center at 80–90 cm, and these we refer to as very thick walls. We note that the 50–60 cm thick walls are *not* concentrated in rooms originally assigned to Di Peso's Diablo phase, which was characterized as having simpler architecture of poorer quality than did the preceding phases. Instead, walls of 50–60 cm occur in particular places on the site; namely, in Units 6 and 12. Both of these are single-story units, but this clearly is not the reason for the presence of some thinner walls: most of the walls in both units are very thick, falling into the 80–90 cm mode. Presently, we do not know why this bimodality of wall thickness exists at Casas Grandes. It could be that the original construction consisted of very thick walls, whereas the slightly thinner ones represent additions and room subdivisions. The data we collected are not sufficient to resolve this point, and we can only say that all of the walls at Casas Grandes are thick, although there is some variability within this pattern.

We also examined wall thickness by room shape at the primate center. Rooms of simple quadrilateral and L shapes show the full range of wall thickness values, from about 40 cm to more than 100 cm. Their mean is 71.7 cm (SD $= 15.0$, $n = 190$). Rooms of compound shapes show almost exactly the same wall thickness range, but their mean is somewhat higher at 83.1 cm (SD $= 13.0$, $n = 40$). This mean difference is statistically significant ($t = -4.462$, df $= 228$, $p < .0001$). The average thickness of the walls of compound rooms with eight or more walls is greater than that of simple rooms with four to six walls.

Wall thickness shows much greater variability in our sample of rooms from the neighbors of the primate center. Closest to the Casas Grandes situation is site 242, where mean wall thickness is 56 cm (SD $= 1.6$). The small standard deviation shows that the excavated walls are fairly uniform in thickness, and they fall into the "thick" category just defined for the major center. The other three neighbors of the primate center have comparable wall thicknesses. The mean at site 204 is 33 cm (SD $= 4.4$), that of site 317 is 29 cm (SD $= 4.6$), and site 231 has a mean wall thickness of 23 cm (SD $= 1.7$). An analysis of variance shows that the three means do not differ at a statistically significant level ($F = .117$, $p = .890$). We here term this thin-walled architecture. We associate thick-walled architecture with Casas Grandes and its administrative satellites, and we consider the more common thin-walled variant to be typical of the common Medio communities of the area.

Outside of the Casas Grandes core area, very thick walls are found at the large Galeana site in the Santa María drainage (Cruz Antillón et al. 2004:153). The site's occupation is Medio period. Some of the exposed walls measure 100 cm across, although the range of thickness values is not known as very little excavation has been done on the site. The Casa Chica site is a smaller and much simpler Medio community in the same drainage. The same source notes that the adobe walls of this site ranged from 34 to 46 cm in thickness, which we would place at the upper end of our thin-walled category. The pattern in this drainage is still incompletely defined, but it appears to be the same as in the Casas Grandes core. That is, the largest and undoubtedly the most influential community in the area shows at least some very thick-walled architecture, whereas a lesser community had thin walls.

## Other Architectural Elements

In this section we consider the patterns of doorways, wall niches, platforms, stairways, and columns in Casas Grandes versus the neighboring sites.

*Doorways.* Doorways numbered 569 in the 282 rooms excavated at Casas Grandes (Di Peso, Rinaldo, and Fenner 1974:4:234–35). Of these, 234 (41.1 percent) were rectangular, and 335 (58.9 percent) were T-shaped. Although Di Peso noted that T-shaped doorways occurred in other parts of the Puebloan world, he described them as "one of the diagnostic Casas Grandes architectural features" (Di Peso, Rinaldo, and Fenner 1974:4:236). We found both rectangular and T-shaped doorways at neighboring sites 204, 231, and 242. The walls at site 317 were eroded below the doorway level, so entryway type and placement could not be determined. As at the primate center, the T-shaped doorways of the neighboring sites always outnumbered the rectangular ones. At sites 204 and 231, T-shaped doorways accounted for 62 percent and 66 percent, respectively, of the excavated entryways. At site 242, the T-shaped doorway percentage was 72 percent. The remainder in every case was made up of rectangular doorways. We do not know what may have been the functional differences between T-shaped and rectangular doorways, or how many of the latter category might be remodeled examples of the former. In any case, both doorway shapes occur in comparable proportions across all excavated sites in the present sample.

Some of these doorways were found open, whereas others had been sealed by filling their openings with large stones and adobe mortar. The sealed opening was then covered with a coat of adobe plaster. At Casas Grandes, most doorways (402, or 74.7 percent) were found open, while 136 (25.3 percent) were sealed as just described. Thirty-one upper-floor doors were not classed as sealed or unsealed, and therefore are omitted from this calculation (Di Peso, Rinaldo, and Fenner 1974:4:234–35). Interestingly, the neighboring sites all showed much higher percentages of sealed doorways compared to Casas Grandes. At site 204, 63.6 percent of doorways were sealed; the figure for site 231 was 58.3 percent; and that of site 242 was 77.8 percent. Site 317, as just noted, had no preserved doorways. Figures 3.3 and 3.4 show examples of open and sealed doorways from site 204.

Sealed doorways are commonly found at Pueblo sites in the U.S. Southwest (e.g., Bluhm 1957:33; Lekson 1986:28; Martin, Rinaldo, and Longacre 1961:37). The presence of many sealed doorways usually is taken to imply renovation and shifting room-use patterns throughout the site's occupational history (e.g., Mindeleff 1891:190). Another explanation for high frequencies of sealed doorways is planned abandonment of a pueblo, or at least parts of it, during a declining occupation. Windes (2003) traces such a situation at Chaco Canyon's Pueblo Bonito. He shows that doorway sealing was a noticeable feature of site-use behavior at Pueblo Bonito in the early 1100s, during the contraction of occupation just prior to the final abandonment of the community. We conclude, then, that doorway sealing in Pueblo architecture results from a range of factors ranging from renovation to abandonment. The curious situation in northwestern Chihuahua is that Casas Grandes contained so few sealed doorways (ca. 25 percent), whereas the smaller neighboring communities had so many (58 percent to 78 percent). This raises the question of whether the neighboring communities had the same occupational histories as the primate center, an issue that will be considered in the final chapter of this volume.

*Wall Niches.* Niches were common features at Casas Grandes, where 304 were recorded in a variety of shapes and sizes. Some of these (116) were described as step-ups for what Di Peso termed "bed platforms," whereas other niches (188) were set higher in the walls. Most wall niches were empty when excavated, but a few contained collections of exotic or unusual items that may have been offerings (Di Peso, Rinaldo, and Fenner 1974:4:229). Niches at the primate center were distributed unevenly among rooms of different shapes. Quadrilateral and L-shaped rooms averaged 1.3 niches per room (SD = 1.7; $n = 195$), whereas rooms of compound shapes contained an average of 2.5 wall niches (SD = 1.9; $n = 40$). This mean difference is statistically significant ($t = -3.94$; df = 233; $p < .0001$).

Wall niches are present but rare among the neighboring sites. Site 317 is omitted from this discussion due to its extensive wall erosion. One niche was present in a room in the small Mound B at site 204. It was built into part of the fill of a sealed doorway (fig. 3.5a); that is, the lower part of the old doorway was left open to form the niche, a practice which also was common at Casas Grandes. Another niche, set into a wall at an unusual angle, was found in a room at site 231 (fig. 3.5b). Both niches were empty. Interestingly, no wall niches were found at site 242, despite that community's generally strong architectural resemblance to Casas Grandes.

*Platforms.* The 282 excavated rooms in Casas Grandes contained 210 platforms that were built into corners or across alcoves (Di Peso, Rinaldo, and Fenner 1974:4:238). These platforms ranged from 1.7 m to 2.8 m wide and from 1.5 m to 2.9 m deep. The

(a)

(b)

**Figure 3.3** Examples of open (*a*) and sealed (*b*) T-shaped doorways at site 204. The scale shows 10 cm intervals.

**Figure 3.4** Examples of open (*a*) and sealed (*b*) rectangular doorways at site 204. The scale shows 10 cm intervals.

**Figure 3.5** Wall niches from neighboring sites: *a*. Room 80, site 204; *b*. an oddly angled niche from Room 1, site 231. The scale shows 10 cm intervals.

top was formed by a layer of adobe plaster spread over closely spaced horizontal poles. Skirting walls of adobe enclosed the space beneath 197 (94 percent) of these platforms. Small "crawl-through" openings gave access to the enclosed space. Di Peso presumed that these were sleeping, or "bed," platforms, and the Casas Grandes report refers to them as such. This could be true, although facilities for so basic a purpose might be expected to be nearly ubiquitous among the site's rooms. In fact, our sample of 233 rooms from Casas Grandes shows that 115 (48.9 percent) did not contain platforms.

Our analyses show that platforms occur in about 85 percent of rooms of compound shapes. Most 8-sided to 10-sided rooms have at least one platform, as do all rooms with 12 to 20 sides. In fact, it is the presence of alcoves (in which platforms often were built) that provides much of the complexity of shape in compound rooms. In contrast, only about 50 percent of the rooms of simple quadrilateral and L shapes contained platforms. This paucity of platforms in simply shaped rooms is not a function of room size. Preceding pages showed that simple-shaped and compound-shaped rooms occurred in about the same range of sizes. The 110 simple-shaped rooms without interior platforms average 20.7 sq m in floor area (SD = 17.8), whereas the 84 simple-shaped rooms that contain platforms average 23.3 sq m in floor area (SD = 13.7). This size difference between simple-shaped rooms with and without platforms is not statistically significant ($t = -1.142$, df = 192, $p = .255$).

We also note that platforms are not homogeneously distributed over the excavated parts of Casas Grandes. Room Units 8, 11, 12, and 14 seem to represent the norm, with platforms in 52 percent to 56 percent of their rooms. Units 6 and 13 fall considerably below these figures, with only 20 percent of their rooms containing platforms. Unit 16 is far above the norm, with platforms in 79 percent of its rooms. Room Units 15, 19, and 22 were omitted from consideration, as each contains only a few excavated rooms. Somewhat similar platforms were found at Pueblo Bonito, Chaco Canyon, although they do not appear to have had skirting walls. They were interpreted as shelves, and it was argued that their presence would have significantly increased a room's storage capacity (Judd 1964:29).

We suggest that the significance of the platforms of Casas Grandes may lie in the enclosed spaces beneath them. Using the average dimensions of these facilities (Di Peso, Rinaldo, and Fenner 1974:4:238), we calculated that the platforms would have enclosed volumes of 4 cu m to 6 cu m. Using a middle figure of 5 cu m, we calculate that the 197 platforms with skirting walls would have enclosed nearly 1,000 cu m. This volume is equivalent to about 100 storage rooms with floor areas of 3 m × 2 m and wall heights of 1.8 m. This storage space would have been private, protected, and readily accessible. Moreover, it is present most often in the site's largest and most elaborate rooms. We emphasize, however, that under-platform areas are unlikely to have been the community's primary kind of storage, as none was present in about half of all excavated rooms of all sizes. Instead, it is more likely to have been supplemental storage associated with some members of society.

Remains interpretable as platforms were very rare among the sites neighboring Casas Grandes. Neither platforms themselves, skirting walls, nor indentations in room walls at platform height or width were observed in most of the excavated rooms. At site 242,

**Figure 3.6** A possible "bed platform" support indentation in Room 3, site 242. The vertical scale is 1.5 m and the horizontal scale is 1 m.

the Casas Grandes look-alike, Rooms 3, 8, and 9 contain horizontal and vertical wall indentations that likely mark where platforms abutted the walls. Figure 3.6 shows one of these from Room 3. In none of these cases, however, were there any traces of skirting walls. Judging by the lengths and widths of the wall indentations, the site 242 platforms would have been a little smaller than those of the primate center. At site 204, Room 61 contained what might be the remains of the skirting walls of a platform (fig. 3.7). Two walls were added to the corner of the room to form a small rectangle measuring about 1.0 m × 1.4 m. This area is on the small end of the range of platform areas at Casas Grandes. The surviving skirting walls were about 80 cm high, which also is within the Casas Grandes range. The enclosed space was entered by a small doorway opening east into an unexcavated room. There were no remnants that could be identified as the top of the purported platform. Room 61 is dated entirely to the late Medio period, as is site 242. The early Medio rooms at site 204 contained no remains interpretable as platforms. These facilities, then, may be a late addition to the Medio architectural complex.

*Other Elements.* Stairways and columns are found at Casas Grandes and at the neighboring communities. About half of the stairways at the primate center were made of stone,

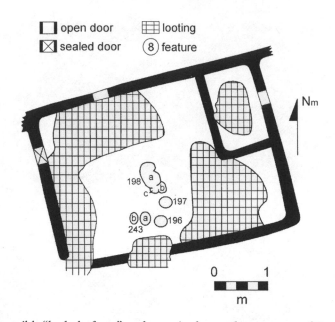

**Figure 3.7** A possible "bed platform" enclosure in the northeast corner of Room 61, site 204.

while the other half were of adobe. Some 82 percent of the stairs at Casas Grandes were found with public or ceremonial structures, with the small remainder occurring in private residential rooms. These stairways were fairly large, the adobe version averaging 11 steps over about 9 horizontal meters (Di Peso, Rinaldo, and Fenner 1974:4:246–47). A single adobe stairway was found in Room 6 at site 204. This room, dated to the early part of the Medio period, is illustrated in figure 3.8a. The stair (fig. 3.8b) was small by Casas Grandes standards, rising only three steps and 80 cm over 1.7 horizontal meters. Two large, flat stones lay atop the third tread of the stair, but it is unclear whether they represent internal reinforcement or a landing atop the stairway. There is no indication that any part of site 204 rose to two stories, so that the stairway presumably gave access to the roof. This could not have been the normal means of roof access, however, as nothing like it was found anywhere else in the pueblo. Despite this unusual feature, the room in which it occurs appears to have been an ordinary domestic space. The presence of the stairway is mysterious, but it at least makes us aware that this architectural element occurred in the early part of the Medio period, as well as in the late Medio contexts at Casas Grandes.

Lastly, quadrilateral adobe columns occur at the primate center in Units 6, 8, 11, 14, and 16. Seven sets of columns are present in these five units, and they always occur in the same context: as the transition from a plaza to interior rooms. The spacing of the columns within a set characteristically is about 2 m, although one set was spaced at an interval of about 1.5 m. The columns themselves are quadrilateral and are cast from puddle adobe. Most of them are 1.0–1.5 m on a side, although the members of one set are unusually large at 1.2 × 2.0 m. All of these sets of columns later had walls built between them on the plaza side to create closed rooms.

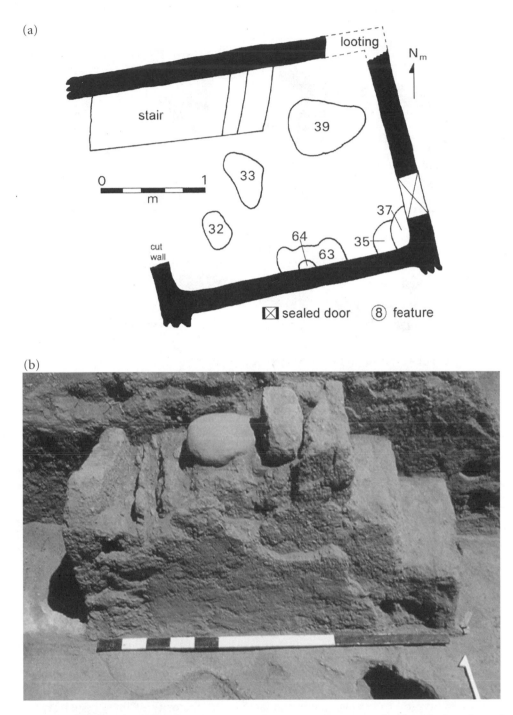

**Figure 3.8** The single adobe stairway at site 204: *a.* Room 6, site 204, showing the location of the adobe stair remnant; *b.* the stair. The horizontal scale is 1.5 meters.

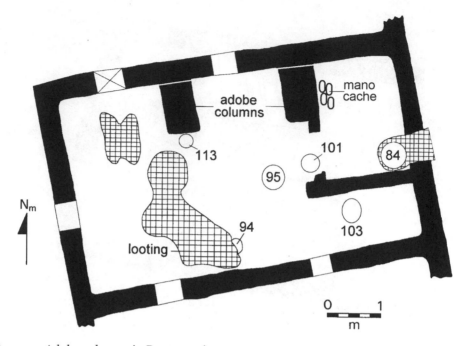

**Figure 3.9** Adobe columns in Room 21, site 204.

A set of apparent columns was found in Room 21 at site 204 (fig. 3.9). As at Casas Grandes, the 204 columns lay at the transition between a plaza and an interior room. There were only two columns in Room 21, each of which measured about 1.3 m long by 75 cm wide. Although substantial, they are somewhat smaller than their counterparts at the primate center. The surviving portion of each colonnade was about 55 cm high, but their original heights are unknown. Their upper surfaces were rough and damaged, as shown in figure 3.10. The columns at Casas Grandes were presumed to have extended to the roof levels. We presume the same was likely at site 204, where the two columns were original features of the room. Their adobe footings extended about 15 cm below the room's floor level and into sterile soil. There is no indication that any part of the room's floor passed beneath a colonnade. Nevertheless, both columns clearly abutted the room's north wall. At Casas Grandes, walls often were added beside or around existing columns to enclose what once had been open, colonnaded space. This may have been done at site 204 as well.

In summary, thick- and thin-walled Medio period rooms from the primate center and its neighbors were built using the same puddle adobe technique. The sample studied here contained considerable variability in room size, room shape, and wall thickness, but a clear typical or average pattern emerged. The majority of investigated Medio period rooms contained 5 to 15 sq m of floor area and were built in simple quadrilateral or L shapes. Their walls were thin at 20 to 40 cm. It is interesting to note that these characteristics were found to be equally applicable to the large site 204 as to the small 231 and 317 communities.

**Figure 3.10** Construction detail of an adobe column. This is the east column of the pair found in Room 21, site 204: *a.* looking north; *b.* looking east. The checkered portion of the scale measures 50 cm.

Two communities stand out from this pattern: Casas Grandes and site 242. Both have large, thick-walled rooms, some of which were built in compound shapes. Earlier (Whalen and Minis 2001b) we argued that the style of building seen in these two communities constituted an "architecture of power" in northwest Chihuahua. That is, a distinctive and elaborate building style was used to emphasize and reinforce the special status of the communities that displayed it. The architecture of power was displayed in its most extreme form at the primate center, and it occurred in simpler form at administrative satellites like 242. Beyond this basic pattern, a series of architectural elements was found at all of the sites discussed here, although the elements were not equally well represented at every site. Predictably, Casas Grandes had the largest and most elaborate set of wall niches, intramural platforms, stairways, and columns. These elements were sparsely represented among the neighboring sites. We see, in other words, a common, basic architectural tradition at all of these sites, which was greatly elaborated upon at the primate center.

## Intramural Features

From the primate center to its small neighbors, all excavated Medio period sites have similar assemblages of intramural features. Nearly all rooms contain at least one small fire pit or hearth, and these fire features are by far the most common category of intramural facility. A number of rooms had post molds in their floors. These did not form discernable patterns, however, and it is unclear what the posts were used for. Their irregular distributions suggest that intramural posts were used to shore up roofs wherever necessary, as well as for a variety of other minor support purposes. Finally, many excavated rooms contained unburned floor pits. These varied greatly in size and construction. Most were of uncertain function, but some were clearly storage pits or ash receptacles for nearby fire pits.

These three categories of intramural features are found at all Medio period sites excavated to date, and we take them to represent the ordinary domestic feature assemblage. The primate center of Casas Grandes goes a little beyond its neighbors in the elaboration of its intramural feature assemblage. For instance, there are a few sub-floor caches and a very few ceramic jars set into room floors. Presently, these have no known counterparts at the neighboring sites discussed in this volume. In general, however, the same fairly simple set of intramural features is found everywhere.

Table 3.2 shows the frequencies of major intramural feature categories at Casas Grandes and at the neighboring communities. Clearly, the primate center has the largest and most varied set of features in its large sample of excavated rooms. The small sites 231, 242, and 317 have the sparsest and simplest assemblages, and the large 204 community falls in between these two extremes. As hearths and fire pits are the largest and most ubiquitous type of intramural facility, we begin with them.

*Fire Pits and Hearths.* First, we note that the fire pits and hearths found in rooms of the Casas Grandes area are similar to, but not exactly like, those of adjacent parts of the U.S. Southwest. Clay-lined, hemispherical fire pits are ubiquitous. Conspicuously absent in Chihuahua, however, are the rectangular, slab-lined fire boxes that have been

**Table 3.2**  Feature Class Frequencies at Casas Grandes and Its Neighbors

| Feature class | Casas Grandes[a] | Site 204 | Site 231 | Site 242 | Site 317 |
|---|---|---|---|---|---|
| Fire features | 66.1% (484)[b] | 59.8% (138) | 85.7% (24) | 88.8% (8) | 73.7% (14) |
| Post holes | 15.3% (112) | 10.0% (23) | 0 | 0 | 0 |
| Unburned pits, ? function | 7.4% (54) | 25.9% (60) | 0 | 11.2% (1) | 10.5% (2) |
| Ash pits | 3.7% (27) | 4.3% (10) | 14.3% (4) | 0 | 15.8% (3) |
| Sub-floor caches | 6.6% (48) | 0 | 0 | 0 | 0 |
| In-floor jars | 0.9% (7) | 0 | 0 | 0 | 0 |
| **Total** | 100.0% (732) | 100.0% (231) | 100.0% (28) | 100.0% (9) | 100.0% (19) |

a. Data from Di Peso, Rinaldo, and Fenner (1974:4:252–58).

b. Counts in parentheses.

reported from early to late Mogollon pueblos (e.g., Lowell 1999; Shafer 2003). The typology developed to classify the intramural fire features at Casas Grandes (Di Peso, Rinaldo, and Fenner 1974:4:252–53) was found applicable to the fire pits and hearths of the neighboring communities, and much of this discussion is phrased in terms of this system. A basic distinction among intramural fire facilities is between those that were excavated into the floors of rooms versus those that were raised above the floor level on adobe platforms. In-floor fire pits always were the most common kind. They characteristically were of shallow basin shape in profile and were circular or ovoid in plan view. Most of them were lined with clay or adobe, probably to increase their refractory properties. This interior coating often was burned to a bright orange. Most of these simple fire pits occurred alone, but some were accompanied by an ash pit. These were small, hemispherical pits that usually were not heavily burned, and their fill of fine ash gives them their name. The fact that ash pits were associated with only a few fire pits argues that they were not essential components of fire feature use.

Other types of in-floor fire pits were much rarer in the Casas Grandes classification system. They were distinguished by particular features such as adobe rims or collars that rose a few centimeters above the floor level. One side of a few fire pits had been dug away to form an air vent. A few fire pits lacked adobe linings, while others were lined by setting a ceramic bowl or large sherds into the floor. Finally, a few in-floor hearths were rectangular in plan view. Some of these hearths had linings of adobe or stone, but others were unlined.

Platform hearths were the second and less common category of intramural fire facility at Casas Grandes and its neighbors. Lekson (1999:106) notes that platform hearths apparently were unique to Casas Grandes and related communities as far north as southwestern New Mexico, apparently being absent in the Chaco, Aztec, Mimbres, and El Paso areas. These distinctive facilities consist of a low adobe platform, usually rectangular in plan view, into which were dug a shallow basin fire pit, an ash pit, and an air vent. Molded geometric decorations sometimes were added to the platform hearths of Casas Grandes. Whether plain or decorated, platform hearths represent an especially elaborate type of intramural fire feature that may have had status implications.

**Table 3.3**  Fire Feature Type Frequencies at Casas Grandes and Its Neighbors

| Type | Type[a] | Casas Grandes[b] | Site 204 | Site 231 | Site 242 | Site 317 |
|---|---|---|---|---|---|---|
| Basin, lined | 1a | 55.8% (263)[c] | 56.3% (81) | 70.8% (17) | 12.5% (1) | 42.9% (6) |
| Basin, unlined | 3 | 2.6% (12) | 26.3% (38) | 12.5% (3) | 37.5% (3) | 21.4% (3) |
| Basin, lined, with adobe collar | 1b | 0.2% (1) | 3.5% (5) | 4.2% (1) | 0 | 21.4% (3) |
| Basin, lined, with ash pit | 1c | 11.9% (56) | 6.9% (10) | 12.5% (3) | 0 | 14.3% (2) |
| Basin, lined, with air vent | 1d | 0.2% (1) | 2.8% (4) | 0 | 0 | 0 |
| Rectangular, unlined | 4 | 1.3% (6) | 0.7% (1) | 0 | 0 | 0 |
| Rectangular, stone-lined | 5a | 0.4% (2) | 0 | 0 | 0 | 0 |
| Rectangular, adobe-lined | 5c | 0.2% (1) | 0 | 0 | 0 | 0 |
| Basin, lined, stone collar | 1f | 0.2% (1) | 0 | 0 | 0 | 0 |
| Basin, ceramic liner | 1h | 1.3% (6) | 0 | 0 | 0 | 0 |
| Basin, ceramic liner, adobe collar | 1i | 0.2% (1) | 0 | 0 | 0 | 0 |
| Platform hearth | 2 | 25.7% (121) | 3.5% (5) | 0 | 50.0% (4) | 0 |
| **Totals** | | **100.0% (471)** | **100.0% (144)** | **100.0% (24)** | **100.0% (8)** | **100.0% (14)** |

a. Types assigned at Casas Grandes (Di Peso, Rinaldo, and Fenner 1974:4:252–53).

b. Data from Di Peso, Rinaldo, and Fenner (1974:4:252–54).

c. Counts are in parentheses.

The frequencies of different types of fire pits and hearths at Casas Grandes and its neighbors are shown in table 3.3. As always, the sample from the primate center contains the greatest number and variety of fire facilities. The small sites 231, 242, and 317 have the smallest samples and the least variety, and the large site 204 falls between these two extremes.

Table 3.3 shows that the dominant intramural fire feature type at the primate center and most of its neighbors was the simple clay-lined basin. In the Casas Grandes classification, this is the Type 1a fire facility (Di Peso, Rinaldo, and Fenner 1974:4:252). The only exception to this statement is site 242, where Type 1a fire pits were rare. The second most frequent type at all of the neighboring sites discussed here was an even simpler type of fire pit: the unlined basin. Lowell (1999) describes the unlined basin as a casual sort of fire pit that represents little labor input. This was classified as the Type 3 fire pit at Casas Grandes, and it was rare in that community. This frequency difference may reflect a more formal or elaborate fire facility assemblage at the primate center than at its rural neighbors. In any case, simple basin fire pits of the lined and unlined varieties made up the majority of intramural fire features at all sites except 242. Even there, basin fire pits constituted half of the fire feature sample. Other variants of basin fire pits with adobe collars or associated ash pits occurred in low frequency at all sites except 242. Figure 3.11 shows examples of this common fire feature from site 204.

Platform hearths represent a different and more elaborate kind of fire facility, and they are not nearly as common as their simple basin counterparts. Table 3.3 shows that platform hearths are well represented at Casas Grandes, where they comprise nearly 26 percent of the sample. Platform hearths made up 50 percent of the sample at site 242, however. One of these is illustrated in figure 3.12a. It is noteworthy that this site had a relatively low frequency of the in-floor basin fire pits that were so common in other communities. Elsewhere (Whalen and Minnis 2001b) we have argued that platform hearths were part of the "architecture of power" that was displayed at the primate center and at its administrative satellites like the 242 community. Platform hearths were not found at the small, simple sites 231 and 317, and they were rare at the large site 204. Figure 3.12b shows one of the 204 platform hearths, all of which were badly damaged by later construction.

*Fire Feature Dimensions.* Here we consider the metric characteristics of the three most common types of fire pits and hearths: clay-lined basins (types 1a–i), unlined basins (type 3), and platform hearths (type 2). These three categories make up nearly all of the intramural fire features at the sites discussed here. Table 3.4 shows their mean dimensions.

The clay-lined basin fire pits show no statistically significant difference in mean area or depth among the neighbors of Casas Grandes. The same is true for unlined basin fire pits, and their dimensions did not differ significantly from those of lined fire pits at the same sites. The primate center could not be included in these tests as all of the necessary statistics were not provided in the site report. Mean dimensions were given, however, and it is apparent that lined basin fire pits were very much larger at Casas Grandes than at the neighboring communities. In fact, the area figure given in the table is nearly four times the comparable figures from the neighboring communities. The lined fire pits of the primate center also were about twice as deep as those of the neighbors. Unlined fire pits at Casas Grandes were considerably smaller than their lined counterparts but still a good deal larger than those of the neighboring sites.

*Fire Feature Uses.* The preceding discussion of intramural fire pit and hearth types leads to the question of their functions. First, we note that fire features, often in multiples, were present in nearly every Medio period room dug in Chihuahua. At Casas Grandes, for example, 484 fire features were found in 230 excavated rooms. Of the total of 259 rooms dug at the primate center, only 29 (11 percent) had no fire feature. At site 204, only three of 31 excavated rooms (10 percent) had no intramural hearth or fire pit. All excavated rooms at sites 231 and 242 contained fire features, as did all but one of the rooms dug at site 317. These figures allow us to estimate that 80–90 percent of Medio period rooms contained fire features.

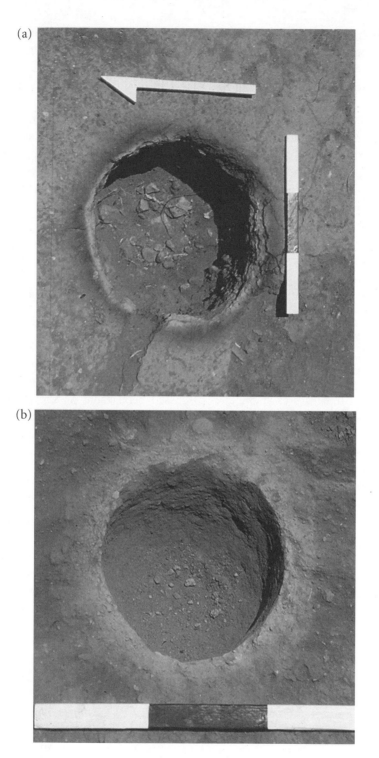

(a)

(b)

**Figure 3.11** Examples of simple, hemispherical hearths from site 204. This is the most common kind of Medio period fire feature. The scale measures 30 cm.

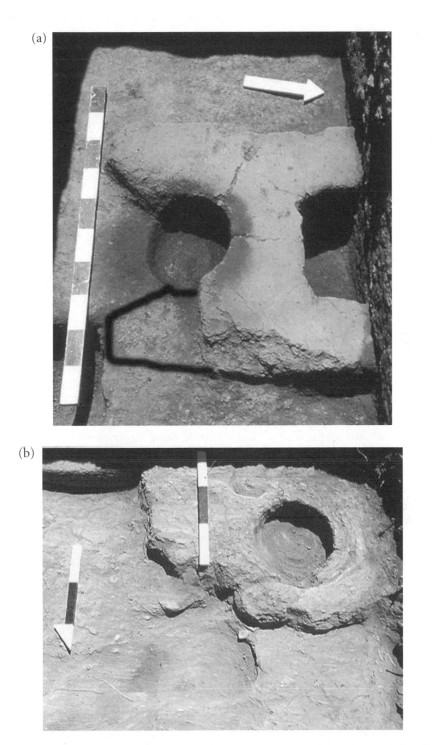

**Figure 3.12** Platform hearths from the neighbors of Casas Grandes: *a.* hearth from site 242; the black line shows where a corner was cut away during excavation; *b.* poorly preserved hearth from site 204.

**Table 3.4**  Fire Feature Dimensions at Five Medio Sites

| Site | Dimensions | Lined basin | | | Unlined basin | | |
|------|------------|------|------|------|------|------|------|
| | | *n* | Mean | SD | *n* | Mean | SD |
| 204 | area | 86 | 1,943 sq cm | 1,480 | 20 | 1,794 sq cm | 1,108 |
| | depth | 86 | 15.4 cm | 5.8 | 20 | 14.2 cm | 6.4 |
| 231 | area | 18 | 1,781 sq cm | 744 | 3 | 1,052 sq cm | 301 |
| | depth | 18 | 11.1 cm | 2.9 | 3 | 12.0 cm | 2.6 |
| 242 | area | 1 | — | — | 3 | 2,699 sq cm | 807 |
| | depth | 1 | — | — | 3 | 15.0 cm | 7.9 |
| 317 | area | 7 | 1,606 sq cm | 620 | 1 | — | — |
| | depth | 7 | 15.1 cm | 3.2 | 1 | — | — |
| Casas Grandes[a] | area | 263 | 6,195 sq cm | —[b] | 12 | 3,510 sq cm | —[b] |
| | depth | 263 | 28 cm | —[b] | 12 | 35.5 cm | —[b] |

a. Data from Di Peso, Rinaldo, and Fenner (1974:4:253).
b. Figures not provided.

Certainly, fire pits and hearths were nearly ubiquitous in Medio period rooms because they served common, essential domestic functions. Heating, illumination, and cooking were argued to be the roles played by the intramural fire features of Casas Grandes (Di Peso, Rinaldo, and Fenner 1974:4:251). At other southwestern pueblo sites, researchers see a good deal of cooking being done inside pueblo rooms but also acknowledge the multifunctional nature of the fire features (e.g., Lowell 1999; Reid and Whittlesey 1982). The in-floor fire pits just described for the primate center were large enough for a variety of tasks, and we agree with the implication that intramural fire pits likely were multifunctional. We suspect that the clay-lined fire pits comprising most of the sample from nearly every site were so-treated to increase their refractory properties, making them more efficient for heating and cooking. The much rarer unlined fire pits may have been more casual constructions for illumination or for other short-term use. Lowell (1999) made a similar interpretation of the uses of lined and unlined basin fire pits at the Grasshopper and Chodistaas pueblos of east-central Arizona.

The uses of platform hearths are less clear, and the facilities have no counterparts in existing fire feature studies (e.g., Lowell 1999; Shafer 2003; Sobolik, Zimmerman, and Guilfoyl 1997). The fire basins of platform hearths often were heavily burned, but those at Casas Grandes were much smaller and shallower than the in-floor basin fire pits. The published mean lengths and widths of the Casas Grandes platform hearth fire basins (Di Peso, Rinaldo, and Fenner 1974:4:256) yield average areas of 2,297 sq cm for oval specimens and 1,590 sq cm for round ones. Depths of both shapes of platform fire basin averaged only 12 cm. This strongly suggests that platform hearths did not serve the full range of functions just ascribed to in-floor fire pits. In particular, the platform hearth fire basins seem too small for effective cooking, as they are only about one-third the area and one-half the depth of their in-floor counterparts.

The disparity just noted in in-floor fire pit size between Casas Grandes and its neighbors is extreme, and it likely has behavioral implications. At this point, it is necessary to consider the factors that likely determined fire feature size at Casas Grandes or in any pueblo community. Several variables come immediately to mind, and these can be summarized under the headings of room size and cooking activities. Each is briefly considered following.

There clearly is a general correlation between fire pit size (expressed here as pit area) and room floor area in the Medio communities discussed here. Casas Grandes has the region's largest rooms (mean area = 23.2 sq m), and these contain the region's largest fire pits (mean area = 6,195 sq cm). Sites 204, 231, and 317 have much smaller rooms (mean area = 8.7 sq m), and they contain smaller fire pits (mean area = 1,777 sq cm). This relationship disappears at a more specific level, however, which suggests that other factors likely are involved. Correlation coefficients were calculated between room floor area and fire pit areas. The resulting coefficients should have values near 1.0 if fire pits were built to fit room sizes. In fact, the correlation coefficients were less than 0.1 at sites 204, 231, 242, and 317. This demonstrates that there is no relationship between fire pit areas and the floor areas of the rooms in which they were found. In other words, hearth size clearly does not depend on room size at any of the neighboring communities. We did not make similar calculations for Casas Grandes, although we suspect that the same result would be obtained.

Cooking activities long have been recognized as affecting intramural fire pit size. The relation likely is not a simple one, however, as noted by Ciolek-Torrello and Reid (1974). Variables influencing intramural fire pit size minimally include the number of people cooked for, the cooking technology used, and the presence versus absence of extramural cooking facilities such as those documented in the Mimbres area (Shafer 2003; Sobolik, Zimmerman, and Guilfoyl 1997). At present, we know too little about all of these variables to be able to make convincing arguments about their influence on fire pit size. Outdoor cooking facilities, for instance, are known to exist on Medio period sites. Our regional surveys (Whalen and Minnis 2001a) noted the presence of extramural fire features around a number of pueblo room blocks. These ranged in size from small to very large, but they never have been systematically recorded or studied. As a result, we know almost nothing about their numbers or characteristics.

Chapter 4 will show that some ceramic vessels at Casas Grandes were much larger than any known from neighboring communities. Larger vessels and larger intramural fire pits are consistent with larger-scale food preparation activities at the primate center. This, in turn, could imply that households were larger at Casas Grandes than among its neighbors. This notion accords well with the large sizes of the rooms at the primate center.

## Room Function

Southwestern archaeologists long have been interested in assigning functions to prehistoric pueblo rooms. Summaries of the many studies of room function are provided by Cameron (1999) and Riggs (2001). There have been two major approaches to the problem of assigning room function. These focus, respectively, on architectural characteristics and activity analysis through artifacts. The architectural approach rests on ethnographic analogy, and it is the oldest way to assign function to pueblo rooms. Ethnographic data, notes Cameron (1999:209), indicate a strong relationship between a room's size and its function. Accordingly, the smallest rooms characteristically are seen as storage facilities, intermediate ones are habitation spaces, and ceremonial or communal functions are ascribed to very large rooms. These functional classifications are supplemented by observation of intramural feature assemblages. Storage rooms, in addition to their small size, have few or no features, and access to them often is restricted by either few doorways or small ones. They also lack architectural elements such as wall niches or ventilators. Habitation rooms are larger and more complex, having hearths, sub-floor burials, and more doorways for a higher level of access. Ceremonial or communal rooms may be the largest spaces, and they contain special features such as wall niches, floor vaults, or perimeter benches. Studies over the last three decades, from Hill (1970) to Shafer (2003) have relied on the architectural approach for assessing pueblo room function.

There are some obvious complications to the method, however. First, the characteristics just used to distinguish room types are norms or central tendencies. This means that some rooms fit neatly into one category or another, but others show a mixture of traits that do not precisely match any of the categories. At the NAN Ranch pueblo, for instance, Shafer (2003:61) considers Room 58 to have had a communal function because of the low bench running around three walls. The room is only 17.3 sq m in floor area, however, placing it considerably below the site's other recognized ceremonial or communal rooms, which measure 34 to 95 sq m. In cases like this, analysts selectively emphasize the architectural characteristics that seem most indicative of room function. The second problem with the architectural approach is room remodeling, which may alter architectural characteristics and obscure their relation to room function. Remodeling was common in pueblos. However, data from the historic Oraybi pueblo indicate that habitation rooms were the most frequently remodeled type of interior space, and they almost always continued to be used for habitation (Cameron 1999:210). It may be, therefore, that the effect of remodeling on functional interpretation is not as severe as has sometimes been argued.

Another approach to identifying pueblo room function is activity analysis based primarily on artifacts from floor contexts. It has been argued that the relation between architecture and room function is too loose and too easily distorted to be reliable (e.g., Riggs 2001), making artifact-based activity analyses more accurate. An obvious requirement of this approach is the presence in rooms of de facto refuse, or material lying where it was left by its prehistoric users. Some pueblos, such as Grasshopper (Riggs 2001), meet this requirement, but others, such as NAN Ranch (Shafer 2003), do not. Where it is applicable, the activity approach usually recognizes a larger number of room uses than does the architectural method (e.g., Reid and Whittlesey 1982).

It will be apparent that these two approaches to room function are not mutually exclusive, although studies characteristically place primary reliance on one or the other. One analysis, however, argues that the results of the two approaches do not correlate well, due to the frequent remodeling of pueblo rooms and to their use for more than one purpose during their occupational histories (Riggs 2001).

*Room Function at Casas Grandes.* All of the excavated rooms at Casas Grandes originally were assigned to at least one of four functional classes: domestic, public, public-ceremonial, or ceremonial. This classification makes no mention of storage rooms. The descriptions of a few Casas Grandes rooms contain the notation that they probably served for the storage of food or exotica. Nevertheless, storage rooms are not included in the summary tables showing the percentages of rooms across time that were devoted to the four functions just listed (Di Peso, Rinaldo, and Fenner 1974:4:198, 200).

The failure to define storage rooms at Casas Grandes is problematic in light of other studies of pueblo communities. Charles Adams (1983:51) asserts that a traditional pueblo community should have two or three storage and granary rooms for each habitation room. A similar figure comes from the Turkey Creek pueblo (Lowell 1991), where 132 storage rooms and 59 habitation rooms were identified (a storage-to-habitation room ratio of 2.2). Other studies of pueblo room use show considerable variation in frequencies of storage rooms, however. At the NAN Ranch pueblo, 21 storage rooms versus 30 habitation rooms were identified, for a ratio of 0.7 (Shafer 2003). The Broken K pueblo contained 17 rooms identified as storage spaces, and 42 classed as habitation rooms (a storage-to-habitation room ratio of 0.4) (Hill 1970). At the Grasshopper pueblo, Riggs (2001) also derives a storage-to-habitation room ratio of 0.4. Although the ratios just given vary widely, all of these studies of historic and prehistoric southwestern pueblos recognize a substantial number of storage rooms. The Casas Grandes classification used by Di Peso and colleagues stands in sharp distinction to this pattern. Indeed, the whole question of storage at Casas Grandes was little considered in the original analysis, and it remains obscure.

The four room classifications employed by Di Peso and colleagues seem to have been based primarily on architectural characteristics and feature assemblages. Artifacts also were used to infer intramural activities. The artifactual data are questionable, however, as the floor levels in Casas Grandes rooms were 25–35 cm in thickness, and all of their contents were analyzed as floor materials. We thus have no idea what was and was not primary refuse. In any case, the following definitions are offered for the primate center's room types (Di Peso, Rinaldo, and Fenner 1974:4:198). Domestic rooms have fire hearths, bed platforms, doorways of all types but of smaller sizes, and their floor levels contain food preparation tools. Public rooms have the characteristics of domestic rooms, plus entryways of larger size, stairways, columns, or large quantities of stored material such as shell. Public-ceremonial rooms have any of the characteristics of domestic and public rooms, plus sub-floor corner caches and "other ceremonial materials." Ceremonial rooms have special associations with ball courts and other ceremonial features.

Clearly, these type descriptions contain high levels of overlap and ambiguity. Our examination of the characteristics of rooms classed in Di Peso's system shows that many rooms have the characteristics of two or three of the four types. Di Peso dealt with this ambiguity by arguing that a very large amount of renovation had taken place,

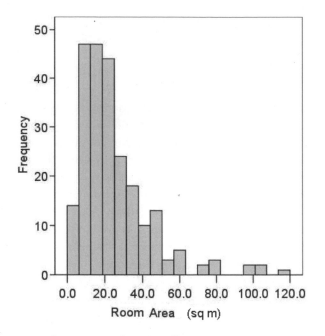

**Figure 3.13** Histogram of Casas Grandes room floor areas.

resulting in drastic changes of room function over the occupation of the site. This could be so, although sealed openings, a frequent result of remodeling, accounted for only 25 percent of the doorways of the primate center but 58–78 percent of the doorways in the neighboring communities. We have also argued earlier that the occupation span of the excavated parts of Casas Grandes was shorter than is usually assumed. Accordingly, it appears that a reconsideration of the primate center's room classification system is in order. This is too large a task to complete here, but some preliminary steps can be taken.

In his original functional classification, Di Peso made no explicit use of room size, even though this variable often plays a central part in studies of pueblo room function. Accordingly, we begin our analysis here. We have already noted that the rooms of Casas Grandes are very much larger than those normally found in pueblo architecture. Nevertheless, we will attempt to apply to them the precepts of functional analysis just discussed.

Figure 3.13 is a histogram of 232 room floor areas at Casas Grandes, and we use it to define four room size classes. Class I rooms range from 1.4 to 34.9 sq m of floor area, with a mean size of 17.6 sq m. Class II rooms are 35.0 to 63.9 sq m in area, and their mean size is 47.1 sq m. Rooms of Class III measure from 64.0 to 99.5 sq m, having an average size of 71.6 sq m. Lastly, Class IV rooms range from 99.6 to 120.0 sq m. The ensuing discussion considers the architectural and feature characteristics of these room size classes. Table 3.5 shows the proportions of rooms in each size class having particular architectural elements or features. Table 3.6 provides the mean frequencies per room of these elements and features, and gives the results of an analysis of variance that was used to compare the mean values within size classes. When a significant mean

**Table 3.5**  Architectural Characteristics of Casas Grandes Rooms, by Size Class

|  | Class I | Class II | Class III | Class IV |
|---|---|---|---|---|
| *n* | 188 | 34 | 5 | 4 |
| All hearths (%)[a] | 86 | 100 | 100 | 100 |
| Platform hearths (%) | 44 | 59 | 60 | 75 |
| Doorways (%) | 95 | 100 | 100 | 100 |
| "Bed" platforms (%) | 50 | 50 | 60 | 75 |
| Wall niches (%) | 41 | 29 | 20 | 50 |
| Sub-floor burials (%) | 27 | 35 | 20 | 0 |
| Sub-floor caches (%) | 0 | 24 | 60 | 0 |
| Simple shapes (%) | 88 | 59 | 60 | 50 |
| Compound shapes (%) | 12 | 41 | 40 | 50 |
| Windows (%) | 34 | 50 | 60 | 50 |

*Source:* Data from Di Peso, Rinaldo, and Fenner (1974: vol. 4 and vol. 5:197–822).
a. % means percentage of rooms in a size class that have the indicated characteristic.

**Table 3.6**  Frequencies of Architectural Characteristics at Casas Grandes, by Size Class

|  |  | Class I | Class II | Class III | Class IV | ANOVA result (Scheffé Post Hoc test) |
|---|---|---|---|---|---|---|
| Room floor | mean | 17.6 | 47.1 | 71.6 | 107.3 | Not tested. Defined by |
| area (sq m) | SD | 8.1 | 7.7 | 4.0 | 8.8 | histogram. |
| No. of hearths, | mean | 1.5 | 3.3 | 3.8 | 4.0 | $F = 19.025, p < .0001$ |
| all kinds | SD | 1.1 | 2.2 | 2.2 | 2.4 | (Class I differs from all others.) |
| No. of doorways, | mean | 2.9 | 4.3 | 5.0 | 5.5 | $F = 9.771, p < .001$ |
| all kinds | SD | 1.6 | 2.3 | 1.9 | 2.1 | (Class I differs from all others.) |
| No. of | mean | 0.5 | 1.1 | 1.0 | 0.8 | $F = 3.404, p = .02$ |
| windows | SD | 0.9 | 1.4 | 1.2 | 1.0 | (Class I differs from all others.) |
| No. of platform | mean | 0.5 | 0.7 | 1.0 | 0.8 | $F = 2.304, p = .07$ |
| hearths | SD | 0.6 | 0.7 | 1.0 | 0.5 |  |
| No. of "bed" | mean | 0.7 | 1.0 | 1.6 | 1.5 | $F = 2.313, p = .07$ |
| platforms | SD | 1.0 | 1.2 | 2.0 | 1.7 |  |
| No. of wall niches | mean | 0.8 | 0.6 | 0.4 | 1.0 | $F = 3.404, p = .72$ |
|  | SD | 1.2 | 1.1 | 0.9 | 1.4 |  |

difference was found, the Scheffé post hoc test was applied to determine which size classes differed significantly from the others.

Some patterns are apparent in these data, and some significant differences were found among the classes. Hearths are present in rooms of every size class, and table 3.5 indicates that there are few rooms without hearths. This is one of the factors that led Di Peso to classify nearly all of the excavated rooms as domestic. Rooms without hearths occur only in Class I, or among the site's smallest intramural spaces. The mean number of hearths per Class I room is significantly smaller than in any of the other size classes. This analysis lumped hearths of all types. Platform hearths, however, are a distinctive and elaborate kind of fire feature (Di Peso, Rinaldo, and Fenner 1974:4:255–56). The next row of table 3.5 shows that platform hearths occur in all room size classes at Casas Grandes, but that their frequency of occurrence rises somewhat with room size. Nevertheless, analysis of variance shows that the mean platform hearth figures shown in table 3.6 barely fail to achieve statistical significance ($F = 2.304$; $p = 0.07$).

Doorways were found in rooms of all size classes, but table 3.6 shows a significant difference among size classes in mean number of doorways per room. Specifically, it is the Class I rooms that differ from all others. The same pattern is apparent for windows: Class I rooms average fewer than their larger counterparts. Wall niches, on the other hand, do not occur at significantly different frequencies across room size classes. Finally, several other room size class characteristics were not tested statistically in the present study. Sub-floor caches of shell and stone beads and pendants never were found in either the smallest (Class I) or the largest (Class IV) rooms. Sub-floor human burials were about equally common in rooms of size Classes I to III, yet none came from the largest rooms of Class IV. Room shape was highly predictable for Class I rooms, nearly all of which were of simple quadrilateral or L shapes. Compound shapes make up about half of all rooms in the larger size classes, although simple shapes continue to be equally well represented.

In sum, Casas Grandes rooms of size Class I average 17.6 sq m in floor area. They show a number of differences from the rest of the sample. They have significantly fewer hearths, doorways, and windows than do larger rooms. They also have the sample's lowest frequencies of platform hearths and "bed" platforms, although both of these mean differences barely failed to achieve statistical significance in the present data set. Class I rooms never have sub-floor caches, and nearly all of them are of simple shapes. Class I rooms thus are the community's smallest, simplest, and least accessible spaces. We stress, however that although Class I rooms are small by the standards of Casas Grandes, they include rooms up to nearly 35 sq m. These rooms are good-sized in comparison to the other Southwestern pueblo rooms discussed earlier in this section.

Some of these rooms could have been storage spaces. Of the 188 Class I rooms, 20 contain no hearths. These hearthless rooms range in floor area from 1.4 to 19.5 sq m, with a mean size of 9.6 sq m (SD = 4.7). About 80 percent of the small, hearthless rooms lack windows and wall niches, and about 70 percent have no "bed" platforms or sub-floor burials. They are, in other words, the smallest and simplest rooms of size Class I. These 20 rooms are not distributed evenly among the excavated parts of Casas Grandes. Instead, more than half of them are concentrated in Units 6 and 12, and the rest are scattered thinly over all of the other excavated room units. It is interesting to note that Units 6 and 12 contain low and medium frequencies, respectively, of the "bed" platforms that we earlier argued to have been intramural storage facilities. Even if all 20 of these rooms served for storage, however, they comprise only 8.6 percent of the 231 excavated rooms in our sample. Other work in pueblos of the U.S. Southwest (e.g., E. C. Adams 1983) leads us to expect that more spaces should have been devoted to storage. This leads us to suspect that intramural food storage at Casas Grandes may not have been done in the manner characteristic of pueblos in the U.S. Southwest.

The largest rooms at Casas Grandes (Class IV) average more than 100 sq m in floor area. There are only four of these rooms in the excavated sample, but they show several characteristics that set them apart. They have the sample's highest frequency of the elaborate platform hearths, no sub-floor caches were found in any of them, and this is the only category of Casas Grandes room that contained no sub-floor human burials. Very large rooms commonly are interpreted as communal or ceremonial facilities in studies of southwestern pueblo room function (e.g., E. C. Adams 1983; Cameron 1999; Shafer 2003), and one of our Class IV rooms originally was characterized as a communal space of some sort (Di Peso, Rinaldo, and Fenner 1974:5:710). This is Room 45 of Unit 14, which had a floor area of 99.8 sq m. Inside the room were four adobe pillars or columns that may have supported a second-story balcony running around all four sides of the space. The other three rooms in Class IV did not contain such unusual features.

It seems likely that Class II and III rooms served a wide variety of purposes. The average floor areas of these two classes are, respectively, 47 and 72 sq m, so that they are large by Southwest pueblo standards. One of the Class III rooms is Room 36 of Unit 14. It had 68 sq m of floor area, and it was described by Di Peso as "one of the most impressive rooms excavated in Unit 14 (Di Peso, Rinaldo, and Fenner 1974:5:671). The room had a compound shape described by the excavators as a butterfly, and beneath its floor were eight caches of shell and stone jewelry. Table 3.6 demonstrates that sub-floor caches were most common in the rooms of Class III size. Apart from a few rooms like the one just described, however, Class II and III rooms differed little from each other. The rooms of Classes II and III contain all of the architectural traits and features discussed here.

In sum, some simple patterns of association among room size, feature types, and architectural traits do exist. At the end of this analysis, however, we must conclude that the Casas Grandes rooms do not sort into neat, easily perceptible functional classes based on size and architecture. Except for a few variables, there is a good deal of trait overlap among the size classes. There are several possible explanations for this situation. It may be that our classification system is inadequate or inappropriate, drawing as it does on the pueblos of the U.S. Southwest. We have here assumed a difference of degree rather than of kind. That is, we see Casas Grandes as the same basic kind of community as other southwestern pueblos, although at a much larger scale. This assumption seems the most parsimonious choice at the present, although it may be incorrect. It could also be that the Casas Grandes rooms have been so extensively modified that their original functions are blurred. Unfortunately, we can only conclude that room function remains imprecisely defined at the primate center.

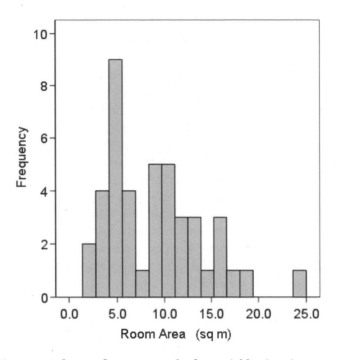

**Figure 3.14** Histogram of room floor areas at the four neighboring sites.

*Room Function at the Neighboring Sites.* Preceding discussion identified two patterns of room usage among the Medio period neighbors of Casas Grandes. The first, and evidently the most common, was termed the small-room pattern. This includes sites 204, 231, and 317. Here, mean room size was about 9 sq m (SD = 5.0). This is quite comparable to the mean room sizes of a sample of 25 prehistoric pueblos assembled by Cameron (1999). The second Medio pattern, however, is composed of much larger rooms. These were present at Casas Grandes and at the small site 242, an administrative satellite of the primate center. None of these sites had any consistent amount of de facto refuse on room floors. Room-use analysis, therefore, relies on architectural characteristics and intramural feature assemblages.

Figure 3.14 shows a histogram of room floor areas at the four neighboring sites, from which three size modes are defined. Small rooms range from 2.4 to 6.9 sq m, medium-sized rooms measure 7.0 to 14.9 sq m, and large rooms have 15.0 to 24.8 sq m of floor area. In this sample, rooms without hearths number only five, or ca. 10 percent of the total of 51. These five rooms are the smallest ones in the small-room size class. Their mean floor area is 3.2 sq m (SD = 0.7), and all of them come from site 204. All five have at least one doorway, although many of these entries had been sealed. Hearthless rooms likely occurred all over site 204, as one was found in every excavation unit except for that of Mound B. Based on their size and simplicity, we suggest that these rooms could have been used for storage. They were not found at small sites 231 or 317.

Large rooms were found at sites 204 and 242, although they appear to have served different purposes in the two communities. Only one room at the former site fell into the large category, whereas there were three such rooms in site 242. The large room at site 204 is Room 21 (refer to fig. 3.9). It measured about 23 sq m and had a simple, rectangular shape. Two doorways opened onto a plaza, and three more doorways led to adjoining rooms on the other three sides. We suspect that looting destroyed another entryway on the east wall. In any case, Room 21 had a high level of accessibility. The room also contained two adobe column bases, as described earlier in this chapter. The room may originally have been an open, colonnaded space leading onto the adjacent plaza, with the north wall being added later to enclose the space. At some point in the history of Room 21, two partition walls were added to enclose about 4 sq m of the northeast corner.

Room 21 had a number of intramural features. One feature, Feature 94 in figure 3.9, was a small, shallow, hemispherical hearth constructed near the room's south wall. The presence of only one small hearth in so large a room is unusual at site 204, where many rooms contained multiple fire features. We also note that badly damaged platform hearths were present in the centers of each of two smaller rooms that adjoined Room 21 to the south. The fire feature assemblage of Room 21, then, is very sparse and simple, and it is not consistent with those of the adjoining, interconnected rooms. We suspect that Room 21 originally had no hearth, the small extant one being added at a late stage of the room's history. Also present in the floor of Room 21 were four roughly cylindrical pits of 40–50 cm in diameter and 25–60 cm deep (Features 84, 95, 101, and 103 in fig. 3.9). The fill of the pits was almost devoid of artifacts.

The artifacts found in other parts of Room 21 are noteworthy, however. In the northeast corner of the room, on the floor and lying against the base of the easternmost adobe platform or column, was a pile of ground stone implements. Five were used manos, and seven other pieces were carefully shaped but unused mano blanks (fig. 3.15). A broken Type 1A metate lay in floor contact in the southeast corner of the room. Room 21 also yielded six broken ceramic vessels, the locations of which were distributed all over the floor. Most of each vessel's sherds were in floor contact. Five were utilitarian jars of common types: Plain (1), Rubbed Scored (3), and Corrugated (1). Their volumes ranged widely from 15 to 43 L. Two of them bore exterior soot, but none had interior pitting. (Refer to chapter 4 for a discussion of these traces of use-wear.) The sixth vessel was a small (9 L) Ramos Black jar with a painted red design. Room 21 thus contained a concentration of utilitarian implements that is without equal in any other excavated room of the present sample. There were other unusual artifacts in Room 21 as well. A cache of four undamaged projectile points, one broken point, and two bifaces was found in the northeast corner, atop the pile of new and used manos. The points were all of the Late Archaic style (fig. 3.16), and they likely represent curated items.

The unusual contents of Room 21 extend into adjoining Rooms 19 and 22 (fig. 3.17). Each room had a central platform hearth. Each was connected to Room 21 by an unsealed, T-shaped doorway. The northwest corner of Room 19 contained a few mano blanks similar to those found in Room 21. Under the floor of Room 22 adjoining the south wall was the burial of a juvenile macaw (fig. 3.18). This is the only macaw burial found to date at any of the neighbors of Casas Grandes. The Room 21-19-22 complex is the most elaborate one in our excavated sample. Rooms 19 and 22 likely were residential spaces, whereas Room 21 may have served as a communal or ceremonial space.

**Figure 3.15** A pile of mano blanks in Room 21, site 204. It lay against one of the adobe columns, the edge of which is visible at the bottom of the picture. The scale shows 10 cm intervals.

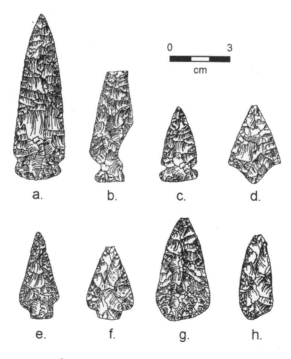

**Figure 3.16** A cache of large points and bifaces from Room 21, site 204. It was found near the cache of mano blanks shown in the previous figure.

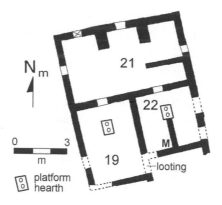

**Figure 3.17** The elaborate Room 19-21-22 complex at site 204. Room 21 contains two adobe colonnades. Rooms 19 and 22 each have a platform hearth, and the macaw burial in Room 22 is shown by the letter *M*. Rooms 19 and 22 each appear to have only one doorway that opens into Room 21. The *x* through a doorway indicates that it was found sealed.

**Figure 3.18** The burial of a juvenile macaw in Room 22, site 204. It lay just beneath the floor, in a corner of the room. This is the common location for human burials in these pueblos.

The 29 remaining rooms at site 204 make up 83 percent of the site's sample. Eleven of these are small and 18 are medium-sized, as previously defined. Most of them (72 percent) have more than one hearth, and a few contain 8 to 13 hearths distributed among several successive floor levels. Nearly all of these are the small, simple, hemispherical features described previously. In the present sample, there is no significant correlation between a room's size and the number of hearths it contained. For instance, the room with 13 hearths had an area of only 4.2 sq m. Platform hearths were found in four of the medium-sized rooms, whereas the small rooms had none of these elaborate fire features. The small and medium-sized rooms had rectangular and T-shaped doorways in about equal frequencies.

All of these rooms could have been residential spaces. The few small, hearthless rooms described earlier could have been used for storage. It will be clear that we use *residential* as a catch-all category for rooms to which no other specific function can be assigned. The pattern just described is comparable to the one just discussed for Casas Grandes. At both sites, a majority of rooms have hearths and were classed as residential spaces. Each site also has a small percentage of large rooms, some with unusual features, which could have served for communal or ceremonial functions. Finally, both the primate center and site 204 have a few small, hearthless rooms that might have been storage spaces.

The three small sites differ somewhat from this pattern. As discussed earlier in this chapter, sites 231 and 317 are small-room pueblos, whereas site 242 is a large-room community. The small-room sites will be evaluated first. A few of these rooms fall at the upper end of the small-room category defined earlier in figure 3.14, but most rooms are medium-sized. There are no large rooms in this excavated sample. All of the site 231 and 317 rooms contained hearths. We found none of the small, hearthless rooms present at Casas Grandes and at site 204. The mean number of hearths per room at site 231 was 6.0 (SD = 1.12, $n = 4$), and that at site 317 was 2.8 (SD = 0.84, $n = 5$). This mean difference is statistically significant ($t = 4.84$, df = 7, $p = .002$). In addition to having more hearths per room than site 317, site 231 also contained several architectural elements not found at its counterpart. All of these occurred in Room 1, and they include a wall niche, a short interior wall, and a stone-and-adobe step or low platform (fig. 3.19). The stone-and-adobe step or platform rose only 13 cm above the floor surface, over which it was constructed. It lay directly beneath a T-shaped doorway that opened into the adjacent Room 3. Despite these architectural embellishments, however, Room 1 was not large, its 8.3 sq m of floor area placing it a little below the average room size of sites 231 and 317. No platform hearths were found at either site, and all rooms were of simple, quadrilateral shapes. In general, the architecture of small sites 231 and 317 was the simplest in our current sample. We ascribe residential functions to all of the excavated rooms at both sites.

Site 242 has already been noted to contain large rooms, some of which were of compound shapes. The site's sample included one hearthless room (No. 8) which, at 9.0 sq m, was also the smallest of the excavated spaces. Room 8 had two sealed doorways, and it was L-shaped. Lying in the middle of the cluster of excavated rooms, it could have been a storage room. Its floor area is comparable to the hearthless spaces at the primate center. This large storage space accords well with the previously expressed idea of site 242 as an administrative satellite of the Casas Grandes system. We note that this potential storage room is considerably larger than those at site 204.

The other excavated rooms in the 242 settlement contain hearths, most of which are of the elaborate platform variety. One of these is shown in figure 3.12a. Three of the five

**Figure 3.19** A step or low platform of stone and adobe in Room 1, site 231. The intervals on the scale are 10 cm.

excavated rooms exceeded 20 sq m in area, which equates to the small-room category at Casas Grandes. Two of the rooms at site 242 (Nos. 3 and 9) had horizontal indentations in their walls that might mark the points of attachment of the intramural platforms that were argued earlier to have been storage facilities (see fig. 3.6). The largest room in the 242 sample (Room 7) had the most complex shape, with 14 walls (refer to fig. 1.27), although it is only a few square meters larger than several other 242 rooms. Room 7 was outlined by wall trenching but was not completely excavated. Accordingly, we lack a full inventory of its features. Those present in the excavated part include a platform hearth and two small, hemispherical fire pits. The small excavated sample at site 242 includes no unusually large room that might have served for communal or ceremonial activity.

In summary, all of the rooms dug at sites 231 and 317 appear to have been residential, at least at some points in their histories. At site 242, Room 8 may have been used for storage, but all of the others likely served domestic functions. The much larger samples from site 204 and from Casas Grandes include examples of what seem to be storage, residential, and communal or ceremonial rooms. We conclude this discussion of Medio period room use by reiterating the paucity of identifiable storage rooms at any of the sites discussed here. This situation contrasts with reports from the Pueblo Southwest, where many more storage rooms usually are identified. This raises the possibility that food storage in Medio period pueblos was accomplished in some different manner than in the southwestern pueblos.

## Architectural Change through the Medio Period

The present data set does not permit a thorough investigation of this topic. Only site 204 has well-dated early and late Medio contexts, and few of these are rooms. Rooms 1–8 and 50–52 have exclusively early Medio dates from floor contact samples. Rooms 61–65 have only late Medio dates, plus a late ceramic assemblage. Rooms 70–72 of Mound B are associated with a midden that contains only late Medio ceramics. We thus have a sample of 10 early and 9 late Medio rooms. The rest of the excavated rooms at site 204 seem to be mixed early and late Medio contexts, as discussed in chapter 2.

Statistical analyses were conducted on the early and late rooms and on their features. Much was found to be consistent across the period, but some patterns were detected. It appears that platform hearths were either rare or absent in the early part of the Medio period. At site 204, the early Medio rooms of Area 1 contained no platform hearths. A few of these facilities were found in Areas 2 and 3 and in a Mound B room. Radiocarbon dates presented in chapter 2 argue that these three areas were last occupied in the late part of the Medio, when they were heavily remodeled. We have argued that the excavated parts of Casas Grandes, with their platform hearths, are late Medio. At the neighboring sites, no platform hearth has yet been found in a context dating to the early part of the Medio period. It thus appears that platform hearths were a late Medio addition to the intramural feature assemblage. The same may be true of rectangular hearths with stone or adobe linings and of the use of ceramic bowls or large sherds as basin liners. Fire pits of these kinds presently are known only from what we will show to be late Medio contexts at Casas Grandes. In contrast, the first five basin hearth variants shown in table 3.3 are found in early and late Medio rooms at site 204. All of these observations indicate that a number of types of basin hearths occurred from early through late Medio times, and that a few new types were added in the late part of the Medio.

Fire feature size also was compared across time. This analysis uses lined and unlined hearths from the nine early Medio rooms of Area 1 at site 204. Eight late Medio rooms came from Area 4 and Mound C at site 204. The sample is regrettably small, as only these few rooms were either exclusively early or late Medio, without occupation across the period. Table 3.7 shows statistics for early and late Medio fire pits of the lined and unlined varieties.

It is apparent from the table that early Medio clay-lined fire pits were somewhat (ca. 29 percent) larger in mean area than their late Medio successors, whereas the depth of these fire pits differs little across the Medio period. In this sample, neither mean difference is statistically significant (area: $t = 1.41$, df $= 43$, $p = .17$; depth: $t = -0.88$, df $= 43$, $p = .39$). The table also shows that unlined fire pits were much less common

Table 3.7  Early and Late Medio Fire Pit Dimensions at Site 204

| Type | Dimensions | Early Medio | | | Late Medio | | |
|------|-----------|-----|------|-----|-----|------|-----|
| | | $n$ | Mean | SD | $n$ | Mean | SD |
| Lined | area | 15 | 2,342.8 sq cm | 1,348.1 | 30 | 1,737.0 sq cm | 1,680.8 |
| | depth | 15 | 14.0 cm | 6.8 | 30 | 15.7 cm | 6.5 |
| Unlined | area | 3 | 1,081.8 sq cm | 544.6 | 3 | 1,953.0 sq cm | 971.1 |
| | depth | 3 | 14.3 cm | 1.5 | 3 | 19.3 cm | 9.0 |

than lined ones all across the Medio, so that the sample analyzed here is too small to do more than hint at patterns of change. Early Medio unlined fire pits are of smaller mean area and depth than those of the late Medio. Nevertheless, the mean differences are not significant (area: $t = -1.66$, df $= 5$, $p = .16$; depth: $t = 0.92$, df $= 5$, $p = .40$). Within the early Medio rooms, clay-lined fire pits were found to be of significantly larger mean area than the unlined pits ($t = 2.67$, df $= 6$, $p = .03$), although the small sample size prevents this result from being conclusive. The depths of lined and unlined fire pit differed little in the early Medio, however. In the late Medio, the mean areas and depths of lined and unlined fire pits were so similar that a test for significance of difference is unnecessary. In summary, this sample hints that the common clay-lined fire pit might have decreased in area, but not in depth, from early to late Medio times in the site 204 sample. In addition, early Medio clay-lined fire pits were larger in area than their unlined contemporaries. This difference was not found in the late part of the Medio period, where lined and unlined fire pits were of about the same area and depth.

No significant differences were found between the early and late parts of the Medio period in mean room area, wall thickness, numbers of rectangular and T-shaped doorways, or numbers of hearths. Wall niches and "bed" platforms did not occur in any early Medio contexts. Such observations do not demonstrate that these architectural features were not present in the early Medio, of course, although the 204 data hint that they were either rare or absent early in the period. The whole data set thus suggests several conclusions. First, there was a good deal of continuity in basic architectural style from early to late Medio times. Second, early Medio architecture may have been somewhat simpler than its late successor, with lower frequencies of elements such as platform hearths, "bed" platforms, and wall niches. Essentially, we argue that the difference between early and late Medio architecture lay more in degree of elaboration than in kind. Finally, we see the "architecture of power" that was displayed at Casas Grandes and at its satellite site 242 as a late Medio addition to the complex. As described elsewhere (Whalen and Minnis 2001b) the architecture of power includes such unusual elements as multistory construction, very thick walls even in single-story units, large rooms, and complex room shapes.

# 4

## Medio Period Ceramic Evolution

Archaeologists have long sought to unravel the sequence of development of the elaborate Medio period ceramic assemblage, especially the many polychrome types. Since early in the twentieth century there has existed the idea of a developmental continuity from the simpler Viejo assemblage to its more complex Medio successor (e.g., Brand 1933; Carey 1931; and Sayles 1936a). E. B. Sayles (1936a) published an early postulation of a specific set of developmental relations among Chihuahuan ceramic types, which is reproduced here as figure 4.1. Sayles' scheme envisions a progression from Dublan and Babícora Polychromes through Ramos Polychrome, the pinnacle of the series. The figure implies a simple succession of different types through time, although the true situation is actually more complex. Nevertheless, Sayles recognized some significant evolutionary relations, as will be apparent later in this discussion.

### Previous Seriation Work

Chihuahuan ceramics never have been seriated at the fine scales that are so common in the adjacent Southwest and Mesoamerica, and the reason was identified long ago. Brand (1933:91) and Lister (1946:433) note Chihuahua's lack of the deep, stratified midden deposits that were so crucial in ceramic chronology development in the neighboring U.S. Southwest. Our own large-scale surveys in the Casas Grandes area (Whalen and Minnis 2001a) confirm the accuracy of these early observations. Among more than 300 Medio period sites, we recorded only a handful of visible midden deposits. Consequently, the early history of Chihuahuan archaeology records only a few stratigraphic excavations, and these were done before chronometric dating techniques were available. Carey (1931) reports on excavation of a small, trash-filled pit of the Medio period in the Casas Grandes area, where he tabulated ceramic frequencies by level. In the absence of modern ceramic type names, Carey used ambiguous descriptive terms such as "Red-and-Black-on-Buff," which could be either Ramos or Babícora Polychromes, or both. Although this greatly diminishes the utility of his results, some temporal trends still were identified. Black and red wares, for example, decrease over time, whereas some kinds of polychromes (the "Red-and-Black-on-Buff") increase in frequency. Later, Lister (1946) described 1936 excavations in two-foot levels in extramural contexts at several Medio sites in the Carretas area northwest of Casas Grandes. Sherd tabulations, now using modern type names, were provided by level, and some changes were

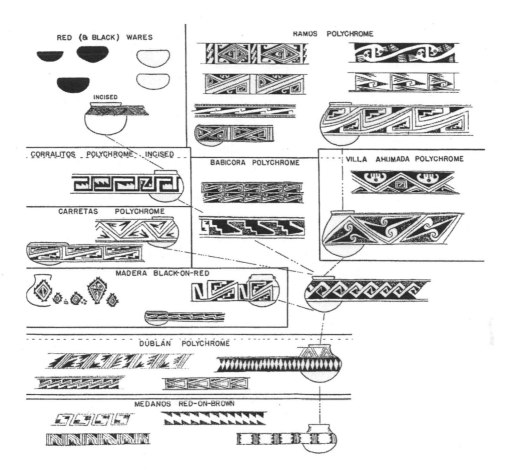

**Figure** 4.1 Evolutionary relationships of the Chihuahuan polychromes, as perceived in 1936 (modified from Sayles 1936a: fig. 17).

evident. These included an increase in Ramos Polychrome frequency through time, a small decrease in Babícora Polychrome in the upper level, and a decrease in Playas Red wares from bottom to top. Beyond these general observations, little more was done for decades with Medio period ceramic evolution.

Work on the nearly 800,000 sherds from the Casas Grandes excavations provided the most detailed look ever at Medio period ceramics (Di Peso, Rinaldo, and Fenner 1974: vol. 6). Many variants of existing types were defined, as were several new types. Nevertheless, most of the ceramic discussion was not phrased in the specific developmental terms of earlier works. This especially true for the complex polychrome types. Accordingly, the substantial contributions of Di Peso and his colleagues to Medio ceramic knowledge did not include expansion or revision of the seriation shown in figure 4.1. Instead, almost all their discussion of inter-type relations consists of notations of trait similarities among types. Babícora Polychrome, for instance, is observed to share a larger number of characteristics with the rest of the Medio ceramic tradition than any other single pottery type (Di Peso, Rinaldo, and Fenner 1974:6:2). The discussion stops here, however, without reference to Sayles' (1936a) assertion that Babícora is one of the oldest of the Chihuahuan polychromes.

The reason for this omission likely lies in the preconception that the elaborate polychrome types of the Medio period did not originate locally but rather in Mesoamerica. The three major types are used here as examples. Ramos Polychrome, the apogee of the Medio assemblage, is described as possibly derived "from some polychrome type made further south in Mexico" (Di Peso, Rinaldo, and Fenner 1974:6:251). Villa Ahumada Polychrome was seen as coming probably "from one of the polychromes made to the south" (Di Peso, Rinaldo, and Fenner 1974:6:300). A more complex lineage was proposed for Babícora Polychrome, which was postulated possibly to originate "from Mata poly and some polychrome type native to an area further south in Mexico" (Di Peso, Rinaldo, and Fenner 1974:6:183). Mata Polychrome is a type from the preceding Viejo period, to which a west Mexican origin is also ascribed (Di Peso, Rinaldo, and Fenner 1974:6:75). This kind of thinking is consistent with Di Peso's entire interpretation of Casas Grandes, which he saw as an exogenic phenomenon; that is, as something stimulated from the outside. Mesoamerican influences, he argued, produced so great a disjunction between the Viejo and Medio periods that it amounted to a "cultural hiatus" (Di Peso 1974:1:100), and Mesoamerican-derived polychromes were simply one part of this process. Elsewhere, we have argued against the exogenic model of the rise of Casas Grandes (Whalen and Minnis 2003), instead seeing the rise of this center and its distinctive material culture as locally stimulated and as growing from local stock.

Whatever position one takes in this interpretive controversy, we are left with little information on what early and late Medio ceramic assemblages looked like. This situation arises from several sources. First, Di Peso and his colleagues divided the rooms at Casas Grandes among his three Medio phases "on the basis of stratigraphy and architecture" (Di Peso, Rinaldo, and Fenner 1974:6:84). Pottery assemblages were then placed in a phase on the basis of their floor or sub-floor associations. Ceramic inventories for each phase were then formed by taking the floors assigned on architectural and stratigraphic grounds to, say, the Buena Fe phase and recording the pottery types found on those floors. The same 22 local pottery types occur in all three of Di Peso's phases of the Medio period (Di Peso, Rinaldo, and Fenner 1974:6:84), and the tabulations that we made from the ceramic data presented with the architectural descriptions show fluctuations of only a few percent in these type frequencies over the three phases. As a result, the three phases do not have the ceramic definitions that we are accustomed to seeing in the U.S. Southwest or in Mesoamerica.

Attempts to use the Casas Grandes data for Medio period ceramic seriation have met with limited success. We attempted to use discriminant analysis to develop a ceramic seriation of Medio contexts assigned by Di Peso to the Buena Fe and Paquimé/Diablo phases (Whalen and Minnis 1996a). Discriminant analysis classifies cases into groups based on a set of selected characteristics, and the analysis provides a statistical measure of how reliable the classification is. For the Casas Grandes analysis, we formed two groups: early Medio (Di Peso's Buena Fe phase) and late Medio (Di Peso's Paquimé and Diablo phases). To represent these groups, we selected 24 proveniences (note that the original paper erroneously says 42) that were assigned by the excavators to either Buena Fe or Paquimé/Diablo phases. The reported frequencies of 19 ceramic types from these contexts were the variables used in the analysis. The classificatory function that was formed by the analysis achieved good discrimination of the two time periods, with the significance of the group mean difference equal to .0002. The function was then applied to a small sample of 18 surface collections from our 1989 survey in the Casas Grandes area, with the surprising result that 16 (89 percent) of the sites were classified as early Medio. We reported these results in Whalen and Minnis 1996a. Problems arose, however, when we sought to expand the discriminant analysis beyond the original set of 24 proveniences. The larger the provenience sample, the greater became the difference between the early and late group means. In other words, the discriminatory power of the function declined, quickly reaching unacceptable levels. Experiments with different proveniences and with differing numbers of these convinced us that the original results were unreliable and that a reliable discriminant function could not be developed from the Casas Grandes data.

Other seriation studies made use of the revised tree-ring dates from Casas Grandes (Dean and Ravesloot 1993) to provide a chronological ordering of deposits, from which ceramic assemblages could be compared. Pitezel (2000) used nine rooms that were ordered by their tree-ring dates between ca. A.D. 1224 and 1390. Using Di Peso's ceramic tabulations for these contexts, Pitezel tabulated type frequencies from each room's floor level. Comparison of these assemblages revealed small percentage changes in a number of type frequencies. For example, Babícora and Escondida Polychromes and Playas Red were observed to decrease over time, while Corralitos Polychrome, Plain ware, and Black-on-Red increased. Ramos Polychrome stayed fairly constant across the time interval. A larger study of ceramic frequencies in tree-ring-dated rooms was done by Rakita and Raymond (2003), who attempted to seriate Medio ceramic types using Di Peso's sherd counts from 25 excavated rooms. They ordered these rooms first by Di Peso's original phase designations, then in a second round of analysis, by the revised tree-ring dates provided by Dean and Ravesloot (1993). The authors note that "no concordance was noted between the estimated tree-ring dates and the frequencies of the various ceramic styles" (Rakita and Raymond 2003:161). The same authors also attempted to construct a frequency seriation (i.e., using Ford or "battleship" curves) for Medio period burials from Casas Grandes. Burials were chosen for analysis because they represent unmixed contexts. The analysis was hampered by the paucity of vessels in grave offerings, but a few patterns were detected. The authors argue that Babícora and Villa Ahumada Polychromes are early, Corralitos and Escondida Polychromes are late, and Ramos Polychrome occurs all through the Medio. These conclusions lend support to some aspects of Sayles' ceramic evolution diagram shown in figure 4.1.

Lastly, Rakita and Raymond attempted to construct frequency seriations of Donald Brand's (1933) survey sites. This analysis suffers from a fundamental problem, however, as Brand did not use modern ceramic type names. The authors note that Brand lumped several polychrome types into a single class termed "Casas Grandes Polychrome," effectively preventing their analysis from recognizing temporal change in some of the most important painted wares (e.g., Ramos and Babícora Polychromes). Brand distinguished

Villa Ahumada Polychrome, which the analysis just described suggests had an early popularity in the Casas Grandes and Santa María areas, but then declined rapidly in the former. This result supports the burial-based seriation of Villa Ahumada Polychrome as an early Medio ware. To recapitulate, Rakita and Raymond (2003) see Babícora and Villa Ahumada Polychromes as characteristic of the early Medio, whereas Corralitos and Escondida are late Medio polychromes. Ramos Polychrome occurs throughout the sequence. Acknowledging the many analytical difficulties that they faced, Rakita and Raymond urge further study of stratified and dated Medio period contexts.

We believe that there is a simple explanation for the ubiquitous difficulties encountered in seriating the Casas Grandes ceramics. That is, we contend that the primate center's ceramic collections represent a single interval rather than the series of distinct intervals that was originally proposed. To illustrate this, we examined contexts from either end of the site's ceramic sequence. The first of these consists of sub-floor deposits from rooms and plazas classed by the excavators as built in the Buena Fe phase, or at the opening of the Medio period. To provide the late end of the sequence, we made ceramic tabulations from a sample of rooms and plazas the excavators considered to have been occupied in the Diablo phase, or at the end of the Medio period.

Polychrome type frequencies were then computed by count and as a percentage of all polychromes for all of the proveniences in each group. The mean percentages of each of the polychrome types in each group were compared using t-tests, e.g., the early mean Ramos Polychrome percentage against the late mean Ramos Polychrome percentage. No statistically significant differences were found for any of the eight types tested. What should be the oldest and youngest ceramic assemblages in the excavated part of Casas Grandes contain the same types in about the same frequencies. Reanalysis of the Casas Grandes tree-ring dates pointed to the conclusion that the site's Medio period occupation likely was a single chronological unit, without the three sequential phases defined originally (Dean and Ravesloot 1993:96). The analysis just described supports this conclusion, suggesting that the site contains a single ceramic unit as well. Extant collections from the primate center, then, do not appear to hold the key to the quest to seriate Medio period ceramics.

Recent years have seen significant progress in Medio ceramic studies due to increased digging and dating in west-central Chihuahua and in the Casas Grandes area. The west-central Chihuahuan work by Jane Kelley and colleagues, termed the PAC (for Proyecto Arqueológico Chihuahua), took place between 1990 and 2000, and it focused on an area some 175 km south of the primate center. The PAC combined survey, excavation, and chronometric dating, providing a welcome body of data on Medio period ceramic evolution. Using material from dated contexts, Burd, Kelley, and Hendrickson (2004) discuss the ceramic characteristics of the Viejo-to-Medio transition, the early Medio, and the late Medio, all as seen at the southernmost limit of the Casas Grandes culture area. This work verifies arguments by Brand (1933), Sayles (1936a), and Gladwin (1936), all of whom saw Babícora Polychrome as the older, cruder predecessor of Ramos Polychrome (refer to fig. 4.1). Burd and her coauthors also see Babícora Polychrome as evolving out of the newly defined Viejo-to-Medio transitional type that they term Santa Ana Polychrome. Unlike Di Peso, then, the PAC researchers envision an in situ developmental process, rather than relying for local inspiration on the introduction of Mesoamerican wares.

Summarizing Burd, Kelley, and Hendrickson (2004:196), the PAC results characterize the early Medio in west-central Chihuahua as occurring with pre–A.D. 1300 radiocarbon dates and as consisting of plain, textured, black, and red wares, Babícora Polychrome, and a few Chihuahuan trade polychromes of unspecified type. Ramos and Villa Ahumada Polychromes are not specifically listed as present in early Medio contexts. The late Medio ceramics associated with post–A.D. 1300 dates include all of the early types, plus increased quantities of Ramos and Villa Ahumada Polychromes. These data contradict the assertion that Villa Ahumada is an early ware (Rakita and Raymond 2003). In addition, the PAC researchers observe that Black-on-Red makes its appearance only in late Medio times. This type, they note, is the only one currently recognized as specific to the late part of the Medio period in southern Chihuahua.

These data have interesting implications. The ideal situation for distinguishing early from late Medio deposits would be to have types that are specific to each subdivision. Unfortunately, the PAC data argue that, with the sole exception of the not-too-common Black-on-Red, diagnostic early and late Medio types do not exist. The same conclusion could be reached with the Casas Grandes data, although one is always uncertain whether mixing of deposits is obscuring actual intra-period ceramic differences. The PAC data, however, argue that intermixing is not the problem. This observation emphasizes the conclusion that Medio period subdivision will have to be based on more subtle differences such as type frequencies or even design element execution patterns (Burd, Kelley, and Hendrickson 2004:204).

## New Data on the Seriation Problem

Recent excavation in the vicinity of Casas Grandes has given us an excellent opportunity to study the developmental sequence of Medio ceramics. In chapter 1 we described the large, deep midden associated with site 204 Mound A, the smaller one with Mound C, and the test pits that were dug into these middens. Each 1 × 2 m pit was dug to sterile soil in 5 cm levels. Most test pits were 16–22 levels, or 80–110 cm, deep, although one reached deeper, ending at 29 levels, or ca. 145 cm, below the surface. All of the Mound A midden test pits shared a consistent characteristic: their lowest levels contained a Medio ceramic assemblage without Ramos Polychrome. These accounted for about one-third of all of the midden test pit levels, and they will hereafter be referred to as the early Medio levels. Ramos Polychrome was present in nearly every higher test pit level. These Ramos-bearing levels made up about two-thirds of all excavated midden deposits, and they are hereafter referred to as the late Medio levels.

At issue now are the ages of the early and late Medio intervals. As discussed in chapter 2, there is a series of radiocarbon dates from the lower levels of test pits 1, 2, 6, and 7. These averaged to cal A.D. 1160–1280 (2σ), and, as noted, contained no Ramos Polychrome. Test pits 3, 4, and 5 have no lower-level dates, but their pre-Ramos ceramic assemblages (to be described presently) closely match those of the dated lower levels.

**Table 4.1** Dating the Appearance of Ramos Polychrome

| Sample[a] | Context | Material | Years B.P. |
|---|---|---|---|
| A-13599 | Test pit 2, Ramos level | wood charcoal | 675 ± 35 |
| A-13600 | Test pit 7, above Ramos | wood charcoal | 645 ± 30 |
| A-13601 | Test pit 7, below Ramos | wood charcoal | 670 ± 30 |

a. A is University of Arizona Radiocarbon Laboratory.

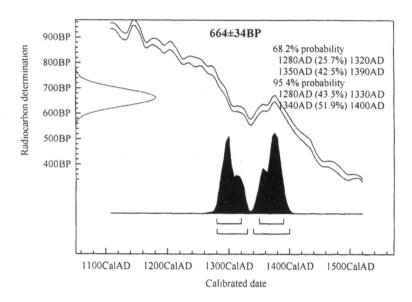

**Figure 4.2** The radiocarbon calibration curve at about 650 years B.P. Figure generated by OXCAL v3.5 (Bronk Ramsey 2000). Atmospheric data from Stuiver et al. 1998.

We also have data from test pit levels that date the first appearance of Ramos Polychrome. We processed a radiocarbon date from the level in which Ramos Polychrome was first seen in test pit number 2. In a second pit (No. 7), two dates come from levels on either side of the first Ramos. Table 4.1 shows these three dates. All were processed with extended counting by the University of Arizona Radiocarbon Laboratory.

The three dates are nearly identical, and the test for coevality confirms that they are all dating the same event ($T' = 0.15$, $\chi^2_{.05} = 5.99$, $p < .001$). It is, therefore, proper to calculate their weighted average, which is 664 ± 34 radiocarbon years B.P. This date pinpoints the appearance of Ramos Polychrome in the Medio ceramic sequence at site 204. There is a problem, however, in converting the date to calendar years, as described in chapter 2 and illustrated in figure 4.2: the B.P. date falls directly on a major "wiggle" in the radiocarbon calibration curve. The B.P. date thus has two calendar dates with nearly equal probabilities of occurrence at 2σ: cal A.D. 1280–1330 and cal A.D. 1340–1400. There is no way to decide which of these calendar-year intervals most probably contains the

**Table 4.2**   Ramos Polychrome Percentages in the Late Medio Levels of the 204 Midden Test Pits

| Test pit number | % Ramos at bottom | % Ramos at top | Mean % in all levels | Standard deviation | Early Medio below? |
|---|---|---|---|---|---|
| 1 | 16.4 | 25.6 | 19.5 | 10.2 | yes |
| 2 | 12.5 | 26.5 | 33.5 | 23.2 | yes |
| 3 | 14.8 | 21.9 | 32.9 | 33.3 | yes |
| 4 | 10.0 | 33.3 | 30.1 | 24.5 | yes |
| 5 | 22.0 | 60.1 | 56.0 | 21.2 | yes |
| 6 | 23.5 | 100 | 53.9 | 26.4 | yes |
| 7 | 16.7 | 72.7 | 62.5 | 12.9 | yes |
| 8 | 50.0 | 100 | 50.5 | 36.3 | no |
| 9 | 100 | 77.3 | 61.3 | 34.0 | no |

true date. Even so, we can say with confidence that in this data set Ramos Polychrome does not appear before about A.D. 1280. Furthermore, we note that essentially the entire time interval covered by the two calendar-year date ranges falls into the 1300s. It is, therefore, most likely that Ramos Polychrome is a late thirteenth- or early fourteenth-century addition to the Medio ceramic assemblage.

It is noteworthy that the dates just discussed are consistent with another series of radiocarbon dates from the Ramos-bearing upper levels of Mound A midden test pits 1, 2, 4, and 7. These dates averaged cal A.D. 1280–1390 ($2\sigma$). Test pits 3, 5, and 6 had no upper-level dates, but their ceramic assemblages were very similar to those of the dated levels. To summarize, the appearance of Ramos Polychrome after A.D. 1280 splits the Mound A midden test pits into two parts. The lower, pre-Ramos levels date to ca. A.D. 1160–1280, which is the early part of the Medio period. These comprise about one-third of the midden deposits. The upper levels, containing Ramos Polychrome, yield dates falling within the interval of A.D. 1280 to at least 1390, which is in the late part of the Medio period. Midden deposition continued for some time beyond 1390, however, as the upper 20–30 cm of each test pit contained no dateable charcoal.

Further division of the midden deposits at site 204 is based on the frequency of Ramos Polychrome. Not surprisingly, Ramos occurs infrequently at first, increasing thereafter to dominate the polychrome assemblage. In the initial deposits of the late Medio period in all of the main midden's seven test pits, Ramos comprises 10 percent to 22 percent of all polychrome sherds. Table 4.2 shows this situation. The only exceptions are test pits 8 and 9, which contain high frequencies of Ramos from bottom to top. These two pits are not located on the main midden. Reference to figure 1.16 shows that test pit 8 lies at the west end of Mound A, and pit 9 was dug into the small midden associated with Mound C. Table 4.2 shows that Ramos Polychrome frequency increases in the upper levels of all test pits, although to variable extents.

These data can be used to postulate two divisions of the late Medio period. The first, which we term the late Medio I, is the only late Medio deposit represented in test pits 1 through 4. Here, the depositional sequence begins with early Medio layers that contain no Ramos Polychrome. Overlying these are layers in which Ramos occurs at low to medium frequency (i.e., 10 percent to 39 percent), and the depositional sequence ends here. Figure 4.3a illustrates the test pit 2 sequence as an example. Note that all four of these pits are adjacent, occupying the western and central parts of the midden.

The second subdivision postulated here is the late Medio II. It succeeds the late Medio I and is defined by Ramos Polychrome frequencies of 40 percent or more of all Polychrome sherds. Table 4.2 shows that test pits 8 and 9 belong exclusively to the late Medio II, and pits 5, 6, and 7 have late Medio II components overlying late Medio I layers. The test pit 5 sequence is illustrated in figure 4.3b to exemplify this situation. Reference to figure 1.16 shows that pits 5, 6, and 7 are adjacent and at the east end of Mound A. The figure shows that the early Medio and late Medio I occupations of the site were extensive, but by the late Medio II occupation had contracted to the west end of Mound A and to the small Mound C. No midden was found with Mound B.

The next question concerns the dates of the late Medio subdivisions just discussed. Preceding pages established the dates of the early Medio as from the late 1100s to about 1280 or 1300, but the chronological placement of the late Medio I and II segments remains to be determined. Clearly required is a comprehensive series of dates from late Medio levels such as those of test pit 5 (fig. 4.3b). Unfortunately, charcoal preservation was poor in the upper five or six levels of every test pit, and many other levels yielded no dateable samples. We have four dates from Late Medio levels in test pits 1, 2, 4, and 7, however, and these are of some assistance. All four pits give dates in the 1300s for levels in which Ramos made up 10 percent to 39 percent of all polychromes (i.e., late Medio I times). We have no dates from the postulated late Medio II levels of any test pit, but test pit 7 is adjacent to Excavation Area 4 (see figs. 1.5 and 1.16), which in chapter 2 we asserted was one of the last occupations in the community, and that area's architecture is of the poorest quality found on the site. The upper limits of this area's 2σ radiocarbon dates are 1400, 1420, and 1435, and these data suggest that the late Medio II falls at least partly in the 1400s, perhaps continuing into the late 1400s, as discussed in chapter 2. Unfortunately, site 204 seems to have been abandoned before the end of the Medio period.

In sum, the late Medio I, with its low frequencies of Ramos Polychrome, began in the late 1200s or early 1300s, and we tentatively postulate that it lasts until the middle 1300s. The succeeding late Medio II interval is tentatively dated from the end of the late Medio I into the middle or late 1400s. We will use this as a working hypothesis in the present study. We do not know what happens to Ramos Polychrome frequencies after the collapse of centralized authority at Casas Grandes. It may well be that the Ramos frequency fell then, necessitating the eventual creation of a late Medio III time interval, but we presently have no data on this point. More dating of midden deposits clearly is crucial to the development of this argument.

## Early and Late Medio Ceramic Assemblage Composition

To this point, we have discussed only Ramos Polychrome and its frequency changes over time. The question now is whether the other components of the ceramic assemblage

(a)                     Test Pit No. 2

| 5 cm level no. | % Ramos | Interval |
|---|---|---|
| 1 | 26.3 | |
| 2 | 33.3 | Late Medio I |
| 3 | 33.3 | |
| 4 | 28.6 | |
| 5 | 12.5 | |
| 6 | 0 | |
| 7 | 0 | |
| 8 | 0 | |
| 9 | 0 | |
| 10 | 0 | |
| 11 | 0 | Early Medio |
| 12 | 0 | |
| 13 | 0 | |
| 14 | 0 | |
| 15 | 0 | |
| 16 | 0 | |

(b)                     Test Pit No. 5

| 5 cm level no. | % Ramos | Interval |
|---|---|---|
| 1 | 50.0 | |
| 2 | 66.7 | |
| 3 | 83.3 | |
| 4 | 19.1 | Late Medio II |
| 5 | 63.3 | |
| 6 | 40.0 | |
| 7 | 69.2 | |
| 8 | 72.7 | |
| 9 | 66.7 | |
| 10 | 34.4 | |
| 11 | 32.1 | |
| 12 | 25.0 | |
| 13 | 34.4 | Late Medio I |
| 14 | 26.7 | |
| 15 | 12.5 | |
| 16 | 18.8 | |
| 17 | 0 | |
| 18 | 0 | |
| 19 | 0 | Early Medio |
| 20 | 0 | |
| 21 | 0 | |
| 22 | 0 | |

**Figure 4.3** Two example test pits showing the proposed intervals of the Medio period: *a*. test pit 2, early Medio and late Medio I; *b*. test pit 5, early Medio through late Medio II

**Table 4.3**    Ceramic Type Frequencies in the 204 Midden Test Pits

| Ceramic type | Early Medio | | Late Medio I (%) | | Late Medio II (%) | |
|---|---|---|---|---|---|---|
| | % | n | % | n | % | n |
| **Polychromes** | | | | | | |
| Babícora | 49.11 | 127 | 34.32 | 198 | 15.41 | 49 |
| White-Paste Babícora | 38.20 | 99 | 25.74 | 149 | 10.38 | 33 |
| Dublan | 9.40 | 24 | 2.20 | 13 | 1.57 | 5 |
| Villa Ahumada | 3.29 | 9 | 5.69 | 33 | 5.35 | 17 |
| Babícora, Ramos variety | 0 | 0 | 1.85 | 11 | 4.09 | 13 |
| Carretas | 0 | 0 | 1.11 | 6 | 1.26 | 4 |
| Corralitos | 0 | 0 | 0 | 0 | 0 | 0 |
| Escondida | 0 | 0 | 0.08 | 1 | 0.31 | 1 |
| Huerigos | 0 | 0 | 0 | 0 | 0 | 0 |
| Ramos | 0 | 0 | 29.01 | 168 | 61.63 | 196 |
| **Total** | **100** | **259** | **100** | **579** | **100** | **318** |
| **Non-polychromes** | | | | | | |
| Plain | 81.89 | 2,898 | 79.70 | 4,256 | 78.46 | 2,306 |
| Scored types | 5.85 | 206 | 5.63 | 301 | 4.63 | 136 |
| Incised types | 2.86 | 101 | 2.64 | 141 | 2.59 | 76 |
| Corrugated types | 2.20 | 78 | 1.70 | 91 | 1.16 | 34 |
| Broad Coil | 0.13 | 5 | 0.28 | 15 | 0.10 | 3 |
| Tool Punched | 0.56 | 20 | 0.37 | 20 | 0.27 | 8 |
| Playas Red types | 2.92 | 103 | 4.70 | 251 | 6.33 | 186 |
| Black | 3.59 | 127 | 4.95 | 264 | 6.36 | 187 |
| Black-on-Red | 0 | 0 | 0.03 | 2 | 0.10 | 3 |
| **Total** | **100** | **3,538** | **100** | **5,341** | **100** | **2,939** |

fluctuate in a similarly regular fashion through the site 204 test pit levels. Table 4.3 shows data to demonstrate that they do. The table's figures are count-based ceramic frequencies found in the seven test pits from the Mound A midden, expressed as percentages of the total number of polychrome and non-polychrome sherds from three parts of the Medio period. A total of 1,156 polychrome and 11,818 non-polychrome sherds came from these levels. For each type, n in the table is the total number of sherds from all test pits. A number of the non-polychrome types were lumped into categories e.g., Plain Scored, Patterned Scored, and Rubbed Scored compose the Scored category. The same is true of the Incised, Corrugated, and Playas Red categories. "White-Paste Babícora" is a variant that will be described in succeeding pages. Corralitos and Huerigos Polychromes do not occur in the excavated test pits.

It is apparent from table 4.3 that the early Medio polychrome assemblage is simpler than its late Medio successors. Present in the early Medio levels are only four of the 10 polychrome types and varieties that characterize the late part of the Medio period at site 204. In this sample, the early Medio ceramic assemblage is dominated by Babícora

Polychrome, which accounts for nearly 50 percent of all painted sherds in the early levels. This is the standard variant of Babícora, as described at Casas Grandes (Di Peso, Rinaldo, and Fenner 1974:6:183–98). Babícora has often been argued to be the oldest of the Chihuahuan polychromes (e.g., Amsden 1928; Brand 1935; Burd, Kelley, and Hendrickson 2004; Carlson 1982; Gladwin and Gladwin 1934; Kidder 1916; Rakita and Raymond 2003; Sayles 1936a), and the data from site 204 support this assertion.

In a fairly close second to Babícora is a ceramic that has not been described in the Medio period literature. Accordingly, it has no established name, and we here use the descriptive term "White-Paste Babícora." At this point, we prefer to consider it a variant of Babícora Polychrome. This usage, of course, implies an evolutionary relationship, about which more will be said presently. The name conveys the principal characteristics of the ceramic. Babícora Polychrome, as described at Casas Grandes, shows a range of paste colors characterized as "light reddish-brown (5 YR 6/6) or light brown (7.5 YR 6/4) through reddish yellow (5 YR 6/6) or pink (7.5 YR 7/4) to a very pale brown (10 YR 7/3, 10 YR 7/4). Typical color is light brown" (Di Peso, Rinaldo, and Fenner 1974:6:184). In the same discussion, most sherds are also noted to have gray cores, of which dark gray (7.5 YR 4/0) was the most common. In contrast, White-Paste Babícora is characterized by a paste color that is outside of the range just defined in the quoted Babícora type description. We do note, however, that a general discussion of Medio period ceramics earlier in the Casas Grandes volume mentions Babícora pastes ranging from "pinkish or white through light brown and very pale brown" (Di Peso, Rinaldo, and Fenner 1974:6:82), although the white pastes are not mentioned in the full type description.

White-Paste Babícora, as the name implies, is made from white-firing clays, which are abundant in the Casas Grandes area. Many examples of White-Paste Babícora have chalk-white paste, but others are a grayish or pinkish white (ca. 5 YR 8/1). The paste is fine, without much visible tempering material. About 70 percent of our sample of White-Paste Babícora sherds have no cores, whereas thin, very light gray cores are present in the other 30 percent. Local potters confirmed that some of the white-firing clays of the Casas Grandes area produce cores much like those we observed in White-Paste Babícora. It is also noteworthy that the paste, core, and temper characteristics just described for White-Paste Babícora are shared by both of the other white-paste wares of the Casas Grandes area. These are Ramos and Escondida Polychromes, which have fine-grained pastes and little visible tempering material. In addition, light gray cores are present in 10 percent to 20 percent of Ramos Polychrome sherds (Di Peso, Rinaldo, and Fenner 1974:6:1).

Figure 4.4 shows photographs of typical examples of White-Paste Babícora. Judging from what can be learned from sherds, the designs of White-Paste Babícora seem to be very similar to those of standard Babícora: thick, imprecise black and red lines forming simple geometric motifs. The White-Paste Babícora motifs also seem to use simple, line-based layouts much like the "Babícora A" style described as "a layout constructed of a series of lines running continuously around the vessel that are appended with or terminate in one or two different triangle-based motifs" (Hendrickson 2003:77). Hendrickson further notes that the simple Babícora A motifs are usually red, which also

**Figure 4.4** Examples of White-Paste Babícora sherds from the 204 midden test pits.

seems to be the case in our sample of White-Paste Babícora. This issue is discussed further in a later section of this chapter.

We wished to determine whether White-Paste Babícora was similarly abundant at Casas Grandes and other Medio sites in the region as at site 204. To establish this, we reexamined a sample of the Babícora sherds excavated by Di Peso at the primate center. Sherds from the 1958–61 excavations are stored at the INAH warehouse in the town of Casas Grandes. They are sorted and boxed by type, presumably as left by Di Peso and his colleagues. The Babícora sherds are in six large boxes, containing an estimated 14,000 sherds. In an unsystematic sample of 850 Babícora sherds from one randomly selected box, we counted some 200 white, pinkish white, and grayish white sherds, or about 22 percent of the total. In a second sample of 100 sherds from another box, we found about 18 percent white or off-white sherds. These are not thorough samples, but they do show that White-Paste Babícora is not simply a ceramic variant confined to site 204 and vicinity. This point is further reinforced by reexamination of a sample of 78 of our 1994–95 survey collections from the Core Zone around Casas Grandes and the Middle Zone some 60–80 km north and west of the primate center. These zones are fully described elsewhere (Whalen and Minnis 2001a). In the restudied survey collections, White-Paste Babícora was identified from 23 of the 78 sites, 11 in the Core Zone and 12 in the Middle Zone. The ceramic thus appears to have a wide distribution in the Casas Grandes area.

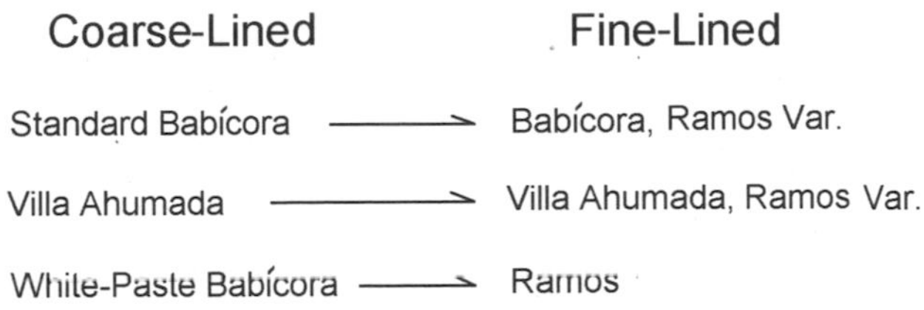

**Coarse-Lined**       **Fine-Lined**

Standard Babícora  ——————➤  Babícora, Ramos Var.

Villa Ahumada  ——————➤  Villa Ahumada, Ramos Var.

White-Paste Babícora  ——————➤  Ramos

**Figure 4.5** Coarse-lined and fine-lined Polychrome variants.

White-Paste Babícora is the earliest-known Chihuahuan polychrome to combine red and black painted decoration with fine-textured, white-firing clays. This is the combination that is refined into a later apogee as classic Ramos Polychrome. Accordingly, we tentatively identify White-Paste Babícora as the antecedent of Ramos Polychrome. It is true that the painting style of White-Paste Babícora is coarser and simpler than that of Ramos Polychrome. Nevertheless, this is a transition that has precedent in the Medio ceramic assemblage. As described in the Casas Grandes volume (Di Peso, Rinaldo, and Fenner 1974:6:183, 299) and shown in figure 4.5, the standard Babícora and Villa Ahumada Polychromes are both accompanied by fine-lined variants. The early Medio test pit levels at site 204 contain none of the fine-lined specimens, which accords well with Hendrickson's (2003) argument on stylistic grounds that all fine-lined polychromes occur late in the Medio period.

There is not a simple coarse- to fine-line progression over time, however. The coarse-lined Babícora and Villa Ahumada Polychromes did not disappear when fine-lined painting began to be used. Instead, both existed until the end of the Medio. The proposed link between White-Paste Babícora and Ramos Polychrome operates the same way, as table 4.3 shows that White-Paste Babícora persists beside fine-lined Ramos until the end of the Medio period. A significant difference, however, is that Ramos Polychrome becomes so much more popular that it is recognized as the "signature" ware of the primate center of Casas Grandes (Lekson 2000:283). It must also be emphasized that all fine-lined Ramos is not equally fine. Our survey collections include many examples of white-paste sherds decorated in the Ramos tradition that are not nearly as finely executed as the splendid examples found in museums and collections. We agree with Sphren's (2003) argument that the best examples of Ramos Polychrome were likely made by specialists, but other, coarser, examples probably were not. In other words, the ceramic tradition does not contain a sudden jump from coarse to exquisitely fine painting. Instead, some of what we term "fine-lined" Ramos is so, but other vessels were significantly less well painted.

In short, we see the Chihuahuan ceramic tradition as having a persistent style of painting across all polychrome types: bold, thick-lined, linear designs in red and black. It presently appears that all painted pottery is like this before about A.D. 1280 or 1300, or in early Medio times. This style continues into the late Medio, but that time also sees the proliferation of fine-lined variants of some of these polychromes, derived from Babícora, Villa Ahumada, and White-Paste Babícora, as described previously.

To conclude this discussion of the early Medio polychrome ceramic assemblage, we return to table 4.3. Two more polychromes are present in the early Medio. These are Dublan and Villa Ahumada, comprising, respectively, about 9 percent and 3 percent of the assemblage in the lower test pit levels. Both are as described in the Casas Grandes volume (Di Peso, Rinaldo, and Fenner 1974: vol. 6). Villa Ahumada stays at a fairly constant, low frequency from the lower to the upper test pit levels. It does not appear from these data to be the diagnostic early Medio ware suggested by a recent study (Rakita and Raymond 2003). In fact, the data in table 4.3 argue that there are no ceramic diagnostics of the early part of the Medio period. Dublan Polychrome is the type that comes closest to diagnostic status, as it continues into the late Medio at reduced frequency. It is the simplest of the Chihuahuan polychromes in terms of its designs, and it is the only painted type that never bears the macaw motif, a symbol that is characteristic of Casas Grandes (Di Peso, Rinaldo, and Fenner 1974:6:99). Researchers at work on the southern edge of the Casas Grandes culture area were recently led to wonder "whether Babícora and Dublan Polychromes might not be regarded as embodying the beginnings of the Chihuahua polychrome tradition" (Burd, Kelley, and Hendrickson 2004:194). The data from site 204 support this supposition.

In summary, the early Medio polychrome assemblage from the lower test pit levels at site 204 consists mostly of Babícora and White-Paste Babícora Polychromes, plus small amounts of Dublan and Villa Ahumada Polychromes. These early deposits contain no Ramos Polychrome. Recognition of early Medio deposits, then, may be based as strongly upon what they do not contain as upon what is present. The data in table 4.3 do not reveal any ceramic type diagnostic of early Medio times. That is, there are no types unique to the early Medio. Type combinations may, however, be useful diagnostics. A sizeable assemblage containing no Ramos Polychrome but some or all of the Dublan, White-Paste Babícora, Villa Ahumada, and Babícora types is likely to be early Medio. The proportions of the wares might also be a useful measure, as others have also suggested (Burd, Kelley, and Hendrickson 2004:202). The most useful ratios would, of course, be those that show considerable difference between the early and late Medio. For example, the ratio of Dublan to Babícora for the early Medio is 0.17, whereas the late Medio figure is about 0.06 in the upper levels. A variety of other ratios could also be calculated. Obviously, however, the validity of these ratios is strongly dependent on sample size.

Next we consider the late Medio I polychromes shown in table 4.3. First, we emphasize that all of the early Medio polychromes continue into the late part of the period, although at lower frequencies. In addition to the persistence of these ceramics, a number of polychrome types seem to make their first appearance in late Medio I times, or after about A.D. 1300. In addition to Ramos, table 4.3 identifies two other late Medio I polychrome types: Carretas and Escondida. Sayles (1936a:29) considered Carretas a derivation of Babícora Polychrome in vessel shape and design, and the similarity of Carretas and Babícora has been noted (Burd, Kelley, and Hendrickson 2004:194; Di Peso, Rinaldo, and Fenner 1974:6:198). The late Medio dating of Escondida Polychrome is not surprising. Many have noted the strong resemblance of Escondida to Gila Polychrome, often classing the former as a local imitation of the latter (e.g., Di Peso, Rinaldo, and Fenner 1974:226). Gila Polychrome is a post–A.D. 1300 trade ware in Chihuahua, and Escondida appears to be contemporaneous with it. Another recent seriation study (Rakita and Raymond 2003) also identified Escondida as a late Medio ware. Corralitos and Huerigos Polychromes were found only in surface levels at site 204, so that we can make no definitive statement about their dating. Data from other sites show them to be late Medio types, however, as will be discussed later in this chapter. Table 4.3 shows that all of the polychrome types of the late Medio I continue into the late Medio II. With the sole exception of Villa Ahumada Polychrome, all continue the trends of change seen from the early Medio to the late Medio I. Babícora and White-Paste Babícora decline the most from late Medio I to II, and this is matched by a large increase in Ramos Polychrome.

The classic Medio assemblage of eight polychrome types and a number of variants seems to occur all together only in the late part of the Medio period, or after about A.D. 1300. This idea has been proposed before on stylistic grounds and by cross-dating with ceramics from the U.S. Southwest (e.g., Carlson 1982:215), and the data from the site 204 test pits provide a chronometric confirmation of it. Lekson (2000:276) is correct in observing that there was "an explosion of local polychrome types after A.D. 1300," although we take exception to his assertion that the types had no local predecessors. In the preceding discussion, we have argued that late Medio types such as Ramos Polychrome were derived from early Medio ceramics. Lastly, we note that sherds of imported ceramics were absent in early Medio test pit levels, although a few sherds of El Paso Polychrome came from early-dated rooms at site 204. This is feasible, as El Paso Polychrome dates from the 1100s (Whalen 1981). One sherd of Chupadero Black-on-White came from a middle-level context that dated to cal A.D. 1280–1390 ($2\sigma$). Chupadero is a long-lived ware from south-central New Mexico, dating from ca. A.D. 1100–1400 (Wiseman 1986). One sherd of Gila Polychrome, which dates from the 1300s onward, came from an upper level. From these sparse data, it appears that most of the Medio period imports come into the area after A.D. 1300.

The polychrome types and varieties just discussed make up only a small, but highly visible, part of the early and late Medio ceramic assemblages, averaging about 7 percent of the total sherd count. Both assemblages are dominated by a wide range of plain, textured, monochrome, and bichrome ceramics. It is clear from table 4.3 that early and late Medio non-polychrome assemblages generally do not differ to the same extent as their polychrome counterparts, although some trends are visible. The only non-polychrome type that is not present in the early part of the Medio is Black-on-Red. Its presence, then, is a true diagnostic of late Medio times. Work in west-central Chihuahua (Burd, Kelley, and Hendrickson 2004:196) also recognized that Black-on-Red was a late Medio type. Unfortunately, table 4.3 shows that Black-on-Red is never a common type.

Other non-polychrome type frequencies also change noticeably between the early and late parts of the Medio. Plain pottery declines somewhat from its early Medio high. Corrugated types decline in frequency from early through late Medio times. Incised, Scored, Broad Coil, and Tool Punched types are essentially unchanged across the Medio in this sample. The Playas Red types show the largest frequency increase, and Black frequencies also rise slightly.

## Application of the Ceramic Sequence

The question now is whether early and late Medio ceramic assemblages can be recognized using the information just provided. In the early Medio, we expect to see high percentages of Babícora and White-Paste Babícora Polychromes, plus a relatively high frequency of Dublan Polychrome. There should be no Ramos, Carretas, Corralitos, Escondida, or Huerigos Polychrome, and Playas Red should be rare. Because the early Medio assemblage contains no types unique to it, however, it is likely to be recognizable only when it is unmixed with late Medio ceramics.

The late Medio is readily recognizable by the presence of all of the polychrome types just listed, especially Ramos Polychrome. Preceding analysis suggested a further division of the late Medio period based on the steadily increasing frequency of Ramos Polychrome. Late Medio I test pit levels had Ramos frequencies of ca. 18 percent to 39 percent of all polychromes, while the late Medio II range was 40–84 percent. Babícora, another common Medio period polychrome, decreased considerably across the Medio, as did its variant, White-Paste Babícora. Ratios offer a useful way to compare several frequencies at once. We used the site 204 test pit data to calculate 16 ratios of one type to another, for instance, Babícora to Ramos Polychromes. The mean values of these ratios were compared for the late Medio I and II intervals using the t-test. The following polychrome ratios were found to differ significantly: Babícora-to-Ramos, and White-Paste Babícora–to–Ramos. The mean differences in the ratios of Villa Ahumada–to–White-Paste Babícora and Villa Ahumada–to–Ramos fell just short of statistical significance in this sample. The single ratio that stands out as the most useful is Babícora-to-Ramos Polychrome. Both are types likely to be present in ceramic assemblages of adequate size, and they occur at quite different frequencies across the Medio period (refer to table 4.3). In this sample, the range of values of the Babícora-to-Ramos ratio for test pit levels that we assign to the late Medio I is 0.2 to 10.0, with a mean of 1.8. For the late Medio II levels, the value of this ratio ranges from 0.1 to 1.5, with a mean of 0.6.

One final caution is that we do not expect this ceramic ratio or the entire seriation scheme just proposed to be perfectly applicable to all contexts. Instead, we expect it to be more easily applied in some situations than in others. Our proposed sequence and ceramic ratios were based on a relatively simple situation: test pit levels ordered by their stratigraphic positions. Other excavated contexts, especially rooms, often lack this advantage. Even adjacent rooms often are not stratigraphically interrelated. Moreover, there can be considerable variability in how they were filled and how rapidly this process occurred. Despite these caveats, there are two sets of excavated contexts to which we will apply the ceramic sequence just proposed. These are Casas Grandes, excavated by Di Peso and colleagues more than 40 years ago, and the four neighboring sites that we report on in this volume. We begin with the primate center.

*Casas Grandes.* The primate center presents a complex situation, with a great deal of building and remodeling in a concentrated area. Its occupational history reaches from Viejo to terminal Medio times, so that the site has the time depth to accommodate all of our proposed intervals. The site's ceramics present a murkier picture, however, as preceding discussion showed that they vary little throughout the excavated sample. This situation alone means that we will not be able to apply all of our proposed sequence to the primate center.

We stress that our early Medio interval is not to be equated with Di Peso's Buena Fe phase, which he defined as the initial Medio period occupation of the site. A defining criterion of our early Medio is the absence of Ramos Polychrome. Examination of the Casas Grandes architectural and ceramic data (Di Peso, Rinaldo, and Fenner 1974: vols. 4 and 5), however, shows that Ramos Polychrome occurs in quantity *under* all of the floors classed as Buena Fe phase by Di Peso, Rinaldo, and Fenner (1974:4:320). In addition, these sub-floor assemblages characteristically contain Gila Polychrome, a ware well dated in the U.S. Southwest from the early 1300s and best represented in the mid- to late 1300s (Adams and Duff 2004; Crown 1994; Lekson 2000). Ramos and Gila Polychromes, then, are present in what should be the earliest Medio deposits excavated at Casas Grandes, and they are virtually everywhere else in the excavated areas as well. Lekson (2000:285) emphasized this situation, noting that it is nearly impossible to find an assemblage of 100 sherds at the primate center that does not contain Gila Polychrome. This is even truer for Ramos Polychrome. In other words, there are no excavated deposits at Casas Grandes that we can recognize as early Medio. As noted earlier, revised tree-ring dates indicate that some of the site's beams date to the 1200s, which is the time of our early Medio interval. We suggest that these beams were reused in later rooms. From these observations, we can only say that the small fraction of Casas Grandes excavated to date includes no early Medio contexts. There are Viejo period deposits at the site, and we presume that early Medio contexts are to be found there as well. It may well be, however, that the early Medio parts of Casas Grandes are much smaller than their late Medio successors.

Our contention, then, is that the excavated contexts at Casas Grandes are all late Medio in the terminology introduced earlier in this volume; that is, they date after about A.D. 1280–1300. The question now is whether these deposits can be subdivided into the late Medio I and II intervals introduced earlier. Table 4.4 shows the relevant data. The table lists late Medio I and II ceramic percentages from the site 204 test pits against percentages from our sample of 90,657 sherds from Di Peso's Buena Fe sub-floors and Diablo (terminal Medio) floor levels. These two sets of contexts should represent the earliest and latest of the excavated materials. These data are combined, as earlier analysis also showed that there were no statistically significant differences between them in any of the ceramic type frequencies.

It is evident that the Casas Grandes ceramic frequencies are not quite like either of the two sets of late Medio figures from site 204. Even so, the Casas Grandes data are more like the late Medio II figures from site 204. The Babícora–to–Ramos Polychrome ratio at the primate center is 0.16, a figure well within the late Medio II range discussed in preceding pages. We think it significant that, in many types, the Casas Grandes deposits continue the trends recognized from our early Medio through late Medio II intervals at site 204. In the early Medio, for example, Babícora Polychrome stands at about 49 percent of all polychromes. By late Medio I, it is around 34 percent, declining to 15 percent by late Medio II. In the Casas Grandes deposits, it is nearly

**Table 4.4**    Ceramic Type Frequencies from the 204 Midden Test Pits and Casas Grandes

| Ceramic Type | Test pits, late Medio I | Test pits, late Medio II | Casas Grandes |
|---|---|---|---|
| **Polychromes** | | | |
| Babícora | 34.32 | 15.41 | 10.59 |
| White-Paste Babícora | 25.74 | 10.38 | ?[a] |
| Dublan | 2.20 | 1.57 | 0.37 |
| Villa Ahumada | 5.69 | 5.35 | 8.11 |
| Babícora, Ramos variety | 1.85 | 4.09 | ?[a] |
| Carretas | 1.11 | 1.26 | 3.03 |
| Corralitos | 0 | 0 | 3.59 |
| Escondida | 0.08 | 0.31 | 5.99 |
| Huerigos | 0 | 0 | 1.09 |
| Ramos | 29.01 | 61.63 | 67.23 |
| **Non-polychromes** | | | |
| Plain | 79.70 | 78.46 | 72.51 |
| Scored types | 5.63 | 4.63 | 4.66 |
| Incised types | 2.64 | 2.59 | 1.83 |
| Corrugated types | 1.70 | 1.16 | 1.07 |
| Broad Coil | 0.28 | 0.10 | 0.37 |
| Tool Punched | 0.37 | 0.27 | 0.93 |
| Playas Red types | 4.70 | 6.33 | 11.62 |
| Black | 4.95 | 6.36 | 5.68 |
| Black-on-Red | 0.03 | 0.10 | 1.33 |

a. These variants were not tabulated in the Casas Grandes analysis.

11 percent. Other polychromes also show consistent patterns of change in table 4.4. White-Paste Babícora and fine-lined Babícora were tabulated in our analyses, but they were not separated at Casas Grandes. Also, the 204 deposits contained no Corralitos or Huerigos Polychromes. The non-polychrome sherds are more ambiguous, although in general they more closely resemble the late Medio II deposits at site 204. The only exceptions are two minor types: Broad Coil and Tool Punched, both of which occur in low frequency in the late Medio II test pit levels at site 204.

     In addition, we note that large differences in table 4.4 result from the decline of Babícora Polychrome and the corresponding rise in Villa Ahumada, Escondida, Carretas, Corralitos, and Huerigos Polychromes. Earlier, we argued that the occupation of site 204 ended in the early 1400s. Tree-ring date analyses and the established chronologies of imported ceramics (e.g., Tonto Polychrome) indicate that the occupation of the primate center was longer, reaching at least to the mid-1400s and quite possibly to the late part of that century. The Casas Grandes ceramic frequencies, then, could be affected by trends of change continuing after site 204 drops out of the picture. Alternatively, it could be that the perceived difference is not entirely a chronological one. It could be that the primate center's wide range of polychrome types served functions that were not as well represented at the neighboring sites. In either case, we contend that the excavated deposits at Casas Grandes, from the Buena Fe sub-floor deposits to the Paquimé/Diablo floor levels, contain ceramics that are most like our late Medio II assemblage. We earlier hypothesized that the late Medio II interval lasted from the mid- to late 1300s to the mid- to late 1400s, and we believe that the apogee of the center was reached by the mid- to late 1300s, or the late Medio I/II juncture. Others have used the revised tree-ring dates to argue that the peak of the site was reached sometime after A.D. 1300 (Ravesloot, Dean, and Foster 1995:247), and Lekson (2000) has asserted on ceramic grounds that the peak of Casas Grandes' development came in the fourteenth century.

*Site 204.* We now turn to the Mound A rooms at site 204, the occupants of which presumably generated the trash that forms the site's midden. Three contexts will be considered here: floor levels, floor features, and sub-floor features. The floor levels are the layers above room floor surfaces. They range from 10 cm to 14 cm thick. Floor features are those facilities clearly built into or upon floor surfaces. Most of them are fire pits, although other types of features also were present. All of these facilities have been discussed in chapter 3. Floor feature fill sometimes contained artifacts, and these are considered as part of floor features. Sub-floor features are facilities that were dug into the ground surfaces upon which the pueblo rooms later were built. They range from fire pits and ovens to large storage pits, and their fill also frequently contained artifacts. We emphasize that all of these proveniences contained much less artifactual material than did the Mound A midden which is the basis of the present seriation. The midden deposits contained an average of 1,360 sherds per cubic meter of fill (SD = 638), whereas room floor levels held only 114 sherds per cubic meter (SD = 46).

We begin with sub-floor features found beneath the early-dated rooms of Area 1 at site 204. These rooms yielded floor-contact dates ranging from the mid 1100s through the 1200s, as discussed in chapter 2. Eight sub-floor features were found beneath rooms 4, 6, 7, and 8 of Mound A. These facilities include fire pits; two large, unburned, cylindrical pits that may have served for storage; and several other unburned pits of uncertain function. The ceramics of these pits match the early Medio assemblage described earlier in this chapter. Babícora Polychrome is overwhelmingly dominant, at 62.5 percent of the sherds. White-Paste Babícora was in second place, contributing 22.9 percent of the polychromes, and Dublan Polychrome made up the remaining 14.6 percent. Ramos Polychrome was absent. Clearly, the early Medio rooms 4, 6, 7, and 8 were built on a ground surface already in use in the early part of the Medio period. This observation suggests that the early Medio rooms we dug were not the first on the site. These earliest Medio structures doubtless remain hidden under unexcavated parts of Mound A, and we are ignorant of their characteristics.

Unfortunately, the set of early Medio room floor features was not as informative. These floor features were mostly ash-filled fire pits, and they contained no polychromes. Accordingly, there was little chronological information in the sherds recovered from the floor features. The floor levels of these rooms present a different and less reliable context than the floor-contact radiocarbon dates. The latter were from burned wood

**Table 4.5**  Polychrome Sherd Frequencies from the Floor Levels of Early-Dated Rooms, Area 1, Site 204

| Polychrome type ($n = 41$) | Percentage |
| --- | --- |
| Babícora | 38.60 |
| White-Paste Babícora | 1.83 |
| Dublan | 1.17 |
| Villa Ahumada | 4.00 |
| Babícora, Ramos variety | 0 |
| Carretas | 0 |
| Corralitos | 0.33 |
| Escondida | 0 |
| Huerigos | 0 |
| Ramos | 54.07 |

lying in direct and unambiguous contact with floor surfaces. Few artifacts were found in direct floor contact, however, and material from the floor levels came from as much as 14 cm above floor surfaces. This clearly is a different depositional situation than that of the radiocarbon samples, and there is consequently a much larger potential for mixing and variability in floor-level artifacts than in floor-contact material. As a result, the early-dated rooms at site 204 show high variability in their floor-level ceramic inventories. Table 4.5 shows these data. Unfortunately, the sample is very small, consisting of only 41 sherds.

If the floor-level ceramics corresponded perfectly with the floor-contact radiocarbon dates, we would expect the ceramic assemblage to be composed of Babícora, White-Paste Babícora, Dublan, and Villa Ahumada Polychromes, and there should be no Ramos Polychrome. A glance at the preceding table shows that these expectations are not fulfilled. There is a high proportion of Ramos in the floor level, and there is also a little Corralitos Polychrome, a type earlier argued to be from the late Medio. In a word, the polychrome frequencies shown in this table are late Medio. We seem to have early-dated rooms with a fill of later trash. There is a high frequency of Babícora Polychrome in the fill, which preceding discussion showed to be at its most common in the early part of the Medio period. If the room's fill were mixed early and late Medio, we would expect to see higher frequencies of White-Paste Babícora, Dublan, and Villa Ahumada Polychromes. On the other hand, the Babícora–to–Ramos Polychrome ratio is 0.7, which is close to the late Medio II mean value of 0.6. The most that can be said of this small assemblage is that it clearly is not early Medio, and it has some of the characteristics of both the late Medio I and II intervals. To find late Medio ceramics in the fill of an early Medio room is not surprising, and it illustrates the fallacy of Di Peso, Rinaldo, and Fenner's (1974:6:80) assumption that all of the pottery in a room's floor level is contemporaneous with the date of the room.

Area 4 of Mound A contains what we believe to be the latest-occupied rooms in the excavated sample. It contains a late Medio ceramic assemblage, from the floor levels

**Table 4.6** Polychrome Sherd Frequencies from the Floor Levels of Late-Dated Rooms, Area 4, Site 204

| Polychrome type ($n = 238$) | Percentage |
| --- | --- |
| Babícora | 34.17 |
| White-Paste Babícora | 0 |
| Dublan | 2.98 |
| Villa Ahumada | 2.61 |
| Babícora, Ramos variety | 3.26 |
| Carretas | 0 |
| Corralitos | 0.33 |
| Escondida | 0.44 |
| Huerigos | 0 |
| Ramos | 56.21 |

and floor features to the uppermost levels. Table 4.6 shows these data from the Area 4 floor levels. Interestingly, these figures bear some resemblance to those just presented in table 4.5. That is, Babícora Polychrome occurs at a fairly high level, but the presence of a large amount of Ramos Polychrome, plus a little Corralitos and Escondida Polychromes, clearly indicates the late Medio age of this fill. In this case, the radiocarbon dates match the ceramics present.

Another question addressable with the seriation data from the test pits is the dating of the rooms of Mound C. The chronology chapter showed that radiocarbon produced unclear results in this case. Each of the two dated rooms had two dates: one early Medio and one late Medio. The mound's ceramics, however, point to a different conclusion, as all levels of the midden test pit contained Ramos Polychrome. This shows that they are more like the upper levels of the Mound A test pits. To maintain analytical continuity with the Mound A pits, all levels of the Mound C test pit are combined in table 4.7, which shows the type and variety percentages.

Although there were only six polychrome sherds in the lower levels, all of them were Ramos, and the type continues to be well represented in the middle and upper levels. The fine-lined variant of Babícora (the Ramos variant) is well represented. Playas Red is present at relatively high frequency, and there is a little Black-on-Red. These are all components of the late Medio ceramic assemblage. The types that dominate the early Medio assemblage, namely Babícora, White-Paste Babícora, and Dublan Polychromes, occur here at relatively low frequencies. It thus appears that the Mound C midden dates entirely to the late part of the Medio period. If the midden were composed of mixed early and late Medio sherds, we would expect higher frequencies of the early-appearing types. In fact, the figures presented in the preceding table look most like the late Medio II ceramic frequencies of table 4.4. The midden just discussed is adjacent to the small Mound C, and there were no other visible middens in the vicinity. Therefore, we presume that the Mound C midden received most of the trash from the nearby occupation. The implication of this argument is that the two early Medio radiocarbon dates

**Table 4.7**  Ceramic Type Frequencies from the Mound C Midden

| Ceramic type ($n = 238$) | Percentage |
| --- | --- |
| **Polychromes** | |
| Babícora | 16.20 |
| White-Paste Babícora | 8.98 |
| Dublan | 0 |
| Villa Ahumada | 0.44 |
| Babícora, Ramos variety | 4.96 |
| Carretas | 0 |
| Corralitos | 0 |
| Escondida | 0 |
| Huerigos | 0 |
| Ramos | 69.42 |
| **Non-polychromes** | |
| Plain | 75.33 |
| Scored (3 types) | 11.10 |
| Incised (3 types) | 2.37 |
| Corrugated (4 types) | 0.64 |
| Broad Coil | 0 |
| Tool Punched | 0 |
| Playas Red (5 types) | 7.14 |
| Black | 3.18 |
| Black-on-Red | 0.24 |

from the Mound C rooms are anomalous, as they do not fit the midden ceramic assemblage just described. The dates may come from beams borrowed from earlier construction. This being the case, we are left with two late Medio dates for the Mound C rooms. These are nearly identical, and they average to cal A.D. 1290–1420 ($2\sigma$). This late Medio date range is consistent with the ceramics of the midden.

*The Small Sites.* These sites were dated by radiocarbon in chapter 2. To recapitulate, site 231 dated to the early and late parts of the Medio period, or A.D. 1220–1450. Site 317 also had early and late components, dating, respectively, to A.D. 1150–1310 and A.D. 1280–1530. Only site 242 appears to belong exclusively to the late pert of the Medio period, with an averaged date of A.D. 1270–1410. Assuming that time is a major factor in Medio ceramic assemblage variability, there should be some perceptible differences between the 242 assemblage and those of the sites with early and late Medio components. Table 4.8 compares the ceramic frequencies for these sites.

Although there is variability among the three sites, they show ceramic markers of the late Medio, including Ramos, Escondida, Corralitos, and Huerigos Polychromes, plus Black-on-Red. This is consistent with the late Medio radiocarbon dates from portions of each site. Nevertheless, these ceramic data indicate that there are differences in

**Table 4.8** Ceramic Type Frequencies from the Small Sites (in %)[a]

| Type or variety | Site 231 | Site 317 | Site 242 |
|---|---|---|---|
| **Polychromes** | | | |
| Babícora | 40.65 | 41.35 | 22.95 |
| White-Paste Babícora | 7.79 | 2.58 | 3.70 |
| Dublan | 3.57 | 1.56 | 0 |
| Villa Ahumada | 14.11 | 36.19 | 9.85 |
| Babícora, Ramos variety | 0 | 0 | 0 |
| Carretas | 5.27 | 0 | 2.80 |
| Corralitos | 0 | 0.56 | 5.86 |
| Huerigos | 0 | 0 | 5.90 |
| Escondida | 4.05 | 0 | 0 |
| Ramos | 24.56 | 17.76 | 48.94 |
| **Non-polychromes** | | | |
| Plain | 87.06 | 80.60 | 87.21 |
| Scored (3 types) | 3.84 | 3.97 | 2.90 |
| Incised (3 types) | 4.74 | 2.79 | 0.72 |
| Corrugated (4 types) | 1.08 | 3.84 | 0.64 |
| Broad Coil | 0.02 | 0 | 1.94 |
| Tool Punched | 0.18 | 0.24 | 0.11 |
| Playas Red (5 types) | 1.19 | 7.81 | 2.73 |
| Black | 1.81 | 0.60 | 2.95 |
| Black-on-Red | 0.08 | 0.15 | 0.80 |

a. Polychromes as percentage of all polychromes. Non-polychromes as percentage of all non-polychromes.

the major occupation episodes of the three sites. It is inadvisable to try to read much from type frequency fluctuations of a few percent, which is the common situation in table 4.8. Still, there are some notable patterns.

First, sites 231 and 317 are alike in their relatively high frequencies of Babícora Polychrome and low percentages of Ramos Polychrome. The Babícora-to-Ramos ratios are high for both sites, at 1.7 for site 231 and 2.3 for site 317. In contrast, site 242 shows the opposite pattern, with a high frequency of Ramos and less Babícora. This Babícora-to-Ramos ratio of 0.47 is dramatically different from those of the other two small sites. Preceding pages showed high Babícora-to-Ramos ratios to be characteristic of the late Medio I interval, whereas the value of the ratio declined greatly in the late Medio II. Of lesser note is Dublan Polychrome, which is present in small quantities at sites 231 and 317 but absent at 242. Reference to table 4.4 shows that Dublan is at its lowest frequency in the late Medio II at site 204 and at Casas Grandes. Villa Ahumada Polychrome occurs at especially high frequency at site 317. There are at least two possible explanations for the observed situation: community size and site occupation span. There is a difference between large and small communities in the observed frequencies of Ramos Polychrome. Both of the large communities discussed here, Casas Grandes and site

204, contain a good deal of Ramos. Small sites 231 and 317, on the other hand, do not. Site 242, although small in size, shows a Ramos frequency more like those of the large sites. This situation is explicable under the assumption that Ramos was an ideologically empowered ceramic linked to the authority of the primate center. It is also noteworthy that sites 231 and 317 were assigned different occupation spans in chapter 2. The date range of site 231 extends as far as 1450, whereas that of site 317 reaches to 1530. It is distinctly possible that site 317 was occupied after the collapse of Casas Grandes, so that its ceramic assemblage may represent shifting regional dynamics. Unfortunately, the data in hand are inadequate for further pursuit of this issue.

Likewise, the non-polychrome data show small fluctuations and thus are not extensively interpretable. We note that Black-on-Red sherds are present in tiny quantity at all three sites, as expected in the late Medio. Table 4.3 shows that their frequency is highest in the late Medio II, as it is in the present sample at site 242. This site also has relatively low percentages of the Scored, Incised, and Corrugated types, as is characteristic of the late Medio II. One unusual characteristic of site 242 is its low frequency of Playas Red, which preceding analysis showed to reach its peak in the late Medio II. Surprisingly, there is more Playas Red at site 317 than at either of the other two small sites. Lastly, site 242 stands out for its high frequency of Plain sherds. A nonchronological connection between this site's sparse Playas Red and plentiful Plain pottery is suggested in the succeeding functional analysis of Medio ceramics (see chapter 5).

## Stylistic Analyses of Medio Period Ceramics

To this point, we have considered the question of temporal change in Medio ceramics solely in terms of type frequencies. There still remains the issue of stylistic variability across the Medio, and we now turn to that investigation. This inquiry confines itself to the region's polychrome ceramics, as these offer the greatest opportunities for stylistic analyses. Perusal of the Chihuahuan archaeological literature shows that relatively little attention has been devoted to stylistic studies, although much progress recently has been made. Succeeding pages review these efforts.

### Stylistic Studies of the Chihuahuan Polychromes

In one of the earliest discussions of Chihuahuan polychrome designs, Alfred Kidder (1916:261–62) described the design layout as "rectilinear." Two parallel horizontal lines defined the space for decoration, which was filled with large triangles and diamonds. These were subdivided into smaller units that were filled with design elements. Kidder classified these elements into two basic categories: geometrics and "life forms." The former included stepped figures, scrolls, and the "club-shaped" elements that likely are what we now term macaw symbols. Life forms included humans, birds, and plumed serpents. A few years later, Chapman (1923:33) expanded Kidder's brief discussion with further description of the layout patterns of Chihuahuan polychromes. Vessel decoration, he observed, occupied a single zone extending from rim to base. This zone was either divided into panels or formed a continuous "zigzag" band. Chapman also

**Table 4.9** Characteristics of Chihuahuan Polychrome Varieties

| Type | Variant | Traits |
|---|---|---|
| Babícora | Standard | Thick, coarse lines (pp. 98, 183)[a] |
| Babícora | Paquimé | Fine-lined painting, "more like Ramos" (p. 186) |
| Ramos | Standard | Usually fine-lined, but occasionally sloppy execution (pp. 250, 255) |
| Ramos | Black-on-White | Same as standard Ramos (p. 250) |
| Ramos | Capulín | Very fine, precise painting (pp. 250, 255) |
| Villa Ahumada | Standard | Coarse lines, like Standard Babícora (pp. 183, 302) |
| Villa Ahumada | Ramos | Fine-lined, with Ramos-style designs (pp. 299, 302) |
| Villa Ahumada | Capulín | Fine-lined, like Ramos Capulín (pp. 299, 302) |
| Villa Ahumada | Memmott | Medium-fine lines (p. 302) |

a. Page numbers refer to Di Peso, Rinaldo, and Fenner 1974, vol. 6.

distinguished between jar and bowl decorative patterns, noting that the more common jars had more complex designs, in which geometric motifs were supplemented by life forms. Bowls, on the other hand, bore largely geometric designs.

A more detailed analysis of Chihuahuan polychrome designs was provided by Carey (1931), who made an early attempt to quantify design element frequencies. He illustrated nine common design elements, noting that they occurred on 80 percent of decorated vessels (Carey 1931:346). He also provided a brief discussion of the compositional rules used in a few of the polychrome designs. All of these studies were based on whole vessels from museum and private collections, so that proveniences were minimal and stratigraphic information was nonexistent. Nevertheless, by the early 1930s a number of basic steps had been taken in analysis of the Chihuahuan polychrome styles. First, design layouts were known to be either panels or continuous bands. Second, there had been an initial inventory and rough quantification of basic design elements. Third, there was preliminary definition of some of the rules of design composition. After this strong beginning, little more was done for decades.

The next significant study of Chihuahuan polychrome style resulted from excavations at Casas Grandes by Di Peso and his colleagues (Di Peso, Rinaldo, and Fenner 1974: vol. 6). For the first time, the analyses were based upon an excavated sample, and sherds as well as whole vessels were examined. In the volume just cited, Gloria Fenner provided the most extensive description to that time of design layout and composition in Medio period painted pottery. There is a summary discussion of all painted wares, plus lengthy descriptions of the design structures and elements found in each type. In addition, some of the polychrome types were further subdivided into named varieties based on their stylistic elements. Table 4.9 summarizes these varieties and their design traits.

To express this situation in graphic form, we plotted the average painted line thicknesses from the type and variety descriptions in Di Peso, Rinaldo, and Fenner (1974: vol. 6), illustrated in figure 4.6. Corralitos Polychrome is omitted here, as its design structure does not use the same type of lines as the others. These figures were not

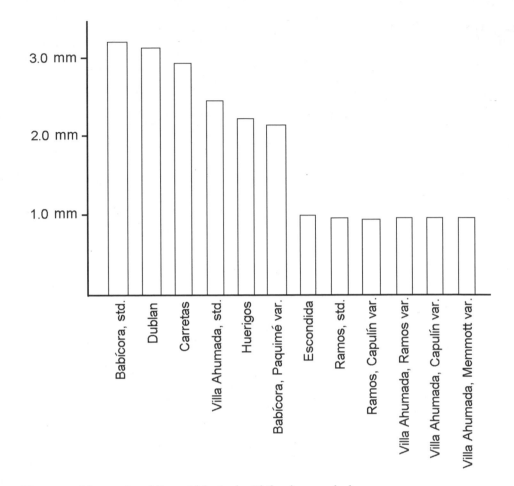

**Figure 4.6** Mean painted line widths in the Chihuahuan polychromes.

available for all of the varieties listed in table 4.9. It is clear that the most finely painted types are Standard Ramos and the Ramos, Capulín variant (data for the other Ramos variants were not available); the Villa Ahumada Ramos, Capulín, and Memmott variants; and Escondida Polychrome. All of these had lines averaging about 1 mm in width. All other types and varieties have painted line widths that average 2 to 3 mm. This includes the Paquimé variant of Babícora Polychrome.

The Casas Grandes analysis goes on to note that Dublan, Standard Babícora, and Standard Villa Ahumada Polychromes were much alike. In addition to the use of thick lines, they all show a lack of uniformity in line width, much overlapping of lines at intersections, inaccuracy of line and figure drawings, and smearing of paint after application (Di Peso, Rinaldo, and Fenner 1974:6:93). In general, the quality of these ceramic types was "at the lower range of that found on Casas Grandes painted types" (Di Peso, Rinaldo, and Fenner 1974:6:98). Elsewhere, it is observed that Carretas and Huerigos Polychromes have many of the same characteristics (Di Peso, Rinaldo, and Fenner 1974:6: 200, 244).

In the tradition of earlier work (e.g., Chapman 1923), the Casas Grandes study recognizes "band" and "paneled" layout patterns. In general, band layouts are defined by horizontal border lines running around the vessel. Repeating motifs fill the space between the border lines in a number of ways and at different levels of complexity. Paneled layouts consist of segments delineated by dividing lines drawn perpendicular to the border lines. These panels are subdivided and filled with design elements in many ways. Altogether, 106 variants of these layout patterns are defined and described (Di Peso, Rinaldo, and Fenner 1974:6:12–13). It is also observed that paneled layouts are most common in the fine-lined style of painting found on Ramos Polychrome and on the non-Standard varieties of Babícora and Villa Ahumada Polychromes. Band layouts, on the other hand, characterize Dublan, the Standard (or thick-lined) variants of Babícora and Villa Ahumada, and the Carretas and Huerigos types (Di Peso, Rinaldo, and Fenner 1974:6:95). In addition, layout variety is highest in Ramos Polychrome and the fine-lined variants of Babícora and Villa Ahumada Polychromes. Dublan, Standard Babícora, Standard Villa Ahumada, Carretas, and Huerigos Polychromes (the thick-lined polychromes) use many fewer layout patterns (Di Peso, Rinaldo, and Fenner 1974:6:201, 245, 305).

Design element variety also is considered for the polychrome types and varieties, although these discussions are not equally thorough for all of them. Consideration of Standard Villa Ahumada design elements is sparse, for instance, and the design characteristics of the variants are scarcely touched upon. In general, types like Dublan, Standard Babícora, and Standard Villa Ahumada seem to use the smallest number of design elements, whereas Ramos and the other fine-lined variants of Babícora and Villa Ahumada have a much larger design element inventory. This variety includes anthropomorphic and zoomorphic figures, which were used much more commonly on vessels done in the fine-lined style of painting than on those of the thick-lined style. For instance, the macaw motif that is so characteristic of Casas Grandes occurs most commonly on Ramos Polychrome and on other variants done in the fine-lined style. Only one questionable fragment of a macaw motif was found on Standard Babícora sherds (Di Peso, Rinaldo, and Fenner 1974:6:94). Likewise, the macaw motif was noted to be more common on the finer varieties of Villa Ahumada (Di Peso, Rinaldo, and Fenner 1974:6:312).

In short, the Casas Grandes study shows a notable correlation between design element variety and the elaboration and style of painting, and this pattern crosscuts types and varieties. The fine-lined, or Ramos, style of decoration uses more varied and elaborate layouts and more motifs, including anthropomorphic and zoomorphic figures. The thick-lined style, in contrast, uses fewer and simpler layout patterns, more geometric motifs, and fewer of the elaborate design elements. There is little consideration of the relation between these two styles of painting, however. The study's implicit assumption is that all of the types and varieties were essentially contemporaneous, and the discussion is a synchronic one. There is, for example, no consideration of variability in design structures or elements among the three phases of the Medio period that were used to characterize the site's architecture.

A quarter-century passed before further pursuit of the question of evolution in Medio period ceramic styles. Then, Mitchel Hendrickson (2000) conducted a study of

Design Horizon A          Design Horizon B

**Figure 4.7** Examples of Design Horizons A and B in the Chihuahuan polychromes. The Horizon A vessel is Babícora Polychrome, and the Horizon B vessel is Ramos Polychrome. (Photographs modified from Sayles 1936b)

stylistic evolution based on 361 whole vessels of the Ramos, Babícora, and Villa Ahumada Polychrome types. The study was published later (Hendrickson 2003), and all subsequent references are to this volume. The unprovenanced vessels came from U.S. and Canadian museum collections.

In the tradition of earlier work, Hendrickson distinguishes continuous or banded versus segmented or paneled layout styles. He also illustrates simple and complex design motifs. The former set contains simple geometrics of various sorts, whereas the latter includes macaws, feathers, zoomorphs, and complex geometrics (Hendrickson 2003:45). Finally, Hendrickson inventories the design motifs found with each layout style. These analyses are used to define two styles of painting, which Hendrickson refers to as Design Horizons A and B. The former is characterized by continuous layouts, a small number and variety of simple design motifs, and the absence of black-bordered red motifs. The latter differs in having segmented or paneled layouts, a greater number of motifs per vessel, and more complex motifs. Black-bordered red motifs are also present. Figure 4.7 shows examples of the two styles.

Hendrickson then discusses the frequencies of these design styles across Ramos, Babícora, and Villa Ahumada Polychromes. Ramos Polychrome, with its near-exclusive reliance on paneled layouts, complex motifs, and black-bordered red elements, falls into Design Horizon B. Babícora and Villa Ahumada, on the other hand, contain examples of both design horizons. Babícora A and Villa Ahumada A are the more common variants of their types. Each has a continuous layout pattern, few and simple motifs, and an absence of black-bordered red elements. Contrasting with this pattern, Babícora B and Villa Ahumada B contain paneled layouts, more complex motifs, and black-bordered red elements. Hendrickson observes that Babícora B and Villa Ahumada B vessels conform to the basic characteristics of Ramos. He further argues that these two Design Horizon B variants "mirror the patterns produced in the Paquimé and Ramos variants of Babícora and Villa Ahumada defined by Di Peso" (Hendrickson 2003:84). Hendrickson's study does not use painted line thickness, uniformity, or overlap, as the Casas Grandes study did. Nevertheless, it seems clear that the design style classifications at Casas Grandes and in Hendrickson's museum sample are recognizing the same stylistic regularities and thus can be blended. Hendrickson's Design Horizon B has the traits just summarized, plus the "Ramos" style of precise, fine-lined painting recognized by Di Peso and his colleagues. Design Horizon A, as defined by Hendrickson, corresponds to the unnamed, thick-lined, imprecise style of painting described at Casas Grandes.

It is at this point that Hendrickson's work goes beyond the Casas Grandes study in pursuit of the issue of temporal variability between design Horizons A and B. He begins by noting that the painted designs on pottery of the preceding Viejo period resembled Design Horizon A but had little in common with B. This observation led to the proposition that the earliest Medio pottery was done in Design Horizon A style, which later evolved to Design Horizon B. This logic implies an evolutionary order among polychrome types. Babícora A and Villa Ahumada A, the standard and most common variants of those types, were argued to be earlier, whereas Ramos (and, presumably, Babícora B and Villa Ahumada B) appeared later in the Medio (Hendrickson 2003:86).

This purely stylistic analysis does not investigate the origin of Ramos Polychrome, or explore its evolutionary relation to Babícora and Villa Ahumada. Accordingly, Hendrickson provides two alternative developmental models. In the first, Ramos originates from an unknown source. Later, it influences the older Babícora and Villa Ahumada types, resulting in the B variants just discussed. It is unclear whether the older A variants ceased to be made at this point. In the second model, the older Babícora and Villa Ahumada types developed into the later Ramos Polychrome. The subsequent fate of the old, simple variants is again uncertain. The author's data did not permit him to decide between the two models, and he concludes that "Since there is no evidence of a Ramos A . . . its origin in the sequence is uncertain" (Hendrickson 2003:86).

This study also provides a seriation of the design motifs used on Chihuahuan painted pottery. The early Design Horizon A contains simple geometric motifs, including triangles in simple, hooked, stepped, and scrolled forms; barbed or ticked lines; and ladder, checkerboard, circle, diamond, and spiral forms. In Design Horizon B, these are supplemented by complex motifs such as macaws, feathers, a variety of zoomorphic forms, and such complex geometric forms as rectangular scrolls, triangles with pendant P motifs, and triangular scrolls in simple and composite forms (refer to Hendrickson 2003:42 for illustrations). This discussion suggests that motifs may be useful in ceramic seriation, a point that will be reconsidered later in this section.

In the second recent stylistic study of Chihuahuan polychromes, Christine VanPool (2003a) makes similar arguments, citing Hendrickson's (2000) original work and using her own stylistic analyses of whole vessels from museum collections. VanPool's discussion of polychrome evolution is phrased in terms of a Paquimé style, which corresponds to Hendrickson's Design Horizon B (VanPool 2003a:109) and to the Ramos style of the Casas Grandes study. VanPool also uses the concept of a "non-Paquimé style," which is less specifically defined. Presumably, it is the absence of the traits used to define the Paquimé style; i.e., fine-lined painting and solid red elements framed by black lines. This non-Paquimé style seems to equate to Hendrickson's Design Horizon A and to the imprecise, thick-lined style of painting described by Di Peso and his colleagues.

Like earlier researchers. VanPool recognizes "running band," or continuous layouts, versus paneled layout patterns (VanPool 2003a:132–33). She assigns chronological significance to these using the same logic as Hendrickson's (2000) study; namely, that the preceding Viejo period is characterized by continuous layouts that continue into early Medio times (VanPool 2003a:132–33). VanPool also argues that the non-Paquimé style of painting characteristically has continuous layouts, and that the Paquimé style and paneled layouts occurred together in the late Medio (VanPool 2003a:150). Lastly, the author conducts a series of statistical tests to evaluate the relative frequencies of particular design elements in the early and late parts of the Medio period. Early in the Medio, she argues, the favored motifs were interlocking scrolls, interlocking "arrow" steps, and interlocking triangular steps. By the late Medio, painters added P motifs, both single and paired; interlocking Right Steps; "Triangle 1" motifs that seem to be much like Hendrickson's Composite Triangular Scroll; and diamonds with ticking on the framing lines. Feathers, macaws, and horned serpents likely also become more common at this time, she suggests. Motifs such as circles, interlocking triangles, running circles, running squares, ticked lines, and hooked triangles were found all through the Medio (VanPool 2003a:144, 152–53).

The stylistic studies conducted by Hendrickson and VanPool clearly are in agreement on the general evolutionary progression found in the Chihuahuan Polychromes. Early in the Medio period, simple geometrics repeat in continuous, horizontal bands that run around the vessel. Paneled layouts rise greatly in popularity in late Medio times. In the late Medio, popular motifs include the pendant P, macaw, feather, serpent, and interlocking geometric forms such as the Composite Triangular Scroll. Both studies make the point that basic geometric motifs are not simply replaced by more complex designs. Instead, the evolutionary process is one of supplementation of simple motifs with complex ones.

Most recently, Maria Sphren (2003) approaches the Chihuahuan Polychromes from a somewhat different angle, by measuring the effort expended in pottery production. The goal of this analysis is to see whether the major Polychromes—Babícora, Ramos, and Villa Ahumada—show comparable levels of investment of labor and skill. These data are used to investigate the question of specialized ceramic production during the Medio period. A set of whole vessels from museum collections provides the data. Through statistical analyses of a set of variables relating to painting quality and effort invested in production, Sphren argues that Babícora was the least skillfully made of the three polychromes. Ramos was the best made, and Villa Ahumada fell in between (Sphren 2003:150). The focus of this study is not on stylistic evolution, but it concludes with a chronological argument: the less skillfully made Babícora and Villa Ahumada types were produced during the early part of the Medio period, when society was less centralized and there was less need to display the symbols of power. By late Medio times, power was being centralized at Casas Grandes, and a part of this process was display of finely made symbols of power. Ramos Polychrome was a primary vehicle for these symbols and, accordingly, it came into florescence then (Sphren 2003:242).

The studies just summarized have proposed some specific evolutionary changes in polychrome pottery across the Medio period. On all grounds of style and design elements, Ramos Polychrome is argued to be a late type that was preceded by Babícora and Villa Ahumada. Some layout patterns, painting styles, and design motifs are argued to be of early or late Medio age. As insightful as they are, all of these efforts share a common limitation: they are based on museum collections of unprovenanced vessels. To date, there have been no stratigraphic or chronometric data that would allow tests of the proposed evolutionary sequence. The stratified and well-dated midden deposits from site 204 provide the first opportunity to do this. Unfortunately, Villa Ahumada Polychrome was so rare in the 204 midden test pits that we cannot include it reliably in the present inquiry. Even so, we can still make some statements about stylistic changes from early to late Medio times.

## Early and Late Medio Polychrome Styles

First, we note that the work reported earlier in this chapter supports and supplements the style-based seriation first proposed by Hendrickson (2000). Our stratigraphic data clearly show that Babícora and Villa Ahumada Polychromes appear in the early part of the Medio period, and that Ramos Polychrome is a late Medio addition to the assemblage. The test pit data also demonstrate that there was no simple replacement of Design Horizon A by Horizon B from early to late Medio times. Instead, Babícora Polychrome, in its Standard variant, persists from bottom to top of the test pits at site 204. Standard Villa Ahumada, although much less common, does the same. Both of these variants fall into Hendrickson's Design Horizon A. The midden test pit data show that this style of painting was supplemented around A.D. 1300 by the fine-lined Ramos that Hendrickson called Design Horizon B. This pattern has further implications for design element seriation. Because Design Horizon A continues throughout the Medio period, it cannot be chronologically diagnostic. Design Horizon B, however, is a marker of the late part of the Medio period.

Identification of the antecedents of Ramos Polychrome is an issue that could not be dealt with by any of the studies just summarized. Hendrickson (2003:86) observed that there is no known Ramos "A," or a proto-Ramos Polychrome made on white paste and painted in the earlier Design Horizon A style. This statement was true when written, but the midden data from site 204 provide the missing element. The White-Paste Babícora described earlier in this chapter could also be classed as Ramos "A"; that is, it has the white paste of Ramos Polychrome, but its painting style uses the thick, imprecise lines and simple geometrics of Hendrickson's Design Horizon A. As described earlier in this volume, it is much like Standard Babícora Polychrome, but done on a white paste. Preceding discussion showed that White-Paste Babícora occurred from the lowest levels of our midden test pits, or from the earliest part of the Medio period. It appears long before Ramos Polychrome, of which it is the most likely ancestor. At one point in his discussion of polychrome stylistic evolution, Hendrickson was led to wonder whether "Ramos is actually a variant of Babícora instead of the other way around" (Hendrickson 2003:86). Hendrickson's data were not adequate to resolve this question, but our results argue that it is.

Earlier stylistic studies (Hendrickson 2000, 2003; VanPool 2003a) proposed sequences of change in design motif popularity between early and late Medio times. The summary just presented showed that these studies agreed on a number of points,

**Table 4.10**   Painted Line Thickness in Midden Test Pit Polychromes

| Polychrome | Line color | Mean thickness, early Medio (in mm) | SD | n | Mean thickness, late Medio (in mm) | SD | n | t-test $p$[a] |
|---|---|---|---|---|---|---|---|---|
| Babícora | black | 3.3 | 0.9 | 44 | 2.9 | 1.2 | 79 | .054 |
| Babícora | red | 3.3 | 0.8 | 35 | 3.0 | 0.9 | 67 | .105 |
| White-Paste-Babícora | black | 3.3 | 1.1 | 31 | 2.6 | 1.2 | 82 | .005 |
| White-Paste-Babícora | red | 3.1 | 0.6 | 26 | 2.8 | 0.8 | 56 | .064 |
| Ramos | black | — | — | 0 | 1.5 | 0.3 | 116 | — |
| Ramos | red | — | — | 0 | 1.6 | 0.4 | 148 | — |

a. The t-tests were done on early Medio versus late Medio mean line thicknesses.

especially on the identification of late Medio motifs. There was less accord, however, on which motifs characterized the early Medio. The cited studies could not resolve this question, as they were based on unprovenanced collections of vessels. Thus, their arguments were made on stylistic rather than stratigraphic grounds.

Now, propositions of early-to-late-Medio design motif frequency change can be tested with stratigraphy and chronometric dating in the site 204 midden test pits. There is a sharp limitation to this endeavor, however. The two studies just cited relied on whole vessels that provided complete layouts and oriented, uninterrupted views of design motifs. In contrast, the test pit data from the site 204 midden consist entirely of sherds. We are thus limited to what can be recognized from these fragments, even the orientations of which were often uncertain. As a result, we were unable to study layout patterns, which were central elements of the earlier studies. In addition, our inventories of design motifs must be taken as minimal sets, because we could not recognize from sherds all of the motifs used by the whole-vessel studies. For example, a triangle could be identified from a partial view, but we usually could not tell if the triangle had a tail, and if so, whether that tail was hooked, scrolled, or stepped. Nevertheless, enough motifs were recognized to show some patterns. The site 204 stylistic analysis focused on three polychromes: Standard Babícora, White-Paste Babícora, and Ramos. Others such as Dublan, Carretas, and Villa Ahumada were too rare to support meaningful analyses. For each analyzed sherd, black and red line thicknesses were measured, the presence of black-bordered red figures was noted, and motifs were identified. The results of each set of observations are discussed below.

*Painted Line Thickness.* This variable was measured reliably from the sherds. Where line thickness varied, the broadest part was measured. Table 4.10 presents these data.

Several trends are apparent in these data. First, early Medio painted lines are on average a little thicker than their late Medio successors. The early/late mean line thickness difference is statistically significant in two cases (the black lines of Babícora and White-Paste Babícora), nearly so in a third case (the red lines of White-Paste Babícora), and

**Table 4.11**    Black-Bordered Red Motifs (BBR) on Test Pit Polychromes

| Polychrome | Sub-period | No BBR | BBR | Fisher's $p$[a] |
|---|---|---|---|---|
| Babícora | early Medio | 58 | 3 | .365 |
| Babícora | late Medio | 142 | 5 | |
| White-Paste Babícora | early Medio | 59 | 1 | .287 |
| White-Paste Babícora | late Medio | 133 | 9 | |
| Ramos | late Medio | 200 | 102 | n/a |

a. Fisher's Exact Probability score, calculated for the 2 × 2 table, shown for each polychrome.

insignificant in the fourth case (the red lines of Babícora). Note that the last comparison would have achieved statistical significance if the late mean line thickness were only 0.1 mm thinner (i.e., 2.9 mm instead of 3.0 mm). It is also evident from the figures in the table that White-Paste Babícora and Standard Babícora line thicknesses were much alike in early and late Medio times. Despite the thinning trend just noted, both are always characterized by fairly broad lines. A last observation is that late Medio Ramos Polychrome had much thinner lines than the other two late Medio polychromes.

*Black-Bordered Red Motifs.* Black-bordered red motifs were recognized reliably on sherds, as the entire motif need not be present for a positive identification. This decorative technique has long been recognized as a characteristic of Ramos Polychrome (Di Peso, Rinaldo, and Fenner 1974:6:254). Recently, Hendrickson (2003) showed that red motifs with black framing lines also occur on Babícora and Villa Ahumada vessels, although much more rarely than on Ramos Polychrome. To this list we can now add White-Paste Babícora. Table 4.11 summarizes the frequencies of occurrence of black-bordered red motifs by type in the site 204 midden test pits.

It is clear from the table that black-bordered red motifs always are rare in Babícora and in White-Paste Babícora. The Fisher's Exact Probability scores shown in the table test the null hypothesis that the frequencies of black-bordered red motifs do not differ significantly between the early versus late Medio. Both Fisher's $p$ scores are far above the critical value of .05, so the null hypothesis of no significant difference is accepted in both cases. Ramos Polychrome occurs only in the late Medio, when 51 percent of our sample showed black-bordered red motifs. Hendrickson (2003) reports this type of motif on 91 percent of Ramos Polychrome, 36 percent of Babícora, and 15 percent of Villa Ahumada. His study, however, used whole vessels, and an occurrence of a black-bordered red motif anywhere on the surface meant that the vessel was counted as having that motif. One such vessel, however, would break into many sherds, a number of which would not contain the black-bordered red motif. Our counts, therefore, are lower than Hendrickson's. In any case, it is clear from all studies that Ramos Polychrome has by far the highest incidence of black-bordered red motifs, far more than all other polychromes. We also note that Hendrickson found black-bordered red motifs in both Design Horizons A and B, suggesting their presence in the early and late parts of

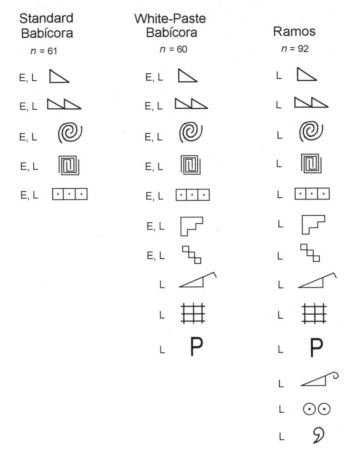

**Figure 4.8** Design motif inventories across polychrome types. Motifs occurring in the early Medio are marked "E," and those from the late Medio are "L."

the Medio period. This conclusion is confirmed by the results in table 4.11, where black-bordered red motifs occur all across the Medio in Babícora and White-Paste Babícora.

*Design Element Variety.* Earlier studies (Hendrickson 2003; VanPool 2003a) argued for particular changes in design motif frequencies from early to late Medio. They had no stratigraphic or chronometric data against which to test their style-based propositions, but we can now do some extent of testing. The midden test pit data from site 204 provide a design motif inventory from dated early and late Medio layers for Standard Babícora, White-Paste Babícora, and Ramos Polychromes. Other types were too rare to inventory. Figure 4.8 illustrates the design element inventories from the 204 midden. The figure should be considered a minimum inventory, as it is derived solely from sherds. The "E" and "L" notations indicate early and late Medio sherd samples, respectively.

The figure shows that Standard Babícora has by far the smallest number of recognized design motifs. The Casas Grandes pottery study also noted the minimal design motif inventory of this type (Di Peso, Rinaldo, and Fenner 1974:6:98). The design motif inventory of Ramos Polychrome, in contrast, is the largest identified. This, too, echoes the Casas Grandes results (Di Peso, Rinaldo, and Fenner 1974:6:2). Interestingly, however, White-Paste Babícora is more like Ramos than Standard Babícora in its design motif inventory. The question now is how these inventories varied between the early and late parts of the Medio period, and reference to figure 4.8 provides these data.

The early/late division shown in figure 4.8 is based on test pit stratigraphy and radiocarbon dating, as discussed earlier in this chapter. The early Medio polychrome assemblage was shown to be dominated by Standard Babícora, with smaller quantities of White-Paste Babícora, and much smaller quantities of Dublan and Villa Ahumada Polychromes. Ramos was added to this set in the late Medio. Figure 4.8 suggests that Standard Babícora used a small variety of motifs all through the Medio period. Accordingly, late Babícora looked much like its early Medio predecessor in both motif inventory and in continued use of the thick-lined style of painting. Recall that preceding analyses showed no significant difference in the type's mean line thicknesses from early to late Medio.

Not surprisingly, figure 4.8 portrays that early Medio White-Paste Babícora had a design motif inventory much like that of the contemporaneous Standard Babícora, although the former may have used a few more motifs than the latter. Even so, it is clear that simple geometrics dominate both types. We emphasize that early Medio White-Paste Babícora is painted in the Design Horizon A style, with thick, uneven, imprecise lines, and that late Medio White-Paste Babícora continues to use this style of painting. Preceding analyses showed that (a) the painted lines of White-Paste Babícora were as broad as those of Standard Babícora all through the Medio; and (b) there was no significant difference in mean line thickness in White-Paste Babícora from early to late Medio times. It is clear that the early Medio thick-lined style of painting was supplemented in the late Medio by the fine-lined style but was never replaced by it.

Figure 4.8 shows that the late Medio White-Paste Babícora design motif inventory was larger than that of the early Medio. Moreover, this increase consisted of motifs that also appear on the Ramos Polychrome of the late Medio. These include the hooked triangle, P, and checkerboard motifs. In its design motif inventory, late Medio White-Paste Babícora more closely resembles Ramos Polychrome than Standard Babícora. Nevertheless, White-Paste Babícora continues to be painted in the thick-lined style all through the Medio period. White-Paste Babícora thus represents a link among a number of the major Polychrome types. It appears early in the Medio period, along with the dominant Standard Babícora, with which it shares thick-lined painting and a relatively small design element inventory of simple geometric figures. Nevertheless, it is made on a white paste that is not characteristic of Standard Babícora, but is the trademark of late Medio Ramos Polychrome. In the late Medio, White-Paste Babícora and Ramos share the same white paste and similar design element inventories, although Ramos designs were the more elaborate of the two. Ramos Polychrome also uses the fine-lined style of painting that does not characterize either Standard Babícora or White-Paste Babícora. The three types clearly are closely interrelated on several grounds. The stratigraphic data we presented earlier argued that Babícora Polychrome represents the origin of the

Chihuahuan Polychrome tradition in the Casas Grandes area, and the stylistic data just reviewed also support this conclusion. We note that Gladwin made the same argument in 1936. Unfortunately, we cannot include Villa Ahumada in this discussion, as it was rare in the site 204 midden test pits.

Earlier in this section we summarized arguments by Hendrickson (2003) and VanPool (2003a) on the question of design motif frequency change across the Medio. Hendrickson recognized a set of simple geometrics that occurs most commonly on continuous layouts. These he suggested to be early Medio. This set of simple motifs was supplemented, but not replaced, by a larger set of complex motifs in the late Medio, and this expanded motif set is mostly found on segmented or paneled layouts. Our stratigraphic study of design elements, as summarized in figure 4.8, argues that Hendrickson's style-based conclusions are generally accurate. We differ on only a few points. First, the rectangular interlocking scroll was classed by Hendrickson as a complex motif (i.e., late Medio). He does not mention the interlocking scroll, however, illustrating only the single variant of that form. Our data show that the simple and rectangular interlocking scrolls are pan-Medio motifs. Hendrickson also classed the checkerboard and triangles with appended hooks and scrolls as simple, pan-Medio motifs that extended all across his sample. In our study, however, both of these motifs were recognized only in late Medio contexts. We must emphasize, however, that Hendrickson's analysis did not distinguish between Standard (or thick-lined) Babícora and Babícora of the Ramos (or fine-lined) variant. The latter variant has a larger design motif inventory than the former. Accordingly, Hendrickson's Babícora design motif inventory is considerably greater than ours, which is based only on Standard Babícora.

VanPool (2003a) posits a more specific inventory of early, late, and pan-Medio motifs. Unfortunately, VanPool's early motifs (arrow steps and triangular steps) could not be reliably recognized on our test pit sherds. We are thus unable to comment on that portion of her argument. Our stratigraphic data agree with VanPool's assertion that P motifs and zoomorphs are late Medio. We disagree somewhat on which motifs are pan-Medio, however. Contrary to VanPool, our data argue that scrolls and right steps extend from early to late Medio times. VanPool also argued that hooked triangles, circles, and running circles were pan-Medio motifs, whereas we find them only in the late Medio.

As figure 4.8 indicates, we recognized no motifs that occur only in the early Medio period. Instead, we see a set of basic, geometric figures that run all across the Medio. These include triangles, running triangles, interlocking scrolls, running squares, and steps of both single and double varieties. This set of motifs is supplemented by others in the late Medio, and it is these new motifs that should prove to be the most useful chronological markers. They include the hooked and scrolled triangle, P, checkerboard, circle, running circle, comma, and zoomorphs. Anthropomorphs and feather motifs likely also belong to this class of design motif, although they were not recognized in our sample. Notably, the P and comma motifs seem to be components of macaw symbols (e.g., Di Peso, Rinaldo, and Fenner 1974:6:282, fig. 292-6), whereas the circle and running circle motifs may be Tlaloc symbols. In a word, late Medio design motifs go beyond geometrics to include a number of representational figures that likely had religious or ceremonial significance. VanPool (2003a) also notes this, and it is also consistent with Sphren's (2003) argument that the finely made late Medio ceramics carried more symbolic information that their early counterparts.

## Diachronic Change in Medio Period Ceramics

The seriation of Medio period ceramics has been a topic of interest for many years. Of special concern are the painted types, which although few in number, are highly visible components of the Medio period ceramic assemblage. This chapter reviewed earlier seriation work and analyzed a large body of new data in consideration of ceramic evolution during the Medio period.

At site 204, we dug test pits into a large, deep trash midden, securing both radiocarbon dates and large ceramic samples. The lower, pre–Ramos Polychrome segments of the test pits were radiocarbon-dated to cal A.D. 1160–1280 ($2\sigma$), or the early Medio. The upper segments dated to cal A.D. 1280–1390 ($2\sigma$), which is late Medio. The topmost 20–25 cm of each pit lacked charcoal and so remain undated. Their ceramics, however, argue that these upper segments are only a little different than the levels immediately below them.

A subdivision of the late Medio was proposed, based on changing percentages of Ramos Polychrome pottery in the large Mound A midden at site 204. Test pits dug into the midden showed that there are two groups of Ramos Polychrome frequencies. The first, which we termed the late Medio I, is characterized by about 12 percent to about 35 percent Ramos. The second set, or the late Medio II, has about 50 percent to 84 percent Ramos Polychrome. These figures refer to Ramos as a percentage of all polychrome sherds in a context, here, test pit levels. Where they occur together in midden test pits, late Medio II deposits always overlie those of the late Medio I. Preceding discussion used radiocarbon dates from the test pits to suggest very tentative chronological definitions for the late Medio I and II intervals. It will be recalled that the early Medio was radiocarbon-dated from the mid- to late 1100s to the late 1200s. The late Medio I was tentatively dated from 1300 through the mid- to late 1300s, and the late Medio II continues from there into at least the mid-1400s and probably later. There are indications from Casas Grandes and other sites that the last part of the Medio period extended into or even through the late 1400s.

This ceramic and chronological sequence enabled us to gain a finer perspective on the history of occupation at site 204. All of the Mound A midden test pits have early Medio lower levels that are overlain by late Medio I deposits. In about 60 percent of these cases, the late Medio I deposits continue to the surface level. All of these test pits lay on the western or central part of the large Mound A midden. The other 40 percent of the Mound A midden test pits have late Medio II deposits overlying late Medio I levels and continuing to the surface. All of these test pits are on the eastern part of the midden. It is thus clear that the late Medio II deposits are not as widespread in the site's major midden as are those of the preceding late Medio I. This is a strong indication that the occupation of Mound A, the community's major room block, declined considerably between the late Medio I and II intervals, or roughly in the mid-to late l300s. The reduced late Medio II occupations continued on the western end of Mound A, on the small Mound C, and, to a lesser extent, on the small Mound B.

In addition to their information on site chronology, these test pits provide the most detailed look ever at Medio period ceramic evolution. The early Medio assemblage, prior to A.D. 1300, contains Babícora, Villa Ahumada, and Dublan Polychromes, plus a heretofore undefined variant termed White-Paste Babícora. In preceding pages, we argued that White-Paste Babícora was the likely predecessor of Ramos Polychrome. White-Paste Babícora shows the simple, broad-lined, red-and-black geometric designs of standard Babícora Polychrome, combined with the white kaolin paste of Ramos. To derive Ramos Polychrome from White-Paste Babícora, it would have been necessary only to refine the line work and to alter the design layouts from what Hendrickson (2003:32) terms "continuous" bands to his "segmented" panels. This would produce most of what we term Ramos Polychrome, as the anthropomorphic and zoomorphic designs for which Ramos is famous actually occur on a small percentage of vessels. We emphasize that this is not an unprecedented change in Chihuahuan ceramics. Both Babícora and Villa Ahumada also have fine-lined forms with segmented panel designs, referred to by Di Peso and his colleagues as "Ramos style" variants of those types (Di Peso, Rinaldo, and Fenner 1974:6:183, 295).

The late part of the Medio period, after A.D. 1300, thus appears to be the time of florescence of fine-lined ceramics in northwestern Chihuahua. Nevertheless, we emphasize that this was not a simple, diachronic, coarse-to-fine line shift. In all three polychromes, coarse-lined and fine-lined variants existed together throughout the late Medio period. The florescence of fine-lined ceramics after A.D. 1300 was attributed to social and political factors. The primate center of Casas Grandes reached its apogee in the 1300s, and regional sociopolitical organization presumably peaked at about the same time. This would, therefore, be the time of greatest need for exotica to reinforce social statuses and alliances and for symbolic transmission of social, political, and ritual information. We see the fine-lined vessels, with their exquisite craftsmanship and complex design motifs as important accoutrements in this developmental process, serving both as exotica and for the transmission of information via their intricate symbolism.

The late Medio assemblage dates from about A.D. 1300. It contains the full set of eight polychrome types, plus several variants of these. In other words, all of the early Medio polychromes are present in the late Medio, and more are added. Relative to the early Medio, the late Medio assemblage also contains less textured ware and more of the Playas Red types. Black-on-Red also appears for the first time in the late Medio levels of the test pits. All of the 16 ceramic types, type groups, and varieties used in our analyses show consistent patterns of change across the late Medio I and II intervals. That is, all trends of increase or decrease in ceramic frequencies recognized from the early Medio to the late Medio I continue in the late Medio II. Figure 4.10 summarizes our findings from the large trash midden at site 204 and from other dated deposits in the Casas Grandes area.

Some of the differences among the findings of the studies just discussed are undoubtedly due to the use of different kinds and quantities of data from a wide variety of contexts. All such differences cannot be explained away so easily, however, and there is likely another factor involved. It has long been known that the different polychrome

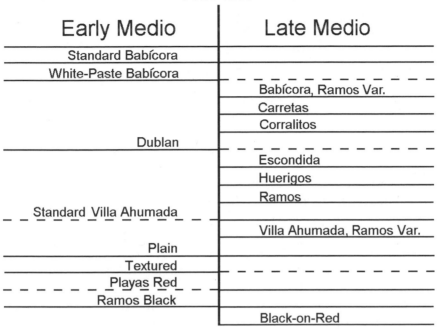

**Figure 4.9** Early and late Medio ceramic assemblages. A solid line shows continuation at the same frequency or greater. A dotted line indicates a reduced frequency.

types do not have the same spatial distributions. A recently published figure (Fish and Fish 1999: fig. 1.6) illustrates the situation. It shows that Carretas and Huerigos Poly-chromes have an epicenter in the Carretas Basin, to the northwest of Casas Grandes. Ramos Polychrome centers on the area around Casas Grandes, whereas Villa Ahumada Polychrome is centered on the lower Santa María River, to the east. Babícora Polychrome centers on the Babícora Basin, to the south. The types obviously are not confined to these areas, as they occur all over northwestern Chihuahua and adjacent parts of the southwestern United States. That their epicenters are geographically distinct, however, argues that their type frequencies may be affected by trade and interaction patterns, as well as by simple geographic distance. Burd, Kelley, and Hendrickson (2004) discuss this issue from the perspective of west-central Chihuahua, on the southern edge of the Casas Grandes world. They conclude that "considerable (ceramic) variability is present at both site and regional levels in this southern area" (2004:202). We presume this to be true all over the Casas Grandes region, although its full extent has yet to be revealed. Accordingly, the fact that a number of common trends were recognized by studies is a heartening indication that progress is at last being made in charting Medio period ceramic evolution. Much clearly remains to be done, however.

# 5

## Medio Period Ceramic Function

The preceding chapter discussed early and late Medio ceramic assemblages in typological terms. The central problem of this chapter is specification of the kinds of activities that are represented in the ceramic assemblage at different times and at different kinds of Medio communities. There are two sources of data: vessel sizes and use-wear traces. Few whole vessels are available from anywhere except Casas Grandes, so that inquiry into container size requires development of methods for estimating Medio period vessel volumes from their sherds. The first part of the chapter is devoted to this end. Studies of ceramic use-wear are more straightforward, as they rely on exterior sooting and interior surface pitting. We use the approach of the previous chapter for this inquiry, first characterizing the early and late Medio assemblages from site 204, where there are large, stratified, well-dated artifact samples. We then compare intercommunity ceramic characteristics and activities based on the samples from excavated rooms on sites 204, 231, 242, and 317.

Before beginning, it is necessary to clarify the ceramic terminology to be used. To maximize sample sizes, analyses are conducted on five groups of sherds or whole vessels. Some groups are composed of a single type, such as Plain or Ramos Black. Other groups are formed by combining a number of the closely related types described in Di Peso's Casas Grandes study (Di Peso, Rinaldo, and Fenner 1974: vol. 6). The Textured group consists of all ten of the Rubbed, Incised, Scored, Corrugated, Broad Coil, and Tool Punched types. The Playas Red group contains five variants of this red-slipped ware, and the Polychrome group contains eight types and several varieties. There is another group composed of Black-on-Red sherds, but these were almost entirely absent in the samples studied here and so are omitted from consideration. The ensuing analyses will be conducted in terms of the Plain, Textured, Playas Red, Ramos Black, and Polychrome ceramic groups. In a few cases, Ramos Polychrome is analyzed separately.

### Vessel Form

The early and late Medio ceramic assemblages are made up primarily of jars and bowls. Identification of these vessel forms was based solely on rim sherds. In some assemblages, jar body sherds can be separated from those of bowls by the finer interior finish of the latter vessel form. This can be problematic in Chihuahua, however. At Casas Grandes, about 50 percent of the Plain jars had well-smoothed interiors (Di Peso, Rinaldo, and

Fenner 1974:6:109), and we found a similarly high frequency of smoothed interiors at the surrounding sites. Accordingly, only rims are used in the following analyses as reliable indicators of jars versus bowls in the Medio period ceramic assemblage.

## Early and Late Medio Vessel Forms within Types

This analysis is based on sherds from the early and late Medio contexts of the large Mound A midden and the small, late Medio Mound C midden. The early and late Medio levels analyzed here are those defined in the preceding chapter on ceramic evolution. Early Medio test pit levels contained 1,118 body sherds and 117 rims, whereas their late Medio successors yielded 3,601 body sherds and 639 rims. The rim sherds from early Medio test pit levels were about 65 percent jars and 35 percent bowls, and the late Medio figures were nearly identical at 68 percent and 32 percent. The translation of rim sherd counts into jar-to-bowl ratios depends, of course, on the jar and bowl orifice sizes of an assemblage. Mean bowl orifice diameter might be twice as large as the mean jar orifice, for instance, necessitating division of the bowl rim sherd count by two in order to use rim sherds to approximate a ratio of jars to bowls. In the sample of 179 whole jars from Casas Grandes (Di Peso, Rinaldo, and Fenner 1974: vol. 6), we calculated mean rim diameter to be 16.6 cm (SD: 6.6), and the mean rim diameter of 106 whole bowls was 18.8 cm (SD: 7.3). These figures produce average circumferences of 52 cm for jars and 59 cm for bowls. Because these two figures are of the same order of magnitude, we assume the simple jar-to-bowl rim sherd count to be about the same as the jar-to-bowl ratio. Based on the data just presented, a jar-to-bowl ratio of about 2:1 seems characteristic of the early and late Medio at site 204.

Jar necks from the site 204 middens were always short, and they were classed as either vertical or flared. This condenses a number of the jar rim form categories used at Casas Grandes (Di Peso, Rinaldo, and Fenner 1974:6:111). Our flared category includes the Recurved A, Recurved B, and Flared designations used by Di Peso and his colleagues, and our vertical category includes their Vertical, Short Vertical, Barely Everted, and Slightly Everted categories. In the middens at site 204, flared rims outnumbered vertical ones by about 2:1 in both the early and late parts of the Medio period.

All of the whole vessels or large, reconstructible vessel segments recovered from some of the site's excavated rooms were either globular or ellipsoidal in body shape, with rounded bases. It appears that the same shapes of jars were present in the middens. Unfortunately, the extensive fragmentation of the midden sherds prevents us from estimating relative proportions of globular and ellipsoidal jars in the early and late Medio. All that can be said at this point is that early and late test pit levels contained nothing to suggest much change in jar body shape across the Medio period.

Bowls from the midden deposits were made in simple, hemispherical shapes in both the early and late Medio. There is variability in their orifices, however, of which two types were recorded. The first is a direct or vertical rim, so that the vessel's rim diameter is equal to its maximum body diameter. The second orifice type is slightly inflected or restricted, so that the orifice diameter is 10–20 percent less than the maximum body diameter. The early Medio sample of 38 bowls was dominated by vertical rims, which

**Table 5.1**    Ceramic Ware Frequencies in the Early and Late Medio at Site 204

| | Early Medio | | | | Late Medio | | | |
| | Jars | | Bowls | | Jars | | Bowls | |
| Ware | % | n | % | n | % | n | % | n |
|---|---|---|---|---|---|---|---|---|
| Plain | 80.1 | 65 | 68.5 | 24 | 72.7 | 317 | 54.4 | 111 |
| Textured | 7.2 | 6 | 7.0 | 3 | 2.5 | 11 | 3.7 | 8 |
| Red | 3.1 | 2 | 7.0 | 3 | 10.5 | 45 | 17.8 | 36 |
| Black | 3.0 | 2 | 7.0 | 3 | 3.6 | 15 | 8.6 | 18 |
| Polychrome | 6.6 | 5 | 10.5 | 4 | 10.7 | 46 | 15.5 | 32 |
| **Totals** | 100 | 80 | 100% | 37 | 100% | 434 | 100% | 205 |

made up 78.9 percent of the assemblage; restricted rims were relatively rare at 21.1 percent. In the late Medio sample of 207 bowls, vertical rims continued to be the dominant form at 65.7 percent of the total. As the late Medio vertical rim percentage declined, the restricted rims increased in frequency to 34.3 percent. The change is not statistically significant in this sample ($\chi^2 = 2.57$, df $= 1$, $p = .108$). Nevertheless, there is another indication that restricted bowl rims may have become more common in the later parts of the Medio period. Data from Casas Grandes (Di Peso, Rinaldo, and Fenner 1974:6:111) show that 60.1 percent of bowls there had vertical or slightly everted rims, whereas 39.9 percent had inverted or restricted rims. In preceding discussion, we have argued that the peak of Casas Grandes comes after that of site 204, so that some of its material postdates most of the late Medio occupation at site 204. The Casas Grandes late Medio bowl sample proportion of 39.9 percent inverted rims is nearly double the 204 midden's early Medio figure of 21.1 percent. Not surprisingly, this difference is statistically significant ($\chi^2 = 8.34$, df $= 1$, $p > .01$). We suggest therefore that inflected bowl rims became more common as the Medio period progressed.

Most of the early and late sherds in the 204 middens are Plain, although Textured, Red, Black, and Polychrome types are also present in both early and late Medio assemblages. A sixth group, Black-on-Red, is known to occur in the late Medio assemblage, but these sherds are absent in the middens at site 204. Although all five of the major ware groups occur in the early and late Medio test pit levels, their proportions are noticeably different. Table 5.1 summarizes these data.

These data show that most early and late Medio vessels were Plain, although Plain ware was slightly more common in the early part of the Medio period. The Textured types diminish from early to late, but Red and Polychrome jars and bowls increased in frequency in the late Medio. Black vessels occur fairly consistently across the period.

## Vessel Forms and Types among Medio Communities

The vessel neck, rim, and body forms described in the preceding section are applicable to all of the sites discussed in this volume. There is, however, a notable difference in jar-to-bowl ratios. We calculated a ratio of about 2:1 for the site 204 middens and for the primate center of Casas Grandes. The rooms at site 204 had a jar-to-bowl ratio of about 2.3:1, which is much like that of the middens. The jar-to-bowl ratio in rooms at sites 231 and 317 is slightly higher, at about 3:1. The normal situation among Medio period communities, then, seems to be a ratio on the order of two or three jar rim sherds for each bowl rim. Yet site 242 is extremely different from this pattern, having a jar-to-bowl rim sherd ratio of about 20:1. Jars clearly made up a much larger percentage of the vessels at site 242 than at other sites, even including the primate center.

The same ceramic types are present at all four sites discussed here, as well as at Casas Grandes. Another similarity among the ceramic samples from the neighboring sites is that most of them lack the Black-on-Red sherds that are known components of the late Medio ceramic assemblage all over west-central and northwestern Chihuahua (Burd, Kelley, and Hendrickson 2004; Di Peso, Rinaldo, and Fenner 1974: vol. 6). Black-on-Red sherds were found only in the enormous pottery samples from Casas Grandes, and they are rare even there, at less than 2 percent of the total. We note that a segment of a small Black-on-Red jar was recovered from site 242, and tabulation by Jones (2002) shows that there are a few (ca. 0.5 percent) of these sherds in the site's assemblage. There were, however, no measurable Black-on-Red rims from any of the four sites, so that Black-on-Red sherds are omitted from the present analyses.

There are some inter-site differences in jar and bowl frequencies within ceramic groups. The data from the four outlying sites are derived from rim sherds alone. The Casas Grandes data are taken from the Di Peso, Rinaldo, and Fenner (1974) report. There, bowl and jar counts are given for all analyzed sherds of every ceramic type, although it is not clear how the two vessel forms were distinguished. These data, therefore, are not exactly the same kind as ours, but they are used for comparison. Our analyses show that Plain jars and bowls are overwhelmingly dominant at all four neighboring sites, as they are at Casas Grandes. Some 60–68 percent of jars are Plain ware at most of these sites, and 40–57 percent of bowls are Plain. The sole exception to this pattern is site 242, where more than 90 percent of the jars are Plain. Textured types comprise 6–16 percent of jars and 3–4.5 percent of bowls at Casas Grandes and at neighboring sites 204, 231, and 317. Site 242 again stands out from the prevailing pattern in having the lowest percentage of Textured jars in the present sample. The site's collection contains no textured bowl rims.

The Playas Red types comprise 7–15 percent of the jar rim sherds in the present sample. Their contribution to the bowl assemblage is higher, however, at 11–21 percent. Site 242 is once again the exception to this generalization, having no measurable Playas Red rims of any kind. Earlier analysis and tabulation of the site 242 collection (Jones 2002:54) demonstrates that there are Playas Red sherds at site 242, although that site has a lower frequency of this ware (1.7 percent) than either sites 231 (5.3 percent) or 317 (5.8 percent). This is surprising for a late Medio site, as the preceding chapter showed that the Playas Red types increase considerably in frequency after the early part of the Medio. Plain, Textured, and Playas Red are the large, utilitarian wares of the Medio period, and the dramatic increase in Plain vessels at site 242 is accompanied by a reduction in the frequencies of Textured and Playas Red.

It may be significant that Plain jars have somewhat wider mouths relative to their body diameters than do either Textured or Playas Red jars. To demonstrate this, we used the whole vessel data from Casas Grandes (Di Peso, Rinaldo, and Fenner 1974: vol. 6), where body and rim diameters were provided for vessels of all types. A ratio of orifice diameter to maximum body diameter was calculated and averages were computed for Plain (0.6615), Textured (0.5998), Playas Red (0.6019), Polychrome (0.6141), and Ramos Black (0.6166). These means were compared with a one-way analysis of variance, which showed a significant difference among them ($F = 3.964$, $p = .004$). The next question is where the significant differences lie among the five types or type groups. The standard solution to this problem is to follow an analysis of variance with one of a variety of "post hoc" tests. These identify the group or groups that differ from each other at a statistically significant level. Selected for the present analysis is Tukey's HSD (for "honestly significant difference") test. This is a widely used post hoc test that is recommended as the second step in analyses of variance, and it identifies Plain jars as the ones whose mean orifice-to-body-diameter ratio differs significantly from those of Textured jars ($p = .018$), Playas Red jars ($p = .021$), Polychrome jars ($p = .022$), and Ramos Black jars ($p = .019$). Furthermore, the test shows that these last four types do not differ significantly from one another in mean orifice-to-body ratios. The values just given show that the orifice-to-body-diameter ratio for Plain jars is the highest of the group by about 8–10 percent. We may thus conclude that Plain jars have, on average, somewhat wider mouths than similarly sized jars of other types. Also possibly of significance is the fact that Plain vessels would have been somewhat cheaper to produce than either textured or red-slipped containers. Here, we are measuring production cost in terms of the effort expended in the vessels' manufacture. At this point, it is not clear why Plain jars are so common at site 242.

Ramos Black makes up only 2–4.5 percent of jars at Casas Grandes and its neighbors, although it is more common among bowls, at 14–29 percent. Site 242 does not stand out from the others in its frequencies of this ceramic type. A different pattern was detected for the Polychrome types, which occur in variable frequencies at Casas Grandes and its neighbors. The highest Polychrome frequencies are found at Casas Grandes, site 204, and site 242. All of these communities had ball courts, parrot cages, and large ovens, as described in chapter 2. Site 242 stands out, however, for the paucity of Polychrome jars. The simpler communities, such as 231 and 317, have lower Polychrome frequencies. The implication of this pattern is that Polychrome vessels, although present in all communities, were more common in those with elite, ritual, and administrative characteristics.

### Vessel Size

How to determine vessel volume from sherds is a long-standing problem in archaeology to which no entirely satisfactory solution has been found. There are two common approaches to estimating the volumes of fragmented ceramic containers. One relies on rim sherds, and the other uses body sherds. Each has strengths and weaknesses, and both will be used in a complementary fashion in the ensuing analyses. Rim sherd analysis is discussed following, and body sherd analysis is considered in a later section.

The estimation of vessel volume from rim sherds requires an adequate number of whole vessels of the type and form in question. Rim diameter and volume are measured for each vessel, providing the raw data for the analysis. The underlying assumption is that there is a consistent relationship between the vessels' rim diameters and their volumes. If this is so, then volume and rim diameter are predictable from each other. For the present analysis, the necessary body of data from whole Medio period vessels came from the Casas Grandes ceramic study (Di Peso, Rinaldo, and Fenner 1974: vol. 6). Rim diameters, body diameters, and volumes were collected for 285 jars and bowls of a range of types and sizes. Miniature vessels were excluded from this data set.

Linear regression is the statistical technique used to build a formula to predict one variable's value from another's, assuming that the two variables are closely related in a linear fashion. Accordingly, our first task was to determine on a type-by-type basis whether rim diameter and vessel volume in the Casas Grandes containers were closely related and whether the relation was a linear one. The extent of the two variables' relation is measured through the statistic $R^2$. The value of $R^2$ ranges from 0, indicating no relation at all (and therefore perfect unpredictability of one variable from another), to 1.0 (reflecting a relationship of identity between the two variables, so that each is perfectly and completely predictable from the other). These extreme values are theoretical, however, and they will not be encountered with real data. An $R^2$ value of .9 has been described as "very high" (Lewis-Beck 1980:24), and values of 0.8 to 0.9 provide solid bases for prediction.

The relation between vessel volume and rim diameter can be shown graphically by a scatter plot of volume and diameter values. If the scatter plot produces a formless cloud of points without apparent linearity, we may safely conclude that the two variables are not related and that one cannot be predicted from the other through linear regression. Apparent linearity of the data points is a more hopeful sign: the more linear their arrangement, the more predictable is one variable from the other. There is, however, a further complication. The plotted data points may approximate an arc rather than a straight line, as illustrated in figure 5.1. This is the plot of Plain jar volumes from Casas Grandes on the $y$ axis against their rim diameters on the $x$ axis. In this case, $y$ is the dependent variable, which we wish to predict from $x$, the independent variable. This analysis is based on 52 whole jars.

In addition to the data points, figure 5.1 shows the least squares line, which is positioned to minimize the distance between itself and every data point. It is clear, however, that the distribution shown in figure 5.1 approximates an arc rather than a straight line. As a result, the least squares line is not highly congruent with the distribution of the data points. The $R^2$ value of .754 quantifies the situation. This is a common problem in regression analysis, and its solution is a systematic alteration of every value of the independent variable ($x$) in order to bring the distribution of points into a more linear form. Bringing the data points closer to the linear relationship required by the regression model has the effect of improving the accuracy of the predictive equation that will ultimately be developed from the analysis. The systematic alteration of the values of $x$ is termed a transformation, and it may take many forms, for example, $\sqrt{X}$, $\log X$, or $X^n$. The kind of transformation used is determined by the shape of the data distribution. Further

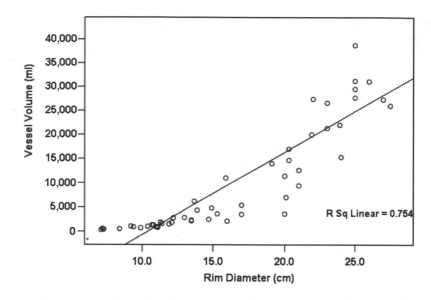

**Figure 5.1** Regression of vessel volume on rim diameter for 52 Plain jars from Casas Grandes.

discussion and illustration of transformations is provided elsewhere (e.g., Drennan 1996:222–25). Transformations were required in some of the regression analyses discussed following.

The first regression analysis was done using rim diameters and vessel volumes of Plain jars from Casas Grandes (see fig. 5.1). Several transformations were applied to the rim diameter variable $(x)$, and $X^3$ was found to produce the strongest linearization of the data points. Figure 5.2 shows the transformed data of figure 5.1. The least squares line and $R^2$ are shown as well. Note that $R^2$ for the untransformed data was .754, compared to .867 for the transformed data. This is a substantial improvement that provides a better basis for estimation of Plain jar volumes from their rim diameters.

The regression analysis illustrated in figure 5.2 calculates the values of the coefficients $a$ and $b$, which are used in the predictive formula $Y = b + aX$. Recall that $Y$ is vessel volume and $X$ is rim diameter. In the present case, $a$ is 1.751, and $b$ is $-1,169.646$. As $X$ was transformed to $X^3$, the latter must be used in the calculation. This is the equation for the least squares line shown in figure 5.2. Substituting terms for symbols, the predictive formula is

$$\text{Plain jar volume} = -1,169.646 + 1.751 \times \text{rim diameter cubed}$$

The Casas Grandes sample we used contained no Plain rim diameters less than 10 cm or greater than 22 cm, so the formula should not be applied to measurements outside of that range. We also emphasize that the volumes resulting from this formula are estimations, not exact measurements. By using the predictive formula just given, we are assuming that every data point falls on the least squares line. Figure 5.2 shows the

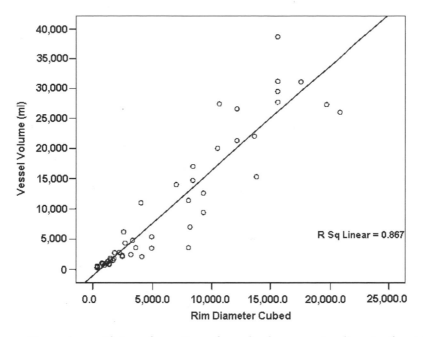

**Figure 5.2** Regression, with transformation, of vessel volume on rim diameter for 52 Plain jars from Casas Grandes.

actual divergence of the data points from the least squares line. If Plain jar volume were perfectly predictable from rim diameter (i.e., if every data point fell on the least squares line), $R^2$ would equal 1.0. The actual $R^2$ value of .843 indicates good predictive potential, but it falls short of perfection. There are many sources of error in this analysis, most notably including irregularities of shape in hand-built ceramic vessels, inaccuracies of measurement, and fluctuation in the orifice-to-volume ratio for individual vessels. The formula just given, therefore, should be understood to produce good *estimates* of Medio period Plain jar volumes for use in succeeding discussion and analysis. The same predictive formulae will be applied to early and late Medio vessels. This procedure may found to be unsatisfactory in the future, when we have more whole vessels that are known to be early or late Medio. In our present state of ignorance, however, we have no alternative but to use the same formulae for all parts of the Medio period.

In addition to the Plain jar analysis just described, regression analyses were carried out for jars of the Textured, Playas Red, Ramos Black, Ramos Polychrome, and other Polychrome types; and for bowls of the Plain, Textured, Playas Red, Ramos Black, Ramos Polychrome, and other Polychrome types. Figures 5.3 to 5.12 show the scatter plots and least squares lines for these analyses. Table 5.2 summarizes all of the regression analyses and presents the derived formulae for vessel volume estimation.

The formulae in the preceding table permit the estimation of jar and bowl volumes from their rim sherds at the four excavated sites. Before proceeding to this analysis, however, we should mention one more point. The assumption underlying the use of Casas Grandes vessels to estimate vessel volumes at neighboring sites is that the ceramics of

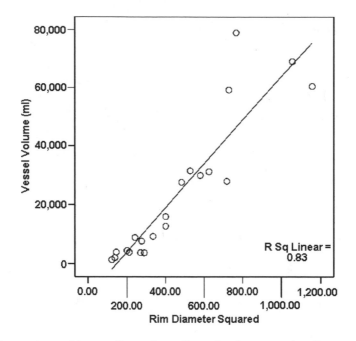

**Figure 5.3** Regression, with transformation, of vessel volume on rim diameter for 21 Textured jars from Casas Grandes.

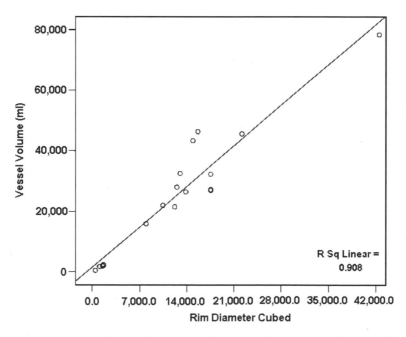

**Figure 5.4** Regression, with transformation, of vessel volume on rim diameter for 14 Playas Red jars from Casas Grandes.

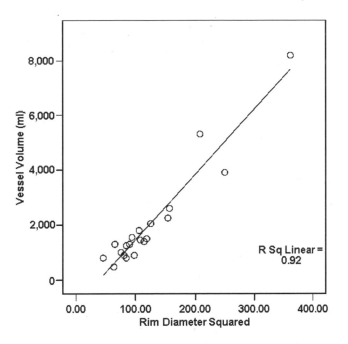

**Figure 5.5** Regression, with transformation, of vessel volume on rim diameter for 19 Ramos Black jars from Casas Grandes.

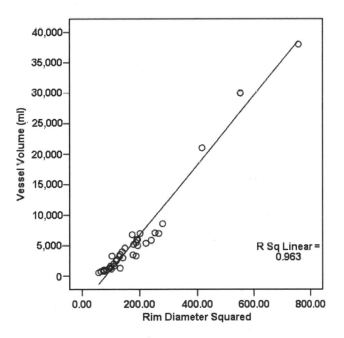

**Figure 5.6** Regression, with transformation, of vessel volume on rim diameter for 36 Ramos Polychrome jars from Casas Grandes.

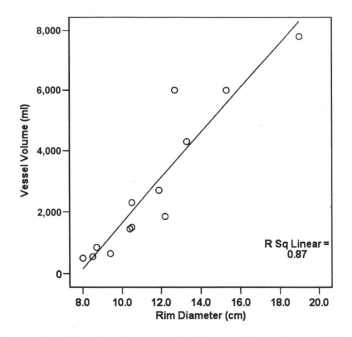

**Figure 5.7** Regression of vessel volume on rim diameter for 13 other polychrome jars from Casas Grandes.

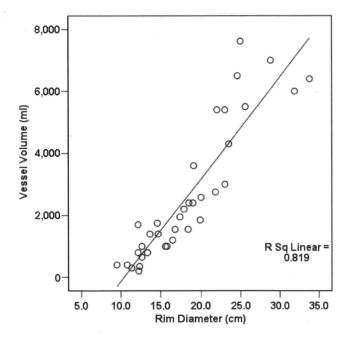

**Figure 5.8** Regression of vessel volume on rim diameter for 36 Plain bowls from Casas Grandes.

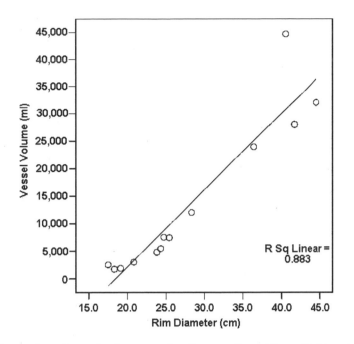

**Figure 5.9** Regression of vessel volume on rim diameter for 13 Playas Red bowls from Casas Grandes.

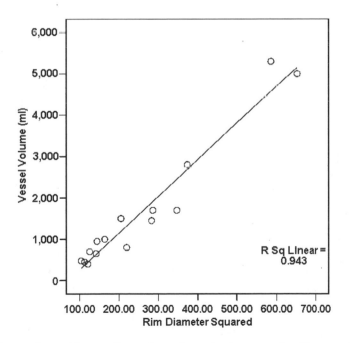

**Figure 5.10** Regression, with transformation, of vessel volume on rim diameter for 15 Ramos Black bowls from Casas Grandes.

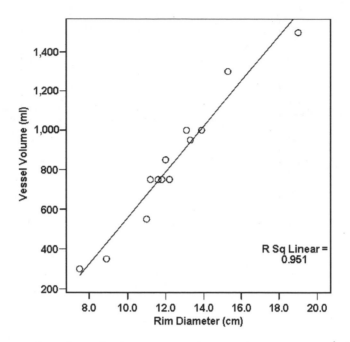

**Figure 5.11** Regression of vessel volume on rim diameter for 13 Ramos Polychrome bowls from Casas Grandes.

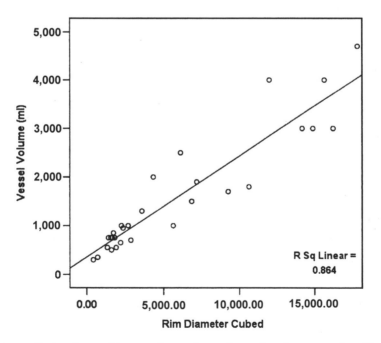

**Figure 5.12** Regression, with transformation, of vessel volume on rim diameter for 30 non–Ramos Polychrome bowls from Casas Grandes.

**Table 5.2**  Results of Regression Analyses on Casas Grandes Vessels

| Type | $n$ | $R^2$ | Predictive formula: volume (ml) = |
|---|---|---|---|
| **Jars** | | | |
| Plain jars | 52 | .867 | $-1{,}169.646 + 1.751 \times$ rim diameter cubed |
| Textured jars | 21 | .830 | $-10{,}946.53 + 74.743 \times$ rim diameter squared |
| Playas Red jars | 14 | .908 | $1{,}522.27 + 1.909 \times$ rim diameter cubed |
| Ramos Black jars | 19 | .920 | $-927.687 + 23.853 \times$ rim diameter squared |
| Ramos Polychrome jars | 36 | .963 | $-4{,}681.165 + 57.249 \times$ rim diameter squared |
| Other polychrome jars | 13 | .870 | $-5{,}575.606 + 741.575 \times$ rim diameter |
| **Bowls** | | | |
| Plain bowls | 36 | .819 | $-3{,}439.018 + 330.210 \times$ rim diameter |
| Textured bowls | 6 | — | sample too small for calculation |
| Playas Red bowls | 13 | .883 | $-25{,}703.83 + 1{,}394.493 \times$ rim diameter |
| Ramos Black bowls | 15 | .943 | $-627.255 + 8.886 \times$ rim diameter squared |
| Ramos Polychrome bowls | 13 | .951 | $-600.680 + 115.727 \times$ rim diameter |
| Other polychrome bowls | 30 | .864 | $358.699 + .207 \times$ rim diameter cubed |

the primate center are much like those of neighboring communities. All of our survey and excavation work to date supports this assumption. The $R^2$ values shown in the table are strikingly high, demonstrating considerable regularity in the relation between size and shape for all categories of vessels. This may indicate that the Casas Grandes area had more centralized production of ceramics of all types than had been thought to be the case. In particular, we observe the very high $R^2$ value for Ramos Polychrome jars. The extremely close fit of the data points to the least squares line (refer to fig. 5.6) argues that these jars were more standardized in size and shape than were other polychrome jars in this sample. A high level of standardization has been proposed as an indication of specialized production (e.g., T. VanPool and Leonard 2002), and Sphren (2003) recently has used other data to argue that Ramos Polychrome was the product of specialists. Our regression analysis lends support to this argument.

Before discussing vessel volumes at the type level, we will use the data from Casas Grandes and the 204 middens to establish size categories for jars and bowls, as these will be useful in comparative discussion of ceramic assemblages. Figure 5.13 shows histograms of whole jar and bowl volumes from Casas Grandes. All types are combined here.

Both the jar and bowl assemblages are divisible into several size categories. In this sample, small jars are less than 10 L in volume, medium jars are 10.1 L to 18 L, large jars are 18.1 to 32.5 L, and very large jars are 32.6 to 50 L. There is a fifth category of extra-large jars that exceed 50 L. Small bowls contain 3.5 L or less, medium bowls hold 3.6 to 9 L, large bowls hold up to 33 L, and very large bowls exceed 33 L in volume. It is clear from figure 5.13 that the vast majority of jars and bowls in this sample are small, although a few are large or very large. These categories are applicable to the data from the other excavated sites, as shown by the histogram in figure 5.14. One difference is

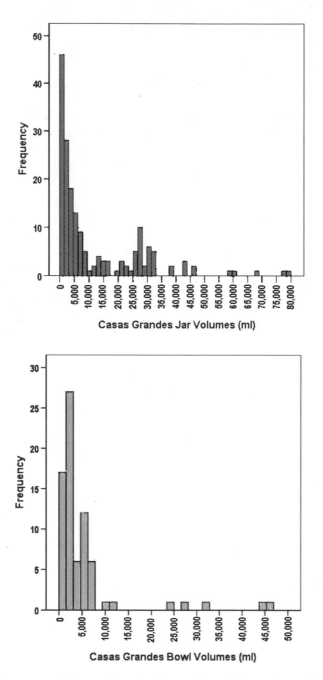

**Figure 5.13** Histograms of jar and bowl volumes (in ml) from Casas Grandes (all vessel types combined).

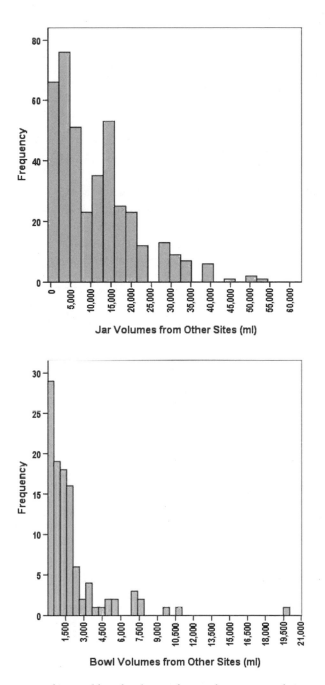

**Figure 5.14** Histograms of jar and bowl volumes from other excavated sites.

immediately apparent, however. There are more of the very large and extra-large categories of jars and bowls at the primate center than among its neighbors. This point will be discussed in more detail later in this chapter. We turn now to the estimation of vessel volume in the site 204 middens in consideration of ceramic assemblage change between the early and late parts of the Medio period.

### Vessel Volumes in the Early and Late Medio

Early and late Medio levels in the Mound A midden test pits contained 514 jar rim sherds, of which 297 were of measurable size (i.e., at least 4 cm). Early Medio levels provided only 43 of these rim sherds, and the remaining 254 were late Medio. There were 245 bowl rim sherds. Of this total, 40 came from early Medio levels, and 205 were late Medio. For the early Medio, there were only 15 measurable rim sherds but there were 63 for the late Medio. All volumes were calculated from rim sherd measurements using the regression-based formulae just given. Table 5.3 shows sample sizes, means, and standard deviations for early and late Medio jars and bowls of different types. Vessel volumes could not be calculated if there were no rims of measurable size in the test pit levels.

No statistically significant differences were found between the early and late Medio for jars or bowls of any type. It is clear from table 5.3, however, that the present sample has limitations imposed by the disproportionate sample size between the early and late Medio assemblages. The late Plain jar rim sherd sample, for instance, is nearly six times greater than its early counterpart, and the late Polychrome sample exceeds the early one by a factor of five. In addition, most of the early Medio type samples are either zero or very small. Small sample sizes mean less perceived variability compared to larger ones. Unfortunately, the question of vessel size differences between the early and late Medio cannot be resolved with the present data set.

**Table 5.3**  Early and Late Medio Vessel Volumes from Site 204 (volumes in liters)

| Vessel | Early Medio | | | Late Medio | | |
|---|---|---|---|---|---|---|
| | $n$ | Mean (L) | SD (L) | $n$ | Mean (L) | SD (L) |
| **Jars** | | | | | | |
| Plain | 36 | 16.7 | 6.3 | 207 | 7.2 | 6.1 |
| Textured | 3 | 13.9 | 15.8 | 7 | 17.4 | 8.7 |
| Red | 0 | — | — | 14 | 11.6 | 6.0 |
| Black | 1 | — | — | 6 | 2.8 | 1.6 |
| Polychrome | 4 | 5.3 | 3.7 | 20 | 7.7 | 5.0 |
| **Bowls** | | | | | | |
| Plain | 14 | 2.1 | 2.0 | 33 | 2.8 | 1.5 |
| Textured | 0 | — | — | 0 | — | — |
| Red | 0 | — | — | 4 | 6.4 | 9.4 |
| Black | 1 | — | — | 14 | 0.7 | 0.6 |
| Polychrome | 0 | — | — | 17 | 2.0 | 1.4 |

Another, rougher, approach to vessel size comparison between assemblages uses templates that are fitted against the inner surface of a sherd, producing an estimate of the diameter of the vessel at the point represented by the sherd. The technique is described in detail elsewhere (Whalen 1998). That study demonstrates that it is impossible to translate individual body sherd diameter measurements into accurate whole vessel volumes. Nevertheless, the diameter estimates can be used to make statements about general ceramic assemblage makeup through reconstruction of the composition of an assemblage in terms of broad vessel size categories. Although the template technique is of lower precision than the rim-sherd-based volume estimates just discussed, it has another major advantage. The body sherds upon which it relies are much more numerous than rims are, and the result is a considerably larger sample of vessel diameter estimates. The template technique was applied to 1,028 body sherds of the Plain, Textured, and Polychrome types from the site 204 middens. Early Medio sherds numbered 271, and there were 757 late body sherds. No statistically significant difference was detected for any type, complementing the rim-sherd-based vessel volume estimates just presented. Two different approaches to vessel size estimation thus point to the conclusion that jar and bowl sizes do not appear to increase from early to late Medio times based on the present sample.

## Jar Volumes among Medio Communities

In table 5.4, the four neighboring sites and Casas Grandes are compared in three ways: maximum, mean, and median jar sizes. One obvious weakness of this data set is the difference in sample size among the five sites for every type. Some of the sample sizes, especially those from site 242, are very small due to the paucity of rim sherds of measurable size.

Three patterns emerge from the table. First, Casas Grandes has the largest mean vessel sizes in several categories. This pattern is especially evident for Plain and Textured jars. Playas Red jars also have a mean greater than those of other sites. We note that Playas Red jars with volumes of more than 70 L were recovered from Casas Grandes, and Plain and Textured jars of this size also were found there. Table 5.4 shows no such jars in the samples from sites 204, 231, and 317. Instead, the largest jars from these sites are Plain vessels with volumes of 33 L to 46 L. This is not proof that there were none of the 70 L jars at neighboring sites, but they were not common enough to be visible in the small samples analyzed here.

The most capacious Ramos Polychrome jars from Casas Grandes were considerably larger than those of neighboring sites, although the primate center's mean Ramos jar volume is the smallest one shown in the table. Clearly, most Ramos Polychrome jars at all sites in this sample were small, with mean volumes of 6 L to 12 L. There were a few specimens with greater volume, of which the largest known came from Casas Grandes. Polychrome jars of types other than Ramos also were small at all four neighbors and at the primate center. In sum, Casas Grandes does not differ from its neighbors in every category and type shown in the table. The community clearly contained many vessels sized for the ordinary domestic unit, but it differs most from its neighbors

**Table 5.4**   Jar Volumes at Five Medio Sites (volumes in liters)

| Type | Site | n | Mean (L) | SD (L) |
|---|---|---|---|---|
| Plain | 204 | 95 | 9.3 | 7.8 |
| | 231 | 19 | 12.0 | 9.8 |
| | 242 | 85 | 14.7 | 7.9 |
| | 317 | 44 | 11.8 | 8.6 |
| | CG | 193[a] | 18.1 | 11.6 |
| Playas Red types | 204 | 51 | 12.9 | 7.1 |
| | 231 | 2 | 10.0 | 12.0 |
| | 242 | 0 | — | — |
| | 317 | 6 | 13.9 | 12.2 |
| | CG | 106[a] | 23.0 | 8.3 |
| Textured types | 204 | 17 | 13.3 | 9.4 |
| | 231 | 8 | 12.2 | 16.0 |
| | 242 | 1 | — | — |
| | 317 | 17 | 13.0 | 12.0 |
| | CG | 21[b] | 23.5 | 24.2 |
| Ramos Black | 204 | 10 | 3.1 | 1.3 |
| | 231 | 7 | 4.5 | 2.6 |
| | 242 | 3 | 3.0 | 1.3 |
| | 317 | 3 | 4.5 | 3.9 |
| | CG | 20[b] | 2.7 | 2.0 |
| Ramos Polychrome | 204 | 12 | 7.4 | 5.7 |
| | 231 | 3 | 10.8 | 8.5 |
| | 242 | 5 | 12.3 | 5.8 |
| | 317 | 10 | 8.8 | 6.5 |
| | CG | 39[b] | 6.2 | 8.6 |
| Other polychrome | 204 | 37 | 6.6 | 3.2 |
| | 231 | 2 | 8.1 | 8.9 |
| | 242 | 4 | 9.1 | 1.9 |
| | 317 | 4 | 4.3 | 1.4 |
| | CG | 14[b] | 4.1 | 2.5 |

a. Sample remeasured for this analysis from the Casas Grandes ceramics.

b. Sample not remeasured. Data from whole vessels illustrated in the Casas Grandes report.

in the presence of at least some very large jars of the Plain, Textured, and Playas Red types, plus some unusually large Ramos Polychrome jars.

A second observation from these data is that site 242 stands apart from the other neighbors of the primate center in the sizes of at least some of its vessels. This pattern is clear in the Plain jars, which form the largest sample of any type from all four neighboring sites. The mean Plain jar volume at site 242 (14.7 L) is noticeably higher than at the other three sites, and it approaches that of the primate center. The Plain jar volume means for the four neighboring sites were tested against each other using one-way analysis of variance. The analysis shows a significant difference among the four sites in mean volume for Plain jars ($F = 8.745$, $p < .0001$). Tukey's post hoc test identifies site 242 as the only one whose mean Plain jar volume differs significantly from those of sites 204 ($p < .0001$), 231 ($p = .045$), and 317 ($p = .008$). Furthermore, the test shows that these last three sites do not differ significantly from each other in Plain jar volume means. Unfortunately, measurable-sized rim sherds of the Textured and Playas Red types are nearly absent at site 242, precluding comparisons like the one just done for Plain jars. Additional analyses of variance show that the mean volumes of jars of other types do not differ significantly among the four sites.

Our findings are consistent with a more generalized result obtained in an earlier study (Jones 2002). Jones used the template technique (Whalen 1998) to estimate jar volume ranges from body sherds. Site 242 was found to have significantly larger jars than sites 231 and 317 did. Site 204 was not included in this analysis. Jars of all types were combined in Jones' analysis, which clearly was detecting the larger Plain jars just discussed. The obvious implication of this pattern is large-scale storage and preparation of food that likely was used in public feasting, and Jones (2002) came to that conclusion. This, in turn, is consistent with our earlier, architecture-based argument that site 242 served as an administrative outpost for the center of Casas Grandes (Whalen and Minnis 2001b).

The third pattern that emerges from the preceding table is based on comparison of jars from site 204 with those of sites 231 and 317. Earlier, it was argued that sites 231 and 317 were small, unremarkable communities that likely reflect only the domestic level of production and consumption. Accordingly, it is most interesting that the much larger site 204 community does not differ significantly from the smaller sites in any of the mean values shown in the table. The implication of this situation is that the 204 community was characterized by production and consumption that remained largely at the domestic level. Recall that no statistically significant difference in early and late Medio Plain and Textured jar volumes was found from the site 204 middens. Only the late Medio test pit levels contained measurable rim sherds of Playas Red, so that they could not be tested against their early predecessors. Nevertheless, the data in hand argue that the proposed situation of domestic-level consumption remained stable across the early Medio and the initial part of the late Medio at site 204. This, in turn, suggests the public feasting used by Casas Grandes and its administrative satellites as an organizational strategy may not have existed at so high a level in the early part of the Medio period.

## Bowl Volumes among Medio Communities

The sample of bowl rim sherds from the four sites is only about one-quarter the size of the jar rim sample just analyzed. There were 107 bowl rims of measurable size from all four sites, and nearly two-thirds of these came from site 204. To the issue of unequal sample size is added the problem of small sample sizes. This analysis of bowl volume is, therefore, of lower reliability than the preceding jar volume study. Data from 97 whole bowls from the Casas Grandes report are also used in this analysis. No new measurements have been made on the bowls of the primate center. Table 5.5 shows bowl size data for Casas Grandes and the four neighboring sites. As noted previously, the sample of whole, Textured bowls from Casas Grandes was too small for regression analysis to calculate a reliable formula for estimation of vessel volume from rim diameter. As a result, Textured bowl volumes cannot be calculated and are omitted from the table. The present sample is so small that Ramos Polychrome bowls are grouped with all other polychromes instead of being analyzed separately, as they were for jars.

There is only one clear pattern in this table. Casas Grandes has bowls of the Plain and Playas Red types that are far larger than those of neighboring communities. The largest Plain and Playas Red bowls at the primate center are around 45 L in volume. Very large Plain and Playas Red bowls from site 242 have estimated volumes of 24, 28, and

**Table 5.5**   Bowl Volumes at Five Medio Sites (volumes in liters)

| Type | Site | $n$ | Mean (L) | SD (L) |
|------|------|-----|----------|--------|
| All types | 204 | 64 | 1.3 | 1.3 |
| | 231 | 12 | 1.5 | 0.9 |
| | 242 | 2 | 2.8 | 3.0 |
| | 317 | 29 | 1.9 | 1.6 |
| | CG | 97 | 4.1 | 7.8 |
| Plain | 204 | 24 | 2.5 | 1.7 |
| | 231 | 5 | 2.7 | 1.1 |
| | 242 | 0 | — | — |
| | 317 | 14 | 2.6 | 1.8 |
| | CG | 38 | 3.9 | 7.3 |
| Playas Red types | 204 | 1 | — | — |
| | 231 | 0 | — | — |
| | 242 | 0 | — | — |
| | 317 | 3 | 5.0 | — |
| | CG | 14 | 12.5 | 13.9 |
| Ramos Black | 204 | 6 | 1.3 | 1.7 |
| | 231 | 4 | 0.9 | 0.5 |
| | 242 | 0 | — | — |
| | 317 | 1 | 1.6 | — |
| | CG | 16 | 1.6 | 1.5 |
| Polychromes | 204 | 9 | 1.0 | 0.4 |
| | 231 | 2 | 2.7 | 1.3 |
| | 242 | 2 | 2.8 | 3.0 |
| | 317 | 0 | — | — |
| | CG | 29 | 1.6 | 1.2 |

32 L. All of these very large bowls are rare, as shown by the means and standard deviations in the table. These rim-sherd-based volumes do not always tell the whole story, however. Excavation at site 204 recovered most of a Plain bowl with a volume of at least 45 L. Nothing so large came from sites 231 or 317, although the samples of excavated material from them were much smaller than the one from site 204. The safest statement thus seems to be that only at the primate center are very large bowls common enough to be visible in the present sample. Ramos Black and Polychrome bowls show no significant difference in volume among the four neighboring sites.

In short, our bowl volume estimates follow the trend recognized for jars. That is, Casas Grandes has more of the largest examples of Plain and Playas Red bowls than do the four neighboring sites. Despite the very large bowl found at site 204, that site's mean Plain bowl volume is only about one-quarter that of Casas Grandes. In this sample, bowl volumes do not follow the second trend identified for jars. That is, site 242 does not stand out as having larger bowls than sites 204, 231, and 317 do. The body-sherd-based bowl volume ranges used by Jones (2002) argue that there were at least some larger bowls at site 242 than at 231 or 317. Our rim-sherd-based bowl volume analysis does not concur, but the measurable bowl rim sample from site 242 is so low as to make questionable any statement about these vessels. Jones' (2002) results, although of lower precision than ours, are probably the more reliable because the sample of measured body sherds greatly exceeds our small sample of rim sherds. The third trend recognized for jars is the similarity between the assemblages at sites 204, 231, and 317. This pattern also holds for bowls, arguing that food preparation in these communities was mostly done on the domestic scale rather than on the large, public one.

## Ceramic Use-Wear

Two kinds of use-wear are conspicuous on Medio period ceramics. These are exterior sooting and interior erosion or pitting. The presence of soot on vessel exteriors clearly shows that the containers were heated over open fires. Extensive interior surface erosion or pitting, however, is less specific in its implications. It has been suggested to result from two sources: acidic by-products of the preparation of fermented drinks (Arthur 2003) and the alkali processing of corn (M. Beck 2001; Di Peso, Rinaldo, and Fenner 1974: vol. 6). Food or drink preparation is the cause in either case, and the two activities are not mutually exclusive. We note that ethnographic data (e.g., Bruman 2000) show that alcoholic drinks were largely absent in the public and ritual activities of the U.S. Southwest. They were much more common all over northern Mexico and Mesoamerica, however.

The ensuing discussion of use-wear on Medio ceramics begins by contrasting the early and late Medio situations as reflected in the midden test pit data from site 204. The study is then expanded to other kinds of sites in the area. Earlier discussion noted that jar and bowl sherds can be difficult to distinguish in Medio ceramic assemblages, as jar sherds do not show consistently coarse interior finishes. Accordingly, sherds were identified as coming from bowls only when interior decoration or a portion of the rim was present. Sherds with coarse to medium interior finishes were classed as jars. Those with finer finishes, which could have come from either jars or bowls, were omitted from this part of the present analysis.

## Interior Pitting in the Early and Late Medio

This study examined a total of 4,720 body sherds: 1,119 from the early Medio midden test pit levels and 3,601 from late Medio levels. Interior pitting is not very common in either assemblage, appearing on 8.9 percent of early Medio jar sherds and on 7.9 percent of their late Medio successors. The intensity of pitting is also about the same. For the early Medio, some 2.1 percent of the jar sherd assemblage is heavily pitted, and light pitting was present on 6.8 percent. The comparable late Medio figures are 2.2 percent and 5.7 percent. Interior surface pitting is also found on bowls in the early and late Medio. In the early Medio test pit levels, 11.4 percent of the bowls showed interior pitting. The late Medio figure differed little at 12.1 percent. Clearly, this sample contains no significant difference in either frequency or intensity of interior surface pitting between the early and late parts of the Medio period at site 204. Rather, pitting occurs there at a low but constant intensity all across the period. This argues that interior surface pitting is not produced by a basic, widespread food processing technique such as alkali corn processing, but rather by an occasional one such as fermentation.

Interior-pitted vessels encompassed a wide range of ceramic types all through the Medio period. Table 5.6 shows the extent of pitting inside the types or type groups found in the site 204 middens.

Several things are evident from the table. First, most vessels with interior pitting are Plain all through the Medio period. The percentage of pitted Plain vessels also increases considerably from early to late Medio times. This shift is accompanied by a dramatic decrease in Polychrome vessels with interior pitting from early to late Medio. Polychromes made up more than 25 percent of the pitted vessel sample in the early part of the Medio, but this figure fell below 2 percent by the late Medio. This observation hints

**Table 5.6**    Interior Pitting on Medio Ceramic Types

|  | Plain | Textured | Red | Black | Polychrome |
|---|---|---|---|---|---|
| **Early Medio** | | | | | |
| No pitting | 597 (98.1)[a] | 112 (92.6) | 18 (100) | 81 (92.0) | 175 (86.6) |
| Light pitting | 39 (6.0) | 9 (7.4) | 0 (0) | 5 (5.7) | 21 (10.4) |
| Heavy pitting | 14 (2.2) | 0 (0) | 0 (0) | 2 (2.3) | 6 (3.0) |
| **Total** | 650 (100.0) | 121 (100.0) | 18 (100.0) | 88 (100.0) | 202 (100.0) |
| **Late Medio** | | | | | |
| No pitting | 1,669 (90.5) | 258 (92.8) | 95 (93.1) | 326 (95.9) | 85 (97.7) |
| Light pitting | 127 (6.9) | 16 (5.8) | 5 (4.9) | 11 (3.2) | 1 (1.1) |
| Heavy pitting | 49 (2.7) | 4 (1.4) | 2 (2.0) | 3 (0.9) | 1 (1.1) |
| **Total** | 1,845 (100.0) | 278 (100.0) | 102 (100.0) | 340 (100.0) | 87 (100.0) |

a. Percentages in parentheses.

at a change in function of polychrome vessels between the early and late parts of the Medio period. In early times, they seem to have been used in domestic activities to a greater extent than in the succeeding late Medio, when Plain vessels took over most of the activities that produced interior pitting.

It is informative to ask what sizes of vessels show interior pitting. Previously we discussed a technique that uses templates to gauge the interior vessel diameters represented by body sherds. Where interior pitting was present, body sherd diameter measurements from the 204 midden test pits ranged from 16 cm to 44 cm in the early Medio period and from 18 cm to 52 cm in the late part of the Medio. Although these figures cannot be taken as precise vessel diameters for the reasons discussed, their distribution of values shows that both early and late Medio times contained a range of small to large vessels with interior pitting. The fact that the late Medio diameter range estimate has higher maximum values than the early range hints that some of the late Medio vessels with interior pitting were larger than their early predecessors. From the data in hand, then, it appears that interior surface pitting occurs on a wide range of vessel sizes in the early and late Medio.

## Interior Pitting across Medio Communities

This study uses 5,456 body sherds from room contexts at sites 204, 231, 242, and 317. The sherds from the 204 midden, discussed in the preceding section, were not included here. Nevertheless, the present sample is still dominated by room-context material from site 204, which provided 2,401 body sherds. Sites 231, 242, and 317 contributed, respectively, 733, 1,093, and 1,229 body sherds to the sample. Unfortunately, the published ceramic data from Casas Grandes are not specific on the question of pitting. In a general discussion of Medio period ceramics from that site, it was noted that "the bottoms and interiors of some jars were pitted and eroded as if they had been subject to some leaching action . . . such as in the preparation of hominy or masa" (Di Peso, Rinaldo, and Fenner 1974:6:86). Beyond this observation, there is no further discussion or tabulation of interior surface pitting on Medio ceramics. As a partial remedy for this situation, we reexamined 1,884 Plain, Playas Red, and Scored jar body sherds from the Casas Grandes ceramic collections, and these data are used here. No bowl sherds were included in this sample.

The first question concerns the frequency of interior surface pitting at each of the four sites. Table 5.7 summarizes these data. There clearly are two frequency classes of pitted vessels. The first, consisting of the primate center and sites 204 and 242, shows interior pitting on 6 percent or more of its body sherds. The second group, formed by sites 231 and 317, shows interior pitting at a much lower level: 1 percent or less. The most consistent difference between the two groups of sites is community elaboration. Sites 231 and 317 were both classified in the "small" site category by our regional survey. They appear to lack any kind of architecture beyond domestic room blocks. Sites 204 and 242 represent very different sizes of communities, but both are relatively elaborate. Both have attached ball courts of the classic I shape, and macaw cage-door stones were found in each community. A macaw burial was excavated at site 204, and macaw cage-door

**Table 5.7**   Frequencies of Interior Surface Pitting, by Site

| Vessel form | Site | *n* | Light pitting (%) | Heavy pitting (%) | All pitting (%) |
|---|---|---|---|---|---|
| Jars | Casas Grandes | 1,884 | 3.9 | 2.8 | 6.7 |
| | 204 | 1,996 | 4.1 | 4.5 | 8.6 |
| | 242 | 1,034 | 2.5 | 4.1 | 6.6 |
| | 231 | 679 | 0.7 | 0.3 | 1.0 |
| | 317 | 1,134 | 0.3 | 0 | 0.3 |
| Bowls | 204 | 405 | 5.1 | 0 | 5.1 |
| | 242 | 59 | 0 | 3.4 | 3.4 |
| | 231 | 54 | 0 | 0 | 0 |
| | 317 | 95 | 0 | 0 | 0 |

stones were found at site 242. Moreover, 242 has elaborate, thick-walled architecture built in apparent imitation of that of the primate center. In this data set, then, there is a correlation between relatively high frequencies of vessels with pitted interiors and sites with ritual, administrative, or elite connotations. The obvious implication is that communities containing elites and discharging ritual or administrative functions were preparing food and drink for groups larger than the ordinary domestic unit, the scale of which is reflected by sites 231 and 317.

A related question is the frequency of occurrence of interior pitting on the five ware groups used in the present study. The Casas Grandes data are not extensive enough to be analyzed. At all four neighboring sites, the vast majority (ca. 88 percent) of interior-pitted vessels are Plain. Polychrome, Textured, and Red vessels are a distant second at ca. 12 percent, and Black containers showed no interior pitting in this sample. We note that Polychrome vessels showed interior pitting at somewhat higher levels in the site 204 midden samples. This was especially true in the early Medio, when more than 25 percent of vessels with interior pitting were polychromes.

The size ranges of interior-pitted vessels can be compared across the four sites. Figure 5.15 shows histograms of body diameter estimates on sherds that show interior surface pitting among the neighbors of Casas Grandes. We lack these data for the primate center. These measurements were made using the template method described in the preceding section. As emphasized there, the figures should not be taken as precise body diameter measurements. Instead, they should be used as relative figures by which to compare ceramic assemblages.

The histograms show that interior-pitted body sherds from all four sites came mostly from medium to large vessels that yielded body diameter measurements of around 30 cm to 40 cm. In fact, this is the only size class represented on sites 231 and 317. Sites 204 and 242 are somewhat different in their wider ranges of body sherd diameter measurements. Most important are the upper ends of these ranges. Both sites 204 and 242 have some interior-pitted vessels that are larger than the common size. These larger vessels

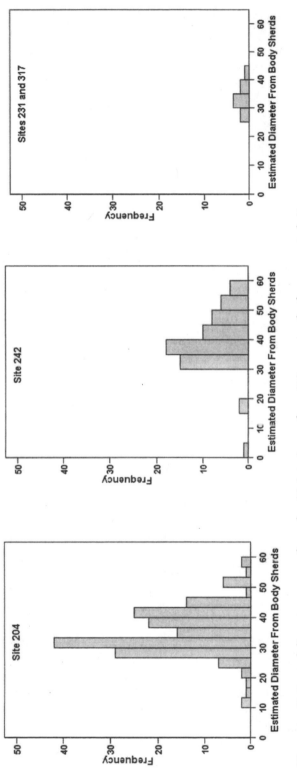

**Figure 5.15** Estimated diameter ranges of vessels with interior surface pitting across the four excavated sites.

are represented by body sherds that gave diameter measurements of 40 to nearly 60 cm. Furthermore, site 242 has even larger pitted vessels than site 204 does. The site 242 mean body diameter measurement of 39.90 differs at a statistically significant level from the 204 mean of 34.96 ($t = -4.150$, df $= 232$, 2-tailed $p > .0001$). Site 242 is suggested to have been an administrative node of Casas Grandes (Whalen and Minnis 2001b), and it has in its assemblage the largest interior-pitted vessels in this four-site sample.

## Exterior Sooting in the Early and Late Medio

The presence of soot on vessel exteriors is the most common and readily observable kind of use-wear in Medio period ceramics. Its source is likewise clear: sooted vessels were heated over fires, most likely for the cooking of food. Fire-clouds—artifacts of open-air pottery firing—also are often present on Medio period ceramics, and they should not be mistaken for soot. To avoid confusing the two, we used the criteria employed at Casas Grandes. There, carbon deposits from cooking fires were described as "generally a dirty matte black in distinction from the more lustrous black of a fire-cloud" (Di Peso, Rinaldo, and Fenner 1974:6:85). In the present study, no magnification was used to detect soot, and only its presence or absence was recorded for each body sherd. This expedient was used because sooting is known to vary widely in intensity on different parts of the same vessel in different degrees of proximity to the fire (Skibo 1992:149).

This study examined 4,719 body sherds from the midden test pits at site 204. Soot was detected on 264 of these sherds, or 5.6 percent of the total. In the early Medio, 115 jar sherds (10.3 percent) showed exterior soot, and 147 late Medio sherds (4.1 percent) were sooted. Sooting was practically nonexistent on bowls, which accounted for only 0.7 percent of the sherds with soot. There were no sooted body sherds that were clearly recognizable as coming from bowls in the early Medio test pit assemblage, and there were only two such sherds in the late Medio levels, or 3 percent of that group. Sparse as they are, the bowl data reinforce the impression given by the jars. That is, exterior sooting is rare in this assemblage.

This is very different from the situation recorded at Casas Grandes. The ceramic study (Di Peso, Rinaldo, and Fenner 1974: vol. 6) gives sooted and unsooted sherd counts and percentages for all pottery types. We combined these to calculate an overall average of 52 percent sooted sherds. We are presently unable to explain a difference of this magnitude. It seems unlikely that vastly different soot recognition criteria were used by our study and the one at Casas Grandes. A point against this possibility is that our 3 percent level of bowl sooting is comparable to the Casas Grandes data, where sooted non-polychrome bowl frequencies ranged from 0.2 percent to 3.4 percent, with a mean of 1.6 percent (SD $= 1.2$). Our technique thus produced comparable numbers of sooted bowls but wildly different numbers of sooted jars. The possibility that some real, functional difference is producing this discrepancy will be discussed in more detail after all of our excavated sites have been analyzed. Finally, we note that sooted jars were very much more common than sooted bowls at the primate center, as in the 204 middens.

**Table 5.8** Ceramic Types with Exterior Sooting in the Site 204 Midden

| Vessel | | Plain | Textured | Red | Black | Polychrome | **Total** |
|---|---|---|---|---|---|---|---|
| **Jars** | | | | | | | |
| Early Medio | n | 89 | 11 | 5 | 4 | 6 | **115** |
| | % | 77.4 | 9.6 | 4.3 | 3.5 | 5.2 | **100** |
| Late Medio | n | 106 | 6 | 5 | 6 | 20 | **143** |
| | % | 74.1 | 4.2 | 3.5 | 4.2 | 14.0 | **100** |
| **Bowls** | | | | | | | |
| Early Medio | n | 0 | 0 | 0 | 0 | 0 | **0** |
| Late Medio | n | 1 | 0 | 0 | 0 | 1 | **2** |
| | % | 50 | — | — | — | 50 | **100** |

The next question is the frequencies with which different ceramic types were sooted in early and late Medio times. Table 5.8 shows the frequencies of exterior sooting on different ceramic ware groups from the 204 middens.

It is clear from these data that most sooted vessels were Plain jars all across the Medio period. This is clearly the major cooking vessel at all times. Other jar types, including the polychromes, appear to have been used for cooking either in much smaller numbers or only occasionally. The largest change in the table is the sharp increase from early to late Medio in the number of polychrome jars with exterior soot.

Like the overall sooted vessel frequency just discussed, the frequencies of sooted vessels of all types at Casas Grandes are much higher than the figures given in the preceding table. Exterior soot was present on 54.1 percent of Plain jars, on 49.1 percent of Textured jars, on 46.6 percent of Red jars, and on 25.5 percent of Polychrome jars. For bowls, sooted percentages were 3.4 percent for Plain, 1.2 percent for Textured, 3.1 percent for Red, and 8.1 percent for Polychromes. Ramos Black sherds were not extensively examined for soot (Di Peso, Rinaldo, and Fenner 1974:6:160). The relatively high percentage of sooted polychrome bowls comes from the Carretas, Escondida, and Huerigos Polychromes, which had, respectively, 27.1 percent, 19.5 percent, and 60.4 percent sooted bowl sherds within each type. It is not clear why bowls of these three types should have been used over fires so much more often than those of other polychrome types. This observation hints at some sort of special use, beyond the everyday domestic chores of food preparation, which did not occur at site 204. The data just summarized also show a much more even distribution of exterior soot across all pottery types than was found in the midden at site 204.

Body sherd diameter measurements were used to give an idea of the relative sizes of sooted vessels in the middens at site 204, as described in the preceding section. Sooted early Medio jars gave body diameter estimates of 14 cm to 56 cm, with a mean of 30.9 cm (SD: 10.2). For the late Medio, sooted jar body sherd measurements ranged from 11 cm to 58 cm, with a mean of 30.3 (SD: 9.5). Obviously, there is no significant difference between these means. The sooted body diameter estimates just given cover most of the range of all body diameter estimates from the middens. We may conclude, therefore, that all sizes of jars occur with exterior soot in the early and late parts of the Medio period. All jar sizes are not equally likely to be sooted, however. Figure 5.16 shows early and late Medio histograms of sooted body sherd diameters from the 204 middens. It is clear that medium-sized jars are the most often sooted in both sub-periods. There are a few small and large sooted jars in the early and late parts of the Medio, but there are not many of either. In addition, despite their near-identical means, the histograms hint that at least some slightly larger jars may have been in use as cooking vessels by the late Medio. Lastly, sooted cooking jars rarely show interior pitting.

## Exterior Sooting across Medio Communities

Examined for this study were 5,456 body sherds. Half of them came from site 204 (2,377 sherds), and smaller samples are from sites 231 (736 sherds), 242 (1,108 sherds), and 317 (1,235 sherds). All of this material came from excavated rooms. In addition, this inquiry will make use of data from the primate center, as the ceramic study (Di Peso, Rinaldo, and Fenner 1974: vol. 6) provides counts and percentages of sherds with exterior soot for each type.

Table 5.9 contains data on the frequency of exterior soot on jars, bowls, and whole assemblages from Casas Grandes and the four excavated sites. The table shows that both jar and bowl sherds bore exterior soot at all five sites. Casas Grandes stands out as different in its jar-to-bowl proportion, however. At the primate center, jar sherds had exterior soot about twice as often as did bowl sherds. This pattern is not reflected at the four neighboring sites, however, where sooted jar and bowl sherds are nearer parity. It appears that bowls were more often used as cooking vessels among the neighbors of Casas Grandes than at the primate center itself. Bowls, of course, have smaller volumes than jars of comparable diameters. The relatively low proportion of sooted bowl sherds at Casas Grandes may, therefore, reflect a larger scale of cooking than existed among any of the neighboring communities.

The table also shows that the five sites can be divided into three groups based on their sooted sherd frequencies, at least for jars. The lowest-frequency group is formed by sites 231 and 317, where sooted sherds make up 15 percent or less of the ceramic assemblage. At the other end of the scale, the highest-frequency group consists of site 242 and Casas Grandes, both of which have ceramic assemblages containing more than 40 percent sooted sherds. Between these two groups is site 204, where about 25 percent of body sherds bore exterior soot.

Because sites 231 and 317 are small, simple, and without distinguishing features, their low percentages of sooted sherds likely represent the normal situation of food preparation at the domestic unit level. In contrast, sites 204, 242, and Casas Grandes are all ball-court communities. Preceding analysis shows that much of the occupation of site 204 mostly dates before the apogee of Casas Grandes at about A.D. 1350. Site 242 was shown to be contemporaneous with Casas Grandes, and it has been characterized as an administrative node of the primate center. The high percentage of sooted sherds at site 242 in this sample is second only to that of Casas Grandes, arguing for food preparation beyond the normal, domestic level. In a word, large quantities of food appear to have

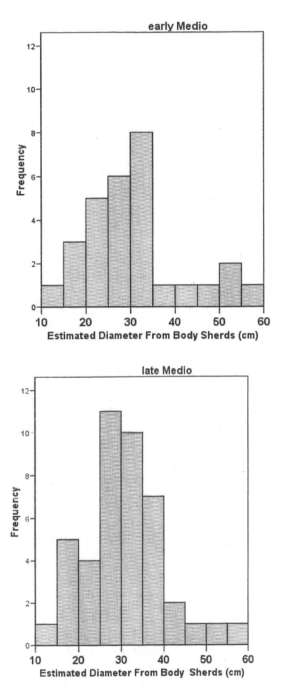

**Figure 5.16** Histograms of sooted body sherd diameter estimates: *a.* early Medio, *b.* late Medio.

**Table 5.9**   Frequencies of Exterior Sooting on Body Sherds, by Site

| Site | All vessels (*n*) | Sooted vessels(%) | All jars (*n*) | Sooted jars (%) | All bowls (*n*) | Sooted bowls (%) |
|------|------------------|-------------------|----------------|-----------------|-----------------|------------------|
| Casas Grandes[a] | 712,807 | 49.3 | 618,459 | 52.6% | 94,348 | 27.4 |
| 204 | 2,377 | 25.3 | 2,363 | 25.2 | 14 | 35.7 |
| 231 | 736 | 15.1 | 682 | 15.2 | 54 | 13.0 |
| 242 | 1,108 | 43.3 | 1,049 | 43.7 | 59 | 37.3 |
| 317 | 1,235 | 13.4 | 1,140 | 13.6 | 95 | 11.6 |

a. Data from Di Peso, Rinaldo, and Fenner 1974:6:92–316.

been prepared in communities where there is evidence of ritual and administrative activities. Where there is no such evidence (e.g., at sites 231 and 317) only domestic-level food preparation is evident.

Also to be considered here are the sizes of vessels bearing exterior soot. Unfortunately, Casas Grandes cannot be included in this part of the inquiry, as there are no diameter measurements on its sooted body sherds. At site 204, 368 body sherds gave a mean diameter estimate of 32.7 cm (SD: 8.3). For site 231, *n* is 98 and the mean diameter estimate is 29.8 (SD: 8.8). For site 242 the corresponding figures are 419 sherds and 38.0 cm (SD: 8.7), and for site 242 they are 138 sherds and 31.2 cm (SD: 8.0). The means just given were compared using analyses of variance, and a significant difference was detected ($F = 48.597$, $p < .0001$). Tukey's post hoc test shows that site 242 differs significantly from the other three ($p < .0001$ in every case). We may conclude, therefore, that site 242 has larger sooted vessels than the other three sites. Because the large site 204 does not differ at a statistically significant level from small sites 231 and 317, we can conclude that about the same sized vessels are being used for cooking at all three sites.

## The Uses of Ceramics in Medio Communities

To conclude this chapter, we offer a brief contrast in ceramic-function terms of the five Medio period sites discussed here. These are the primate center of the region (Casas Grandes); a large ball-court community (site 204); a small administrative center, also with a ball court and a small platform mound (site 242); and two small, simple communities that lacked any kind of public architecture (sites 231 and 317). The primate center could not be compared to the other four neighboring sites in all aspects, as some of the analyses that we used were not carried out there.

We begin this site characterization with 231 and 317, the small, simple sites that seem to represent the present sample's lowest level of food processing. Both small sites show the following characteristics. They have a range of small to large jars and bowls, but they contain none of the largest vessels in our sample. Their sherds have the lowest levels of exterior sooting found in this sample. Interior surface pitting was rare, occurring at a level of less than 1 percent. Finally, these small sites have few polychrome sherds relative to the others in this sample. We argue that these characteristics represent the basic, household level of food storage, processing, and consumption.

At the other end of the scale is the primate center of Casas Grandes. The analyses that were done with these data showed that the center had a range of small to large jars and bowls, as did the four neighboring sites. However, the Casas Grandes assemblage also included at least a few extra-large jars and bowls that were not found in the present sample from the neighboring communities. These vessels were of the Textured and Playas Red types, which we earlier characterized as somewhat more expensive to produce than the Plain utility ware that dominates all Medio ceramic assemblages. In this cheapest and most common ware, Casas Grandes showed the same range of sizes as its neighbors.

The primate center stands out in two categories of use-wear. It had a higher frequency of sooted vessels than any other site in the present sample. The limited data that we collected suggest that Casas Grandes had one of the region's higher frequencies of interior-pitted vessels, and it also had the highest ratio of sooted jars to sooted bowls in this sample. That is, more jars and fewer bowls were being used over fires there than at the four neighboring sites. All these four sites showed about as many sooted jars as sooted bowls.

We take all of the characteristics just enumerated to be reflections of the same activities: the large-scale preparation of food and drink. Moreover, at Casas Grandes we see a level of food production that is much greater than the basic, domestic situation just described for small sites 231 and 317. An obvious context for this level of food processing is public feasting. This is a well-recognized integrative and organizing strategy in mid-level, or chiefdom, societies (Dietler and Hayden 2001; Mills 2004; Minnis and Whalen 2005). In such societies, feasting often takes place in association with public rituals, and we note the large quantity of ritual architecture at Casas Grandes.

A final characteristic of Casas Grandes is its high frequency (18 percent) of Polychrome pottery. The same figure for the small sites is 3–5 percent. Most of this pottery is Ramos Polychrome. Researchers have argued that its intricate designs and symbolism played important roles in the organization and integration of Medio period society (e.g., Moulard 2005; VanPool and VanPool 2007). Ramos Polychrome may also have served as a luxury ware or a status marker, so that its high frequency at Casas Grandes reflects the concentration there of society's elite. The primate center thus stands apart in many ways from the small, simple sites just discussed.

In terms of ceramic function, sites 242 and 204 fall between Casas Grandes and small sites 231 and 317. Site 242, the postulated administrative satellite of the primate center has a number of characteristics that set it apart from the other neighbors discussed here. The first of these is a huge jar-to-bowl ratio of 20:1. It seems that the storage and cooking activities in which jars play a part were unusually intensive at site 242. Among these many jars were the largest Plain and Playas Red jars found among the neighboring sites. Site 242 also showed a high frequency of vessels with interior surface pitting. Sooted jars and bowls occurred in higher frequency at site 242 than at the other neighbors, and at least some of these vessels were larger than their counterparts at the neighboring sites. Together, these ceramic characteristics add up to a picture of significantly greater food processing at site 242 than at the small sites. Site 242 has been characterized on architectural grounds as an administrative satellite of Casas Grandes (Whalen and Minnis 2001b). Its ceramic assemblage, although simpler than the primate center's, shows the same ability to produce food and drink at a level far above the domestic one.

Site 204 also falls between Casas Grandes and the small sites in the ceramic characteristics just summarized. Vessel sizes, including sooted vessel volumes, were not significantly different at site 204 than at small sites 231 and 317. Nevertheless, site 204 is unlike the small ones in other ways. The 204 proportion of sooted vessels (25 percent) is substantially greater than those of the small sites (13–15 percent), but less than those of Casas Grandes and site 242 (40–50 percent). The proportion of vessels with interior pitting at 204 (8.6 percent) is similar to the figure of 6.6 percent at site 242, and it greatly exceeds the fraction of pitted vessels at the small sites (less than 1 percent). Finally, site 204 has a high frequency (12 percent) of polychrome pottery, ranking second only to Casas Grandes (18 percent) in the present sample. We interpret these data as showing some evidence for food preparation above the ordinary domestic level, but clearly not at the same scale as at Casas Grandes and site 242. We have argued that the main occupation of site 204 came before the apogee of Casas Grandes in the mid- to late 1300s. The ambiguity of the data for large-scale food and drink preparation at site 204 may be a reflection of the simpler organizational system that characterized the region before the ascendancy of the primate center.

We tentatively suggest that the use-wear characteristics of sites 204 versus 242 reflect the development of an increasingly effective regional hierarchy in the late part of the Medio period. Site 204 was likely a prominent community in the early Medio and the initial part of the late Medio periods, and it has more sooted vessels than the small, simple sites 231 and 317. This argues for a level of food preparation at site 204 that was somewhat above the domestic level reflected at the smaller sites. By the late part of the Medio, however, site 242 and Casas Grandes have considerably increased frequencies of sooted vessels, and both sites appear to have had more cooking capacity as well. Our analyses argue that the domestic level of cooking stayed about the same throughout the Medio period. It is the supra-domestic level of food production that seems to increase from early to late Medio times, and we suspect that this change was closely tied to the organizational needs of Casas Grandes.

# 6

## Medio Period Lithics

In the history of northwest Chihuahuan archaeology, much less attention has been devoted to the study of stone than to ceramics. The Casas Grandes report, for instance, devotes only 80 pages to chipped stone in contrast to 239 pages devoted to the site's Medio period ceramics (Di Peso, Rinaldo, and Fenner 1974:6:77–317). Ground stone implements, in contrast, have been much more thoroughly studied and described. The Casas Grandes report (Di Peso, Rinaldo, and Fenner 1974:7:38–335) contains nearly 300 pages of inventory, description, and illustration of the primate center's large assemblage. Site 204 provides the area's second largest assemblage of stone of all kinds, and its analysis is the focal point of this chapter. Also considered here are the much smaller collections from small sites 231, 242, and 317. We begin with the chipped stone.

### Chipped Stone

Although it was the first major study of Medio period chipped stone, the Casas Grandes report does not provide a comprehensive look at the complete assemblage. For instance, the total data set from this enormous site is reported as only 3,714 pieces. Of these, 1,103 are classified as various sorts of tools, 122 as cores, and 2,611 as debitage (Di Peso, Rinaldo, and Fenner 1974:7:341). The latter group contains flakes and debris that were "left without a functional category" (1974:7:340).

The study's reported ratio of tools to debitage is very high at 0.42, and this implies that data collection at Casas Grandes was strongly biased toward recognizable implements. Moreover, the absence of consistent, fine-mesh screening during the site's excavation means that few of the smaller lithic artifacts would have been recovered. As a point of comparison, all excavated deposits at site 204 were screened through one-quarter-inch mesh, yielding a total of 23,029 pieces of chipped stone. It is also noteworthy that the total excavated area at site 204 was only a fraction of that at Casas Grandes. The tool-to-debitage ratio at site 204 was less than .001. Even allowing for considerable difference in classification, it is clear that the Casas Grandes data set omits most of the material studied at site 204 and the other sites examined in the present study.

Nevertheless, the essential character of the Medio period chipped stone assemblage emerges from the Casas Grandes study. The inventory of raw materials used at the primate center is the same set found in all later studies. This includes "several varieties of chert, jasper, chalcedony, and obsidian, as well as quartz, quartzite, and coarser grained (materials) such as rhyolite and basalt" (Di Peso, Rinaldo, and Fenner 1974:7:339). It is further noted that the coarser-grained igneous materials were used for all large tools, such as choppers and scrapers, where thick, tough edges were required. In contrast, most of the smaller and more finely made tools used obsidian or fine-grained siliceous stones. Pressure-flaking was found almost exclusively on these implements (Di Peso, Rinaldo, and Fenner 1974:7:339).

This observation has stood the test of time, but it now appears that the Casas Grandes chipped stone sample was heavily biased toward fine-grained pieces. For instance, data are presented for 261 scrapers from the primate center (Di Peso, Rinaldo, and Fenner 1974:7: 344–48). Of these, 235, or 90 percent, were made from the fine-grained raw materials just listed, whereas only 26, or 10 percent, were of the coarse-grained rhyolite and basalt. Later studies find nothing like this proportion of fine and coarse materials at other Medio period sites. Study of a portion of the lithic assemblage from site 204 (Rowles 2004) found that 45 percent of scrapers were of fine-grained material, whereas 55 percent were coarse grained. The magnitude of this difference argues either that much finer raw materials were in use at Casas Grandes than among its neighbors, or that different collection strategies were employed on excavated materials at the two sites. We favor the latter explanation in light of the very small chipped stone sample (ca. 3,700 pieces) collected in the extensive excavations at the primate center. Our excavation experience in Chihuahua suggests fine-grained artifacts are the most conspicuous and easily recognized elements of the chipped stone assemblage. It could still be, of course, that the primate center enjoyed the finest lithic raw material in the region, as has been suggested before by others, so that both factors may have contributed to the different pattern (Van Pool et al. 2000).

Finally, the Casas Grandes study shows that the dominant reduction technique in use was direct, hard-hammer percussion on minimally prepared cores. Other assemblage characteristics include production of flakes of a wide range of sizes and shapes, minimal retouching, little bifacial flaking, and the presence of few formal tools (Di Peso, Rinaldo, and Fenner 1974:7:336–415). This pattern fits well into the "expedient technology" model described by many (e.g., Parry and Kelly 1987:287) and characteristic of the Late Prehistoric period over much of the Southwest. Closer to the present area of interest, expedient technologies are found everywhere among the Pueblo cultures of the U.S. Southwest and northwestern Mexico. The Casas Grandes assemblage, then, is entirely representative of its region and time.

The twenty years following the Casas Grandes study saw little more study of Medio period chipped stone. In the past decade, however, a number of lithic analyses have been carried out in conjunction with renewed survey and excavation work in northwestern Chihuahua. These provide a second round of lithic studies that supplement the Casas Grandes results. Three master's thesis studies produced detailed analyses of small collections of chipped stone from site surfaces (Miller 1995) or from recently excavated contexts in the Casas Grandes core area (Rebnegger 2001; Rowles 2004). A published article deals with chipped stone from test excavations at the Galeana site, a large Medio community in the Santa María drainage, to the southeast of the primate center and outside of its core area (VanPool et al. 2000).

These studies confirm a number of the initial observations from Casas Grandes, especially the expedient, informal nature of the assemblage and patterns of raw material use. In a word, there seems to have been considerable continuity among Medio communities in raw material use, reduction strategies, and tool types. The results of these recent studies will be mentioned as appropriate in the ensuing discussion of chipped stone from the four Medio communities that are the focus of this volume. One limitation all of these studies share, however, is a lack of chronological control within the Medio period. This means that the period could be considered only as a single unit. To date, no study has been able to address questions of change in chipped stone industries between the early and late parts of the Medio period. The new data analyzed in this chapter begin to remedy this situation.

These data consist of 26,694 pieces of chipped stone from sites 204, 231, 242, and 317. Analyses were carried out at two levels, here termed preliminary and detailed. Preliminary analyses were done on all 26,694 pieces. These were first sorted into flake, core, tool, and debris categories, and raw material was noted for each piece. Flakes were subdivided into whole and broken categories. Whole flakes were classed as primary, secondary, or tertiary based on a simple scale of proportion of visible cortex, i.e., >50 percent cortex present; <50 percent cortex present; cortex absent. Cores were classed as whole or fragmentary. A tool was defined as any piece showing visible use-wear. Little magnification was used, so that the reported number likely understates the actual situation. The leftovers from this process were classed as debris, and these were simply counted.

Detailed analyses were done on a much smaller sample of 10,202 pieces, or ca. 38 percent of the total. This sample was drawn unevenly from a number of contexts. The first includes all of the chipped stone (7,076 pieces) from the stratified midden deposits at site 204. The second is a sample (2,831 pieces) from site 204 Areas 1 and 2 of Mound A, plus material from Mound B (refer to chapters 1 and 3 for discussion of these areas and mounds). The third is a sample (295 pieces) from sites 231, 242, and 317. Detailed analyses include measurements of flake, core, and tool dimensions. Observed flake characteristics are platform type, presence of platform lipping, dorsal surface flake scar direction(s), bulb prominence, and type of termination. Core characteristics were direction(s) of flake removal, core shape, and evidence of utilization. Tools were classified into cutting, chopping, scraping, perforating, projectile point, or preform categories. Multifunction tools were so-classified when recognized. All areas of all four sites were not examined with equal thoroughness. Nevertheless, the extant preliminary and detailed data are adequate for three analyses. First is the question of change over time in the site 204 midden and in dated rooms on the site. Second is intra-site comparison of different parts of site 204. The third analysis is inter-site comparison of site 204 versus its neighbors.

## Diachronic Change in Medio Period Chipped Stone at Site 204

The best source of data for consideration of the largely unexplored issue of diachronic change in lithics is the deep midden at site 204. Preceding discussion described the midden deposits and how they were divided into early and late Medio units. Some test pit levels were dated by radiocarbon samples. The rest were classed as early versus late Medio by the absence or presence of Ramos Polychrome, which are established as belonging exclusively to the late part of the Medio period. The site 204 midden test pit excavations included 5.0 cubic meters of early Medio deposits, whereas the late Medio accounted for 10.6 cubic meters. These deposits yielded a total of 7,076 pieces of chipped stone: 2,063 belonging to the early Medio, and 5,013 from the late part of the period. The early Medio chipped stone density was 381.8 pieces per cubic meter, but that of the late Medio was 490.8. We will argue that smaller piece size in the late Medio produced this difference in density. All of this material was analyzed at the primary level, whereas the 2,009 whole flakes, cores, and tools received additional, detailed study. We turn now to specific analyses, which were conducted on whole and broken cores, flakes, and tools.

*Core Analyses.* Cores make up a small percentage of the chipped stone assemblage in the site 204 midden deposits across all of the Medio period. The combined frequency of whole and broken cores in the early Medio is 2.8 percent, and that of the late Medio is 1.7 percent. In the early Medio sample, there were 59 cores and core fragments (expected frequency 45.6 under the null hypothesis of no significant difference), whereas there were 86 pieces (expected frequency 99.4) for the late Medio. These data show a significant difference in core frequency between the early and late Medio midden deposits ($\chi^2 = 5.74$, df $= 1$, $p < .02$). The direction of difference is evident from the counts just given: cores are more common than expected in the early Medio and less so in the late part of the period. We can suggest several possible interpretations of this trend. First, it may be that on-site core reduction was less common in the late Medio than in the early part of the period. Alternatively, it may be that different reduction strategies were in use, or that core reduction was more intense in the late part of the period, so that fewer whole cores survive in the archaeological record. Subsequent analyses will discriminate among these alternatives.

Core raw material types and frequencies are very similar in the early and late Medio. Most cores (ca. 60 percent) are rhyolite, about 35 percent are chert, and the remaining few are basalt or chalcedony. As there is no statistically significant difference in the early and late frequencies of these raw materials, material type may be considered a constant in succeeding analyses. Early and late Medio cores also were of about the same size. Mean length was about 57 mm, mean width about 50 mm, and mean thickness about 35 mm. None of these dimensions differed at a statistically significant level across the period.

One point is significant, however. The early Medio broken-core sample contains five fragments of small obsidian nodules that we have classified as broken cores. These nodules were split by bipolar percussion, as evidenced by crushing on both ends. The late Medio sample contains no obsidian nodule fragments. We also note that early Medio midden deposits contained eight chips or chunks of obsidian that were classified as debris, but only two pieces of obsidian came from the late Medio midden test pit levels. These data hint that at site 204 obsidian was in more common use in the early part of the Medio period than later.

**Table 6.1**  Core Shape Frequencies in the Early and Late Medio

| Age | Irregular | Round | Conical | Bifacial | Tabular | Total |
|---|---|---|---|---|---|---|
| **Early Medio** | | | | | | |
| Count | 19 | 8 | 8 | 6 | 3 | 44 |
| Pct. | 43.2 | 18.2 | 18.2 | 13.6 | 6.8 | 100 |
| **Late Medio** | | | | | | |
| Count | 38 | 13 | 6 | 2 | 1 | 60 |
| Pct. | 63.3 | 21.7 | 10.0 | 3.3 | 1.7 | 100 |
| **Total** | 57 | 21 | 14 | 8 | 4 | 104 |

Core shape was recorded for the early and late Medio in the five categories shown in table 6.1. The table contains too many low cell counts for a reliable chi-squared test. Accordingly, the test was run without the tabular cores, as this is the least common shape class. No significant difference in core shape proportions was detected between the early and late Medio samples ($\chi^2 = 6.79$, df $= 3$, $p = .079$). We note that irregularly shaped cores were the most common throughout the site 204 midden deposits, and their frequency rises considerably from early to late Medio times. Accordingly, a second chi-squared test was done using the observed total of irregular cores and the sum of all other core shape classes for the early and late Medio (as listed in table 6.1). In this case, a significant difference was detected ($\chi^2 = 4.16$, df $= 1$, $p = .033$). The table shows the direction of the difference: irregularly shaped cores are more common in the late Medio than earlier.

Also examined was direction of flake removal from these cores. The recorded states of this variable were multidirectional, bidirectional, and unidirectional. Unidirectional cores have a single striking platform from which flakes were removed. Bidirectional cores have two platforms, and multidirectional cores show multiple striking platforms (Andrefsky 1998:138–39). Of the early Medio cores, 36.4 percent are multidirectional, 47.7 percent are bidirectional, and 15.9 percent are unidirectional. For the late Medio, the same figures are 51.1 percent, 40.6 percent, and 8.3 percent. Early and late Medio directional frequencies do not differ at a statistically significant level.

The high frequency of multidirectional flaking accords well with the idea of random, opportunistic core reduction all through the period. Also notable is the common occurrence of bidirectional cores in the early and late Medio deposits. Some of these were no doubt produced in the course of freehand reduction. Some, however, may result from bipolar flaking. Experiments with this technique show that two flakes occasionally are removed with one blow, one from the striking platform and one from the distal end in contact with the anvil. Kobayashi (1975:117) notes that this situation produces cores that appear to be bidirectional. Bipolar flaking may, therefore, inflate the number of bidirectional cores observed throughout the Medio at site 204. About 40 percent to 48 percent of all whole cores were classed as bidirectional. Some cores also show the distinctive crushing at each end that is a signature of bipolar flaking (Crabtree 1972:9; Jeske and Lurie 1997:144; Odell 2004:61).

**Table 6.2**   Flake Raw Materials in the Early and Late Medio

| Age | Chert | Rhyolite | Basalt | Chalcedony | Obsidian | Other | **Total** |
|---|---|---|---|---|---|---|---|
| **Early Medio** | | | | | | | |
| Count | 271 | 222 | 50 | 13 | 0 | 2 | 558 |
| Pct. | 48.6 | 39.8 | 8.9 | 2.3 | 0 | 0.4 | **100.0** |
| **Late Medio** | | | | | | | |
| Count | 695 | 485 | 89 | 19 | 0 | 2 | 1,290 |
| Pct. | 53.9 | 37.6 | 6.9 | 1.5 | 0 | 0.1 | **100.0** |

*Flake Analyses.* Table 6.2 shows raw material counts and percentages for the 1,769 whole flakes from early and late Medio midden test pit levels at site 204. Throughout the period, around 90 percent of these flakes were either chert or rhyolite. Deposits from both sub-periods contained some flakes of basalt and chalcedony, although these clearly were never major tool-making materials. Ignimbrite, silicified rhyolite, and quartzite were represented in minute quantities and are lumped in the "Other" category. Notably, no obsidian flakes were recovered from the midden deposits. We note that chipped stone assemblages dominated by chert and rhyolite are the norm in northwest Chihuahua (e.g., Miller 1995; Rebnegger 2001; Rowles 2004; VanPool et al. 2000). The early and late Medio figures shown in table 6.2 are quite similar in every category, demonstrating that there was no significant change in either material or frequency across the period. Raw material type and frequency for broken flakes are almost identical to the data shown in the table. Accordingly, raw material type and type frequency may be considered to be constants in succeeding analyses of whole and broken flakes in the early and late Medio midden test pit levels.

Flake size is the next issue to be considered. Table 6.3 presents mean dimensional data for 1,769 whole flakes of the early and late Medio. These means were compared with t-tests, and the results appear in the table. It is apparent that early Medio flakes are, on average, longer and wider than their late Medio successors. Early and late Medio flake length and width differ at statistically significant levels. Mean flake thickness is a little greater in the early than the late Medio, but the difference does not achieve statistical significance. Nevertheless, we may conclude from these data that flakes were larger, on average, in the early part of the Medio, declining in size by the late part of the period. The ranges shown in table 6.3 argue that flake size was fairly variable all across the Medio period. The large standard deviations make the same point, as they are 50 percent to 65 percent of the mean values in all cases.

Application of the $F$ test for equality of variances shows that the standard deviations of early and late Medio flake width variances differ at a significant level ($F = 4.37, p = .037$), but length and thickness variances do not (respectively, $F = 2.42, p = .120$; and $F = 1.71, p = .191$). The conclusion arising from these data is that early and late Medio flake dimensions are fairly variable all across the Medio period. It is also apparent that site 204 midden flake dimensions in this sample are about as variable in the early Medio

**Table 6.3**  Flake Dimensions and Ranges in the Early and Late Medio

| Dimension | Age | $n$ | Mean | SD | Range | $t$ | df | $p$ |
|---|---|---|---|---|---|---|---|---|
| Length | early | 562 | 28.97 | 14.47 | 6.0–90.1 mm | | | |
| | late | 1,207 | 27.51 | 14.17 | 7.0–111.1 mm | 2.013 | 1,767 | .044 |
| Width | early | 562 | 26.66 | 13.92 | 7.1–102.9 mm | | | |
| | late | 1,207 | 25.29 | 12.73 | 6.1–125.5 mm | 1.982 | 1,011 | .048 |
| Thickness | early | 562 | 8.44 | 5.60 | 0.9–38.8 mm | | | |
| | late | 1,207 | 8.05 | 5.43 | 0.8–40.8 mm | 1.376 | 1,767 | .169 |

**Table 6.4**  Levels of Cortex Removal on Early and Late Medio Flakes

| Age | Primary | Secondary | Tertiary | **Total** |
|---|---|---|---|---|
| **Early Medio** | | | | |
| Observed | 66 | 231 | 265 | 562 |
| Expected | 50.5 | 219.5 | 292.0 | |
| Adj. residual[a] | 2.77 | 1.21 | −2.76 | |
| **Late Medio** | | | | |
| Observed | 93 | 460 | 654 | 1,207 |
| Expected | 108.5 | 471.5 | 627.0 | |
| Adj. residual[a] | −2.76 | −1.20 | 2.76 | |
| **Total** | 159 | 691 | 919 | 1,769 |

a. Adjusted residual values greater than 1.96 indicate cells that contain significant differences between the observed frequencies and those expected under the null hypothesis of no significant difference. The sign shows the direction of the difference.

as in the late part of the period. These observations are consistent with the idea of expedient core reduction, which produces flakes of irregular shapes from unprepared cores (Kooyman 2000:82; Parry and Kelly 1987:287; Silva 1997:10–11).

Cortex on flake dorsal surfaces was recorded as primary (>50 percent cortex), secondary (<50 percent), or tertiary (no cortex visible). Table 6.4 is a cross-tabulation of these data for the early and late Medio. The observed frequencies in the table were tested against those expected under the null hypothesis of no significant difference in extent of cortex removal between the early and late Medio. The test result rejects the null hypothesis, showing instead that levels of flake decortication differ significantly between the early and late Medio midden test pit levels ($\chi^2 = 11.51$, df = 2, $p < .01$). The adjusted residuals show which cells contain significant differences between observed and expected frequencies. The early Medio has a higher than expected frequency of primary flakes, but the observed frequency of tertiary flakes is lower than expected. The late Medio reverses this situation, containing fewer primary flakes and more tertiary ones. This argues that either less early-stage reduction occurred on-site in the late than the early Medio, or that reduction was more intensive in the late than in the early part of the period.

These data show that broken flakes were very common in the midden test pits, constituting ca. 67–72 percent of the assemblages in the early and late Medio. The next step is to test observed frequencies of early and late Medio whole and broken flakes against the frequencies expected under the null hypothesis of no significant difference in flake condition. There were 562 whole flakes in the early Medio sample (508.4 expected), and there were 1,373 broken flakes (1,426.6 expected). Late Medio whole flakes numbered 1,207 (1,260.6 expected), plus 3,591 broken flakes (3,537.4 expected). The test result ($\chi^2 = 10.76$, df $= 1$, $p < .002$) shows a significant difference in whole and broken flake frequencies between the early and late parts of the Medio period. Specifically, early Medio test pit levels contained more whole flakes and fewer broken ones than expected, whereas late Medio levels reverse this trend, with fewer whole flakes and more broken ones.

Flakes can break into a number of pieces at any stage of reduction, use, and deposition (Andrefsky 1998:81), so that many factors influence the number of broken flakes in an assemblage. Material type is one commonly cited factor (e.g., Amick and Mauldin 1997:25). Raw material types and frequencies in the present assemblage were just shown to vary little from the early to late Medio deposits, however, and so they are not at issue here. Experimental studies show that core reduction produces more broken flakes than does tool manufacture (e.g., Prentiss and Romanski 1989:2), and that hard-hammer percussion breaks more flakes than does use of a soft hammer (Mauldin and Amick 1989:83–84). We may also infer that increasingly intensive hard-hammer core reduction should raise the number of broken flakes in an assemblage. Finally, experimentation demonstrates that post-depositional trampling produces "a drastic reduction in numbers of complete flakes" in an assemblage (Prentiss and Romanski 1989:94). This factor cannot be omitted from consideration, as the flake samples being analyzed here came from gradually accumulated midden deposits located on the edge of the large site 204 pueblo. They were, therefore, likely trampled a good deal, and this accounts for some of the large broken flake assemblage just described. We suggest, however, that the significant increase in broken flakes from early to late Medio times may also reflect increasingly intensive reduction in the latter part of the period. We turn now to other analyses to pursue this issue.

Bulbs of percussion on flake ventral surfaces were recorded as either prominent or diffuse (the latter category also included bases where no bulb was observable). The frequency of diffuse bulbs in the early Medio was 44.5 percent, whereas prominent bulbs accounted for 55.5 percent of the sample. For the late Medio, the same figures were 39.7 percent and 60.3 percent. There is no significant difference in bulb type frequencies across the period, but notably both the early and late Medio deposits contain substantial numbers of flakes with diffuse and prominent bulbs. Hard-hammer percussion is known to produce prominent bulbs of percussion, whereas soft-hammer flaking does not (Cotterell and Kamminga 1990:134). In the same discussion, these authors observe that another frequent by-product of soft-hammer percussion is the presence of lips on flake platforms. The early and late Medio assemblages under discussion here contained

**Table 6.5**   Platform Type Frequencies in the Early and Late Medio

| Age | Cortical | Smooth | Faceted | Crushed | Nonexistent | **Total** |
|---|---|---|---|---|---|---|
| **Early Medio** | | | | | | |
| Observed | 116 | 229 | 90 | 84 | 28 | 547 |
| Expected | 94.9 | 225.6 | 77.7 | 106.9 | 41.9 | |
| Adj. residual[a] | 2.9 | 0.4 | 1.8 | −3.0 | −2.7 | |
| **Late Medio** | | | | | | |
| Observed | 176 | 465 | 149 | 245 | 101 | 1,136 |
| Expected | 197.1 | 468.4 | 161.3 | 222.1 | 87.1 | |
| Adj. residual[a] | −2.9 | −0.4 | −1.8 | 3.0 | 2.7 | |
| Total | 292 | 694 | 239 | 329 | 129 | 1,683 |

a. Adjusted residual values greater than 1.96 indicate cells that contain significant differences between the observed frequencies and those expected under the null hypothesis of no significant difference. The sign shows the direction of the difference.

almost no lipping, however, which argues that soft-hammer percussion did not produce the many diffuse or absent bulbs on the flakes found in the midden levels.

Another factor known to influence bulb prominence is bipolar flaking. Several authors (e.g., Kooyman 2000:17; Odell 2004:61) cite diffuse bulbs as one of the signatures of bipolar flaking. By this logic, the presence of a substantial number of diffuse bulbs of percussion in the early and late Medio test pit levels suggests that a good deal of bipolar flaking took place in addition to the hard-hammer, freehand reduction implied by the many prominent bulbs. Bipolar flaking, notes Shott (1986:5, 16), does not imply any specific application or activity, but it is a reduction strategy commonly found in expedient technologies. Bipolar flaking has been characterized as an intensive reduction strategy, and studies point to its efficacy in conserving scarce materials such as obsidian (e.g., Andrefsky 1998:119–20; Parry and Kelly 1987:301).

Other flake attributes can be examined to pursue the question of bipolar reduction frequency across the Medio period. Flake platform characteristics were recorded for 1,683 specimens from all levels of the midden test pits. In this and some subsequent analyses, a small percentage of flakes were classed as indeterminate for the variable in question, often due to small flake size. These unclassified flakes are omitted from the analyses, producing totals smaller than the total of 1,769 whole flakes given earlier in this chapter. Table 6.5 presents the observed frequencies across the Medio period of five different platform types: faceted, crushed, cortical, smooth, and nonexistent. Also shown are the frequencies expected under the null hypothesis of no significant difference in platform type frequencies between the two sub-periods.

There is a significant difference in platform type frequencies between the early and late Medio midden levels ($\chi^2 = 24.06$, df $= 4$, $p < .0001$). Examination of the adjusted residuals shown in table 6.5 reveals that six residuals exceed the critical value of 1.96, indicating significant differences between the observed and expected frequencies. Significant differences occur in the cortical, crushed, and nonexistent platforms. In particular, platforms with cortexes are present at higher than expected frequency in the early Medio levels of the midden test pits, and are less common than expected in late Medio deposits. This is consistent with the significantly higher frequency of flakes with dorsal surface cortexes in the early Medio sample, as demonstrated previously. This is another piece of evidence for more intensive reduction in the late part of the Medio period.

In addition, the late Medio levels are characterized by higher than expected frequencies of crushed and nonexistent platforms, whereas the early Medio levels had lower than expected frequencies of these two platform types. We note that elevated frequencies of platforms that are crushed, small, or nonexistent have been linked to the technique of bipolar flaking (Kooyman 2000:56; Odell 2004:61). The bipolar technique, which can be an intensive reduction strategy, is often found in expedient core technologies (Parry and Kelly 1987:287; Shott 1986:5), and the data suggest that its frequency increased from early to late Medio times. This observation fits our previous arguments for increasingly intensive reduction in the late Medio period at site 204.

A postulated late Medio increase in the frequency of bipolar flaking also agrees with our preceding analyses of flake size. There, mean flake length and width were shown to decline significantly from early to late Medio times, whereas flake thickness did not differ at a significant level. Experimental data on flake production (Jeske and Lurie 1997:141) demonstrate that flakes produced by the bipolar technique are shorter and narrower than those made by freehand percussion. Flake thickness did not differ significantly between the two techniques. Accordingly, we ascribe the observed reduction in flake length and width from early to late Medio in the site 204 midden at least partially to increasing use of bipolar flaking in the latter part of the period. Finally, Jeske and Lurie (1997:144) note that one of the attributes of bipolar flaking is a relatively low ratio of flake-to-nonflake debris. Data presented earlier in this chapter permit calculation of this ratio. For the early Medio, its value is 0.46, whereas the late Medio figure is 0.32, a decline of about one-third from the early Medio and a further indication of the increasing use of bipolar flaking in the late Medio at site 204.

Two other flake characteristics do not bear on the question of freehand versus bipolar flaking, but are included here to complete the flake analysis. The first is dorsal surface scarring, data for which were recorded from 1,659 whole flakes. Scar patterns were recorded as longitudinal (scars parallel to the long axis), transverse (scars perpendicular to the long axis), medial (scars converging on the center of the piece), or irregular. The early versus late parts of the Medio period did not differ at a statistically significant level in frequencies of dorsal surface scarring patterns. Irregular scarring is by far the most common pattern all across the Medio, suggesting expedient core reduction, where flakes are struck opportunistically from a number of different directions (Silva 1997:10–11).

The final flake characteristic considered here is termination type, which was recorded as feather, hinge, or step for 1,604 whole flakes from early and late Medio test pit levels. Frequencies of the three termination types do not differ between the early and late Medio in the 204 midden sample. Feather terminations overwhelmingly dominate the assemblage all through the period. In their experimental study Jeske and

Lurie (1997:153) found that feather terminations occurred at nearly identical frequencies in bipolar and freehand reduction.

*Tool Analyses.* Throughout the Medio period, chipped stone implements ranged from formal tools to expediently produced flakes and cores utilized without further modification. The latter is by far the most common category of Medio chipped stone tool. The few formal tools found in the site 204 midden deposits include tiny projectile points and a few drills or borers. These implements are identical to those illustrated in the Casas Grandes report (Di Peso, Rinaldo, and Fenner 1974: vol. 7). Found at Casas Grandes and other sites but absent in the 204 midden were fragments of small to medium-sized bifacial tools termed "knives" (Di Peso, Rinaldo, and Fenner 1974:7:374–75). As noted earlier in this chapter, the chipped stone assemblage from Casas Grandes was not recovered by the sort of consistent, fine screening in use today. Accordingly, the proportion of tools in that assemblage cannot be estimated. In the site 204 midden excavations, tools comprised 2.3 percent of the early Medio assemblage and 1.7 percent of the late Medio collection. The vast majority of the 136 tools from the midden were irregularly shaped, expediently produced pieces used without modification. These were classified by morphology and use-wear into three main categories. Cutting tools had thin, sharp edges that contained visible use-wear. Scraping tools had thick, blunt edges with use-wear suggestive of scraping, especially step fractures. Formal tools are listed in subcategories of perforating tools, tabular knives, and projectile points.

A specialized category of large, heavy implement used for cutting and coarse scraping was termed a tabular knife. These are similar to the "agave knives" and "scraping or pulping planes" recognized in the southern Arizona archaeological record (Fish, Fish, and Madsen 1992:83–84) and described in ethnographic studies as agave-processing implements. These are distinguished from general-purpose cutting and scraping tools by their large size and coarser material. Figure 6.1 shows examples of these implements. Several additional subcategories of formal tools were noted. Perforating tools have long, narrow points that are retouched into drill shapes. There is visible wear in these points' tips and edges. Projectile points are small and bifacially retouched, usually showing a triangular form with side notching and a concave base. Table 6.6 shows frequencies of these tool types in the early and late Medio midden deposits at site 204. These data show no significant difference in type frequencies between the early and late Medio ($\chi^2$ = 1.233, df = 4, $p$ = .873). This suggests that tool-using activities were about the same all across the period.

Although tool type frequencies remained similar across the Medio period, their sizes did not. In this analysis, we use tool weight as a single measure of size. Table 6.7 shows descriptive statistics for tool weights in the type classes just discussed. These means were compared by t-tests, the results of which are shown in the table. It is clear that general-purpose cutting and scraping tools were much larger in early Medio times than in the late part of the period. In fact, the table shows that early Medio mean weights for these tools are about double the comparable late Medio figures. Not surprisingly, the t-test shows a significant difference in each case. The large, coarse tabular knives do not vary significantly in mean weight between the early and late Medio. We suggest

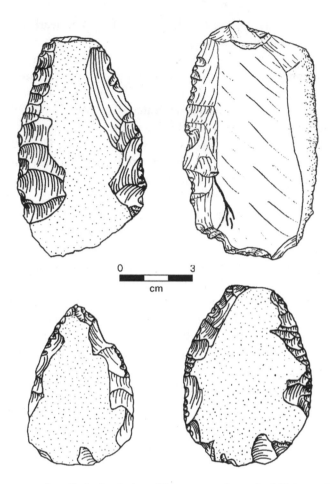

**Figure 6.1** Four examples of tabular knives. These come from the hillslope above site 204.

**Table 6.6**  Tool Types in the Early and Late Medio

| Age | Cutting | Scraping | Perforating | Tabular knife | Point | Total |
|---|---|---|---|---|---|---|
| **Early Medio** | | | | | | |
| Observed | 6 | 25 | 3 | 13 | 2 | 49 |
| Expected | 7.2 | 24.5 | 2.2 | 13.7 | 1.4 | |
| **Late Medio** | | | | | | |
| Observed | 14 | 43 | 3 | 25 | 2 | 87 |
| Expected | 12.8 | 43.5 | 3.8 | 24.3 | 2.6 | |
| **Total** | 20 | 68 | 6 | 38 | 4 | 136 |

**Table 6.7**  Descriptive Statistics for Tool Weights in the Early and Late Medio

| Type | Age | n | Mean wt. | SD | t | df | p |
|---|---|---|---|---|---|---|---|
| Cutting | early Medio | 6 | 38.7 | 14.1 | 2.925 | 18 | .009 |
|  | late Medio | 14 | 17.6 | 15.0 |  |  |  |
| Scraping | early Medio | 25 | 83.6 | 69.25 | 2.760 | 35.5 | .009 |
|  | late Medio | 43 | 41.2 | 34.0 |  |  |  |
| Perforating | early Medio | 3 | 2.3 | 2.0 | −.844 | 2.2 | .482 |
|  | late Medio | 3 | 7.4 | 5.9 |  |  |  |
| Tabular knives | early Medio | 13 | 89.1 | 47.5 | .064 | 36 | .950 |
|  | late Medio | 25 | 88.1 | 39.7 |  |  |  |
| Points | early Medio | 2 | 0.2 | 0.1 | — | — | — |
|  | late Medio | 2 | 0[a] | 0 | — | — | — |

a. Both are fragmentary, so that accurate weights could not be determined.

that this category of tool was focused on the needs of agave processing, making it the most specialized of those discussed here. It is likely that the properties of tabular knives were closely tailored to their use, the job dictating the necessary size. Accordingly, we are not surprised to see the consistency of tabular knives across the Medio period even though many other, general-purpose tools become smaller in late times. We argue that this reduction in size of the much more common general-purpose tools is another aspect of the increasingly intensive reduction in the late Medio indicated in preceding analyses of cores and flakes.

Raw material types and frequencies, by tool type, are shown in table 6.8. In the general-purpose cutting, scraping, and perforating categories, the most common tool-making materials were always chert and rhyolite. This is the common pattern for all kinds of chipped stone artifacts in northwest Chihuahua. Two other tool categories used somewhat different raw materials. Tabular knives are the most notable, in that nearly all of them in the 204 midden were made of rhyolite. This is likely a practical matter, as rhyolite is more commonly available than fine-grained basalt, and as chert, chalcedony, and obsidian usually do not occur in pieces large enough for such implements. In addition, rhyolite provides a more durable, less brittle cutting edge than do the finer-quality raw materials discussed here. The tiny projectile points recovered from the midden mostly were made of obsidian, although similar chert and chalcedony points were found in other parts of site 204 and at neighboring communities. Points are the one tool type whose size is appropriate to the small obsidian and chalcedony nodules found in the region. Chert is more common, and it comes in somewhat larger pieces. Accordingly, it was fashioned into a wider variety of small and medium-sized tools.

This table has too many low cell counts to support a chi-squared analysis. Accordingly, for each tool type, chi-squared tests were run on the two most common raw material types, chert and rhyolite, in the early and late Medio. There are no significant differences between the two time periods in the proportions of chert and rhyolite used

**Table 6.8**   Raw Material Frequencies, by Tool Type, in the Early and Late Medio

| Type | Age | n | Rhyolite | Basalt | Chert | Chalcedony | Obsidian |
|------|-----|---|----------|--------|-------|------------|----------|
| Cutting | early Medio | 6 | 4 | 0 | 2 | 0 | 0 |
| | late Medio | 14 | 7 | 0 | 6 | 1 | 0 |
| Scraping | early Medio | 25 | 13 | 0 | 12 | 0 | 0 |
| | late Medio | 43 | 17 | 0 | 26 | 0 | 0 |
| Perforating | early Medio | 3 | 0 | 0 | 3 | 0 | 0 |
| | late Medio | 3 | 0 | 0 | 3 | 0 | 0 |
| Tabular knives | early Medio | 13 | 12 | 1 | 0 | 0 | 0 |
| | late Medio | 25 | 24 | 1 | 0 | 0 | 0 |
| Points | early Medio | 2 | 0 | 0 | 0 | 0 | 2 |
| | late Medio | 2 | 0 | 0 | 1 | 0 | 1 |

for the different tool types. The other raw material types are too rare to show significant differences. The site 204 midden deposits thus indicate that the same sorts of tools were being made out of the same raw materials in both early and late Medio times.

A final chipped stone analysis done at site 204 focuses on the projectile points. Only four points were recovered from the midden deposits, so that diachronic change cannot be addressed here. A larger sample of 22 points and two bifacial knives came from the rest of the site. These artifacts can be divided into two groups: those that seem to be contemporaneous with the Medio period occupation of the site and those clearly dating to earlier times. The 16 Medio period points are considered first. Six of these were made of obsidian, the remaining ten were of chert. Figure 6.2 illustrates the chert points, all of which are typical Medio period sizes and styles. All of the points are small, with a mean length of 1.8 cm, and they are fairly standardized in shape. All are triangular and side-notched, with concave bases. This is a common type of point at Casas Grandes as well, where they are classed as types IA and IA1 (Di Peso, Rinaldo, and Fenner 1974:7:392).

The six obsidian points are illustrated in figure 6.3. These are about the same size as the chert specimens, with a mean length of 1.5 cm. The obsidian points are not nearly as standardized in shape as their chert counterparts, however. Some have the familiar triangular shape, some are side-notched, and most have concave bases, although these traits are seldom combined in a single specimen. A possible explanation for the variability of obsidian points is that some may have been made in earlier time periods, before the popularity of the style shown in figure 6.2. Obsidian is a rare raw material in the region, and any artifacts made from it may well have been picked up by later people. The minute size of these points is explicable, given that obsidian occurs in small nodules in northwestern Chihuahua (Shackley 2005). We note that two of the oddest-looking obsidian points (fig. 6.3 a, b) came from early Medio midden test pit levels. The others are from undated surface contexts or from upper levels of room fill. Obsidian projectile points are always rare in Medio period contexts, even at Casas Grandes.

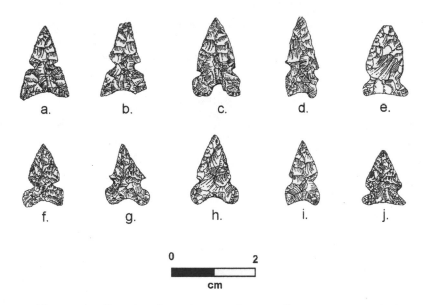

**Figure 6.2** Chert projectile points from site 204. These small points are typical of the Medio period.

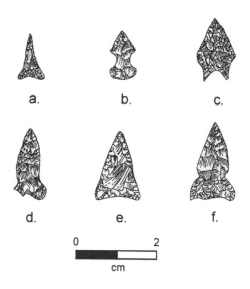

**Figure 6.3** Obsidian projectile points from site 204.

There, obsidian points make up only 7 (or 16 percent) of the 43 whole points that are described and measured (Di Peso, Rinaldo, and Fenner 1974:7:392–93). Most of the primate center's points were chert, with a few of chalcedony, jasper, and quartz.

## Intercommunity Analyses: The Small Sites

Small sites 231, 242, and 317 yielded, respectively, 1,574, 564, and 2,471 pieces of chipped stone, for a total of 4,609 specimens. All were studied at the preliminary level discussed earlier in this chapter. Subsequently, 3,116 of these artifacts were analyzed in detail by Rebnegger (2001). From site 231, 1,152 pieces (73 percent of the total) were examined. The analyzed sample from site 317 totaled 1,566 pieces (63 percent). The site 242 sample consists of 385 pieces (68 percent). It is divided into two parts: (a) the rooms and (b) the fill of the stone arcs described in chapter 1. From the 242 rooms, 186 pieces were studied, and the other 199 came from the arcs. The discussion that follows is abstracted from Rebnegger (2001). Little statistical analysis was done there, however, so we have applied analyses to the data set where useful.

Chipped stone frequency is the first and most obvious point of difference between the three sites' assemblages. We do not expect the densities of chipped stone, or any other class of artifact, to be equal at each site. Although all of the excavated contexts are of the same general kind—room fill—there is no guarantee that comparable activities formed the excavated deposits in each case. To illustrate this point, the mean density of chipped stone in the site 204 rooms is 43.3 pieces per cubic meter. The figure at site 231 is a comparable 51.6 pieces per cubic meter, but at site 317, chipped stone density is 99.9 pieces per cubic meter. Accordingly, we can say only that chipped stone density in the excavated rooms varies widely, from ca. 40 to 100 pieces per cubic meter of fill. Site 242 stands out as dramatically different: its excavated room deposits contained only 4.7 pieces per cubic meter. The stone arcs at site 242 had a much higher density of all kinds of artifacts than did the rooms, suggesting that they may have been used as middens at some point in their histories. Chipped stone density in the arcs averaged 33.1 pieces per cubic meter. The midden deposits at site 204, in contrast, contained ca. 436 pieces of chipped stone per cubic meter. All indications, then, are that activities involving chipped stone were performed on a smaller scale at site 242 than at the other sites studied here.

Mass analysis was done on nearly all of the chipped stone from the three small sites. Pieces were passed through a series of six screens that ranged from 0.6 cm (0.25 inch) to 2.5 cm (1 inch). Table 6.9 shows the observed frequencies of these size classes by site, plus expected frequencies, group percentages, and adjusted residuals. The arcs and the rooms of site 242 are separated for this analysis, giving four contexts. The observed size class frequencies differ significantly across these contexts ($\chi^2 = 250.11$, df $= 15$, $p <$ .0001), and the adjusted residuals show where the differences lie.

It will be observed from table 6.9 that the 242 room and 317 room cells contain all but two of the significant residuals, identifying these as the major sources of the table's variability. The uniformly positive signs of the 242 room residuals from 2.5 cm upward demonstrate significantly greater than expected frequencies of medium to large pieces

**Table 6.9**  Mass Analysis Results for the Small Sites

| Site | 0.6 cm | 1.3 cm | 2.5 cm | 3.8 cm | 5.0 cm | 6.3 cm | **Total** |
|---|---|---|---|---|---|---|---|
| **231 rooms** | | | | | | | |
| Observed | 109 | 958 | 372 | 92 | 22 | 39 | 1,592 |
| Expected | 101.0 | 937.2 | 394.2 | 104.6 | 23.9 | 31.1 | |
| Adj. residual[a] | 1.0 | 1.3 | −1.6 | −1.6 | −0.5 | 1.8 | |
| **242 rooms** | | | | | | | |
| Observed | 13 | 98 | 82 | 36 | 14 | 32 | 275 |
| Expected | 17.5 | 161.9 | 68.1 | 18.1 | 4.1 | 5.4 | |
| Adj. residual[a] | −1.1 | −8.1 | 2.0 | 4.5 | 5.0 | 12.0 | |
| **242 arcs** | | | | | | | |
| Observed | 7 | 106 | 41 | 22 | 4 | 3 | 183 |
| Expected | 11.6 | 107.7 | 45.3 | 12.0 | 2.7 | 3.6 | |
| Adj. residual[a] | −1.4 | −0.3 | −0.8 | 3.0 | 0.8 | −0.3 | |
| **317 rooms** | | | | | | | |
| Observed | 154 | 1,463 | 609 | 143 | 27 | 13 | 2,409 |
| Expected | 152.9 | 1,418.2 | 596.4 | 158.3 | 36.2 | 47.0 | |
| Adj. residual[a] | 0.1 | 2.7 | 0.9 | −2.0 | −2.3 | −7.4 | |
| **Total** | 283 | 2,625 | 1,104 | 293 | 67 | 87 | 4,459 |

a. Underlined adjusted residual values greater than 1.96 indicate cells that contain significant differences between the observed frequencies and those expected under the null hypothesis of no significant difference. The sign shows the direction of the difference.

in this context. In contrast, the uniformly negative signs of the 317 room residuals from 3.8 cm upward show significantly smaller than expected frequencies of medium to large pieces. Size class frequencies in the 231 rooms and the 242 arcs are mostly as expected. In other words, the largest chipped stone pieces come from the site 242 rooms, where the largest two size categories make up 16.7 percent of that sample. The smallest chipped stone pieces come from the site 317 rooms, where the largest two size categories amount to only 1.7 percent of the assemblage. In the 231 rooms and the 242 arcs, the largest two classes contribute 3.8 percent of each collection. These data can be combined with the preceding data on chipped stone density. The 242 rooms have a very low density of stone, but the pieces are somewhat larger. The 317 rooms contain a higher density of somewhat smaller pieces.

The same raw materials were in use at all of the small sites; namely, chert, rhyolite, basalt, and chalcedony, plus traces of obsidian and a few other stones such as ignimbrite and quartzite. The first three materials dominate all the small-site assemblages. Interestingly, fine-grained basalt was well represented at all small sites, although it was almost absent at site 204. To some extent, this likely reflects local resource availability, as we see no evidence that people went far beyond their local environs to procure stone for chipping. Recall that the three small sites are located in the same area of the piedmont of the Sierra Madre, whereas site 204 lies some 10 km away, in another drainage.

**Table 6.10**    Raw Material Frequencies at the Small Sites

| Site | Chert | Basalt | Rhyolite | Chalcedony | Obsidian | Total |
|---|---|---|---|---|---|---|
| **231** | | | | | | |
| Observed | 174 | 186 | 1,075 | 138 | 1 | 1,574 |
| Expected | 417.0 | 387.6 | 641.0 | 119.2 | 9.2 | |
| Adj. residual[a] | −17.1 | −14.5 | 27.4 | 2.2 | −3.3 | |
| **242** | | | | | | |
| Observed | 247 | 201 | 85 | 17 | 14 | 564 |
| Expected | 149.4 | 139.8 | 229.7 | 42.7 | 3.3 | |
| Adj. residual[a] | 9.9 | 6.5 | −13.2 | −4.4 | 6.3 | |
| **317** | | | | | | |
| Observed | 800 | 748 | 717 | 194 | 12 | 2,471 |
| Expected | 654.6 | 608.5 | 1,006.3 | 187.1 | 14.5 | |
| Adj. residual[a] | 9.7 | 9.6 | −17.4 | 0.8 | −1.0 | |
| Total | 1,221 | 1,135 | 1,877 | 349 | 27 | 4,609 |

a. Underlined adjusted residual values greater than 1.96 indicate cells that contain significant differences between the observed frequencies and those expected under the null hypothesis of no significant difference. The sign shows the direction of the difference.

Despite their similar locations, however, the three small sites vary in their raw materials. Table 6.10 shows raw-material frequencies by site, using the full data set rather than Rebnegger's (2001) sample. In this case, room and arc deposits are combined to produce the figures for site 242. Also shown here is the adjusted residual for each cell. The frequencies of raw materials differ significantly among the three sites ($\chi^2 = 931.5$, df = 8, $p < .0001$).

Of the 15 cells in the preceding table, all but 2 (site 317, chalcedony and obsidian) show significant differences, attesting to the high level of variability in the three sites' raw material frequencies. The site 242 assemblage is dominated by chert and basalt, whereas site 317 shows about equal proportions of chert, basalt, and rhyolite. Site 231, in contrast, has a high proportion of rhyolite. We note that the Galeana site (VanPool et al. 2000:17) also has a high frequency of stone classified as igneous, which we presume to consist mostly of basalt and rhyolite. Presently, we cannot ascribe this variability to any factor beyond local availability, although we realize that this may not be the entire explanation. Obsidian, although never common, occurs in highest frequency at site 242. It is noteworthy that in the present sample the region's two finest raw materials, chert and obsidian, occur in the highest relative frequencies at site 242. We have argued elsewhere (Whalen and Minnis 2001b) that site 242 was a high-status community, serving as an administrative node of the Casas Grandes system.

The most common kinds of cores at all three small sites were multidirectional. The mean weight of whole cores at site 231 is much greater than those of the other two sites. At site 231, 15 whole cores had a mean weight of 306 g (SD 310.7). The mean weight of six whole cores at site 317 was a good deal lower at 98.6 g (SD 186.3), and the corresponding figure for 4 specimens at site 242 was 143.7 g (SD 238.5). Nevertheless, a test of the three means by analysis of variance detected no significant difference among them ($F = 1.487, p = .248$). This counterintuitive result is produced by the large range of each set of measurements, as reflected in the standard deviations. These are so large that the distributions overlap considerably, and the analysis thus is unable to conclude that the three samples likely come from different populations.

We now turn to flake characteristics. These were observed in Rebnegger's (2001) sample rather than in the full data set. In Rebnegger's study, examination of a number of flake and core characteristics led to the conclusion that the same technology was in use at all three sites; namely, expedient core reduction, primarily by freehand, hard-hammer percussion but with some use of bipolar flaking as well. The technology, in other words, is the same as that just described for site 204.

All three small sites have assemblages dominated by tertiary flakes, that is, ones with no dorsal surface cortex. These comprised 60 percent of the flakes at site 242, 79 percent at site 317, and 82 percent at site 231, so that the proportions of primary and secondary flakes are low at all these sites. Other excavated Medio period contexts show a different pattern. Room fill at site 204, for instance, yielded 5,333 flakes, of which 14.5 percent were primary, 35.3 percent were secondary, and 50.2 percent were tertiary. Additional data come from the Galeana site (VanPool et al. 2000). Here, cortex levels were tabulated for 607 pieces of debitage from intramural excavations. This category includes all whole and broken flakes, plus all debris. Using our categories, we calculate that primary pieces amounted to 14.5 percent of the sample, whereas 24.9 percent was secondary and 60.6 percent was tertiary. Even allowing for classificatory differences, it is clear that site 204 and Galeana show similar proportions of levels of cortex removal. Both are large communities. Unfortunately, the Casas Grandes report (Di Peso, Rinaldo, and Fenner 1974: vol. 7) does not describe extent of cortex present on most of the recovered flakes. Nevertheless, these data argue that all three of the small sites have low frequencies of primary flakes and, presumably, of the early-stage reduction that these pieces represent. There was no statistically significant difference in flake type frequencies among the three small sites. Mean flake dimensions also failed to differ at significant levels across these sites.

The frequencies of chipped stone artifact categories are shown in table 6.11, as are adjusted residuals. These frequencies vary significantly across the three sites ($\chi^2 = 141.01$, df = 12, $p < .0001$), and examination of the residuals shows where the differences lie. Cores and core fragments make up small parts of each assemblage, and their frequencies do not differ significantly across the three sites. Debris is significantly variable, with less than expected amounts in the rooms at sites 231 and 242, the expected amount in the site 242 arcs, and more than would be expected at site 317. The whole flake count at site 231 is about as expected, but it is higher than expected in both the rooms and arcs at 242 and lower than expected at 317. Flake fragments are less common than expected everywhere at 242 and at site 317, but they are more common than expected at site 231.

To express the situation in another way, the ratios of whole to broken flakes at sites 231 and 317 are, respectively, 0.53 and 0.57. Site 242 rooms, in contrast, have a whole-to–broken flake ratio of 1.32, and that of the arcs is 0.85. In the excavated rooms at site 204, the ratio is 1.1, but the same ratio in the midden deposits is 0.47. Using data

**Table 6.11**    Chipped Stone Artifact Types, by Site, in Room Fill

| Site | Flakes | Flake fragments | Cores | Core fragments | Debris | Total |
|---|---|---|---|---|---|---|
| **231 rooms** | | | | | | |
| Observed | 372 | 703 | 16 | 1 | 55 | 1,147 |
| Expected | 373.5 | 626.6 | 13.5 | 2.6 | 130.9 | |
| Adj. residual[a] | −0.1 | 5.7 | 0.9 | −1.3 | −8.9 | |
| **242 rooms** | | | | | | |
| Observed | 83 | 64 | 4 | 0 | 10 | 161 |
| Expected | 52.1 | 87.4 | 1.9 | 0.4 | 18.3 | |
| Adj. residual[a] | 5.4 | −4.0 | 1.6 | −0.6 | −2.1 | |
| **242 arcs** | | | | | | |
| Observed | 78 | 92 | 0 | 0 | 23 | 193 |
| Expected | 62.8 | 105.4 | 2.3 | 0.4 | 22.0 | |
| Adj. residual[a] | 2.4 | −2.0 | −1.6 | −0.7 | 0.2 | |
| **317 rooms** | | | | | | |
| Observed | 463 | 813 | 16 | 6 | 261 | 1,559 |
| Expected | 507.64 | 851.6 | 18.3 | 3.6 | 177.9 | |
| Adj. residual[a] | −3.4 | −2.8 | 0.8 | 1.8 | 9.5 | |
| **Total** | 996 | 1,672 | 36 | 7 | 349 | 3,060 |

a. Adjusted residual values greater than 1.96 indicate cells that contain significant differences between the observed frequencies and those expected under the null hypothesis of no significant difference. The sign shows the direction of the difference.

from the Galeana site (VanPool et al. 2000), the whole–to–broken flake ratio in the excavated rooms at that site is 1.36, and in an open, non-intramural area, it is 0.86. Among excavated Medio period contexts, then, there are two clusters of values for the whole–to–broken flake ratio. The first group has about half as many whole as broken flakes, so that the values of the ratio are around 0.5. In this group are the large site 204 midden (0.47), plus small sites 231 and 317 (respectively, 0.53 and 0.57). The second group of contexts contains about as many (or more) whole as broken flakes, so that the value of the ratio is around 1. Included here are the rooms at site 204 (1.1), rooms at the Galeana site (1.36), and site 242 (1.32). The open-air area at the Galeana site has a value of 0.86, and the ratio in the arcs at site 242 is 0.85, placing both of them closer to the second group than to the first.

In earlier discussion of the site 204 midden sample, we noted that the frequency of broken flakes in an assemblage is affected by a number of factors, from raw material to type and intensity of reduction to use to post-depositional trampling. We argued that the whole–to–broken flake ratio in the 204 midden (0.47) likely was lowered by trampling, whereas the less-trampled room fill showed a higher value (1.1). The open-air part of the Galeana site also showed a lower ratio value than the rooms (0.86 vs. 1.4), as did the shallow deposits of the arcs versus the deeper room deposits at site 242 (0.85 vs. 1.3).

It is not clear that this explanation accounts for the low ratio values at sites 231 and 317, however, as both assemblages come entirely from room fill. Also considered in all these contexts was use of different qualities of raw materials. Stone types of whole and broken flakes were tabulated and compared by context. The analysis was not fruitful, however, as no interpretable patterns of raw material use characterize contexts with higher or lower values of the whole-to-broken flake ratio.

An experimental study (Prentiss and Romanski 1989:92) shows that tool manufacture produces many more whole than broken flakes, whereas core reduction results in some whole flakes and many broken ones. As subsequent discussion will show, there is no indication of much difference in the kinds or frequencies of tools being made at any of the sites under discussion here. Instead, all investigated Medio period contexts show that this lithic technology was overwhelmingly dominated by simple core reduction and production of expedient implements for short-term use. We suggest that the intensity of reduction being practiced at a locality could affect the proportion of broken flakes in the assemblage. By this logic, sites 231 and 317 may have been the scenes of more intensive core reduction than usually took place elsewhere (including at site 242). A similar argument was made in preceding analysis of the site 204 midden. There, the late Medio decrease in the ratio of whole to broken flakes was argued to reflect increasing intensity of core reduction.

Rebnegger's (2001) analysis recognized similar kinds of tools at all three small sites. As at site 204, these are almost all informal implements, i.e., pieces that were utilized with little or no intentional retouching. Rebnegger classifies most of these tools as scrapers, although the specimens she illustrates suggest that this category includes both steep-edged pieces and those with fine edges. In our site 204 analysis, the fine-edged tools would have been classed as cutting implements rather than as scrapers. Classificatory differences aside, however, the informal tool assemblages seem similar at all of the sites discussed in this volume. Rebnegger (2001:78) also notes that all of the largest tools were made from rhyolite. These are much like the tabular knives discussed earlier in this chapter (refer to fig. 6.1) and elsewhere (Fish, Fish, and Madsen 1992), and they make up a large proportion of the implements recognized at all three small sites. These communities were located in upland, piedmont settings where agave cultivation appears to have been common (Minnis, Whalen, and Howell 2006).

It is also noteworthy that site 242 had the highest proportion of tools among the three small sites, despite its low density of chipped stone. Tools made up 9.1 percent of the 242 room assemblage and 3.0 percent of that of the arcs. In contrast, tools comprised only 0.4 percent and 0.9 percent of the 231 and 317 collections. The presence of more tools at site 242 likely is related to the vast systems of agricultural terraces that lie near the site (Minnis, Whalen, and Howell 2006). We have argued elsewhere (Whalen and Minnis 2001b) that site 242 was an administrative node of the Casas Grandes system and that its function was to organize agricultural production in this part of the uplands.

Formal tools were rare at all three of the small sites, as they were at site 204. Only projectile points and a few fragments of bifacial knives were found. Site 317 produced the largest collection of formal tools, including four projectile points and two biface

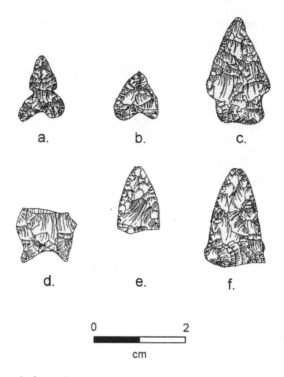

**Figure 6.4** Formal tools from site 317.

fragments. One more biface fragment came from site 242. Figure 6.4 illustrates the site 317 formal tools. Specimen a is a typical Medio period chert point, much like those illustrated earlier in figure 6.2. Specimen b, also of chert, is more ambiguous. It appears to be either a preform or a reworked piece of a larger point. Specimens c, d, and e are made of obsidian. The first of these is a whole projectile point. Specimen d is a point base, and e is a fragment of a biface of unknown kind. Specimen f also is a biface fragment. It is unusual in that it is made of rhyolite, a material not usually used for formal tools in this area. Specimens c and d are not of Medio period size or style, resembling instead points of late Archaic or early Ceramic times. It will be recalled that curated points like these also were found at site 204.

## Ground Stone

More than 7,000 pieces of ground stone were recovered from Casas Grandes, and analysis of this large data set (Di Peso, Rinaldo, and Fenner 1974:7:38–335) established types that provide a standard of comparison for all subsequent studies. As was the case with chipped stone, the collection of ground stone artifacts at the primate center appears to have been biased toward whole pieces. For instance, the ratio of whole or nearly whole metates to metate fragments at the primate center was 137 to 106, or 1.29. At site 204, where an intensive effort was made to recover all ground stone fragments from the excavated areas, the ratio of whole to fragmentary metates is 14 to 59, or 0.24. This difference results from the recovery of a much larger number of fragments at site 204. These data indicate that the Casas Grandes sample is less reliable for some kinds of comparisons (e.g., density calculations), although it remains a useful guide for whole-piece analysis.

The area's second largest Medio period ground stone data set comes from site 204. At 567 pieces, however, it is only about one-twelfth the size of the Casas Grandes sample. Ground stone was recovered from a number of contexts at site 204: the trash midden, the room fill in all three mounds, and the site's surface. Unfortunately, only a small part of the total assemblage came from the trash midden, and these pieces usually were fragments of larger implements. It appears that large pieces of ground stone were not often discarded in the trash midden. This is understandable, as such pieces are reusable in a variety of ways. As a result, our analyses were unable to detect any significant changes in the ground stone assemblage between the early and late parts of the Medio period. This is not to assert that no such changes occurred, only that they were not apparent in the present sample. Most of the site's ground stone came from room fill, and it likely did not travel far from where it was used. In addition, there were many ground stone fragments on the site's surface. This is undoubtedly a result of the heavy looting that has taken place at the site. Looters carry away whole pieces of ground stone that are dug from rooms, discarding any fragments. The surface material above each excavation unit was collected and analyzed, but the rest of the surface stone was not studied. As our analyses could detect no early/late Medio period differences in the 204 ground stone sample, the entire assemblage—midden, room, and surface—is treated as a single sample. The mean density of ground stone at site 204 was 2.15 pieces per cubic meter of excavated soil.

Much smaller ground stone assemblages came from sites 231, 242, and 317, summing to 18, 32, and 21 pieces, respectively. Nearly all of this material came from the fill of excavated rooms, as these sites had very little ground stone on their surfaces. We note that this is the common situation at small Medio period communities. As at site 242, most of the ground stone was from room fill, although some came from the stone arcs. There is no apparent difference between the two collections, however, and they will be analyzed as one. Ground stone density at site 231 was 0.6 pieces per cubic meter. At site 242, the figure was 0.68, and it was 0.79 at site 317. These small-site density figures are quite comparable, and they are dramatically lower than the figure of 2.15 just given for large site 204.

Subsequent analyses will focus on the collections from Casas Grandes and site 204, as they are so much larger than those of the three small sites. The Casas Grandes sample already has been extensively described. The 204 collection recently was described and compared to that of Casas Grandes by McKay (2005). The present study utilizes these results and expands upon them in two ways. First, statistical analyses are added where useful. Second, small sites 231, 242, and 317 will be included in the comparison to give an idea of variability in ground stone assemblages at Medio communities ranging from the primate center to small villages.

## Implement Frequencies

As the first step in his analysis, McKay (2005) sorted the 204 collection into the types established for Casas Grandes. This was readily accomplished, as nothing was found at site 204 that did not have a counterpart at the primate center. The remainder of the study was a rank-order comparison of the Casas Grandes and site 204 assemblages. For each collection, ground stone implement categories were ranked in order of decreasing frequency, expressed as a percentage of the whole ground stone assemblage. Because the Casas Grandes assemblage is some 12 times larger than that of site 204, it is not surprising to find that the larger sample shows much more variability than the smaller one (McKay 2005:45, table 6.2). This variability is not proportionate to sample size, however. The table just cited shows that Casas Grandes has 36 ground stone implement categories, whereas site 204 has 23. The 204 assemblage thus contains about 64 percent of the diversity of Casas Grandes' sample, although it is only about 8 percent as large. This observation shows that the two assemblages are alike in many ways. The difference between them, as McKay's rank-order table indicates, is produced mostly by the presence of a number of rare things that occur almost exclusively at Casas Grandes. These include cruciform objects, stone cylinders, effigies of several sorts, pipes, stools, rasps or ringing stones, altar stones, ceremonial axe and hammer heads, palettes, and decorated stone bowls. Together, these items comprise a class that is not as strictly utilitarian as the more common manos, metates, mortars, pestles, axes, and abraders. The individual frequencies of these nonutilitarian implements are less than 1 percent of their assemblage totals, and their summed frequencies are only about 5 percent of the total piece count at each site. In this discussion, we omit large stone disks, large stone slabs, and nesting box doors and the stone plugs used to close them. All of these ground stone items occur at Casas Grandes at frequencies of 1 percent or more, but we consider them to be architectural elements rather than implements.

Removing all of the nonutilitarian and architectural items from the rank-order lists leaves very similar assemblages at Casas Grandes and site 204. Included in the new short lists are manos, metates, abrading stones, pestles, undecorated stone bowls, axes, mauls, and small stone disks. We consider these items to be the standard utilitarian ground stone assemblage of the Medio period. This idea is reinforced by the fact that almost nothing outside of the assemblage just described was found at small sites 231, 242, and 317. Table 6.12 illustrates this by listing the frequencies of these utilitarian implements at the five sites under discussion here. This is not a rank-order list, as the frequencies of some items are quite different across the five sites.

The table shows that there are similarities and differences in ground stone implement frequencies among the five sites, even though all share most of the categories shown. Stone bowls, which seem often to have functioned as mortars, are present at all of the sites except 231. There is, however, a pestle at 231, so we attribute the absence of bowls to an accident of discovery. Axes occur at all sites except 242. None of the small sites have mauls or the enigmatic stone disks that were found in the larger communities.

The frequencies of some of these basic tools are highly variable across the five sites, but others are not. Stone bowls and pestles everywhere constitute similarly small

**Table 6.12**  Frequencies of Utilitarian Ground Stone Implements at Five Medio Sites (counts in parentheses)

| Tool | Casas Grandes | Site 204 | Site 231 | Site 242 | Site 317 |
|------|---------------|----------|----------|----------|----------|
| Manos & fragments | 27.3% (1,293) | 39.2% (204) | 58.8% (10) | 78.6% (22) | 63.1% (12) |
| Metates & fragments | 6.9% (327) | 14.1% (73) | 5.9% (1) | 3.6% (1) | 5.3% (1) |
| Abrading stones | 28.6% (1,352) | 27.3% (142) | 17.6% (3) | 7.1% (2) | 15.7% (3) |
| Pestles | 4.2% (197) | 4.6% (24) | 5.9% (1) | 3.6% (1) | 5.3% (1) |
| Stone bowls | 6.5% (308) | 4.2% (22) | 0 | 7.1% (2) | 5.3% (1) |
| Axes | 19.9% (943) | 2.7% (14) | 11.8% (2) | 0 | 5.3% (1) |
| Mauls | 3.5% (165) | 2.5% (13) | 0 | 0 | 0 |
| Stone disks | 3.1% (149) | 5.4% (22) | 0 | 0 | 0 |

percentages of the assemblage. Abrading stones are usually common, although site 242 stands out as having an unusually low frequency of these abundant, general-purpose tools. The frequency of axes is highly variable across the sites. The largest differences, however, are in the frequencies of manos and metates. Metates consistently make up a small percentage of the assemblages from Casas Grandes and from the three small sites. An apparent deviation from this pattern is at site 204, which has an unusually high metate frequency in the excavated deposits as well as on the surface. This may not be an actual deviation, however. As previously mentioned, the recovery of ground stone at Casas Grandes was biased toward whole specimens and against fragments. Thus, the reported percentage of metates at the primate center is artificially low compared with that of site 204, where nearly all fragments were recovered. We contend that complete recovery of metate fragments at Casas Grandes would raise the frequency shown in table 6.12 at least to that of site 204. The situation then would be that metates were more common at the two large sites than at the three small ones.

Manos and their fragments were the most common implements at site 204 and at the small sites, but not at Casas Grandes. In fact, the three small sites show very high frequencies of manos that are out of proportion to their low frequencies of metates. The site 204 mano percentage falls in between those of Casas Grandes and the small sites. It is not clear whether the low frequency of manos at Casas Grandes is a real situation or results from the incomplete recovery of fragments. The question of why mano frequency is so high at the small sites will be considered in succeeding discussion of mano types. At this point, we turn to consideration of individual ground stone implement type differences among the five sites.

*Metates.* Table 6.13 shows frequencies of metate types across the sites discussed here. It is clear from the table that the primate center has by far the highest frequency of the finely made, sharp-cornered Type IA metates. VanPool and Leonard (2002: fig. 3) published a photograph of a cache of apparently unused IA metates that was excavated at the primate center after the work of the Joint Casas Grandes Project. Table 6.13 also shows that the less carefully shaped, round-cornered Type IB metates make up a low proportion

**Table 6.13**    Metate Types at Casas Grandes and Its Neighbors (counts in parentheses)

| Metate type | Casas Grandes | Site 204 | Site 231 | Site 242 | Site 317 |
|---|---|---|---|---|---|
| IA, sharp cornered | 78.3% (94) | 21.1% (4) | 0 | 0 | 0 |
| IB, round cornered | 19.2% (23) | 36.8% (7) | 100.0% (1) | 100.0% (1) | 0 |
| ID irregular trough | 0.8% (1) | 15.8% (3) | 0 | 0 | 0 |
| II unshaped slab | 1.7% (2) | 26.3% (5) | 0 | 0 | 100.0% (1) |

20 cm

**Figure 6.5** Examples of metate types from site 204: *left* Type IA, *right* Type IB.

of the Casas Grandes assemblage. Irregular or unshaped specimens were present at the primate center only in trace quantities. In contrast, site 204 reverses the pattern of the primate center, having a smallish proportion of IA metates and a much larger Type IB assemblage. An example of each type is illustrated in figure 6.5. In addition, site 204 also yielded much higher percentages of the irregular trough and unshaped slab metates (Types ID and II). Compared to the primate center, then, site 204 has a much lower proportion of the most carefully made metates.

VanPool and Leonard (2002) analyzed the most common types of metates from Casas Grandes in consideration of the question of specialized manufacture. They argued that the precisely made, square-cornered Type IA metates were more uniform in their metric attributes than were their round-cornered Type IB counterparts. Based on this conclusion they argued that IA metates were the products of specialists, whereas the Type IB were not. The authors then statistically compared the IB metates to the similarly shaped trough metates of the Classic Mimbres area. It has never been suggested that the Mimbres trough metates were produced by specialists. The analysis revealed that the IB metates have about the same level of variability in metric characteristics as do the Mimbres trough metates. The authors take this as an indication of nonspecialized production of the Casas Grandes Type IB metates. This study did not include Casas Grandes Type ID metates, but these are much less regular in shape than the Type IB specimens.

By this argument, the primate center and site 204 differ dramatically in their frequencies of specialist-produced metates, which are the most common kind found at Casas Grandes. We note that our statistical analysis showed no significant difference in any size dimension of Type IA metates between Casas Grandes and site 204, which is a further argument for the uniformity of this kind of grinding implement. Table 6.13 also shows that no Type IA metates or identifiable fragments thereof were found at any of the small sites, which contained only the less formal Type IB metates and one informal, unshaped grinding slab.

*Manos.* Manos from Casas Grandes were classified into 24 types (Di Peso, Rinaldo, and Fenner 1974:7:172–202), although some of these seem to us to be simply reflections of different degrees of wear on the same kind of implement. There is, however, a basic division into one-handed versus two-handed specimens. The former is the least common at Casas Grandes, whereas the latter is abundant. In fact, the typical mano at the primate center can be described as a two-handed, sub-rectangular piece with grinding wear on opposing faces. It is of the "trough type," which is defined as convex from end to end on both faces, so as to fit the transverse contour of a typical metate. All are made of vesicular basalt. Of 919 classified manos at the primate center, we calculate that 688 (75 percent) were of the sort just described, which encompasses Casas Grandes Types IVa through IVm.

This also is the case at site 204, where 83 manos were classed in the Casas Grandes types (McKay 2005:119–21). The description just given for the most common sort of mano at Casas Grandes fits most (79.5 percent) of the site 204 sample as well. McKay (2005:52) notes that the means of mano length, width, and thickness at Casas Grandes are nearly identical to those at site 204. The frequency of manos at Casas Grandes also is about the same as at site 204, comprising 13.3 percent of the ground stone assemblage at the former site and 14.6 percent at the latter. A difference between the two sites, however, lies in the frequencies of one-handed manos of Types I–III. These are one-handed, shaped, sub-rectangular or oval stones with one or two grinding surfaces. They are rare at the primate center (2.8 percent) compared to site 204 (16.8 percent). We use the Casas Grandes identification of a one-handed mano as being 16 cm or less in length (Di Peso, Rinaldo, and Fenner 1974:7:172).

The mano assemblages from small sites 231, 242, and 317 number, respectively, only 10, 14, and 12 pieces. Nevertheless, they show several differences from the large-site pattern just described. The first difference is the high frequency of one-handed manos. They comprise 50 percent of the mano sample at sites 231 and 317, and 43 percent of the manos from site 242. At 40–50 percent, the frequency of one-handed manos at the small sites is much higher than at Casas Grandes (2.8 percent) or site 204 (16.8 percent). These one-handed manos come in oval, circular, sub-rectangular, and irregular shapes. The most common sort of one-handed mano at the small sites is oval in shape, is 10–12 cm long, has a single grinding surface, and does not show extensive wear. These implements are most like the Type IB manos that occurred so infrequently at the primate center (Di Peso, Rinaldo, and Fenner 1974:7:173). Fine-grained basalt manos comprise 44.5 percent of the one-handed mano collection from the small sites. Rhyolite manos make up 27.8 percent of the sample, 22.2 percent are vesicular basalt, and 5.5 percent are silicified sandstone. It is worth emphasizing that the vesicular basalt so commonly used for two-handed manos is not the major raw material type for their one-handed counterparts. Instead, most of the one-handed manos appear to have been made from locally available raw materials.

Although one-handed manos were common at the three small sites, they made up only about half of the mano assemblage. The other half consisted of two-handed implements greater than 16 cm in length. Beyond this commonality, however, lies an important difference. The two-handed manos at sites 231 and 317 differ greatly from those just described at Casas Grandes and at site 204. The site 231 shape class frequencies were two irregular, two oval, no circular, and one sub-rectangular. Of the site 317 manos, none were irregular, 4 were oval, 1 was circular, and 1 was sub-rectangular. Site 242 had no irregular, 1 oval, no circular, and 7 sub-rectangular manos.

Sites 231 and 317 have few of the sub-rectangular manos shaped for trough metates that dominated the Casas Grandes and site 204 assemblages. Instead, most of the 231 and 317 manos have about the same range of shapes as the one-handed implements just described. The one- and two-handed manos also are made from the same raw materials. Fine-grained basalt overwhelmingly dominates at 73 percent, followed by vesicular basalt at 18 percent and rhyolite at 9 percent. In short, the two-handed manos from small sites 231 and 317 seem simply to be larger versions of their one-handed counterparts. These implements show much less energy input in their creation than do the more symmetrical and precisely made manos of the large sites. In addition, they are made of local raw materials. These observations may go far toward explaining the high frequency of manos at these two sites (refer to table 6.12): they are cheap products made of local materials.

Such is not the case at small site 242. All but one of the large manos from 242 are of the sub-rectangular, trough-metate type that dominates the assemblages at Casas Grandes and site 204. Furthermore, all of the 242 two-handed manos are made of vesicular basalt. In both form and raw material, then, the 242 mano assemblage looks more like those found on the area's large sites and less like those of the other small sites. VanPool and Leonard (2002:720) believe that the vesicular basalt used at Casas Grandes is not locally available but was transported into the area from a source or sources still unknown. If this is the case, then it can be argued that small site 242 shared in the distribution of vesicular basalt to a much greater extent than did sites 231 and 317. All of the vesicular basalt manos from 242 were very heavily worn, however. This was not the case at either the primate center or site 204, and it argues that site 242 was not high on the vesicular basalt distribution ladder despite its postulated status as a minor administrative node of the Casas Grandes system.

Blanks, or preforms, are the final category of mano to consider here. At Casas Grandes, these are described as pieces of vesicular basalt that have been pecked and ground into a rectangular, or "brick-shaped," form with rounded corners. Their dimensions are slightly larger than those of in-service manos. There are no individual descriptions of these pieces, and their number is not specified. The Casas Grandes report only notes the recovery of "a number of mano blanks" (Di Peso, Rinaldo, and Fenner 1974:7:172).

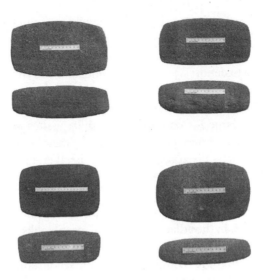

**Figure 6.6** Front and side views of four of the mano blanks recovered from Room 21, site 204. Scales measure 100 mm.

These are described as occurring in a variety of shapes: thick block, thin block, loaf, and turtle-back (Di Peso, Rinaldo, and Fenner 1974:7:172).

In addition to mano blanks, the Casas Grandes typology also contains "block planes," which are described as pieces of vesicular basalt that have been pecked and ground to rectangular shapes with rounded corners. This description sounds very like that just given for mano blanks, although the block planes are described as "unusually well made and symmetrical" (Di Peso, Rinaldo, and Fenner 1974:7:57). There are 64 of these implements, and they are classified into two types. Type I, comprising 70 percent of the sample, has sharper, squarer corners. The less common Type II block plane has more rounded corners. The mean dimensions of the two types are nearly identical. These implements were classed as block planes solely by analogy with smaller tools used for woodworking by the modern Hopi (Di Peso, Rinaldo, and Fenner 1974:7:57). There is no other morphological or contextual indication of this use of the Casas Grandes block planes.

It is unclear what distinguishes block planes from mano blanks at Casas Grandes. In fact, the report notes that some of the Type II block planes "may have been mano blanks" (Di Peso, Rinaldo, and Fenner 1974:7:57). We favor discarding the unsubstantiated block plane category, as we feel that all of the pieces just described are mano blanks, some of which were more neatly made than others. That there should be some neatly made mano blanks at the primate center is consistent with the very precisely shaped metate blanks also found there, made of the same material, and pictured by VanPool and Leonard (2002:fig. 3).

Site 204 yielded 23 vesicular basalt mano blanks, which is the region's second largest sample, and figure 6.6 shows some of them. Mean length, width, and thickness of these implements was tested against dimensions of the block planes from Casas Grandes.

No statistically significant difference was found in width or thickness. Only length differed significantly between the two sites, with specimens from Casas Grandes averaging 3 cm longer than those of site 204. All of the mano blanks from 204 have the rounded edges and corners used to define Type II block planes at Casas Grandes. This agrees with the metate data just presented. That is, the most precisely made items—Type I blocks (or mano blanks) and Type IA metates—are most common at the primate center, but are rare or absent at the large 204 community. Both large sites were well provided with vesicular basalt implements, however. It is noteworthy that no mano blanks were found at any of the three small sites discussed here. It may be, therefore, that mano blanks are to be expected only at the large communities of the region.

Most of the 23 mano blanks from site 204 were found in Excavation Area 2 of Mound A (refer to fig. 1.5). In a corner of Room 21 was a pile of ground stone implements that included 10 mano blanks. In the adjacent Room 19, three blanks were found in a corner, and one blank was found in each of the nearby Rooms 23 and 24. Some 65 percent of the site's sample of mano blanks thus comes from a single set of rooms. Beyond the concentration of mano blanks, these rooms stood out from the others on several other grounds. They contained elaborate architectural elements, including two adobe column bases and two platform hearths. Also found here were two caches of Archaic projectile points. The only macaw burial yet found in the region outside of Casas Grandes lay beneath the floor of one of these rooms. It could be that the vesicular basalt mano blanks were being obtained through a regional network by the elites of large communities.

In chapter 2 we analyzed radiocarbon dates from floor contexts in the rooms where mano blanks were concentrated. We argued that the last occupation of the rooms was in the late part of the Medio period, which presumably also is the date of the piles of mano blanks. One blank was found in a floor level of one of the early Medio rooms in Excavation Area 1, but it could represent a later deposit in an abandoned room. The other blanks come from late Medio parts of Mounds A and C. It thus appears that mano blanks were much more common in the late Medio than in the early part of the period.

*Other Items.* The last of the common ground stone implements to be discussed here is what was termed the abrading stone at Casas Grandes. This is a catchall category of small implements thought to have been used as abrasive implements in the shaping and polishing of a wide range of materials, including wood, bone, shell, and turquoise (Di Peso, Rinaldo, and Fenner 1974:7:49). These tools occurred in a variety of shapes and sizes, although nearly all could be grasped and used with one hand. They represent a variety of raw materials and degrees of coarseness.

Abrading stones were the most common category of ground stone tool at Casas Grandes, and they were a fairly close second at site 204 (see table 6.12). Both of these large sites showed abrading stone frequencies of 27–29 percent of the total assemblage. For site 204, McKay (2005:870) identified 105 abrading stones. Most were irregular ovoid shapes. About two-thirds of them had wear on only one surface, and most had heavily battered ends. Some bore traces of the red or black pigments that they had been used to grind, as was also the case at Casas Grandes (Di Peso, Rinaldo, and Fenner 1974:7:49). In a word, these appear to be expedient tools that were used for a wide range of tasks, both at Casas Grandes and at site 204. Most of the abrading stones from 204 came from room fill, but 22 were found in the site's trash midden. There, they occurred in late Medio levels at a density of 1.2 pieces per cubic meter of excavated soil. The figure for the early Medio levels was only 0.6 pieces per cubic meter. We note that the overall densities of ground stone were about the same in the early and late Medio midden test pit levels.

Abrading stones also were the second most common category of ground stone tool at small sites 231 and 317, but, at 16–18 percent, their frequencies were only about half those of the larger sites. The data in hand thus show that abrading stones occurred in all investigated Medio communities, but their frequencies were higher in large than in small communities. This may reflect a differential level of craft activity at large versus small Medio communities. Beyond this observation, we note that site 242 stands out as having abrading stones in unusually low frequency (7.1 percent). Samples are small and interpretation should therefore be cautious, but this finding may indicate a lower than normal level of craft activity at site 242, which has been characterized as a minor administrative outpost of Casas Grandes. For the same reason, it may also be significant that 242 is the only site from which no stone axes were recovered (refer to table 6.12). We do not discuss the rest of the ground stone assemblages of the sites analyzed here. This material closely fits the descriptions and illustrations from Casas Grandes (Di Peso, Rinaldo, and Fenner 1974:7).

## Stone Tool Use in Medio Communities

Early and late Medio chipped stone assemblages from the midden at site 204 have much in common. In every category of chipped stone artifact, the same local raw materials, in about the same proportions, were in use all across the period. These raw materials are often available as cobbles in the area's water channels and piedmont gravels. Our presumption is that the lithic raw material found in the site 204 midden was procured in the vicinity of the community throughout the Medio period. It is clear that expedient core reduction was the primary activity represented throughout the midden deposits. Reduction seems largely to have been freehand work, although there is evidence of some bipolar flaking at all times.

Most flake and core attributes did not vary at statistically significant levels between early and late Medio midden deposits. Flakes and cores were always highly variable in size. All across the period, flakes also were irregular in shape and cores characteristically showed multidirectional flake removal scars. This argues for the minimal core preparation that characterizes expedient technologies. The same classes of tools were found from top to bottom of the midden deposits. Tool type frequencies did not differ significantly between the early and late Medio, nor did the types and frequencies of their raw materials. These observations argue for minimal changes in activities between the early and late parts of the Medio period.

Despite their broad similarity, there were some notable differences between the early and late Medio chipped stone assemblages studied here. Obsidian is always rare in Medio lithic assemblages, and it was present in a predictably small quantity in the 204 midden deposits. A total of 10 small pieces came from this context, having a combined weight of 13.6 g. Of this total, 8 pieces weighing 12.2 g came from early Medio levels. The early Medio thus has 90 percent by weight of the midden test pits' obsidian. This figure is especially impressive given that the volume of excavated late Medio deposits (10.6 cu m) was approximately double that of the early Medio (5.0 cu m). These data argue that although it was always rare, obsidian was much more common in the early Medio than in the late part of the period.

Also documented in preceding pages were several statistically significant differences in flake and core characteristics. Compared to their early Medio predecessors, late Medio flakes were smaller, they had less cortex, more of them were broken, and more had striking platforms that were shattered or nonexistent. Whole cores also were less common in late Medio deposits than in early ones. Keep in mind that the same raw materials were used in both assemblages. The sizes of early and late Medio tools, as measured by weight, were found to differ significantly. General-purpose cutting and scraping implements were smaller in late Medio than in early Medio times. Given that these implements accounted for about two-thirds of the tools all across the period, a real difference in size is present.

The early and late Medio chipped stone assemblages were both products of expedient core reduction. Nevertheless, preceding analyses argued that reduction became more intensive in the late Medio. In brief, much of the late Medio chipped stone assemblage was smaller and more broken up than its early Medio predecessor, despite being made of the same raw materials. The larger question is why the late Medio population at site 204 should have needed to practice the more intensive reduction that we postulate. We presently cannot provide a satisfactory answer. The population of the Casas Grandes area reached its apogee in the late Medio, which may have reduced the procurement zones for all sorts of resources. The late Medio also was a time of increasingly effective regional organization, which doubtless imposed a whole set of the technological and social constraints, especially on the communities of the Core Zone.

The three small sites have been found to be alike in many ways. All show the same pattern of reduction of minimally prepared cores into flakes of a wide variety of sizes and shapes. The common raw materials of the region—chert, rhyolite, basalt, and chalcedony—were in use at all the sites discussed here, although their relative proportions are quite variable from site to site. We presume that Medio populations used whatever stone was readily available in the immediate vicinity of their communities. Most sites contained tiny percentages of obsidian as well.

All three small sites have low frequencies of primary flakes (ca. 3–6 percent), combined with high tertiary flake frequencies (ca. 65–80 percent). Comparative data showed that this is not the pattern in evidence at the large Medio period sites (e.g., 204 and Galeana). There, primary flakes were not so heavily outnumbered by tertiary ones. The high proportion of tertiary flakes at all three small sites has several possible explanations. It could be that much early-stage reduction was being done off-site, resulting in low primary flake counts and elevated numbers of tertiary pieces.

All three small sites showed the same kinds of expedient tools for cutting and scraping, much of them likely associated with plant processing. Many of the tools on all three sites were the large rhyolite implements referred to earlier in this chapter as tabular knives, probably for agave processing. The presence of these implements is consistent with the upland locations of the small sites. Finally, all three sites had very few formal chipped stone tools. A few projectile points, some of earlier type and obviously curated, plus a few biface fragments, complete the sparse assemblages.

Despite these broad similarities, however, there were some notable differences among the small sites. The most obvious of these is chipped stone density. On average, site 242 stands out as having the lowest chipped stone density of any of the Medio communities discussed here. Despite this, 242 has somewhat higher frequencies of the finer-quality raw materials—obsidian and chert—than its two small counterparts.

The ratio of whole to broken flakes was variable across the three small sites, and once again, 242 stands out. There, about as many whole as broken flakes were found. At sites 231 and 317, in contrast, whole flakes were outnumbered by broken ones by about two to one. This pattern was taken to indicate more intensive reduction at sites 231 and 317 than at 242, a hypothesis consistent with the low density of chipped stone of all kinds at the last site. In addition to having the most whole flakes, 242 also has a higher frequency of expedient tools than its two small neighbors do. Site 242 does not, however, have correspondingly large quantities of production debris. These observations suggest that at least some of the site's implements and flakes were made elsewhere and brought to the site. Among the three small sites, then, 242 stands out as somewhat distinct, a condition likely related to its special status as an administrative node of Casas Grandes.

The preceding discussion compared the ground stone assemblages of five Medio period sites: the primate center of Casas Grandes, the large neighboring site 204, and small sites 231, 242, and 317. For this analysis, the ground stone was divided into two categories: utilitarian implements likely used in everyday life, and exotic items that probably had more restricted uses. The utilitarian assemblage was common to the sites discussed here. It consists of manos, metates, abrading stones, stone bowls, pestles, and axes. Rare or exotic items (e.g., palettes, effigies) occurred only in large communities and in the small site 242 that likely was closely affiliated with the primate center.

Much of the variability in the ground stone assemblages in this sample can be dichotomized into large-site versus small-site patterns. For instance, metates at large sites include the precisely made Type IA specimens as well as other types that are less formal. The small sites of the present sample, in contrast, do not contain any IA metates. Instead, their sparse assemblages show only the less formal types. Preceding discussion also argued that metates and their fragments are common at large sites but rare at small ones. We are puzzled by the very low frequencies of metates at all three of the small sites, especially as this dearth of metates is not matched by a corresponding lack of manos.

Manos were by far the most common implements in the ground stone assemblages of all three small sites. Manos comprised one-half to three-quarters of the small-site ground stone totals, but only about one-quarter to one-third of the samples from Casas Grandes and site 204. In addition, one-handed manos were much more common at the small sites than at the large ones, where two-handed specimens overwhelmingly dominated. It is noteworthy that small-site manos often were less carefully made than those at the large sites. Moreover, the small-site manos seldom were made of vesicular basalt but were instead produced from locally available raw materials. Conspicuously absent at the small sites are the vesicular basalt, trough-type manos that are common at Casas Grandes and site 204. Among the small sites, 242 is the only one where most manos were of this type. Finally, well-made, vesicular basalt mano blanks were accumulated only at the large sites. None were found at any of the small sites.

The presence of many implements of vesicular basalt clearly is a major point of difference between the large and small sites discussed here. This raw material is thought to have been imported or controlled at a regional level, likely by the primate center of Casas Grandes. Here, vesicular basalt implements were the most numerous and the most finely made. The distribution network appears to have included the large 204 community, where vesicular basalt implements were plentiful, although most of them were not as finely made as those of Casas Grandes. Also included in the distribution chain at a low level were small communities like 242, which were closely connected to the primate center as minor administrative nodes. Small, rural communities such as sites 231 and 317 seem either to have been outside of the network or far down the chain of distribution. No ground stone exotics of any sort were found at small sites 231 and 317.

Distinctive ground stone assemblages appear to be characteristic of large and small Medio period communities. Large-site assemblages include more formal or carefully made manos and metates, as well as stockpiles of mano blanks. Nearly all of these implements are made of vesicular basalt. Exotic or nonutilitarian items also are present. In contrast, the small sites have few or no formal manos and metates, no mano blanks, very limited use of vesicular basalt, and no exotic items. These small-site assemblages seem to be strictly utilitarian. Small site 242 is the only exception to this generalization. It blends some large-site ground stone characteristics (e.g., vesicular basalt, trough-type manos and exotic items) with its predominantly small-site traits.

# 7

## Farming, Gathering, and Hunting

The Casas Grandes Valley has long been recognized as a particularly good place for making a living. After a long journey through northern Mexico, Francisco de Ibarra's party arrived at the ruins of Casas Grandes in 1564. "This is the most useful and beneficial of all rivers we found in the provinces," wrote the expedition's chronicler, Baltasar de Obregón. "Its shores are covered with beautiful and tall poplars, willows, and savins. It can be readily and at little cost be utilized for irrigating the fertile shores," he continued, and he also mentioned the abundance of edible plants and animals (Hammond and Rey 1928:206). In later years, the bounty of the Casas Grandes environment was stressed by many, from Bandelier (1890) to Doolittle (1993). This chapter examines the use of floral and faunal resources among Medio communities and across the period. One of our arguments is that the bountiful environment described by Obregón was significantly affected by increasingly heavy human activities in the late Medio.

### Medio Period Plant Use

Relationships between society and food were likely complex during the Medio period. We envision at least some centralized control of food production by the primate center in Medio times (Minnis, Whalen, and Howell 2006). Specialized food production may also have been practiced as communities took advantage of the differing potentials of their local settings. Groups away from prime floodplain locations, for instance, could have augmented their productivity by growing agave. This plant is better suited to drier, hillslope settings, and it has long been an important resource for indigenous peoples in the Southwest (e.g., Castetter, Bell, and Grove 1938; Gentry 1982). Although humans clearly respond to the potentials of their surroundings, they also play important roles in shaping those potentials. The Medio period population was dense, and it must have had a significant impact on its environment. Anthropogenic environmental alterations likely led to changes in resource availability and farming potential, and these changes could have resulted in modified subsistence strategies. In pursuit of these lines of thought, in the present chapter we examine Medio period plant and animal use, first in our sample of communities and then across the period.

## The Paleoethnobotany of Casas Grandes

The subsistence foundations of Casas Grandes and its neighbors have long been of secondary interest in Chihuahuan archaeology. This is not due simply to the intrinsic aesthetic appeal that exotica like macaws and copper bells have over burned maize cobs and bone fragments, but rather to deficiencies in the available data. The problem is that most excavation of Medio period contexts was done before the widespread use of such modern recovery techniques as fine screening and flotation. This helps to explain the paucity of recovered material. During three years of excavation, only 355 lots of plant remains were collected. Interpretation of these data was sparse as well. Only some of the small recovered sample was identified in detail. Other remains "were crushed beyond recognition by the time they were studied or lacked key characteristics" (Di Peso, Rinaldo, and Fenner 1974:8:308). Plant remains are dealt with in nine pages in the Casas Grandes report, whereas Medio period ceramics and ground stone each have some 300 pages of description and discussion.

An additional problem is that some of the most important plant remains apparently were not identified by trained ethnobotanists, leading to inconsistencies in classificatory terminology. For instance, plant remains from five large pit-ovens were identified in the field as "sotol." There is terminological confusion between sotol, a member of the genus *Dasylirion,* and agave or mescal, of the genus *Agave.* Both agave and sotol can be cooked in pit-ovens, and their names often were used interchangeably in the Casas Grandes volume. It is impossible to clarify this situation now, as no agavaceous plant remains from the ovens appear to have been saved. The only agave identified in the Casas Grandes report is one sample from a small, round, stone-lined oven in a plaza of Unit 12 (Di Peso, Rinaldo, and Fenner 1974:8:316). The identification of agave from this sample seems less than certain, as it is classified in one place as an *Agave* leaf base. On the same page, however, the fragment is referred to simply as a monocotyledon, a more inclusive taxon that could include *Yucca, Dasylirion,* and other plants. Accordingly, although we suspect that the plant remains in the five large pit-ovens were agave, definitive proof is lacking.

The list of plant remains recognized at the primate center is a short one (Di Peso, Rinaldo, and Fenner 1974:8:316). Among the cultigens were maize, squash, gourds, and cotton. Beans are not included in this list, although we recovered beans from the neighbors of Casas Grandes. Most likely, then, they also were present at the primate center. Agave remains were found at Casas Grandes, but the plant was placed in the uncultivated list. As will become apparent, we believe that the plant was cultivated. Other uncultivated plant remains from the primate center include seeds of hackberry and purslane, saltbush, a mesquite pod, walnut shell fragments, and a piece of a piñon nut shell. Even this brief inventory shows exploitation of floodplain and upland resources.

## The Paleoethnobotany of Casas Grandes' Neighbors

There are two bodies of paleoethnobotanical data to be considered here. The first consists of a few analyses of plant remains from sites excavated after Casas Grandes but before the excavations reported in the present volume. The material collected by our excavations comprises the second, and larger, data set. Earlier studies are from the Joyce Well site in New Mexico and Cuarenta Casas in the mountains of Chihuahua. Skibo, McCluney, and Walker (2002) recently published an updated and expanded version of McCluney's report of his 1963 excavations at the Joyce Well site. The original report on plant remains is included in the volume, but it identified only maize, bottle gourd, and cotton. The amount of shelled corn was impressive, amounting to some 20 bushels. Bottle gourd and cotton were the only other plant remains identified at Joyce Well (Skibo, McCluney, and Walker 2002:46). This paucity of identified plant species is characteristic of assemblages recovered before flotation, and it reflects a focus on cultivated plants. Guevara Sánchez (1986) and Montúfar López and Reyes Landa (1995) published much wider inventories of plant remains from Cuarenta Casas, a Medio period cliff dwelling located in the mountainous area southwest of Casas Grandes. Present on the site were remains of a range of wild and cultivated plants. Cuarenta Casas shows a pattern that is well known from the U.S. Southwest (e.g., Huckell and Toll 2004): cultigens provided an important part of the subsistence base but were supplemented by many collected wild plant foods.

The most recent post–Casas Grandes data set to be considered here is the large one collected from the four Medio period sites analyzed in the present volume. Flotation samples were taken and large plant remains were recovered by hand during excavation of sites 204, 231, 242, and 317. Remains were also collected from excavations in several large ovens of the Core Zone. All this work yielded 237 flotation samples containing propagules (i.e., seeds, fruits, and associated structures). Wood charcoal was identified from these flotation samples, from larger pieces collected directly, and from specimens used for radiocarbon dating. Two-thirds of the flotation samples are from site 204, where 36 rooms and a number of extramural features were excavated. Only fourteen rooms were investigated at small sites 231, 242, and 317, so that the macroplant data are much more limited than for site 204. Flotation samples were usually taken from features or floor levels. Few samples were taken from the upper fill of rooms in light of the extensive looting of these sites and the difficulty in determining which room fill was disturbed until the floors were exposed.

Samples were floated either in a water-conserving system described elsewhere (Minnis and LeBlanc 1976) or in the water of the Arroyo la Tinaja that runs by site 204. Cloth with a mesh of about 0.3 mm was used to strain the samples' light fractions. These were dried and sorted under a dissecting microscope. Heavy fractions were examined in the field, but they yielded almost no plant remains. The light fractions were screened to remove material smaller than 0.3 mm, which received only a cursory examination. Samples of the larger material that exceeded 15 g were divided with a sample-splitter, and the subsample closest to 15 g was fully sorted. Samples smaller than 15 g were sorted in their entirety.

Taxa recovered from Medio period sites are listed in table 7.1, and ubiquity values are given. The ubiquity of a taxon is the percentage of all flotation samples in which it occurs. Only those taxa with ubiquity values of 1 percent or more are shown here. All taxa recovered from prehistoric contexts are present in northwestern Chihuahua today,

**Table 7.1**   Ubiquity of Propagules at Four Medio Period Sites[a]

| Taxon | Site 204 | Site 231 | Site 242 | Site 317 |
|---|---|---|---|---|
| **Maize** (all categories)[b] | 73.2 | 77.4 | 52.9 | 65.5 |
| **Maize** cupules | 70.7 | 71.0 | 35.3 | 65.6 |
| Goosefoot-Pigweed | 32.5 | 51.6 | 35.3 | 21.2 |
| Purslane | 21.7 | 41.9 | 68.8 | 9.4 |
| **Maize** kernels | 21.0 | 25.8 | 11.8 | 6.6 |
| Goosefoot | 15.9 | 12.9 | 11.8 | 15.6 |
| Agave (all categories) | 10.8 | 22.6 | 5.9 | 6.3 |
| Agave tissue | 8.9 | 9.7 | — | — |
| Pigweed | 7.6 | 6.5 | 11.8 | — |
| Nightshade family | 7.6 | — | — | — |
| Bean family | 5.8 | — | — | — |
| Agave (other) | 5.1 | 12.9 | — | — |
| **Cotton** | 5.1 | 3.2 | — | — |
| Bean family | 3.8 | — | — | — |
| Acacia/Mesquite | 3.8 | — | — | — |
| Locoweed/Rattlebox | 3.8 | 6.5 | — | — |
| Grass family | 3.8 | 12.9 | 11.8 | 3.1 |
| Prickly pear | 3.8 | — | — | — |
| Saltbush | 1.9 | — | — | — |
| Nutshell | 1.9 | — | — | — |
| Monocot | 1.9 | — | — | 6.3 |
| Knotweed | 1.9 | — | — | 3.1 |
| Plantain | 1.9 | — | — | — |
| **Bean** | 1.9 | 6.5 | 5.9 | 6.3 |
| cf. Mock Pennyroyal | 1.3 | 9.7 | — | — |
| **Squash** | 1.3 | — | — | — |
| Aster family | 1.3 | 3.2 | — | — |
| Juniper | 1.3 | — | — | 3.1 |
| Agave spine | 1.3 | 2.2 | 5.9 | — |
| Piñon | 1.3 | — | — | — |
| **Gourd** | 1.3 | — | — | 1.3 |
| Gymnosperm | 1.3 | — | — | — |
| Carpetweed | 1.3 | 3.2 | — | — |
| cf. Beargrass | 0.6 | — | — | — |
| Misc. tissue | 0.6 | — | — | 15.6 |
| Cholla | 0.6 | — | — | — |
| Dock | 0.6 | — | — | — |
| Dropseed | 0.6 | 3.2 | — | — |
| False Purslane | 0.6 | — | — | — |
| Grape | 0.6 | — | — | — |
| cf. Pink family | 0.6 | — | — | — |
| Ragweed | 0.6 | — | — | — |

**Table 7.1** (*Continued*)

| Taxon | Site 204 | Site 231 | Site 242 | Site 317 |
|---|---|---|---|---|
| Sorrel | 0.6 | — | — | — |
| Sunflower | 0.6 | — | — | — |
| Vervain | 0.6 | — | — | — |
| Morning glory family | 0.6 | — | — | — |
| Mustard family | — | 6.5 | — | — |
| Kallstroemia | — | — | — | 3.1 |
| Unknown | 18.5 | 19.4 | 29.4 | 9.4 |
| Unidentifiable | 17.2 | 6.5 | 29.4 | 12.5 |
| No. of samples | 157 | 31 | 17 | 32 |

a. Ubiquity is the percentage of all seed-containing samples when a taxon is present.

b. Cultivated plants are shown in bold type.

and there is no evidence of long-distance trade in foodstuffs or other plant resources. The primate center contains macaws, marine shells, and copper from areas to the south and southwest, but the same is not true of plants. Chile (*Capsicum*) and cacao (*Theobroma*) are two southern products that could have been brought into northwestern Chihuahua, although neither is present in the assemblage of recovered propagules.

Several plant resources available in the region are rare or absent in the preceding table but are likely to have been used by the people of Casas Grandes. These include acorns, piñon nuts, and mesquite seeds. The wood charcoal data to be discussed shortly show that oaks were common in the area, and the absence of acorns in the samples likely is a result of their poor preservation. The same is true of piñon nut hulls and mesquite seeds. All of these remains characteristically are poorly represented in plant assemblages from the U.S. Southwest. Other potentially edible plants that also are absent from the prehistoric samples include squawbush, buckthorn, and devil's claw.

As can be seen in table 7.1, most propagule taxa are uncommon in flotation samples from all sites, and a few categories make up the most abundant taxa. All four sites contain the remains of maize, beans, cotton, squash, and gourds. Weeds like goosefoot, pigweed, and purslane dominate the noncultivated plant remains. Agave is relatively common among the four communities. We have recorded upland fields containing many "rock-mulch" piles where we suspect that agave was grown (Minnis and Whalen 2005; Minnis, Whalen, and Howell 2006), although its cultivation remains unproven. In any case, the data show that Medio period people in the Casas Grandes Core Zone were heavily dependent on cultivated crops. These were supplemented with wild plant foods, as is the common situation all over the adjacent Southwest.

Flotation samples were taken from the five conical pit-ovens that we excavated at outlying sites. We also took a sample from a small, hemispherical oven at site 188, another Medio period pueblo in the Core Zone. Unfortunately, these remains (table 7.2) do not provide any clear indication of the ovens' uses. Although maize, agave, weed seeds, and other remains are present, none is abundant enough to argue that it was the

**Table 7.2**  Charred Propagules from Oven Flotation Samples

| Taxon | 188-1 | 204-1 | 204-2 | 239-1 | 257-1 | 317-1 |
|---|---|---|---|---|---|---|
| Maize cupules | 1 | 3 | 3 | 1 | — | — |
| Agave spine | 4 | — | 1 | — | — | — |
| Purslane | 2 | — | 1 | — | — | — |
| Goosefoot | — | — | 1 | — | — | — |
| Pigweed | — | — | 1 | — | — | — |
| Goosefoot/Pigweed | — | 62 | — | — | — | — |
| Knotweed | — | 1 | 1 | — | — | — |
| Grass family | — | — | 1 | — | — | — |
| Tissue | — | 1 | 1 | — | 1 | 171 |
| Unknown | 4 | — | 5 | 6 | — | 2 |
| No. of identifications | 11 | 67 | 15 | 7 | 1 | 173 |
| No. of samples | 1 | 3 | 7 | 1 | 1 | 2 |

primary resource being processed. The site 188 oven was of a different size and kind than the others, but the table shows that it contained about the same remains.

## Diachronic Change in Plant Use

The Medio period was a time of considerable change in settlement and in regional organization, and there likely were concomitant changes in subsistence patterns and plant use. The site 204 midden deposits have proven the best place to study early-to-late-Medio change in ceramic and lithic artifacts, but they contained relatively few plant remains. An alternative approach is to examine ethnobotanical data from early and late Medio rooms at site 204. Only early radiocarbon dates were recovered from floor contexts in Rooms 1–8 and 50–52 in Area 1 of Mound A, and only late dates came from the floors of Rooms 60–65 in Area 4 of the same mound. Rooms 70–72 of Mound C have also been classed as a late occupation based on the presence of Ramos Polychrome from top to bottom of the adjacent midden deposit. Feature and floor contexts in these rooms yielded 42 early Medio flotation samples and 25 late ones. Clearly, these data are not as good as those from the midden, but they support some preliminary observations. Table 7.3 shows counts and proportions of the most common taxa. The table's figures sum to more than the totals just given, as some samples contained several taxa.

Early and late Medio plant remains are similar in this sample. Maize always is the most common taxon, and ubiquity figures are uniformly high for maize cupules. Maize kernel ubiquity is somewhat higher in the late Medio, although a chi-squared test of ubiquity counts for kernels and cupules shows no significant difference between the early versus late parts of the period ($\chi^2 = .659$, df $= 1$, $p = .417$). No agave was recovered from the early Medio samples, but it was present in 12 percent of those of the late Medio. Fisher's exact probability test on the agave ubiquity counts falls just short of statistical significance ($p = .072$). Had agave been present in four late Medio samples rather than

**Table 7.3**   Frequencies of Major Propagules from Early and Late Medio Contexts at Site 204

| Propagule | Early Medio | | Late Medio | |
| --- | --- | --- | --- | --- |
| | No. of samples | Pct. of samples | No. of samples | Pct. of samples |
| Ubiquity of maize kernels | 6 | 14.3 | 6 | 24.0 |
| Ubiquity of maize cupules | 32 | 76.2 | 19 | 76.0 |
| Ubiquity of agave | 0 | 0.0 | 3 | 12.0 |
| Ubiquity of chenopod/amaranth | 9 | 21.4 | 3 | 12.0 |
| Ubiquity of purslane | 1 | 2.4 | 7 | 28.0 |

three, the early/late difference would have been statistically significant. This hints that agave production increased at site 204 from early to late Medio times, although the present sample is too small to support a firm conclusion.

The predominant weed shifts from chenopod/amaranth (e.g., pigweed and goose-foot) during the early Medio period to purslane in the late Medio. Although this ubiquity count difference is statistically significant (Fisher's $p = .020$), we cannot assign practical meaning to it. Pigweed, goosefoot, and purslane all are weedy annuals whose seeds were used as food by prehistoric populations all over the adjacent Southwest, and goosefoot and purslane seeds appear together in more than 60 percent of the samples from the southern Colorado Plateau (Huckell and Toll 2004:58). It is clear that these wild plant seeds were important supplements to maize agriculture everywhere that it was practiced.

These weedy species are meaningful to archaeologists in another way as well. They are recognized as "disturbance taxa," "field weeds," and "co-products of agricultural intensification" (Huckell and Toll 2004:61). Huckell and Toll (2004:65) cite studies in which rises in frequencies of these weeds in prehistoric assemblages are taken as "a predictable consequence of replacement of native vegetation by anthropogenic communities such as cultivated fields." Table 7.3 shows that pigweed, goosefoot, and purslane seeds were identified in 23.8 percent of the samples from early Medio contexts at site 204. By the late Medio, their ubiquity had nearly doubled to 40.0 percent. This is a crude measure, but it hints at an increase in the frequency of "disturbance taxa" from early to late Medio times at site 204. This, in turn, points to increasing clearing of fields and other soil-disturbing activities around the community. Succeeding sections will make the same argument from different data.

## Wood Use in the Medio Period

The samples analyzed here all come from floor-contact levels or floor features. Whenever possible, 20 pieces of wood were identified from each flotation sample. The wood pieces identified were chosen at random from those retained in a 4 mm screen. When samples contained fewer than 20 such pieces, all were identified. Identification sometimes stopped at the super-genus level for expediency. For instance, cottonwood and

**Table 7.4**    Percentages of Charred Wood from Flotation Samples

| Taxon | Site | | | |
|---|---|---|---|---|
| | 204 | 231 | 242 | 317 |
| Pine | 38.1[a] | 7.0 | 87.7 | 28.8 |
| Oak | 36.0 | 3.6 | 3.3 | 46.5 |
| Mesquite | 6.8 | 14.0 | 0.9 | 18.6 |
| Cottonwood/Willow | 5.2 | 0.0 | 0.5 | 0.0 |
| Piñon | 4.7 | 3.7 | 0.0 | 4.4 |
| Juniper | 2.1 | 1.5 | 0.6 | 1.5 |
| No. of identifications | 3,433 | 408 | 845 | 566 |
| No. of samples | 156 | 31 | 46 | 33 |

a. Percentage of all seed-containing samples where a taxon is present.

willow are similar woods that grow in the same settings, and time-consuming observations are necessary to differentiate them. Piñon wood is assumed to be *Pinus cembroides,* the only piñon species present in northern Mexico (Martin and Hutchins 1981). Ponderosa pine (*Pinus ponderosa*) dominates the non-piñon pines found in archaeological sites in much of the U.S. Southwest. There are many *Pinus* species in the Sierra Madre of Chihuahua, however, and they presently cannot be differentiated (Camacho Uribe 1988; Minnis 1987). Their identification thus is only to the genus level. Fortunately, all of these pines are found in the mountains, and only piñon comes from the foothills. Therefore, specimens identified as pine, but not as piñon, are from the mountains.

The wood identifications shown in table 7.4 are based upon a total of more than 5,200 individual fragments from 266 flotation samples. Almost the same woods are present at each site, although the sample from 204 is far larger than those of the other three sites combined. The table shows only the most common taxa, all of which are found around the sites today.

The high frequency of oak shows that the tree was at least as abundant in the upland locations of the sites in Medio times as it is today. Mesquite presently is one of the most common woody plants around the sites. It is an excellent fuel that was found consistently in the prehistoric samples. It occurred at relatively low frequency, however, suggesting a more limited distribution in the past than today. In fact, mesquite is known to have increased all over the region in the last hundred years (e.g., Humphrey 1987; Turner et al. 2003; Webster and Bahre 2001). Juniper and piñon also were found at low frequency in the archaeological samples. This indicates that both trees, although present on the piedmont slopes, were less common than oak during the Medio period. Cottonwood and willow are present in significant quantity only at site 204, which is situated beside a large drainage that still contains these trees. The other three sites are not near drainages large enough to support cottonwoods or willows, so that this type of charcoal is rare at all of them.

The most notable feature of the preceding table is the high frequency of pine charcoal at all four sites. As noted earlier, pines are native to the high foothills and mountains,

**Table 7.5** Wood Charcoal from Excavated Ovens[a]

| | 188 | | 204-1 | 204-2 | 239 | 257 | | 317 | |
|---|---|---|---|---|---|---|---|---|---|
| | Genl[b] | C-14[c] | Genl | Genl | C-14 | Genl | C-14 | Genl | C-14 |
| Pine | 92.9 | 92.1 | 4.0 | 95.2 | 77.2 | 100 | 100 | 98.2 | 83.3 |
| Oak | 7.1 | 7.9 | 56.0 | 0 | 4.5 | 0 | 0 | 0 | 14.6 |
| Monocot | 0 | 0 | 4.0 | 0 | 0 | 0 | 0 | 0 | 0 |
| Cottonwood/Willow | 0 | 0 | 0 | 1.9 | 0 | 0 | 0 | 0 | 0 |
| Dicot | 0 | 0 | 24.0 | 0 | 0 | 0 | 0 | 0 | 0 |
| Walnut | 0 | 0 | 0 | 0 | 11.4 | 0 | 0 | 0 | 0 |
| No. of samples | 3 | 5 | 5 | 6 | 5 | 1 | 3 | 4 | 3 |
| No. of identifications | 14 | 63 | 25 | 105 | 44 | 11 | 37 | 55 | 48 |

a. Numbers are the percentage of all seed-containing samples where a taxon is present.

b. Genl = charcoal identification sample.

c. C-14 = radiocarbon sample.

not to the low foothills that contain all of the sites discussed here. One explanation may be that wood in the sites' immediate areas could have been overexploited, forcing wider procurement. Such a situation has been documented in the nearby Mimbres area of the U.S. Southwest (Minnis 1985). It is also possible that the inhabitants of the Core Zone expended extra effort to obtain pine as a preferred fuel. Site 242 has been characterized as an administrative node of the Casas Grandes polity that likely contained low-level elites, and it stands out in the preceding table for its near-exclusive reliance on pine in all contexts.

The 242 community shows another fuel difference as well. Its assemblage of propagules contained many maize kernels but few charred cupules. The latter generally result from use of corncobs as fuel. That this was a common practice in the Medio period is shown by the much higher incidence of charred cupules at the other three sites (refer to table 7.1). The use of corncob fuel thus seems to have been more limited at site 242 than at its large and small neighbors. Instead, the most common fuel in the 242 community was pine, which certainly was more costly than locally available alternatives.

Charcoal samples also were recovered from the conical pit-ovens that were discussed earlier in this volume. (The site 188 oven is again included in this table, although it is not of the large, conical type discussed in chapter 1.) Table 7.5 summarizes the most common wood taxa identified. For all ovens except those on site 204, additional wood identifications were made from radiocarbon samples before they were processed. These also are shown in the table. It is clear that pine is the most common wood used in these large ovens. The only exception to this statement is one of the large ovens at site 204 (refer to chap. 1), where oak was the most common fuel.

It is well known that fuel selection reflects choices about the physical characteristics of different woods, including availability, form, size, and cultural or symbolic significance (e.g., K. Adams 2004). All these factors can be invoked to explain the dominance of pine charcoal in the ovens and in the platform hearths of site 242. The combustion properties of the wood may have been especially important in the ovens. Pine is an excellent, fast-burning fuel that produces a rapid rise in temperature. Rapid heating to a very high temperature is consistent with both the extensive cracking observed in the rock linings of all of the conical pit-ovens, and the sintering of some of the adobe plaster covering the middle and lower parts of their walls. Refer to chapter 1 for discussion and illustration of conical pit-oven construction.

Fuel abundance and piece size also are considerations in explaining the choice of pine for conical pit-oven fuel. Pit-ovens use a great deal of fuel, and their extensive use could rapidly deplete local wood resources. In an experimental study, Dering (1999:665) found that 224 kg of wood was required to heat 250 kg of rock in a hemispherical baking pit that measured only 1.5 m in diameter by about 0.75 m in depth (about 0.9 cu m in volume). The four conical pit-ovens we excavated had volumes that averaged 8.6 cu m (see table 1.1). The large ones at Casas Grandes averaged 16 cu m, and the largest oven at the primate center was a vast 25 cu m in volume. Our smallest conical pit-ovens are about eight times the volume of the hemispherical one used by Dering. We cannot say, however, that his figure of 224 kg of wood should be multiplied by a factor of eight in the Chihuahuan case, as so little is known about the efficiency of conical pit-ovens. Without experimentation, we can only say that hundreds of kilograms of fuel would have been needed per firing. Moreover, the intense heat required for the baking episode would best be produced by large pieces of wood. It may well be that pine was the only fuel available in such quantities and piece sizes by late Medio times. In a succeeding section of this chapter, we contend that substantial environmental change was produced by the field clearing and fuel needs of the large human populations of the late Medio period.

This explanation also could account for the just-discussed preponderance of pine in intramural hearths at late Medio site 242. Recall that these mostly were platform hearths of a much more elaborate kind than was found in other neighboring communities. Pine was an equally elaborate fuel that could have been a costly solution to the deteriorating late Medio fuel supply in the lowlands. It is unfortunate that we do not know the proportions of different fuels from the primate center of Casas Grandes, where the region's most elite people likely resided and where the platform hearths were especially elaborate. We can envision a situation in which high-status lowland people controlled the supply of imported pine, reserving some for their own use and allocating some to fueling the large ovens that supported public feasting. We have asserted elsewhere that the large, conical pit-ovens were likely used for public feasting, which was an activity under the auspices of the regional elite (Minnis and Whalen 2005).

Finally, there is the possibility that pine had significance beyond its combustion properties and availability. As a plant from higher, moister elevations, for example, it could have had symbolic associations with water or rainfall. Ethnographic studies show that plants frequently have ritual and symbolic connotations to their users (e.g., Castetter, Bell, and Grove 1938; Huckell and Toll 2004). Particular plants also may be associated with status, either by being directly under the control of leaders or by playing prominent roles in activities such as feasting (Lepofsky 2004).

**Table 7.6**  Wood Charcoal from Early and Late Medio Contexts

| Taxon | Early Medio | | Late Medio | |
|---|---|---|---|---|
| | Ubiquity[a] | Abundance[b] | Ubiquity | Abundance |
| Oak | 97.4 | 54.0 | 70.6 | 42.1 |
| Pine | 68.4 | 20.9 | 64.7 | 27.0 |
| Mesquite | 44.7 | 6.9 | 35.3 | 13.3 |
| Piñon | 39.5 | 11.7 | 23.5 | 9.1 |
| Juniper | 21.1 | 3.6 | 0 | 0 |
| Cottonwood/Willow | 15.8 | 2.9 | 35.3 | 8.5 |

a. Ubiquity is the percentage of flotation samples containing a taxon.
b. Abundance is the percentage of individual pieces of a type.

**Table 7.7**  Wood Charcoal Frequencies in Early and Late Medio Contexts

| | Oak | Pine | Mesquite | Piñon/ Juniper | Cottonwood/ Willow | **Total** |
|---|---|---|---|---|---|---|
| **Early Medio** | | | | | | |
| Observed | 314 | 119 | 40 | 89 | 17 | 579 |
| Expected | 294.2 | 129.9 | 49.6 | 79.8 | 25.5 | 579 |
| Adj. residual[a] | 3.0 | −2.1 | −2.7 | 2.4 | −3.3 | |
| **Late Medio** | | | | | | |
| Observed | 90 | 58 | 27 | 19 | 18 | 212 |
| Expected | 107.8 | 48.2 | 18.4 | 28.2 | 9.5 | 212 |
| Adj. residual[a] | −3.0 | 2.1 | 2.7 | −2.4 | 3.3 | |

a. Adjusted residual values greater than 1.96 indicate cells that contain significant differences between the observed frequencies and those expected under the null hypothesis of no significant difference. The sign shows the direction of the difference.

## Diachronic Change in Wood Use

Site 204 provides the best data set with which to examine change in wood use through the Medio period. Table 7.6 contrasts wood remains from early and late Medio rooms. Thirty-eight samples were analyzed from floor and feature contexts in early Medio Rooms 1–8 and 50–52, and 579 pieces of wood were identified. For the late Medio Rooms 60–65 and 70–72, the count is 17 samples and 212 identified pieces from floor and feature contexts.

Table 7.7 shows observed and expected abundance counts for each type of wood. There is a significant difference in the proportions of the different types of wood charcoal between the early and late parts of the Medio period in the present sample ($\chi^2 = 30.09$, df = 4, $p < .0001$). The adjusted residuals show that significant differences in proportion were found in every cell of the table. This suggests a substantial difference in wood-use patterns between the two time intervals. In the early part of the Medio, oak and piñon/juniper were present at significantly higher than expected frequencies, whereas pine, mesquite, and cottonwood/willow were found at significantly lower than expected frequencies. The late part of the Medio reverses these trends, with oak and piñon/juniper at significantly lower than expected frequencies and the frequencies of pine, mesquite, and cottonwood/willow significantly higher than expected.

Changes in wood species proportions in ethnobotanical samples often have been interpreted as reflections of human impact on prehistoric environments (e.g., K. Adams 2004; Huckell and Toll 2004; Kohler and Matthews 1988; Minnis 1985). In the Classic Mimbres area, for example, charcoal species proportions are used to trace increasing floodplain clearing, the consequent exhaustion of riparian firewood sources, and the necessity to travel to uplands to secure wood from coniferous trees (Minnis 1985). Kohler and Matthews (1988) demonstrate reduction of piñon and juniper forests and the establishment of a more open, shrubby vegetation pattern as a result of human agricultural activity around Mesa Verde.

Today, site 204 lies in an open setting surrounded by grass and shrubs. Mesquite is common, and cottonwoods and willows grow in the bottom of the adjacent drainage. We do not see this as the community's original environment, however. Instead, the adjacent hillslopes likely had a heavier covering of oak, piñon, and juniper than is presently the case. The early Medio wood charcoal data support this interpretation, as table 7.7 shows that oak, piñon, and juniper charcoal were well represented there. The abundance of all of these woods declines significantly in the late Medio, and we take this pattern to represent decreasing tree cover in the environs of the community. Like Kohler and Matthews (1988), we attribute the reduction of these trees to field clearing as well as their use for fuel. Preceding discussion of propagule frequencies made the same point, attributing the increasing presence of weedy annuals to field clearing. Even so, the area obviously was not entirely deforested. Oak, piñon, and juniper charcoal still are present in the fire pits of the site's late Medio occupation.

The observed decline in the use of oak, piñon, and juniper in the late Medio was compensated for by an increase in several other woods: pine, mesquite, and cottonwood or willow. Like the inhabitants of the Classic Mimbres area (Minnis 1985), the late Medio population of the 204 community obtained an increasing proportion of their fuel supply from the conifers of higher elevations. The Arroyo la Tinaja, on which the site is located, is one of the region's major access corridors from lower elevations into the mountains. Increased use also was made of the wood of shrubby plants (e.g., mesquite) and of cottonwoods and willows that still grow in the adjacent arroyo bottom. We consider it probable that the changes just discussed resulted from human activity rather than from climatic change. This statement is verified by the presence of the same wood species in early and late Medio contexts. It is their proportions that differ, and anthropogenic factors are the most likely causes of this change.

## Animal Foods

Animals supplemented plant foods as the second aspect of Medio period subsistence, although their contribution traditionally has been minimized. Di Peso characterized the Casas Grandes people as "virtually vegetarians" (Di Peso 1974:2:618). He based this statement on "the surprisingly small amount of trash material" contributed by animal remains (1974:2:744, n. 10). As succeeding discussion will show, we suspect that animal remains were significantly under-recovered at the primate center and that they played a more important role in subsistence than originally believed. This section examines animal use, first at the primate center and its neighbors and then across the Medio period.

## The Zooarchaeology of Casas Grandes

Remains of a wide variety of animal species came from the primate center. Bison, antelope, deer, rabbit, dog, and some rodents such as gophers were seen as food resources. Others like fox, wolf, skunk, bobcat, mountain lion, bear, turkey, and macaw were classed as "socio-religious objects" (Di Peso, Rinaldo, and Fenner 1974:8:248–308). Unfortunately, we do not know the total number of animal bones that were recovered. The Casas Grandes report contains a table of bone counts for some species, which sum to 2,689 specimens (Di Peso, Rinaldo, and Fenner 1974:8:fig. 299-8). In subsequent discussion, all references are to volume 8 of the Casas Grandes report, and only page and figure numbers are given. The figure of 2,689 is not the total assemblage size, as the table just cited does not include some of the mammals shown in a minimum-number-of-individuals count in another table (fig. 296-8). Rather, the bone count just given appears to include only the common taxa. The full count from Casas Grandes likely was around 3,000 bones, excluding the many macaw and turkey remains that were analyzed separately in the original study.

The mammal bones from the primate center were combined into what were termed "minimum faunal counts," abbreviated as MFC. These are "the smallest number of individuals of a species that can be demonstrated from a given provenience by age, sex, size, and duplication of elements" (p. 246). This equates to the minimum number of individuals measurement in use in today's faunal studies. The number of individuals represented at Casas Grandes by the MFC units is variably reported as 862 (p. 242), 824 (p. 244), and 860 (p. 253). The MFC figures for each species were then multiplied by the weight of meat expected from an individual of that type, and the resulting product is the contribution of that species to the total amount of meat available for consumption in the Medio period. The figures and percentages that result produced the often-cited conclusion that "bison provided far more meat than any other wild species in all periods" at Casas Grandes (p. 244, figs. 297-8 and 298-8).

For bison, the analysis seems to have been done as follows. There were 152 bison bones recovered at Casas Grandes (p. 245, fig. 299-8). These included "cranial material and post-cranial skeletal elements" (p. 253). This amounted to 5 percent of the site's total bone sample of ca. 3,000 pieces. These 152 bison bones were combined into an MFC of 29 bison and 19 unspecific bovids (p. 242, fig. 296-8). All came from apparently unmixed Medio period contexts, so that the 19 bovids were assumed to be bison, for a total of 48 individuals. The MFC percentage of bison is given in another table as 5.8 percent of an MFC total of 824. This percentage equates to 45 individuals, and we will use this figure for subsequent discussion. This means that, on average, each individual bison was represented by 3.4 bones.

**Table 7.8**    Frequencies of Small and Medium-Sized Game Animals at
Casas Grandes

| Animal | No. of bones | Pct. of bones[a] | Pct. MFC |
|---|---|---|---|
| Jackrabbit | 211 | 7.0 | 19.6 |
| Deer | 431 | 14.4 | 11.4 |
| Antelope | 1,602 | 53.4 | 33.5 |
| Bear | 220 | 7.3 | not given |

a. Based on our site-wide estimate of 3,000 bones.
*Source:* From data in Di Peso, Rinaldo, and Fenner 1974: vol. 8.

The total estimated weight of Medio period meat is given as 59,699 pounds (p. 245), of which 52 percent is estimated to have come from bison (p. 244, fig. 297-8). This percentage equates to 31,027 pounds of bison meat, or an average of 685 pounds for each of the 45 animals. This seems optimistic, as Wheat (1967) provided a considerably smaller estimate of edible meat from an adult bison: 550 pounds for a bull and 400 pounds for a cow. The very questionable assumption here, however, is that 100 percent of the edible meat from 45 bison entered the Medio period food supply. The analysis seems to have assumed that 3.4 bison bones equals 1 complete bison equals 685 pounds of bison meat available at Casas Grandes. We find this logic fallacious and see no evidence to support the claim that massive quantities of bison meat were consumed at the primate center. Instead, all available data indicate that bison was a minor meat source, although it may have been a prestigious one that was available only to a select few.

Instead of heavy reliance on bison, we envision Medio period meat procurement as based primarily on the small and medium-sized animals that make up most of the bone count at Casas Grandes (p. 245, fig. 299-8). Table 7.8 shows the proportions of the most common species, based on their bone counts (p. 245, fig. 299-8). Other animals represented at the primate center were cottontail rabbits, dogs, and rodents. These cannot be included in the table, as we have no bone counts for them. In any case, it seems clear from the table that antelope and deer were by far the most common game animals at Casas Grandes, accounting together for two-thirds of the site's faunal material. The inclusion of rabbits pushes this figure to about three-quarters of the whole assemblage. The Casas Grandes faunal analyst noted that dogs may have been eaten, as the remains often came from young animals. The bones of bears, on the other hand, were concentrated in a few locations, and many of the bones were worked. It is thus argued that bears were used more commonly in trophy contexts and were not eaten to the same extent as common food animals (p. 252).

## The Zooarchaeology of Casas Grandes' Neighbors

Deposits from the four sites discussed in this volume were screened through one-quarter-inch mesh. A total of 773 bones came from site 204, 81 from site 242, 391 from site 231, and 327 from site 317. Table 7.9 shows counts and percentages of identified

**Table 7.9**  Faunal Remains from the Neighbors of Casas Grandes[a]

| | Site 204 | Site 231 | Site 242 | Site 317 |
|---|---|---|---|---|
| Antelope | — | — | — | — |
| Artyodactyl | — | 1.5% (6) | — | 0.3% (1) |
| Bear | — | — | — | — |
| Bird | 3.8% (29) | 0.5% (2) | — | 2.5% (8) |
| Bison | — | — | — | — |
| Carnivora | 0.4% (3) | 0.3% (1) | — | 0.6% (2) |
| Cats | — | — | — | — |
| Coatimundi | 1.3% (10) | — | — | — |
| Coyote/Dog/Fox | 6.0% (46) | — | — | — |
| Deer | 1.3% (9) | — | — | — |
| Fish | 0.1% (1) | — | — | 0.31 (1) |
| Gopher | 0.8% (6) | 0.5% (2) | — | 1.5% (5) |
| Mammal, small | 1.0% (8) | 0.5% (2) | — | 6.1% (20) |
| Mammal, sm–med | 15.5% (120) | — | — | — |
| Mammal, med | 3.2% (25) | 0.3% (1) | — | 2.5% (8) |
| Mammal, med–lg | 4.7% (36) | — | 18.5%(15) | — |
| Mammal, large | 0.1% (1) | 1.0% (4) | 38.3% (31) | 1.5% (5) |
| Mammal, ? size | — | — | — | — |
| Mouse | 1.0% (8) | — | 1.2% (1) | — |
| Muskrat | — | — | — | — |
| Rabbit, unspecific | — | — | — | 6.1% (20) |
| Rabbit, cottontail | 6.7% (52) | 0.3% (1) | — | 1.5% (5) |
| Rabbit, jackrabbit | 23.7%(184) | 3.3% (13) | — | 4.9% (16) |
| Raccoon | — | — | — | — |
| Rat | 1.4% (11) | 0.3% (1) | 2.5% (2) | 0.3% (1) |
| Reptile | 3.2% (25) | 23.3%(91) | — | 2.5% (8) |
| Rodent | 0.1% (1) | — | — | — |
| Sheep, bighorn | — | — | — | — |
| Squirrel | 1.3% (9) | — | 1.2% (1) | 7.8% (25) |
| Skunk | 0.3% (2) | — | — | — |
| *Sigmodontine* rodent | — | 1.8% (7) | — | 2.2% (7) |
| Unidentified | 24.1% (187) | 66.4% (260) | 38.3% (31) | 59.6% (195) |
| **Total** | 100.0% (773) | 100.0% (391) | 100.0% (81) | 100.0% (327) |

a. Figures given as percentages, with counts in parentheses.

*Sources:* Identifications from sites 231 and 317 by Cannon and Etnier (1997); identifications from sites 242 and 204 by Schmidt (2005).

bone from each site. The faunal remains recovered from sites 231 and 317 were identified by Cannon and Etnier (1997), and the remains from sites 242 and 204 were studied by Schmidt (2005). Although these analysts did not identify the remains to identical groups, the results are close enough to allow comparison between the assemblages.

Several patterns are evident in the faunal data, in particular the distinctive nature of the assemblage from site 242. The community is unusual in two ways. First, few bones were recovered there. The other two small sites (317 and 231) yielded more than four times as many bones as site 242, even though a little less excavation was done at each of these two sites than at 242. The same excavation techniques and screen mesh size were in use at all three sites. We doubt that preservation was at issue, as the soils at the three sites are not significantly different. Rather, we suspect that the paucity of faunal remains from site 242 is due to different consumption behavior.

A second characteristic of the faunal assemblages reinforces the idea that meat consumption was different at site 242. There, the most common analytic taxon is large mammals, accounting for 38 percent of all bones from the site and 62 percent of the few identifiable bones. In this category, our analyst included animals the size of cows and bison (Schmidt 2005). As the remains all came from apparently undisturbed Medio period contexts, we presume the large mammals to be bison. Large mammal bones are far less common at the other three sites studied here, where they constitute 1.0 percent at 231, 1.5 percent at 317, and 0.1 percent at 204. Furthermore, the next most common category recovered at site 242 is medium-to-large mammals, in which category our analyst included creatures of deer and antelope size (Schmidt 2005). Large and medium-to-large mammal remains combined account for 92 percent of the site's identified bones, and the preceding table shows that this is a far higher percentage than was found at any other site. A disparity of this magnitude likely represents a different pattern of meat consumption between site 242 and the other Medio period communities studied here.

Larger mammals often constitute preferred foods, and their concentration in elite contexts is a common situation in hierarchical societies such as Chaco (Plog 1997), the Hohokam (Gasser and Kwiatkowski 1991), and the Mississippians (Knight 2004). In the present sample, large mammal remains occur in the greatest proportion at the primate center and at an administrative node (site 242). Both of these places likely contained elite people, although those of Casas Grandes undoubtedly stood much higher than the inhabitants of the 242 community. Even so, the best-quality meats were likely most available to the upper segment of the Medio population for their consumption or under their control, for instance during feasting events. In contrast, what appear to be ordinary residential sites have more diverse faunal assemblages that are dominated by smaller game, especially rabbits. The preceding table shows that cottontails and jackrabbits are the most commonly recovered taxa from sites 317 and 204, and they are among the most common remains from 231. Rabbits evidently were a commonly used resource in Medio times, not only in the Casas Grandes area, but in more distant areas as well. About 97 percent of the animal bones from Villa Ahumada, ca. 140 km northeast of Casas Grandes, are from rabbits (Cruz Antillón et al. 2004). The faunal assemblage from the Joyce Well site, ca. 150 km north of Casas Grandes in southwestern New Mexico, also was dominated by rabbits (Skibo, McCluney, and Walker 2002).

The suggested association between elite people and consumption of the meat of larger mammals in turn implies that the faunal recovery from Casas Grandes may not be as biased as previously thought. We earlier ascribed the dominance of large mammals in the primate center's assemblage to lack of fine screening, and this factor doubtless had some effect. Fine screens were used at site 242, however, where large animal remains also were present in high proportions. The primate center's bone assemblage thus may be as much a reflection of a pattern of elite consumption or control as of a lack of fine screening.

Also to be considered here is the organization and scale of hunting. The typical faunal assemblage from residential sites during the Medio period emphasizes rabbits and other small animals, suggesting that large game was not easily obtained. How, then, did communities like Casas Grandes and site 242 acquire the meat of larger mammals? Several options are possible. Tribute or offerings of meat may have been required by the primate center, so that the population intensified hunting, probably by going farther afield than they would have for domestic provisioning. Alternatively, there may have been a large-scale exchange in food whereby communities better situated for hunting traded meat for other items. We know that animals from the Sierra Madre were present at the primate center. These include bear, white-tailed deer, mountain lion, and striped skunk (Di Peso, Rinaldo, and Fenner 1974:8:250). The sites studied in this volume are close to the mountains, yet they do not provide evidence of much hunting of animals like deer. We do not know of Sierra Madre communities that specialized in hunting for trade, but too little research has been done there to permit consideration of the issue.

## Diachronic Change in Animal Use

We have shown that the late Medio period was characterized by substantial landscape change from firewood collecting and soil-disturbing activities such as field clearing. Heavy use of faunal resources likely was a parallel process that could have led to more use of small game as well as to greater diversity in hunted species. Changes in the political and ritual organization of Casas Grandes also could have affected the distribution of faunal remains. High-quality meat was likely associated with elites, and changes in their numbers or status could have affected the demand for high-quality foods. The best way to monitor change in animal use through time is to examine early and late Medio assemblages from the deep trash deposits at site 204. The midden test pit levels yielded a total of 442 pieces of bone, of which 373 were identified either as specific animals or as members of a size class (e.g., medium-sized mammal).

Bone abundance was compared in the early and late midden test pit levels. For the early Medio, the figure is 18.5 g of bone per cubic meter of excavated soil. The late Medio figure is a comparable 22.4 g per cubic meter. This indication of little change in bone abundance over time is confirmed by a t-test of mean bone weight in early Medio levels ($n = 42$, mean weight = 2.14, SD = 2.51) versus those of the late Medio ($n = 101$; mean = 2.16; SD = 4.79). Although the standard deviations show that the late Medio levels were more variable in their bone weights, the t-test did not detect a significant difference in mean bone weight between early and late Medio midden test pit levels ($t = -.024$, df = 141, $p = .981$). This suggests that animals were used similarly all through the Medio period.

Animal variability in the early and late Medio is expressed simply by counting the numbers of different taxa identified in each site 204 midden test pit level. Mean numbers of identified taxa were then computed for the early levels ($n = 29$; mean = 2.52,

**Table 7.10** Densities of Faunal Taxa in the Site 204 Midden

| Taxa | Early Medio | Late Medio |
|---|---|---|
| All rabbits | 13.0[a] | 9.5[a] |
| Jackrabbit | 9.0 | 7.8 |
| Cottontail | 4.0 | 1.7 |
| Dog or Coyote | 1.8 | 2.3 |
| Small-to-medium mammal | 4.0 | 5.0 |
| Medium-sized mammal | 0.2 | 0.4 |
| Medium-to-large mammal | 0.8 | 0.3 |

a. pieces per cubic meter of excavated soil

SD = 1.33) and for the late ones ($n$ = 68, mean = 2.22, SD = 1.28). These means are very similar, and a t-test showed no significant difference in the number of identified taxa ($t$ = 1.034, df = 95, $p$ = .304). The implication is that exploitation of particular types of animals was about the same throughout the entire Medio period.

Table 7.10 shows the frequencies of identified taxa and mammal size classes in early and late Medio levels of the site 204 midden. The data are densities, or bone counts per cubic meter of excavated soil. It is clear from the data that the early and late Medio inhabitants of site 204 were using much the same kinds of animals.

The preceding table indicates that not all of the animals listed were being taken in the same frequencies in early and late Medio times. Rabbits clearly were used heavily throughout the period, although the table shows a decline in the density of rabbit bone from early to late Medio. The significance of this difference was established by a single-variable chi-squared test, where the expected frequency was provided by the proportion of early and late Medio deposits (respectively, 32 percent and 68 percent) in the midden sample. There were 65 rabbit bones from early test pit levels (expected value: 53.1), and 101 bones came from late levels (expected value: 112.9). The difference between the observed and expected frequencies is significant ($\chi^2$ = 3.92, df = 1, $p$ < .05). Early Medio midden test pit levels contain more rabbit bone than expected, whereas late Medio levels have less.

There are differences in the frequencies of jackrabbits and cottontails between the early and late Medio. Table 7.11 shows these data, plus the frequencies expected under the null hypothesis of no significant difference in proportions. Calculation of chi-squared shows that there is a significant difference between the observed and expected frequencies of the two kinds of rabbits in the early and late parts of the Medio period ($\chi^2$ = 4.57, df = 1, $p$ < .05). The table shows the direction of the difference: there were fewer jackrabbits and more cottontails than expected in the early Medio, whereas the late Medio deposits contained more jackrabbits and fewer cottontails.

Proportions of these two kinds of rabbits long have been known to provide data relevant to environmental conditions and to hunting practices (e.g., Flannery 1966). Of particular utility here is the lagomorph index, which is simply the number of identified cottontail rabbit specimens divided by the total number of identified specimens

**Table 7.11**    Rabbit Type Frequencies in the Early and Late Medio

|  | Jackrabbit | Cottontail | **Total** |
|---|---|---|---|
| **Early Medio** | | | |
| Observed | 44 | 21 | **65** |
| Expected | 49.7 | 15.3 | |
| **Late Medio** | | | |
| Observed | 83 | 18 | **101** |
| Expected | 77.3 | 23.7 | |
| **Total** | **127** | **39** | **166** |

of all lagomorphs. Resulting values can range from 0 to 1.0. The index can be a useful reflection of prehistoric environmental conditions because cottontails and jackrabbits have somewhat different habitat preferences. Southwestern archaeological data (Bayham and Hatch 1985; Szuter 1991b) show cottontail remains to be more abundant on heavily vegetated upland sites, where they can hide successfully from predators. Jackrabbits, on the other hand, predominate in sparsely vegetated alluvial plain settings, where their speed enables them to flee from pursuers. From this observation, it has been argued that the proportion of cottontail rabbits in lagomorph assemblages can provide a rough measure of ground cover in a particular environment (e.g., Bayham and Hatch 1985; Szuter 1991a, b; Szuter and Bayham 1989). Further, Szuter and Bayham (1989) and Szuter (1991a, b) have demonstrated that Hohokam sites occupied for great lengths of time show a decrease in the lagomorph index (i.e., the frequency of cottontail rabbits declines). The longer a site is occupied, they argue, the more of the surrounding ground cover is destroyed. This renders the area more favorable to jackrabbits and less so to cottontails. These conclusions are based on the assumption that jackrabbits and cottontails were taken in rough proportion to their actual abundance. From the data in table 7.11, the lagomorph index for the early Medio midden deposits at site 204 is 0.44, and that of the late Medio declines considerably to 0.21. Following the studies just cited, we conclude that increasingly heavy use of site 204 after ca. A.D. 1300 led to change in the surrounding environment. The dense vegetation favored by cottontails is seen as declining somewhat, shifting toward the more open habitat preferred by jackrabbits. This is the same conclusion we reached from analysis of weed and wood charcoal ubiquities.

## Plants and Animals in the Medio Period

The Casas Grandes excavations were conducted before modern data-recovery techniques of fine screening and flotation were widely used. Therefore, the plant and animal remains from the four sites discussed in this volume offer the first large, modern data set from which to examine diet, environmental conditions, and the political economy of the Casas Grandes heartland. As has long been assumed, domesticated plants were the major components of the subsistence economy. Maize was preeminent, and other cultigens included beans, squash, gourds, cotton, and probably agave. We do not know the exact proportions in which Medio period cultigens were used, and there may have been variability across communities. Everywhere, however, locally available wild plants were collected to supplement agricultural productivity. Agave always was important to Medio populations, but there is the possibility of its increased use in the late part of the period at site 204. Site 242 has been postulated to be an administrative node of Casas Grandes, and it likely was the residence of rural managers who may have been low-level elites. Preceding chapters have shown that site 242 stands out from its neighbors in every analyzed artifact category. Its food plants are about the same as those of its neighbors, but its wood charcoal data were very different. There was little use of the corncob fuel commonly burned in Medio period intramural fire pits. Instead, nonlocal pine fueled the 242 fires, which clearly were burning a more costly fuel than their neighbors were.

The faunal remains from Casas Grandes and its neighbors offer clues about the ecology and subsistence of the polity. Faunal remains demonstrate that meat sources differed between communities, with the primate center and site 242 utilizing more desirable large mammal species. We refute the often-cited statement that bison were the major meat source at Casas Grandes. Bison appears to have been a relatively rare food, although it probably was a prestigious one. Medium-sized animals such as antelope appear to have provided much of the community's meat. This still is a desirable, high-status meat source, a point emphasized by comparison of the primate center's faunal remains with those of the four neighboring sites. All of these communities made relatively more use of small mammals such as rabbits, as is common among prehispanic peoples in the desert areas of the North American Southwest. Although it was a large ball-court community, site 204 shows little use of the more desirable meat of bison, deer, and antelope. Instead, it displays the common pattern of reliance on small mammals.

There are several indicators of anthropogenic change in the environs of site 204 between the early and late parts of the Medio period. First, weedy annuals such as goosefoot, pigweed, and purslane increase in frequency from early to late Medio times. These weeds are widely recognized as "disturbance taxa" that thrive in anthropogenic contexts such as cultivated fields. Second, the frequencies of oak, juniper, and piñon charcoal decline from the early to late Medio. These are piedmont slope trees from the vicinity of the site, and we attribute their decline to increasing field clearance. Third, we documented a decline in cottontail rabbits and a concomitant increase in jackrabbits from early to late parts of the Medio period. This situation is attributed to decreasing vegetation cover around heavily occupied sites. It seems, then, that the inhabitants of the 204 community had a noticeable impact on the ecology of their surroundings by the late part of the Medio period.

# 8

## Exotic and Ritual Items

Casas Grandes long has been famous for the quantity and variety of such imported and exotic items as marine shell, parrot cages and burials, minerals of many sorts, and copper ornaments. Also present is a category of items that likely functioned in ritual contexts. Sometimes, of course, the two categories overlap in the same object (e.g., conch-shell trumpets). The primate center unquestionably possessed a more impressive array of exotica and ritual items than any other site in the U.S. Southwest or northern Mexico. Nevertheless, some of these items were found at the neighboring sites we excavated. This chapter presents a comparative discussion of the exotica and ritual paraphernalia from these communities.

### Exotic Items

The full set of exotica at Casas Grandes already has been extensively described and illustrated in the site report. Here, we present only summary information on the classes of exotica useful to this study: shell, macaws, minerals, and copper.

### Shell

Marine shell was used for ornaments in northwest Chihuahua at least since Viejo times, although those assemblages include only a few common species from the Gulf of California (Di Peso, Rinaldo, and Fenner 1974:6:385). A much greater quantity and diversity of shell was brought from the same area to the primate center in the succeeding Medio period. The Casas Grandes report presents an extensive description and analysis of the shell and the ornaments made from it, including an ornament typology of which the present study makes use. Finally, as much as possible of the Casas Grandes shell is identified to genus and species.

Shell ornaments at Casas Grandes were classified in an elaborate system of types and subtypes, and these are condensed into a few large groups for the present study. These condensed groups are the same ones used by Bradley (1999: 216–17) in a large study of shell ornaments from a number of sites in the U.S. Southwest and northern Mexico. Table 8.1 shows these categories and their frequencies at Casas Grandes and at the neighboring sites studied in this volume. Site 242 is not shown, as no shell items were recovered there. The regional imbalance in shell frequency is clear from the table: Casas

**Table 8.1**   Shell Items at Chihuahuan Sites

| Item | Casas Grandes | Site 204 | Site 231 | Site 317 |
|---|---|---|---|---|
| Truncated shell bead | 11,542 | 6 | | |
| Whole shell bead | 3,738,650 | 17 | 1 | |
| Disk bead | 41,994 | 5 | | |
| Other type of bead | 275 | 1 | | |
| Tinkler | 21,852 | 11 | | |
| Pendant | 4,218 | 17 | 3 | 1 |
| Bracelet | 435 | 2 | | |
| Other worked pieces | 141 | 23 | 7 | 5 |
| Unfinished pieces | 42 | | | |
| Unworked pieces | no data | 48 | 6 | 6 |

*Source:* Data for Casas Grandes are from Di Peso, Rinaldo, and Fenner (1974: vol. 6).

**Figure 8.1** Four examples of shell pendants from site 204. The scale is in millimeters.

Grandes had an enormous quantity, whereas its neighbors had very little. Among the neighboring sites, 204 had by far the largest inventory of worked and unworked shell. The site yielded examples of all of the major artifact categories found at Casas Grandes, even though its assemblage was only a small fraction of the primate center's. Figure 8.1 shows some of the shell pendants from site 204.

One category of shell item that is absent at the neighboring sites is unfinished pieces. These were present at Casas Grandes, where they consisted of unfinished pieces that showed clear evidence of working, e.g., a partially drilled hole or an incompletely cut line. There was much other evidence for shell working at the primate center, including tools, manufacturing debris, and caches of unworked shells. Most of these categories of evidence are absent at the neighboring sites studied here. There are no unfinished items, nor are there recognizable tools or shell caches. Table 8.1 shows that there are worked and unworked fragments of shell at all of the neighboring sites, but it is not clear whether these represent production or breakage of ornaments. Site 204 has the largest number of worked and unworked shell fragments, which were spread thinly over all of the excavated areas. There was nothing like the heavy concentrations of shell debris that marked Hohokam workshops at Snaketown (Haury 1976:306). We see no compelling indication that anything more than occasional shell working was done at site 204, and the same is true for small sites 231 and 317. From the data in hand, it appears that most of the region's shell working was done at the primate center.

Whether or not they were made there, the greatest variety of shell ornaments outside of Casas Grandes is present at site 204. This situation seems to have been consistent across the site's occupation. About the same number of shell items came from early and late Medio midden levels and room contexts, and the diversity of early and late ornaments also was similar. Some small differences were apparent, however. Simple disk beads were much more common in the early Medio than in the late part of the period, but the opposite is true of shell tinklers. The Casas Grandes report noted that most late Viejo shell items were disk and whole-shell beads, with pendants, tinklers, and bracelets being less common (Di Peso, Rinaldo, and Fenner 1974:6:385). The site 204 early Medio shell assemblage dates immediately after the late Viejo, and it evidently carries on the tendencies of its predecessor. Unworked shell fragments were about twice as common in late Medio deposits as in early ones. We suspect that this is due to the types of shell being used in each time interval, and this question will be considered in more detail presently. To conclude this discussion, we note that shell count and ornament diversity were extremely low at small sites 231 and 317 (refer to table 8.1). Most of each site's assemblage consisted of worked and unworked fragments of shell rather than complete ornaments. The latter apparently were in very short supply in both communities, and the few fragments present likely came from broken ornaments. It seems that there was little, if any, ornament production in these small communities.

In addition to an enormous quantity of shell and a large variety of ornaments, Casas Grandes also stands out for the considerable number of marine genera represented in its shell assemblage. The site report lists 53 genera (Di Peso, Rinaldo, and Fenner 1974:6:405), and table 8.2 shows the frequencies of the most common of these. Also included are the frequencies of marine genera at the primate center's neighbors (Vargas 2004). Note that the Casas Grandes shell frequencies are calculated without the 3.7 million *Nassarius* shells, as the inclusion of so vast a number would have reduced all other generic frequencies nearly to zero. Lastly, we note that the shell identifications from Casas Grandes and from the neighboring sites were done by different analysts working more than a quarter-century apart, which could be a source of variability in the data set. For instance, the identification of *Petaloconchus* at site 204 but not in the much larger Casas Grandes sample could simply be an artifact of classification, or it could reflect a real difference in shell procurement. Generic frequencies also could be affected by classification and by the enormous disparity in the sample sizes. In general, however, the two analyses gave comparable results.

The table clearly shows the great diversity of the Casas Grandes assemblage compared to those of its neighbors. It is also clear, however, that most of the primate center's assemblage is composed of a few common genera. It is impossible to make precise frequency comparisons between Casas Grandes and its neighbors, as the latter samples are

**Table 8.2**  Types of Shell from Four Chihuahuan Sites

| Genus[a] | Casas Grandes | Site 204 | Site 231 | Site 317 |
|---|---|---|---|---|
| *Nassarius* | 3.7 million[b] | 1 (1.0%) | | |
| *Conus* | 31,365 (62.6%) | 16 (16.5%) | 1 (5.9%) | |
| *Olivella* | 11,856 (23.6%) | 5 (5.2%) | 1 (5.9%) | 2 (15.4%) |
| *Chama* | 4,765 (9.4%) | | | |
| *Laevicardium* | 1,144 (2.2%) | 1 (1.0%) | | |
| *Glycymeris* | 590 (1.2%) | 7 (7.2%) | | |
| *Aquipectin* | 147 (0.3%) | | | |
| *Dentalium* | 48 (0.1%) | | | |
| *Argopectin* | (<0.1%)[c] | 1 (1.0%) | | |
| *Turritella* | (<0.1%)[c] | 1 (1.0%) | | |
| *Cerithedia* | (<0.1%)[c] | 1 (1.0%) | | |
| *Petaloconchus* | | 2 (2.1%) | | |
| *Pinctada* | (<0.1%)[c] | 4 (4.1%) | | |
| Freshwater shell | 116 (0.2%) | 58 (59.9%) | 15 (88.2%) | 11 (84.6%) |

a. Forty other marine genera identified from Casas Grandes are not listed here, as they were not identified at any of the neighboring sites. The percentages for Casas Grandes reflect only the genera listed in this table.

b. This figure is excluded from percentage calculations due to its distorting effect.

c. Not included in the percentage calculations.

*Sources:* Data for Casas Grandes from Di Peso, Rinaldo, and Fenner (1974:6:405); data for other sites from Vargas (2004).

so much smaller than the former ones. Even so, we note that the same genera—*Conus, Olivella,* and *Glycymeris*—are among the most common at all four sites. Interestingly, however, the frequency order is not the same for all sites. A prodigious quantity of *Nassarius* shell was recovered from a single storage room at Casas Grandes, but that genus is rare or absent at all of the neighboring sites. It also was not recorded on the surfaces of our intensive survey sites. This observation hints at regional disparities in shell procurement or distribution.

The 53 marine genera reported from Casas Grandes represent the regional pinnacle of assemblage diversity. Site 204 takes second place with only 10 genera. Small sites 231 and 317 have impoverished assemblages that contain, respectively, two and one genera of marine shell. Table 8.2 shows another interesting pattern, which is the use of freshwater shell. Some was identified at Casas Grandes, where it was classed as *Rabdotus scheideanus,* but the table shows that it accounts for only a tiny fraction of the whole assemblage, nearly all of which was of marine origin. The situation is dramatically different among the neighboring sites, however, where 60 to 88 percent of the assemblages was freshwater shell. This appears to be a regional pattern: during our regional survey shell was collected whenever found on site surfaces. As many as possible of these were identified to genus (Vargas 2004). About 75 percent was found to be freshwater shell. The few marine specimens were mostly the common *Conus, Olivella,* and *Glycymeris* genera. The regional situation, then, is that the shell assemblage of the primate center was characterized by a great diversity of marine genera and little use of freshwater shell. The center's neighbors reverse this pattern, with much freshwater shell and few marine genera. Freshwater shell was available in local streams, and it doubtless was a low-cost alternative to marine shell. The 204 assemblage shows that freshwater shell was being used in place of marine shell, as it was made into a variety of ornaments.

The implication of this pattern is that Casas Grandes at its apogee controlled the regional marine shell supply and made little of it available to neighboring communities. Preceding chapters showed that the pinnacle of Casas Grandes' development was reached in the late Medio period. The proposed shell monopoly thus would date to that time interval. It is revealing to look at the composition of the early Medio shell assemblage at site 204, which predates the apogee of the primate center. Ten genera of marine shell were found there. Eight different genera came from early Medio midden levels or room contexts, whereas only two different genera were present in their late Medio successors. Hence, in the late Medio period, site 204 looks much like small sites 231 and 317 in terms of marine shell genera richness. In addition, freshwater shell made up 48 percent of the early Medio 204 assemblage, swelling to 78 percent by late Medio times. All of these data indicate considerably wider access to marine shell in the early part of the Medio period. By the late Medio, when Casas Grandes was reaching its peak, regional access to marine shell appears to have diminished sharply, and increasing use was made of lower-grade, and apparently uncontrolled, freshwater shell. The survey data support this conclusion, in that 75 percent of the identified shell on site surfaces was freshwater. Most of the ceramic assemblages of these sites contained Ramos Polychrome, demonstrating the presence of late Medio occupation components. This postulated control of marine shell seems to have extended only to the primate center's neighbors of the Inner and Middle Zones. Farther away, in what we termed the Outer Zone, the Casas Grandes–related Joyce Well site contained abundant marine shell of *Olivella, Glycymeris, Ostrea,* and *Nassarius,* and no freshwater shell was reported (Skibo, McCluney, and Walker 2002:35).

Lastly, we consider the absence of shell at site 242. As much earth was excavated there as at small sites 231 and 317, so that the lack of shell does not seem likely to be a function of small sample size. We cannot conclude that there was no shell whatsoever in the 242 community, of course, although almost certainly there was very little. This is a surprising observation, as site 242 was a relatively elaborate community. It had Casas Grandes–style architecture, macaw cages, a ceramic assemblage indicative of feasting, and the largest ritual complex known outside of the primate center. The site was interpreted as an administrative satellite of Casas Grandes whose role was to organize agricultural productivity in its part of the uplands.

The apparent paucity of shell at site 242 leads us to wonder how that commodity was used in the political and prestige economies of Casas Grandes. The question is a complex one that cannot be resolved with the small amount of data currently in hand. The original supposition was that shell at Medio period Casas Grandes served primarily for trade rather than for local use, and this was seen as a major departure from the pattern of the preceding Viejo period (Di Peso, Rinaldo, and Fenner 1974:7:385). Bradley (1999) also developed an argument that saw Casas Grandes as an active shell trader rather than simply as a passive recipient. Instead of interpreting shell as a purely commercial commodity, Minnis (1988, 1989) asserted that the shell of Casas Grandes represented hoards of elite wealth. Still others (e.g., Fish and Fish 1999; Whalen and Minnis 2001a) considered shell ornaments to be prestige goods. These interpretations are not mutually exclusive, and they may be recognizing different aspects of a multifaceted situation. Shell likely was valuable in some contexts, but probably not in all. The concept of value is a flexible construct, as discussed by Rissman (1988), who distinguishes between sacred and secular and public and private valuables in the same cultural context. Moreover, he shows that the use and ubiquity of these valuables are strongly dependent on which facet of status or authority is being displayed in a particular situation.

Whatever the case in the site 242 community, the data currently in hand indicate a relatively open situation of shell procurement and distribution in Viejo and early Medio times, followed by sharply limited distribution of marine shell in the late Medio. Further, the late Medio primate center of Casas Grandes was the procurer and controller of marine shell in northwest Chihuahua.

## Macaws

The remains of macaws and other parrots are widespread in the Pueblo Southwest, although there never were many of them. The top three macaw-yielding sites are Wupatki, with 41 birds; Pueblo Bonito, with 29; and Point-of-Pines, also with 29 (McKusick 2001:74–77). Sizeable macaw counts for the Southwest thus are on the order of tens of birds. In sharp contrast to this situation is Casas Grandes, where excavations produced the remains of 322 scarlet macaws (*Ara macao*), 81 military macaws (*Ara militaris*), and 100 specimens identifiable only to the genus *Ara* (Di Peso, Rinaldo, and Fenner 1974:8:274–75). This is far more birds than the combined total for all sites ever reported from the U.S. Southwest. Other evidence of aviculture at Casas Grandes is abundant, including at least 10 complete cages in the plaza of Unit 12, and a further 125 of the distinctive cage-door stones from other localities all over the site. All these data suggest that macaw husbandry was widespread in the community (Di Peso, Rinaldo, and Fenner 1974:2:734). Still unclear is whether macaws were bred at Casas Grandes, as their captive reproduction is notoriously difficult (see McKusick 2001:78 for a list of problems). The alternative is that macaws were kept but not bred at Casas Grandes, the supply being constantly replenished by the import of new, young birds. Whatever the case, it is abundantly clear that Casas Grandes stood orders of magnitude above any other community in the extent of its aviculture.

Although the vast majority of the region's macaw population was located at Casas Grandes, there is evidence that the birds were present at other neighboring sites as well. Observed on the surfaces of 15 communities were whole specimens or (more commonly) fragments of the perforated ground-stone disks that formed the doors of macaw cages at the primate center. A cage diagram, including the door stone, can be found in the Casas Grandes report (Di Peso, Rinaldo, and Fenner 1974:8:269). The cage-door stones observed on site surfaces were unearthed by looters, and broken or unattractive examples were discarded. In one case, the door stone and the stone plug used to

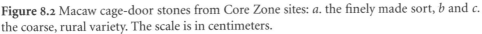

**Figure 8.2** Macaw cage-door stones from Core Zone sites: *a*. the finely made sort, *b* and *c*. the coarse, rural variety. The scale is in centimeters.

close it lay side-by-side on a room-block mound. Figure 8.2 shows some of these stones. Note that two different levels of quality are apparent in the cage-door stones. The finer variety is exemplified by the specimen in figure 8.2a. These cage-door stones are carefully ground all over, so that their faces and edges are as symmetrical as their central openings. Cage-door stones of this sort typify the primate center and closely related communities. The one shown in figure 8.2a is from site 242, the administrative node of Casas Grandes. The other type of macaw cage-door stone is simpler and cruder. It is represented by the specimens shown as figure 8.2b and c. Here, the central opening was carefully made, but the surfaces and outer edges were only partially smoothed, retaining much of the surface contour of the original stone. All of the cage-door stones found in the Core Zone, except for those at the primate center and at site 242, were of this rough, simple type. Only one of the 15 sites with cage-door stones has been excavated. This is site 204, where excavation revealed a macaw burial beneath the floor of Room 21 (see fig. 3.18). We therefore contend that the presence of cage-door stones on site surfaces is a reliable indicator of the practice of aviculture in a community.

All of the 15 sites with cage-door stones occurred in a specific part of our intensive survey area: the outer part of the Core Zone, or the area lying ca. 15 km to 30 km of the primate center. In the outer Core Zone, sites with cage-door stones were found in all environmental settings, from river valleys to uplands. The total number of outer Core Zone sites with macaw cages likely is greater than the observed 15 cases, as identification was dependent on chance exposure of the doors by looting and upon their discard on the sites after discovery. Unfortunately, we have no way to estimate how many of the sites of the outer Core Zone might contain macaw cages. Nevertheless, given that cage-door discovery is as chancy as it is, the fact that they were found on 15 sites raises the possibility that a good many more had unrevealed cages.

It is clear that cage-door stones were much rarer outside of the outer Core Zone. Our intensive survey of the Middle Zone, an area some 40–60 km from the primate center, did not locate a single cage-door stone among 172 Medio period room-block mounds. Looting was as extensive on these sites as on those of the Core Zone, and survey crews were instructed to look carefully for the stones. The fact that they found none does not mean that there were no macaw cages in Middle Zone communities, but it is clear that they were rarer there than in the Core Zone. Three cage-door stones were found on sites in southern Chihuahua and in the Sierra Madre, to the west (Minnis et al. 1993:273). It is clear, however, that most of the region's cages were concentrated at the primate center, with the second-largest set present on the sites of the outer Core Zone. A few cages were present in more distant areas.

Core Zone cage-door sites are of all sizes, and their room-block mounds range from very small (150 sq m in area) to very large (11,950 sq m). According to the mound-size classification system of our intensive survey (Whalen and Minnis 2001a:110), the group with cage-door stones contains six small sites (40 percent), six of medium size (40 percent), and three large ones (20 percent). The question now is whether the observed cage-door stones are distributed among Medio period communities with or without regard to site size. If the latter is true, then the just-presented proportions of small, medium, and large sites with cage-door stones should be about the same as the proportions of those size categories in the outer Core Zone site sample. The site sample proportions are 74.4 percent small sites, 21.0 percent medium sites, and 9.6 percent large sites. Thus, small sites made up 74 percent of the site sample but contributed only 40 percent of the observed cage-door stones. Medium and large sites, in contrast, had disproportionately high numbers of cage-door stones. In short, although cage-door stones were found on the surface of sites of all sizes, they were more likely to be present on medium-sized and large communities than on the many small ones. In the four excavated sites discussed in this volume, cage-door stone fragments were found on the surface of large site 204, and another was discovered during excavation of site 242. Although it is a small community, 242 is interpreted as an administrative node of Casas Grandes. No cage-door stones or their fragments were found on or in small, simple sites 231 and 317.

The chronology of macaw use in the Casas Grandes area seems to parallel that of the U.S. Southwest. It is likely, in fact, that the former fueled the latter. McKusick (2001:76) notes that macaws were rare in the Pueblo Southwest in early times, and that there was a large increase in their frequency from the late 1200s to the middle 1300s. In the Casas Grandes area, macaws appear to have been rare in Viejo times, as a single bone assignable only to the genus *Ara* was recovered from extensive excavations at the Convento site (Di Peso, Rinaldo, and Fenner 1974:8:274). The original work at Casas Grandes showed that many more macaws were imported in the succeeding Medio period. No macaw remains have yet been found in any early Medio contexts (those dating from the late 1100s through the late 1200s). This is not proof that none were present then, of course. Instead, we envision a low frequency of macaws in Viejo and early Medio times, paralleling the better-documented situation in the U.S. Southwest.

All macaw finds that can be dated in northwest Chihuahua fall into the late part of the Medio period. Preceding ceramic analyses in chapter 4 demonstrated that the excavated pueblo parts of Casas Grandes all date to the late Medio, as does the cage-door-yielding site 242. At site 204, the macaw burial shown in figure 3.18 was found beneath the floor of a room with floor-contact radiocarbon dates in the late Medio. Lastly, we have shown that Ramos Polychrome, the principal ceramic carrier of macaw motifs, was introduced in the late Medio period. This clearly is the time of florescence of the macaw trade in northwest Chihuahua.

The final question to consider here is the uses to which macaws were put in the Casas Grandes culture. Original interpretation saw the birds as serving both commercial and religious purposes (Di Peso 1974:2:599), and both purposes seem reasonable. Macaws and vast numbers of their feathers were traded into the U.S. Southwest at the time that Casas Grandes was rising to its peak (McKusick 2001:129), and the primate center certainly was the region's epicenter for aviculture. Macaws and their feathers also could have served as prestige goods (e.g., Minnis 1989). Whatever their other uses may have been, the ceremonial role of the birds certainly is beyond question. They are extensively portrayed on ceramics, both as birds and as composite creatures (e.g., bird-men), and all who have written about Casas Grandes symbolism see macaws as supernaturally powerful creatures and as potent symbols of belief and ritual systems (e.g., Moulard 2005; Townsend 2005; C. VanPool 2003a; C. VanPool and T. VanPool 2007). It is highly significant to this argument that most of the macaws found at Casas Grandes had been beheaded and carefully buried (Di Peso 1974:2:273).

The supernatural role of macaws recently has been interpreted in several different ways. One study (McKusick 2001) asserts that the birds had powerful supernatural ascriptions in Mesoamerican religions and that bird sacrifices were crucial parts of religious rituals. Further, particular kinds of birds were offered to individual Mesoamerican deities. Scarlet macaws, for instance, were sacrificed to Quetzalcoatl in that deity's association with flowing water and, by implication, with water-control systems. McKusick projects this pattern into northwestern Mexico and the U.S. Southwest after about A.D. 1000, with Casas Grandes as the likely center.

A different view of the role of macaws in Casas Grandes cosmology recently has been presented (C. VanPool 2003a; C. VanPool and T. VanPool 2007). The VanPools do not disagree that macaws were creatures of considerable supernatural power, but they do not emphasize either the transmission of Mesoamerican ritual systems to the Casas Grandes area and beyond or the association of macaws with specific Mesoamerican deities. Instead, they see imported macaws as being used in local contexts, as creatures associated with the spirit journeys of the shamans and priestly leaders of the primate center.

The intricate symbolism of Casas Grandes cosmology has just begun to be analyzed, and much remains uncertain. Whatever specific ideas existed at the primate center, however, there is wide agreement that birds, especially macaws, played important roles in ritual and were potent supernatural symbols. Such symbols characteristically reflect and emphasize shared belief systems, and they may also imply an accepted system of ritual authority. The center of these belief and authority systems surely was Casas Grandes, where every component of ritual and ceremonialism was amplified to regionally unique levels. Accordingly, we take the spread of macaws and macaw symbols as one of Emerson's (1997) signifiers of the archaeology of power. We further take the distribution of macaws and their symbolic representations over the area around Casas Grandes to reflect the spread of the primate center's supernatural power and authority. This authority may have existed at multiple levels. The first conceivably involved actual possession of the birds, which mostly was restricted to Casas Grandes and its neighbors of the outer part of the Core Zone. Macaw symbols also were plentiful here. Possession of macaws could imply a more direct or more intensive participation in ritual systems, as well as a more comprehensive extension of the ritual authority of the primate center. The second level of participation and extension of ritual authority may be reflected in the absence or near-absence of the birds with the common presence of macaw symbols on ceramic vessels. This pattern would include our Middle Zone survey unit to the north and areas such as the Santa María drainage to the south. Christine and Todd VanPool (2007) have suggested that a cult of supernatural beliefs emanated from Casas Grandes to surrounding areas. This belief system, they contend, was expressed in the elaborate symbolism of the Polychrome ceramics, in which the macaw played a prominent part.

## Minerals

A large variety of minerals came from Casas Grandes, and the specimens are described and illustrated in the site report (Di Peso, Rinaldo, and Fenner 1974:8:435–81). The center's exotic items recently have been restudied by Szarka (2006). It is apparent that not all kinds of minerals are equally well represented in the community. As illustration, table 8.3 shows the frequencies of the most common minerals from the primate center. Pigments such as kaolin and azurite are omitted from this list. Also shown in the table are counts for all of the minerals recovered from site 204. No minerals were found in the excavations at small sites 231, 242, and 317.

It is clear from table 8.3 that site 204 contains a number of the most common minerals found at the primate center, although the sizes of the two assemblages are radically different. The 204 assemblage contains many of the same materials as the primate center, but their frequencies are different. The primate center's assemblage is dominated overwhelmingly by specular hematite, a type of iron ore with a metallic luster. It breaks into thin plates, and it was much used for mosaic inlays and for other types of ornaments. In second through fourth places are, respectively, selenite, malachite, and quartz crystals. Selenite, a translucent form of gypsum, is the most commonly found mineral at site 204. In second and third places are mica and turquoise, followed by specular hematite and crystals of calcite and quartz. Figure 8.3 shows some of the worked minerals from the 204 community.

At Casas Grandes, large fractions of the mineral assemblage were found concentrated in a few localities. Tabulations by Szarka (2006:116–21) show that the multistoried room units 8, 14, and 16 have rich mineral assemblages containing all of the

**Table 8.3**  Minerals from Casas Grandes and Site 204

| Mineral | Casas Grandes | Site 204 |
|---|---|---|
| Specular hematite | 14,192 | 4 |
| Selenite | 4,236 | 47 |
| Malachite | 2,692 | 0 |
| Quartz crystals | 2,419 | 4 |
| Fluorite | 632 | 0 |
| Turquoise | 383 | 13 |
| Serpentine | 340 | 1 |
| Calcite | 274 | 4 |
| Thenardite | 272 | 0 |
| Mica | 57 | 14 |
| Copper ore | 54 | 0 |
| Petrified wood | 35 | 2 |

*Source:* Compiled and modified from Szarka (2006, tables 11 and 14).

**Figure 8.3** Turquoise and stone pendants from site 204. The top four are turquoise. The bottom left pendant is an unidentified stone, and the bottom right is gypsum. The scale is in millimeters.

44 types recognized in the community. In addition, some of the rooms in these units contain quantities of particular minerals that contribute large fractions of the total site sample. Finally, the mineral concentrations often occur in contexts with other exotic and imported items. Di Peso saw these as commercial stockpiles, Minnis (1989) has interpreted them as elite hoards, and Szarka (2006) refers to them as prestige goods. Whatever the case may be, the primate center's minerals frequently occurred in concentrations. The obvious implication of this pattern is that some members of the community had greater access to minerals than did others. Interestingly, we see no vestige of this pattern at site 204, where minerals were found thinly scattered over nearly all excavated contexts.

Although a few minerals were found all over the 204 community, it is evident that they did not occur with equal frequency in all parts of the Medio period. Eight rooms with early Medio floor-contact radiocarbon dates (Rooms 2, 3, 4, 6, 8, and 50–52) made up 23 percent of the excavated sample but contained 66 percent by count of all of the minerals recovered from the site. The mineral assemblage of these rooms also was diverse, containing 70 percent of the site's mineral variety. In contrast, a set of nine late-dated rooms (Rooms 60–65 and 70–72) was much poorer in minerals. These rooms made up 26 percent of the excavated sample but contained only 10 percent of the site's minerals. Moreover, this set had only half of the variety of the early-dated room sample. Although sparse, these data suggest the presence of more minerals of more different kinds in early Medio than in late Medio contexts. Unfortunately, the site 204 trash middens contained too few minerals to be useful in this analysis.

With this situation in mind, we return to Casas Grandes. All of the excavated pueblo deposits there were shown earlier to be of late Medio age. So, therefore, are the minerals and their postulated concentration in the hands of a limited segment of the community. The site 204 data indicate that this concentration may have extended beyond the primate center. In the 204 community, minerals were more numerous and more diverse in the early Medio, which predates the apogee of Casas Grandes. This situation changed by the late Medio, when both quantity and diversity declined, likely in concert with increasing control of the materials or of trade networks by some elements of the Casas Grandes population. The early Medio period, in other words, may have seen a decentralized situation in which communities procured their own minerals. Distribution may have become more restricted and centralized at Casas Grandes in the late part of the Medio. This would be another component of the extension of the primate center's authority and control into its hinterland, and it mirrors the situation just described for shell.

Lastly, small, simple communities like 231 and 317 evidently never had much access to imported minerals or to shell. The absence of precious items in these kinds of communities is predictable. A more perplexing case is the small administrative node, site 242. It had neither shell nor minerals, despite its elaboration of secular and ritual architecture. Assuming that both shell and minerals represented items of wealth and economic status, the rural functionaries in residence at site 242 were not much wealthier than their neighbors. Their authority, then, was based not on greater wealth and economic status, but rather on ritual and a close connection with the primate center. The point here is that status in early complex societies likely was not equally encoded in all aspects of life. It is more so in mature complex societies, but Lesure and Blake (2002:1), in making the preceding argument, observe that "social processes operate at a variety of different scales" in the kinds of polities that we have described as chiefdoms.

## Copper

Items of cold-hammered and cast copper have been found in prehistoric contexts from Panama to southern Colorado (Di Peso, Rinaldo, and Fenner 1974:7:508.9), and copper is one of the more spectacular artifact categories from Casas Grandes. Nearly 700 copper items were recovered there, and no single community in northwest Mexico or the U.S. Southwest has anything even close to this assemblage. Copper items at the primate center include cold-hammered sheets, needles and awls, wire, many sorts of jewelry, and an axe head (Di Peso, Rinaldo, and Fenner 1974:7:507). Cold-hammered beads were the most common component of this assemblage, contributing 73 percent of the total. Cast-copper bells were the next most common at 17 percent, and all other forms make up the remaining 10 percent. It is noteworthy that the copper items at Casas Grandes were small and portable.

The original interpretation saw Casas Grandes as a production center for these copper items (Di Peso, Rinaldo, and Fenner 1974:7:501–7), and this interpretation was widely accepted until recently. A restudy of copper at Casas Grandes throws serious doubt on the notion of local smelting and casting of copper items, however (Vargas 1995). While acknowledging that the many cold-hammered items (e.g., beads and tinklers) could have been made in the community from imported copper sheets, Vargas finds no convincing evidence that smelting or casting was done there. It is more likely that the cast-copper bells and other items were brought to the primate center in finished form. The source of the copper and the manufacturing area remain undetermined, but western Mesoamerica is the most likely candidate. Copper sheets and cast items, then, should be seen as another kind of imported valuable at Casas Grandes.

Bells are the most widely distributed copper item in northwest Mexico and the southwest United States (Pendergast 1962; Vargas 1995). Tabulations of copper bell finds in the Southwest (Vargas 1995:53) sum to only 206 specimens for the entire region. In contrast, 115 bells came from Casas Grandes alone. Despite this abundance, Vargas (1995:67) uses a stylistic analysis to argue that the primate center was a consumer of bells rather than a large-scale exporter of them. Only a handful of sites in New Mexico, she asserts, received a few bells from the primate center. This is similar to Bradley's (1999) contention that Casas Grandes was more a consumer of shell than an exporter of it.

It also is apparent that copper items, especially bells, were largely restricted to the primate center. Copper items of any sort are rare among the other sites of northwestern Chihuahua. In fact, we are aware of only a few bells and other copper items among the 391 Medio period room-block mounds recorded by our intensive surveys in the Core and Middle Zones. Sayles (1936b:59, plate XIX) illustrates three pendants, two bells, a wire ring, and a tinkler, all of copper, from the Ramos site. The site was mapped and

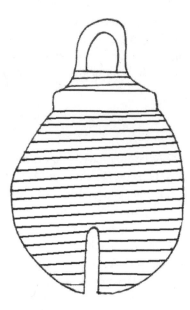

**Figure 8.4** Type IC12a copper bell. (Adapted from Vargas 1995:27).

surface-collected by our Core Zone survey in 1989. It is a complex of four mounds that shows ceramic evidence of an occupational history reaching back at least to the early Medio. The property owner told us that macaw cage-door stones had been found there. Sayles' illustrations include finely made ground-stone bowls; pestles of equally good quality; a variety of shell ornaments that includes a frog effigy; stone beads and pendants, including one of turquoise; a stone cruciform; and a variety of the stone carvings that are described as ceremonial items at Casas Grandes (Di Peso, Rinaldo, and Fenner 1974:291–302). The site clearly had a rich and elaborate assemblage of exotica, despite the fact that its total room-block mound area sums to only 5,400 sq m, which makes it a medium-sized settlement in the typology of our intensive survey (Whalen and Minnis 2001a:124–25).

The second copper-yielding site is 204, the one extensively reported upon in this volume. A single copper bell was found on the surface of Mound B a few years before our work there. The bell most likely was uncovered in the course of the extensive looting of the entire site, and its original context is unknown. The bell was turned over to the regional museum. It was not photographed at the time of its discovery, and it cannot now be located. It was described as similar to the Type IC12a bell illustrated by Vargas (1995:63). Figure 8.4 shows a bell of this type. Both site 204 and the Ramos site are medium to large communities located on the outer edge of the Core Zone. Both had macaw cages, a range of shell and mineral jewelry, and copper ornaments. We do not know how many other sites in the Core Zone contain copper, although no copper has yet been found at any small community.

All of the copper items from Casas Grandes come from contexts that also contain Ramos Polychrome pottery. This dates them to the late Medio, or after about 1300. At present, no copper items are known from early Medio contexts, although they likely were present, at least in small numbers. We suppose so because of the discovery of a piece of copper sheet and a tinkler rolled from similar copper sheet at the Viejo period Convento site (Di Peso, Rinaldo, and Fenner 1974:7:499). No cast-copper items were found there. Copper casting was present in Mesoamerica from ca. A.D. 900 (Pendergast 1962:527), and there are cast-copper bells at Chaco Canyon's Pueblo Bonito in the tenth, eleventh, and early twelfth centuries (Vargas 1995:32). Cast-copper items thus may have been present in the Casas Grandes area before late Medio times, although they have yet to be discovered.

In any case, there seem to be two levels of copper work in the Casas Grandes area: cold-hammering of copper sheets, beads, needles, awls, wire, and tinklers; and lost-wax casting of bells and other ornaments such as the often-pictured turtle effigy. The first of these technologies is by far the simplest, and it seems to have appeared by Viejo times in northwest Chihuahua. Its frequency expands greatly in the succeeding Medio period, and it could have been practiced at the primate center using imported sheet copper. Lost-wax casting, which requires ore smelting, is a much more complex set of techniques that probably never was practiced at Casas Grandes. The data presently in hand suggest that cast-copper items were not brought into the area in quantity until the late part of the Medio period.

## Ritual Paraphernalia

Often, there is no clear-cut distinction between exotic and ritual items. Ornaments of exotic materials, for example, may signify ritual offices. The macaws considered in the last section clearly had both economic and ritual significance. The material discussed in this section differs from the exotica just considered in one important way: all of it except for the shell trumpets is made of local materials. Table 8.4 shows the most common items classed as ritual paraphernalia at Casas Grandes. This material is not discussed here, as it is extensively described and illustrated in the site report (Di Peso, Rinaldo, and Fenner 1974:7:283–336). Also listed in the table are the ritual paraphernalia recovered from neighboring sites 204 and 242. None of these items were found at small sites 231 and 317.

Casas Grandes stands far above its neighbors in the amount and variety of ritual paraphernalia found there. This is consistent with the center's concentration of ritual architecture and with interpretations of the site as a pilgrimage center (Fish and Fish 1999). Renfrew (2000:17) characterizes Chaco Canyon as a "Location of High Devotional Expression," and the same phrase likely is applicable to Casas Grandes. Table 8.4 also shows that site 204 is a distant second to the primate center in the quantity and variety of its ritual paraphernalia.

The excavations at site 204 produced a carved-stone effigy head similar to the Type IC head illustrated for Casas Grandes (Di Peso, Rinaldo, and Fenner 1974:7:295). Also present at 204, as at the primate center, was a small effigy figure carved from shell, and representing a macaw. Both of the 204 effigies are shown in figure 8.5.

**Table 8.4**　Ritual Paraphernalia from Casas Grandes and Its Neighbors

| Item | Casas Grandes[a] | Site 204 | Site 242 |
|---|---|---|---|
| Effigies | 83 | 2 | |
| Crystals | 33 | 7 | |
| Cruciforms | 5 | 1 | |
| Pipes | 11 | 1 | |
| Musical rasps | 2 | 3 | |
| Tools | 61 | 1 | |
| Altar stones | 3 | 1? | |
| Effigy vessels | 49 | 2 | |
| Phalli | 11 | | 1 |
| Polished stone bowls | 21 | | |
| Hand-drums | 109 | | |
| Shell trumpets | 175 | | |

a. Data from Di Peso, Rinaldo, and Fenner (1974:7:38–336).

A number of quartz crystals, which were likely cave formations, came from Casas Grandes, and a few were found at site 204. More common in the latter community, however, were crystals of calcite. These were like the quartz crystals in size and shape, although they were amber-tinted rather than clear. They, too, likely were cave formations. Most of the crystals of both sorts were small, measuring 2 cm to 4 cm in length. One of the quartz crystals clearly had been worked, and it is shown in figure 8.6. Similar worked crystals were found at Casas Grandes, where their worn, pointed tips led to their interpretation as engraving tools. They would have been suitable for working shell or soft stone. At Casas Grandes, these implements were not considered to be ordinary tools but were assigned dual technological and ceremonial roles (Di Peso, Rinaldo, and Fenner 1974:7:335).

The tubular pipes found at Casas Grandes appear to have been used in a smoking ritual (C. VanPool 2003b:699; VanPool and VanPool 2007:28), and they were ground from stone. An apparent pipe fragment was found at site 204, although it was ceramic rather than stone (fig. 8.7). Its tapered body and large interior bore diameter resemble the specimens from Casas Grandes, suggesting that the 204 find was a pipe rather than, say, the hollow handle of a ceramic ladle. The 204 pipe certainly would have been of lower quality than those in use at the primate center. The items listed as tools in the preceding table are axes or pecking hammers that have the familiar shape of the utilitarian implements but that clearly were not meant for use. The Casas Grandes report notes that these implements were made of soft, colorful stones, and they were unusually finely finished (Di Peso, Rinaldo, and Fenner 1974:7:313). Exactly what was done with them is unclear, but they certainly represent a distinctive category of nonutilitarian item. The one found at site 204 has all the characteristics just listed. It takes the form of a pecking hammer, but it is smaller than the utilitarian implement, it was made from a soft, fine-grained green stone, and it was smoothly polished (fig. 8.8).

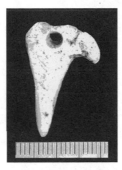

**Figure 8.5** Two effigies from site 204. The upper piece is ground from stone, and the lower macaw effigy is carved from shell. The lower scale is in millimeters.

**Figure 8.6** Worked quartz crystal from site 204. The scale is in millimeters.

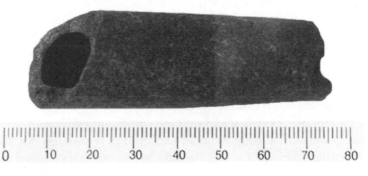

**Figure 8.7** Ceramic pipe from site 204. The scale is in millimeters.

**Figure 8.8** Ceremonial pecking hammer from site 204. It is ground from a fine-grained, greenish stone. The scale is in millimeters.

Elongated, notched pieces of polished stone were characterized as musical rasps at Casas Grandes, and Di Peso, Rinaldo, and Fenner (1974:7:283) list ethnographic analogies to support this interpretation. Three fragments of what appear to be musical rasps were found at site 204, but all were made from bone rather than from polished stone (fig. 8.9). The most complete fragment was made from the scapula of a large mammal. The bone is notched along its superior border, or the part extending away from the glenoid fossa. Two smaller notched bone fragments were found in other contexts on the site. Lastly, an oddly shaped stone piece was found at site 204. It is made from pumice, which is an uncommon raw material (fig. 8.10). Its function is unknown, but it may be a small version of the pieces described as "altar stones" at Casas Grandes (Di Peso, Rinaldo, and Fenner 1974:7:324–25). The stone could also be some type of fetish.

Table 8.4 shows that a number of the ritual items found at Casas Grandes were absent from site 204. These include phalli, finely polished stone bowls, shell trumpets, and ceramic hand-drums. This situation is even more extreme at the three small sites. Of all of the ritual paraphernalia listed in the table, only a finely made stone phallus (fig. 8.11) was recovered from site 242, the presumed administrative extension of the primate center. Sites 231 and 317 yielded nothing at all that could be classed as ritual paraphernalia. If these items, especially the smaller ones, were used primarily on an individual level, e.g., in personal "medicine bundles" like the one described at Casas Grandes (Di Peso, Rinaldo, and Fenner 1974:7:292), then we would expect to find some of them even in the smallest communities. If so, our sample of excavated material simply was not large enough to recover them.

An alternative explanation is that much of the ritual paraphernalia discussed here was associated with a Casas Grandes–centered ritual system that did not extend conspicuously into the area's smallest and simplest communities. Instead, the inhabitants of those villages may have gone to nodes like the 242 community for public, ritual activities. Elsewhere, for example (Whalen and Minnis 2001a), we noted that no Core Zone community lay more than a few kilometers from a ball court. Interestingly,

**Figure 8.9** Two bone rasps from site 204. The small piece in the upper photo is broken from the larger one. The lower photo shows front and side views of the same piece. The scale is in millimeters.

Di Peso's discussion of ritual paraphernalia at Casas Grandes notes in case after case that these items were not found in contexts of the preceding Viejo period (Di Peso, Rinaldo, and Fenner 1974:7:303, 304, 306, 324, 325).

This leads to the question of the chronological placement within the Medio period of the items under consideration here. All of the large assemblage from Casas Grandes can be dated to the late Medio, or after about 1300, as argued in chapter 2. Of the site 204 assemblage, nothing came from well-dated early Medio contexts. Instead, all of the items classed as ritual paraphernalia came either from securely dated late Medio contexts or from the upper fill of rooms. All of this upper fill contained Ramos Polychrome and so dates to the late Medio. The phallus from site 242 likewise is of late Medio age. The data presently in hand are admittedly sparse, but they hint that the early part of the Medio might resemble the preceding Viejo period in paucity of recognizable ritual paraphernalia. This is not to argue that there were no magico-religious practices in those time intervals, of course. Instead, the implication is that supernatural activities were decentralized and unstandardized before about 1300, making them hard to recognize in the archaeological record. After 1300, in the late Medio, the paraphernalia

**Figure 8.10** Pumice-stone object from site 204. The scale is in millimeters.

associated with supernatural activities becomes more conspicuous and standardized, suggesting that magico-religious activity in the late Medio was more centralized than in preceding times. Casas Grandes, with its extensive and elaborate ceremonial facilities and ritual paraphernalia, is the obvious choice for the centralizing agency. We thus envision a situation in which a significant part of the authority of the primate center was supernatural, as is common in chiefdom-level societies. This magico-religious package spreads over the surrounding area, appearing in recognizable form in larger communities like 204 and at administrative nodes like site 242. It is not apparent at small communities such as 231 and 317, however. This is explicable by postulating that the people in the rural hinterland continued to practice the old, unstandardized (and thus largely unrecognizable) Viejo–early Medio supernatural activities at home, while publicly subscribing to the primate center's belief system. The ethnographic record shows that this is a common occurrence when an older, simpler belief system is overlain by a new and more powerful one.

### Exotica and Ritual in the Casas Grandes Polity

The great majority of the region's exotic and imported items were concentrated at Casas Grandes. Little of this material was present in neighboring communities, even in

30 cm

**Figure 8.11** Stone phallus from site 242. The scale is in millimeters.

a large one (site 204) or in an administrative node (site 242). Clearly, the primate center was the region's major consumer of exotica, although there does not seem to have been much redistribution of this material.

It is interesting to note that a similar situation has been described at Chaco Canyon. Kantner and Kintigh (2006:166–69) show that Chaco Canyon was outstanding in its region in the acquisition of relatively large quantities of exotic and imported items, with outlying communities having much less. The situation, then, seems to be that much imported material flowed into Chaco Canyon, but little came back out. Kantner and Kintigh observe that this does not fit well with the in-out cycles envisioned by classic models of prestige goods redistribution. Based on the data just presented, the same argument can be made for Casas Grandes. In both cases, there is need for a fundamental reconsideration of the roles of exotic and imported items in social, political, ritual, and economic organization. Such a study is beyond the scope of the present volume, however.

Ritual items were distributed much like exotica, in that they were concentrated at the primate center. Some of this material came from the large neighbor (site 204) and from the administrative node (site 242), but none was found in the smallest and simplest communities (sites 231 and 317). The late Medio period appears to have been the time of greatest visibility of ritual paraphernalia in northwest Chihuahua. Significantly, this is also the time of the apogee of Casas Grandes.

We see the primate center as the promoter and principal displayer of a ritual system that spread into the region's more prominent communities after A.D. 1300. Ball courts may have been an important part of the package. Preceding discussion dated most courts to the late Medio, when no Core Zone community was far from one. Ritual thus appears to have been a critical tie that bound the Casas Grandes polity. This idea is discussed in more detail in the following chapter.

# 9

## The History and Structure of the Casas Grandes Polity

Chapter 1 raised several issues important to our continuing investigation of the history and organization of the Casas Grandes regional system. The first is clarification of the occupational histories of the primate center and its near neighbors. The contemporaneity, or lack thereof, of these communities obviously has the strongest implication for models of regional organization, and we are now in a position to begin to consider that question. The second question is the nature and extent of the control that Casas Grandes was able to exert over its neighbors of the Core Zone, which was the most organized part of the polity. Chapter 1 identified signifiers of the spread of power and authority in regional contexts, and our task is to monitor their distribution over time and space in northwest Chihuahua. This concluding chapter uses the analytical results of preceding pages to address these issues and to present our latest thinking on the history and operation of the Casas Grandes polity, with specific focus on the organization of the Core Zone.

### The Growth of Casas Grandes and Its Neighbors

The origin and occupational history of Casas Grandes are questions that have been much discussed but still have not been resolved. The presently accepted dating of the excavated parts of the site is ca. A.D. 1250 to 1450. This is based upon a reanalysis of some of the tree-ring samples taken during the original excavation of the site (Dean and Ravesloot 1993), which is discussed in detail in chapter 2. This study indisputably was a major step forward in understanding the chronology of the primate center. Continuing on from the tree-ring study, Lekson (2000) provides an insightful evaluation of the Casas Grandes chronology from the perspective of ceramic cross-dating. Dean and Ravesloot (1993:97) maintained that the Paquimé phase (Di Peso's middle Medio time unit) began around A.D. 1300, and they see the preceding Buena Fe phase as predating 1300. This fits with their idea that some of the site's construction dates to the 1200s but that much of the rest was built in the 1300s. Lekson challenges this idea, however, noting that at Casas Grandes almost every sizeable ceramic collection includes some Gila Polychrome, which appeared after 1300. Because Di Peso's Buena Fe contexts also include Gila Polychrome, they cannot predate 1300. Gila Polychrome is a sensitive chronological monitor, and Lekson argues convincingly that the Chihuahuan polychromes with which it is associated and the site of Casas Grandes itself all were phenomena of the fourteenth and fifteenth centuries.

Some of this argument is strengthened and confirmed by the ceramic seriation work described in chapter 4. We have shown that Ramos Polychrome was a fourteenth-century addition to the Medio ceramic assemblage. Examination of the Casas Grandes ceramic counts and contexts shows that Ramos Polychrome appears in quantity *under* floors assigned by Di Peso to the Buena Fe phase. This observation strengthens Lekson's argument that the excavated contexts at Casas Grandes date after A.D. 1300. As a dating tool, Ramos has the advantage of being much more common than Gila Polychrome, and its abundance permits us to investigate the dating of another prominent component of the primate center: the ritual architecture. The site's two large I-shaped ball courts (Courts I and II) and the smaller, T-shaped court (Court III) did not yield sub-floor ceramics of any kind. A test pit was dug to sterile soil in the south end-field platform of Court I, however, revealing high proportions of Ramos Polychrome to the bottom of the deposits. The same is true of the Mound of the Offerings. Mound 1, the Mound of the Cross, the West Platform Mound of Court II, and the Serpent Mound had no sub-structure excavations, but Ramos Polychrome was present all through their fill. Although there are no sub-floor ceramic data for the small Court III, there was a considerable amount of Ramos Polychrome in its floor level. The Mound of the Bird yielded almost no ceramic data, and no excavations were done on the Mound of the Heroes. Despite these gaps in the data, it is clear that much of the excavated public and ritual architecture of Casas Grandes postdates A.D. 1300. Old and new ceramic data, then, argue that the excavated components of the primate center date to the late part of the Medio period. We stress that our early and late Medio intervals do not equate to Di Peso's original phases. All of the Buena Fe, Paquimé, and Diablo phase deposits contain Ramos Polychrome and so all date from about 1300 onward, or from what we term the late part of the Medio period.

The notion of a fourteenth- and fifteenth-century date for the excavated parts of Casas Grandes returns us to an issue introduced a few years ago: the "thirteenth-century gap" in the prehistory of northwestern Chihuahua. Lekson (2000) proposed this idea based on his observation that the Chihuahuan and Salado Polychromes occur together at Casas Grandes. The Salado Polychromes, especially Gila, are known to date from A.D. 1300, and the logical assumption is that the accompanying Chihuahuan Polychromes do so as well. Casas Grandes thus appears to have no ceramic antecedents from the thirteenth century. As a result, Lekson sees the fourteenth-century Casas Grandes Polychrome ceramic assemblage as emerging essentially *de novo* (2000:285) on the other side of an occupational gap in the area during the thirteenth century.

That there were no known candidates for a pre-fourteenth-century ceramic assemblage was true when written in 2000. In the present volume, however, we have demonstrated that there is an early Medio ceramic assemblage that dates from the early thirteenth century. Its polychromes include Babícora, White-Paste Babícora, Dublan, and Villa Ahumada. All of them were painted in the coarse-line, geometric style of decoration described in chapter 4. Also present were plain, textured, red, and black wares. In chapter 4, we argued that early Medio ceramics contain the antecedents of much of the late Medio assemblage. It is therefore necessary to modify slightly Lekson's (2000:278) assertion that the Chihuahuan Polychromes belong to the fourteenth and fifteenth centuries. Many of them do, but we have shown that Babícora, White-Paste Babícora, Dublan, and Villa Ahumada Polychromes were made in early Medio times, or throughout the thirteenth century. In short, the full Chihuahuan Polychrome assemblage does indeed belong to the fourteenth and fifteenth centuries, although it has thirteenth-century antecedents. Earlier (Whalen and Minnis 2003), we cited architectural and chronometric data to show that there is no thirteenth-century gap in settlement or building styles either.

This observation leads us to another question. Where are the thirteenth-century ceramic and architectural precedents at the primate center itself? The distributions of Gila and Ramos Polychromes demonstrate the fourteenth-century date of most of the excavated parts of Casas Grandes. This does not fix the date of the entire site, of course, and several points should be emphasized. First, Viejo period pit houses are known to exist beneath some Medio construction at the primate center (Di Peso, Rinaldo, and Fenner 1974:4:316–17). We have no idea how widespread was this early occupation of the site, but it is reminiscent of the situation described in this volume for site 204. There, Viejo pit houses were succeeded by early Medio occupation. In the second place, the revised tree-ring date estimates produced by Dean and Ravesloot (1993) leave open the possibility of early Medio occupation of the site. The analysts cite five estimated felling dates that fall at or before 1200. They note that all of these early dates come from rooms with younger estimated felling dates on other beams. Their plausible conclusion is that the early-dated beams represent salvage of material from earlier construction and its reuse in later rooms. The analysts note that these dates "raise the possibility of building activity earlier than that represented by the rooms with which they are associated and may place some activity at the site in the late twelfth or early thirteenth century" (Dean and Ravesloot 1993:96).

Lastly, only a portion of Casas Grandes has been investigated. Di Peso dug on the part of the site with the largest room-block mounds and the most plentiful ritual architecture, but even that part was not completely investigated. There is, therefore, still-unexplored space in which thirteenth-century Casas Grandes could lie hidden. We think it likely, therefore, that Casas Grandes was occupied in the thirteenth century, forming a continuous sequence from the Viejo period through the end of the Medio. We also suspect that the thirteenth-century occupation was considerably less elaborate than its fourteenth-century successor. We see rapid, perhaps even explosive, growth at the primate center after A.D. 1300.

The rapid fourteenth-century development of Casas Grandes must have been accompanied by an equally speedy rise in its population. The crucial question, then, is where these people came from. The most detailed consideration of this problem to date is provided by Stephen Lekson (1999, 2000, 2002). His idea is that there were substantial movements of people from the U.S. Southwest into northwestern Chihuahua in the late thirteenth and the fourteenth centuries. In fact, the notion of northerners moving into the Casas Grandes area is a venerable one (e.g., Gladwin 1936). Neither is the argument without modern, general precedent, as many discuss significant population shifts in the ancient Southwest (e.g., Cameron 1995; Clark 2001; Cordell 1995; Lyons 2003; Mueller and Wilcox 1999; Spielmann 1998).

Although we are not inherently opposed to migration models, we have argued for substantial pre-Medio populations in northwestern Chihuahua, thus reducing the need for a large influx of outsiders (Whalen and Minnis 2003). Obviously, the two ideas are not mutually exclusive, and our purpose is not to insist that no people from the outside came into the Casas Grandes area in Medio times. They certainly could have, but we do not see the major population movement into a nearly empty area that some have suggested.

If, as in our view, migration from the outside is no more than a part of the picture of Casas Grandes' growth, then local people must have played a significant role in populating the growing primate center. Natural increase in the community's population would have been too slow a process to have fueled the rapid growth that we envision. A plausible alternative is growth through absorption of the regional population. This is a pattern recognized in many contexts and in many kinds of complex societies, from Teotihuacán and Monte Albán in Mesoamerica to the Mississippians. It also characterizes the Pueblo Southwest, for example at Chaco Canyon (Wilshusen and Van Dyke 2006), Homol'ovi (E. C. Adams 2002), and Grasshopper (Reid and Whittlesey 1990). Indeed, it would be surprising if a primate center like Casas Grandes did not draw in population from its neighbors. In general, primate centers show strong tendencies toward population concentration (e.g., Smith 1977), although the extent and comprehensiveness of the process depend on many political, demographic, and economic factors.

The question now is whether there is archaeological evidence of this process in the late Medio period of northwestern Chihuahua. To seek this evidence, we examine the occupational histories of the neighbors of Casas Grandes, especially the large community represented by site 204. There are three ways to approach the question of site occupational history. The first involves study of radiocarbon date frequencies, the second is ceramic analysis, and the third is relative volumes of midden debris.

Examination of chronometric date frequencies has long been regarded as an effective way to investigate the occupational histories of settlements or areas. It has been done in a number of contexts, from the Southwest (Berry 1982; Nelson 1999) to Preceramic Peru (Rick 1987). In all such studies, the number of extant dates from a locality is assumed to be related to the magnitude of its occupation. This, of course, measures occupation duration in relative rather than absolute terms. Several graphic techniques have been used to express these data, and here we make use of Berry's (1982:32) method for drawing a histogram of calibrated radiocarbon dates. The dates are plotted on graph paper as horizontal lines showing the range of each. Berry (1982:32) used the $1\sigma$ range, whereas we plotted dates at $2\sigma$ in the present application. Vertical lines then are drawn at 25-year intervals across the plotted date ranges. The number of horizontal lines intersecting each vertical line is the basis for the resulting histogram. Figure 9.1 shows this plot for the 52 radiocarbon dates from site 204.

It is clear from the figure that the number of dates increases steadily from the inception of the Medio period at ca. A.D. 1200 to about the mid-1300s. This pattern suggests a steady increase in the intensity of site occupation through the early Medio and the

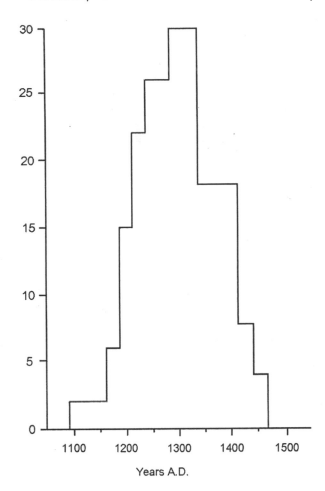

**Figure 9.1** Histogram of site 204 radiocarbon dates. The vertical axis is number of dates.

late Medio I intervals defined in chapter 4. Thereafter, there are two substantial drops in date frequency and, presumably, in site occupation. The first drop comes in the early 1300s, when the number of dates falls by about 40 percent. We cannot say from this that site occupation fell by precisely 40 percent, but the decline certainly was a considerable one. The second major drop is about 1400, when radiocarbon date frequency at site 204 falls to almost nothing.

The ceramic analyses provide another avenue of approach to the question of the occupational history of the 204 community. In chapter 4, we divided the late Medio into two smaller time units based on the frequency of Ramos Polychrome. The late Medio I was tentatively dated from A.D. 1300 to 1350 or 1375, after which the late Medio II interval begins. It is revealing to look at the distribution of midden deposits containing the ceramic signatures of the early, late I, and late II parts of the Medio period. Figure 9.2 displays these data. Listed above each test pit symbol are the Medio period time intervals represented there.

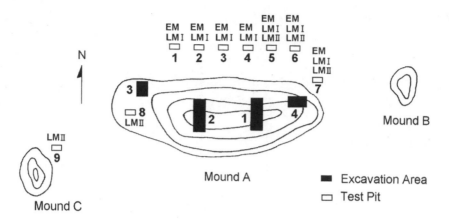

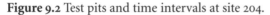

**Figure 9.2** Test pits and time intervals at site 204.

The figure shows that all of Mound A lies opposite a midden containing early Medio deposits. We presume that the inhabitants of each section of the mound dumped trash in the nearest part of the midden. Thus, we argue that almost all of Mound A was occupied in the early Medio. Radiocarbon dates from the excavation areas bear out this supposition. Chapter 2 showed that Excavation Area 1 was entirely early Medio. The rooms of Area 2 overlie early deposits, and some of them may be early Medio constructions that continued to be used in the late part of the period. Area 3 presented a mix of early and late occupation and also was asserted to be early construction that was used into later times. Only Area 4 yielded no early dates or deposits, although the adjacent midden test pit (number 7) contained extensive early Medio trash deposits. The situation is almost the same for the late Medio I deposits, which occurred in nearly all parts of the Mound A midden. Late Medio II deposits were greatly reduced in extent, occurring only on the east and west ends of Mound A (pits 6, 7 and 8) and in the Mound C midden (pit 9). Unfortunately, we were unable to locate midden deposits around the small Mound B, to the east of Mound A. Mound B, therefore, cannot be included in this discussion.

The relative magnitudes of these occupations can be compared in another way as well, by simply counting the numbers of levels in the Mound A midden test pits that belonged to each time interval. Levels were of the same area and thickness, and thus were of equal volume, in all test pits. For the Early Medio, there were 50 levels. The Late Medio I had a similar 58 levels, but only 32 levels could be assigned to the Late Medio II. This is a decline of about 45 percent, and it fits well with the previously discussed 40 percent decline in radiocarbon date frequencies in the late 1300s or early 1400s. All analyses thus indicate that the 204 community reached its maximum size around the early to mid-1300s and maintained that population for only a short time. Occupation declined considerably thereafter, and the community appears to have been largely abandoned by the early 1400s.

Our earlier argument that the primate center began its explosive growth after 1300 means that its peak development likely was not reached for some years. We estimate that the center's apogee came around the mid-1300s. In this scenario, the primate center holds its developmental peak for about a century and then declines in the mid- to late 1400s. An important implication of this conclusion is that the period of growth of the primate center seems to coincide closely with the time of decline of the 204 community. The data in hand thus permit the hypothesis that the growth of Casas Grandes was fueled at least in part by absorption of neighboring populations. At present, we cannot say much about how widespread this population absorption might have been.

## Evaluating Community Complexity

The preceding discussion leads to the second question that this study set out to pursue. That is, when, how, and to what extent were the authority and power of Casas Grandes projected into its rural hinterland? An earlier study (Whalen and Minnis 2001a) provided a preliminary model of the control strategies used by the primate center in its Core Zone and in more distant areas, and these were reviewed in chapter 1. Data reviewed in the present volume permit a more specific pursuit of the question of the spread of the primate center's authority.

We model this inquiry upon Thomas Emerson's (1997) productive study of the spread of power from the preeminent Mississippian center of Cahokia. As discussed in greater detail in chapter 1, Emerson identifies specific forms of an architecture of power, exotic and prestige goods, an architecture of ideology, sacred items, and sacred landscapes that mark the spread of Cahokia's political and ideological power in its rural countryside. To begin a similar inquiry in Chihuahua, we must identify the signifiers of power in the Casas Grandes case. We then must monitor their spread over time and space in northwest Chihuahua. Preceding chapters have provided the required chronological, architectural, and artifactual data for these endeavors. We begin with the primate center, so that it may serve as a benchmark for comparisons among the neighboring sites.

## Signifiers of Power at Casas Grandes

One of the most obvious signifiers of power is the distinctive architecture of the primate center. Di Peso's work showed that Casas Grandes is characterized by large rooms with very thick walls, rooms of intricate shapes, and a number of elaborate architectural elements such as "bed" platforms, platform hearths, and colonnaded rooms. Comparison in chapter 3 of this architectural complex with those of the excavated neighbors strongly emphasized how elaborate was the construction of the primate center. Accordingly, we consider the distinctive building style of the primate center to define the architecture of power for the region. Casas Grandes also was rich in the architecture of ideology, as the site contains the region's largest and most elaborate concentration of ritual structures of several sorts. These include ball courts and platform mounds, as well as large ceremonial rooms.

The community yielded many ideologically empowered items, from altars, offerings, and fetishes to finely made Ramos Polychrome vessels. Ramos Polychrome has been described as the signature type of Casas Grandes, and the strong symbolic content of its elaborate design motifs has long been recognized. The vessels have been seen as a visual language that communicated concepts critical to the religion and authority structure of the center and its surrounding region (e.g., Moulard 2005; Townsend 2005; C. VanPool 2003a; VanPool and VanPool 2007). The presence of a number of relatively elaborate burials evinces an elite population in the community (Rakita 2001; Ravesloot 1984). Some of these are deposited in what appear to be multigenerational tombs that likely reflect their occupants' membership in high-status descent groups. No such elaborate burials have yet been reported from any other site in the region, and thus it appears that the elite of Casas Grandes represent the apogee of regional social differentiation.

Control of at least some of a region's productivity is widely recognized as an essential component and signifier of chiefly power. The presence of supra-community productive facilities is a good indicator of regional centralization, and the case is strengthened if the architecture of power is associated with these large productive facilities. In the Casas Grandes area, conspicuous productive facilities are trincheras, or low terraces built in upland areas for soil and moisture control (Minnis, Whalen and Howell 2006). Trincheras are common features of the Casas Grandes Core Zone, and our intensive surveys showed that they were rare in the more distant Middle Zone. This situation is unlikely to be attributable entirely to population density, which does not appear to have been vastly greater in the Core than in the Middle Zone. An alternative explanation is that Core Zone communities were required to contribute to the support of Casas Grandes to a greater extent than were their more distant neighbors.

In addition to the common systems of small trincheras, the Core Zone also contained a few huge systems that were up to ten times larger than their small, community-based counterparts. These very large trinchera systems occur in sparsely populated parts of the uplands, and they are near sites that display the architecture of power. Site 242 is adjacent to the two largest systems in the region. Another large system is near the evidently special-purpose site of El Pueblito (Pitezel 2003, 2007). We contend that these agricultural systems were built and administered under the auspices of Casas Grandes, their productivity fueling what Lightfoot (1984) has described as "the funds of power" of society's leaders.

The second type of productive facility to be considered here is the conical pit-ovens described and illustrated in chapter 1. They likely were used for baking agave, a common food resource in the area. We interpret the ovens as large-scale food preparation facilities that probably were used to support public feasting (Minnis and Whalen 2005). Like the large systems of trincheras, these ovens are concentrated in the Casas Grandes Core Zone.

Large storage capacity for food and valued goods is required to build up the funds of power of central places. In chapter 3 we asserted that Casas Grandes had a number of kinds of storage, from large ceramic vessels to dedicated rooms to the "bed" platforms that many (from Pepper 1920 to Bustard 2003) regard as intramural storage facilities. The calculations in chapter 3 show that these facilities provide a considerable volume of secure, private storage space.

Elite artifact assemblages characteristically contain implements associated with feasting (Garraty 2000), and these are abundant at Casas Grandes. The comparative analysis of vessel volumes in chapter 5 showed that the primate center had by far the largest Plain, Textured, and Playas Red jars and bowls in the present site sample. These three types were characterized as the "workhorses" of the Medio domestic assemblage, but even the volumes of the largest Ramos Polychrome jars at Casas Grandes exceeded any of those at the neighboring sites. In chapter 5 we also demonstrated that the primate center had the highest frequency of vessels with exterior sooting, indicating a great deal of cooking. Other Casas Grandes jars had the site sample's highest frequency of vessels with the heavy interior erosion associated with the preparation of fermented drink. In general, Casas Grandes displays evidence of a level of production of food and drink that far exceeds the normal, household-level situation.

The analyses of chapter 7 indicated that some foods were of higher quality at Casas Grandes than among its neighbors. The same agricultural produce was present in all of the sites investigated in this study, but it was supplemented to variable degrees with meat from hunting. Small animals, especially rabbits, were the most common game animals at most of the sites in this sample, and they are presumed to have been taken in the vicinity of each community. At Casas Grandes, however, large mammals such as antelope and deer were common food resources. It is evident that at least some of the inhabitants of the primate center consumed more of these high-quality meats than did their neighbors.

Lastly, Casas Grandes is famous for the huge quantities of exotic and imported items found there, and the community obviously was a wealthy one. Emerson (1997) plausibly maintains that the quantity of exotic, valuable goods in a community is a sensitive monitor of the relative status of its inhabitants. By this logic, the principal inhabitants of Casas Grandes stood far above their neighbors. In addition, we have maintained that supplies of exotica (e.g., marine shell) were controlled at the regional level by the primate center.

## Signifiers of Power at the Neighboring Communities

The most significant question now is the extent to which these signifiers of power extended from the primate center into its hinterland. The analyses of preceding chapters point to considerable differences in the extent of visibility of indicators of power and community complexity in the present site sample, and we now turn to these. The four neighboring sites are considered in order of their evident complexity: 242, 204, 231, and 317.

*Site 242.* This community was described in chapter 1 as small, rural, and located in the sparsely populated uplands of the outer part of the Core Zone. The site has only about 20 rooms, and its resident population, therefore, could not have been very large. Even so, chapter 3 showed that this is the only site in the excavated sample to display the architecture of power just described at Casas Grandes. According to the comparative analyses of chapter 3, the architecture of site 242 differed dramatically from what was found at the other neighboring sites. In addition, there was a large, I-shaped ball court and a small associated mound beside the 242 room block. This one of the largest courts known in the region, and the court-and-mound complex are unique among the known neighbors of Casas Grandes. In fact, the small site 242 has the largest and most elaborate concentration of ritual architecture at a single site, apart from the primate center.

No burials were recovered from the excavated rooms at 242, despite their largely unlooted condition. This could be a function of the small excavated sample size, it may reflect the small size of the resident population, or it could mean that the dead of this special community were not disposed of by the common practice of sub-floor interment in room corners. In any case, there are no mortuary data upon which to base an assessment of the relative social status of the site's inhabitants.

Some ideologically empowered material is present at site 242. Chapter 4 demonstrated that the community had a much higher frequency of Ramos Polychrome than any other small site in this sample. In fact, the small site 242 has a Ramos frequency comparable to that of large sites like Casas Grandes and 204. We argued earlier that the symbols of power and authority were carried on this pottery. A finely made stone phallus from site 242 was illustrated in chapter 8. Several similar phalli have been recovered from Casas Grandes, where they were interpreted as items used in fertility rituals (Di Peso, Rinaldo, and Fenner 1974:7:303). None came from any other excavated site, and the implication is of primate center–based ritual projected into the rural countryside. The ball court and mound complex at 242 give the same impression.

High-quality food is another widely recognized marker of elite status. Site 242 was shown in chapter 7 to differ little from any of the other sites in basic plant foods consumed. There appears to have been some difference in meat consumption, however. Animal bones were few in the 242 community, showing that its inhabitants did not practice as much of the generalized, small-animal hunting as residents of all of the neighboring sites in the present sample did. Instead, many of the bones at 242 were from large mammals. They could not be identified to taxa, but this category includes antelope, deer, and bison. Discussion in chapter 7 characterized meat from these animals as preferred food, as opposed to the rabbits and rats that dominated lower-status assemblages. Casas Grandes also was observed to contain a good deal of the bone of these preferred species. Chapter 7 made another observation relevant to the status of the inhabitants of site 242. The hearths of that community were found to contain high percentages of pine charcoal. At the other neighboring sites, in contrast, hearth fuel consisted of at least equal proportions of oak and pine, plus corn-cobs. We suggested in chapter 7 that pine was the more costly fuel, as it had to be brought to the lowlands from the Sierra Madre.

There are strong indications that the 242 community was much involved in the generation of what Lightfoot (1984) has termed the "funds of power." Site 242 was positioned beside one of the largest agricultural terrace systems known in the region, and a second system of comparable size lay nearby. We expect that the 242 community organized the scattered rural population of this part of the uplands to construct and farm the surrounding terrace systems. Moreover, we contend that the produce of these systems went to the community with which 242 was closely tied: Casas Grandes. The data of preceding chapters indicate that this organizational activity at site 242 was facilitated by three strategies.

First, the 242 community replicates the architecture of the primate center, providing a visual statement of the close linkage between them. The prestige and power of

Casas Grandes thus were projected onto its administrative satellite. Ritual is the second cornerstone by which the inhabitants of site 242 managed their neighbors. The community's ball-court-and-mound complex was remarkably elaborate by regional standards, and we presume that it served the same ritual function as its larger and more numerous counterparts at the primate center. The stone phalli found at Casas Grandes have been linked to fertility, a constant concern for farmers. The phallus from site 242 suggests projection into the countryside and to the site's rural managers of an aspect of the ritual system of the primate center.

The third management strategy evidently in use at site 242 is public feasting. The ceramic analyses of chapter 5 demonstrated that site 242 had the largest Plain jars of any of the sites studied here, except for Casas Grandes. Of the four neighboring sites studied here, 242 also had the highest frequency of vessel sooting and interior surface pitting, using the largest vessels. These data were interpreted to reflect preparation of food and fermented drink at a level above ordinary, domestic needs. Finally, the 242 community was distinguished by a jar-to-bowl ratio of about 20:1. The other three neighboring sites had ratios of about 2:1, which we take to be the normal, domestic situation. The very large number of jars present at site 242 suggests large-scale storage and preparation of food and drink.

In sum, although 242 was a small community with few permanent residents, it was quite elaborate in domestic and ritual architecture, and it shows a number of other signifiers of power. Architecture suggests a close link between Casas Grandes and site 242, and the radiocarbon dates of the latter community support this supposition. Site 242 thus marks a projection of the authority of Casas Grandes into the outer part of the Core Zone.

*Site 204.* This large community was occupied primarily in the early Medio and late Medio I intervals. Occupation of the site seems to have declined significantly at the end of the late Medio I or beginning of the late Medio II, in the middle 1300s. The data and analyses of preceding chapters allow us to attempt the first consideration of community complexity in the early and late parts of the Medio period.

No elements of architectural elaboration (e.g., wall niches, platform hearths, or bed platforms) were found in the early Medio rooms. One room contained an adobe-and-stone stair, but the early Medio level of architectural elaboration still remains low. Rooms and fire hearths were about the same sizes as those of small sites 231 and 317. Storage at early Medio site 204 does not appear to have been done in exactly the same way—or perhaps to the same extent—as at Casas Grandes and site 242. Early rooms at site 204 had no bed platforms, seemingly relying solely on small, hearthless storage rooms. A similar room was found at site 317, and this may be the typical situation for Medio period communities.

Facilities for communal activities are not conspicuous in the early Medio at site 204. The small excavated sample contains no unusually large rooms, although these could be present elsewhere on the site. If a ball court existed at early Medio site 204, it could have been covered or destroyed by human or natural processes, and the most that can be said at present is that there is no trace of a court anywhere around the 204 community.

Likewise, neither of the two conical pit-ovens near the site yielded early Medio dates. They and all of their regional counterparts were argued earlier in this volume to belong to the late part of the Medio. This is not to argue that communal activity did not take place at site 204, which would be contrary to generally accepted models of Puebloan social organization. Instead, we suggest that early Medio communal activity did not have the conspicuous, public form that it later assumed.

A related observation is that early Medio site 204 yielded little recognizable ritual paraphernalia. In chapter 8 we described the early Medio as much like the late part of the preceding Viejo period in their shared lack of the ritual items that later were so much in evidence at Casas Grandes. There must have been ritual activity in the late Viejo and early Medio intervals, but we suggested that it was decentralized and unstandardized before about A.D. 1300. This would make its artifactual concomitants difficult to recognize in the archaeological record. We note the similarity of this argument to one made earlier (Rakita 2001). Rakita envisions simpler, clan-based ritual systems operating in the region before the rise of the primate center. This system was supplanted by the new, standardized, and centralized set of religious beliefs promoted by the primate center to strengthen and legitimize its growing authority. The present volume's new data suggest that this transformation, or something like it, was not effective until after A.D. 1300, that is, the late part of the Medio period. The site 204 data indicate an unstandardized and likely simpler ritual system in the early Medio.

One indication of this simplicity is the symbolism on polychrome pottery. The design motifs on this pottery commonly are seen as reflective of the supernatural concepts of the Medio period, especially in its late part. Discussion in chapter 4 showed the early Medio ceramic assemblage to contain few polychromes, all of which were decorated with simple geometrics done in broad, coarse lines. The symbolic content of these ceramics was characterized as relatively low.

Early Medio site 204 had little of the evidence for public feasting that was just discussed for Casas Grandes and site 242. All of the vessel size and use-wear analyses of chapter 5 showed that early Medio site 204 was more like small sites 231 and 317 than like Casas Grandes and site 242 in ceramic characteristics. Small sites 231 and 317 were taken to represent the ordinary, household level of production and consumption.

Finally, there is at least the hint of greater community autonomy in the early part of the Medio period. In chapter 8 we showed that the early Medio component at 204 contained nearly all of the site's total count of marine shell genera, whereas late Medio contexts contained little marine shell and much from freshwater sources. These data argue for wider access to marine shell during the early Medio than in the late part of the period, when the commodity appears to have been controlled on a regional scale by the primate center. Early Medio communities thus may have been freer to procure marine shell than their successors were. It is unfortunate that there are no mortuary data with which to pursue the question of early Medio social differentiation. Di Peso saw differentiation as increasing through the late Viejo, and this trend presumably continued through the early Medio. Another study of the Casas Grandes material draws this conclusion (Rakita 2001). We would expect a simpler situation at site 204 than at the primate center in the late Medio.

Despite the deficiencies of the small data set, our impression is that early Medio site 204 was a relatively simple and relatively autonomous community where most activities were carried out at the household level. We see no indication of the public ritual and associated economic activity that characterized later times. As we have suggested elsewhere (Whalen and Minnis 2003), early Medio communities likely existed in a sort of peer-polity situation, without strong regional centralization.

The late Medio occupation of site 204 was contemporaneous with the beginnings of Casas Grandes' ascent to regional prominence. The 204 community at first continued to be a relatively large one, and much of the excavated room sample (24 of 35 rooms) belongs to this interval of the site's occupation. There were significant architectural continuities with the preceding early Medio occupation. Even so, it seems that the site's late Medio architecture was somewhat more elaborate than its predecessor, as adobe columns and platform hearths were found in some late Medio rooms. Storage at this time appears to have been primarily in small, hearthless rooms, as in the early occupation. In addition, there was what may have been a corner platform or storage alcove in one of the late-occupied rooms, but this was the only one found in the excavated sample. Late Medio site 204 appears to have had about the same proportion of storage rooms (3 of 24 rooms) as did the preceding early Medio community (1 of 9 rooms). Finally, we note that the late Medio room sample contains no trace of the regional architecture of power.

Communal activity is represented on several levels at late Medio site 204. Chapter 3 contained several illustrations of Room 21, the largest in the site's excavated sample. It contained a pair of adobe columns, and there was no substantial fire feature. The only hearth present in the room was characterized as a later addition. The room was interpreted as a communal space, and it had a high level of access to adjacent rooms and to a large plaza. The rooms with columns at Casas Grandes also opened onto plazas. Two of the adjoining rooms were excavated, and each contained a central platform hearth. Beneath the floor of one of these rooms was the only macaw burial yet found in the region outside of the primate center. Caches of pre-Medio projectile points and of unused grinding stones of vesicular basalt were found in this suite of rooms, which was the most elaborate in the excavated sample. All of it was dated to the Late Medio I interval.

The second level of public activity in the 204 community was a ball court of the formal, I-shaped type. Its playing field was of average size, but it was completely surrounded by a tall, earthen embankment. The court is undated, but we have argued that it belonged to the late Medio occupation.

Some large-scale productive facilities are present on the site. Chapter 1 illustrated the two large ovens that likely were used for the baking of agave at a supra-household scale. One of them is near the ball court, an association noted at several other sites in the region. This observation suggests a link between the ball-court ritual and public feasting, a pattern that is strong in Mesoamerica. We do not know the full spans of the ovens' use, but all dated examples in the small regional sample belong to the late Medio.

Artifacts as well as facilities indicate the large-scale production of food and fermented drink at Casas Grandes and site 242. There is no indication, however, that this pattern existed at a similar scale in the late Medio 204 community. The site's late Medio vessel volumes do not differ significantly from those of small sites 231 and 317. As noted earlier, these two sites were taken to represent the basic, household level of production. On the other hand, use-wear analyses showed that the percentage of vessels with interior pitting in the 204 midden test pits was much greater than that of the small sites. In fact, the frequency of interior-pitted vessels at site 204 was comparable to that of site 242, although the vessels in use were not so large. This was so in both the early and late parts of the Medio period. Other use-wear patterns present a cloudier picture. Early Medio midden levels contained more than twice as many vessels with exterior soot as did either the late midden levels at 204 or the entire assemblages at sites 231 and 317. The late Medio decrease in exterior sooting at site 204 may reflect increasing use of the vessels for storage rather than for cooking.

Another late Medio trend at site 204 is a substantial increase in the recovered quantity of ritual paraphernalia. Many of these items are of the same types found at Casas Grandes, and most of them were absent in early Medio deposits at site 204. This was taken as an indication that late Medio ritual activities were becoming more conspicuous than ever before. They probably were more centralized as well, as Casas Grandes stands out as the regional pinnacle of ritual activity of all sorts. Others (e.g., Harmon 2005, 2006; Rakita 2001; VanPool and VanPool 2007) envision the spread throughout the hinterland of ritual sponsored and promoted by Casas Grandes, and the new data from site 204 support their position.

Early and late Medio community autonomy is difficult to measure from our small data set, although there are some hints that it may have been declining by the late Medio. The aforementioned introduction into the community of ritual promoted by the primate center is one indication of reduced autonomy. The same may be true of the ball game, as Harmon (2005, 2006) interprets the late Medio's I-shaped courts as stages for a new variant of the game that was introduced and spread by the rising community center of Casas Grandes. None of this appears to have been present at early Medio site 204. In addition, chapter 8 showed that the number of marine shell species found in late Medio contexts at the site declined dramatically from early to late Medio times. There was a concomitant increase in the use of locally available freshwater shell in the late Medio. This situation was interpreted as showing increasingly effective control of the marine shell supply in the late Medio, when little of it reached even large communities like 204. Macaws also appear on site 204 in the late Medio, and the one copper bell found there likely also is late Medio. Casas Grandes is the most likely controller of all of these categories of exotica. Lastly, there was a large reduction in the site's population in the early to mid-1300s, and we maintained that the people were absorbed by the growing center of Casas Grandes. The power of the rising primate center thus appears to have been felt in unprecedented ways in the late Medio community at site 204.

Unfortunately, no late Medio burials were recovered from site 204, as all had been looted. It can be noted, however, that the only kind of empty graves found in our excavations were simple sub-floor pits in room corners. Human bone was lightly scattered over the site surface, as were a copper bell and a few turquoise and shell ornaments. Several broken shell ornaments were found in a looted grave pit. These few data hint that the common pattern at site 204 was burial in simple circumstances, with exotic or valuable material included in some cases. The amount of effort spent on site 204 by looters suggests that they were well rewarded, and we expect that there were at least a few burials on the site that were more elaborate or better accompanied than the norm. This is reminiscent of the Casas Grandes burial pattern, where about 50 percent of the interments had no offerings, whereas a few were more elaborately treated. We do not suggest that the most elaborate burials at late Medio site 204 rivaled those at the primate center, of course. In fact, the general level of wealth in evidence in the community is only moderate. Earlier we cited Emerson's (1997) opinion that wealth in a community indicated the presence of high-status people. By this logic, the prominent people at site 204 were of only moderately high status relative to their counterparts at the primate center.

*Sites 231 and 317.* Both sites 231 and 317 seem to represent the lowest level of complexity evident in this sample of Medio period communities. Chapter 3 described the simple architecture of both sites. Walls were thin, room shapes were always simple, and room sizes averaged around 9 sq m. This was previously noted to be about the same as the mean size of rooms in a sample of 26 prehistoric pueblos of the U.S. Southwest. There was almost no architectural elaboration in these rooms, none of which contained platform hearths or bed platforms. No ritual architecture was found on either site.

It appears that each community's agricultural productivity was at the level of its own subsistence needs. Small systems of agricultural terraces were found in the vicinity of each community, but no large-scale systems were in evidence. Earlier, we noted that site 317 had two large, conical pit-ovens, as did the 204 community. Sites 231 and 242, in contrast, had none. This observation leads us to wonder whether all of the large ovens were facilities used to support elite-sponsored feasting. Some likely were, as we have asserted earlier (Minnis and Whalen 2005). Others, however, occur scattered across the uplands and at seemingly unimportant communities like 317. We presently do not know whether these facilities were used under any sort of centralized direction, or if they were even contemporaneous. Both sites 231 and 317 displayed low frequencies of vessels with exterior soot and interior pitting. The volumes of the vessels in which food and drink were prepared and served did not differ significantly across sites 204, 231, and 317. In addition, the largest vessels present at the primate center and at site 242 were either absent or rare at small sites 231 and 317. We take all of these data to represent the ordinary, domestic level of food and drink preparation in these two small communities.

The two sites were poor in exotic, imported, and symbolic items. In chapter 8 we noted the presence of a little shell at both sites, although most of it was freshwater rather than marine. We presume that freshwater shell was the easiest and cheapest to obtain. No exotica of any other sort came from either site. Neither site had much Polychrome pottery, and inhabitants seldom used the high-quality vesicular basalt for grinding tools, relying instead on readily obtained local materials such as rhyolite. Both small sites contained remains of common sorts of food: basic cultigens, agave, and small animals, principally rabbits. In short, sites 231 and 317 seem to have contained little if anything that was special, elaborate, or expensive. We presume that these small, poor, rural communities contained no elite people. Our settlement pattern surveys show that small, simple sites like 231 and 317 were the most common kind of Medio period settlement all over the region, and they would have housed a large fraction of the population.

## The Structure of Authority in the Casas Grandes Core

In this volume, we set out to make an intensive, excavation-based study of some of the near neighbors of the primate center of Casas Grandes. We wished to evaluate a survey-based model of the organization of these communities into the primate center's regional polity. Chapter 1 described this model of inner and outer Core Zone organization. We hypothesized that a relatively small area (i.e., the inner Core Zone) was dominated heavily and completely by the primate center, and we saw a different and somewhat looser organization in the outer Core Zone. The new data analyzed in this volume argue that our original model's area of strong centralization should be extended to include the outer Core Zone. The two parts of the Core Zone clearly had different kinds of organization, but preceding discussion indicates that much of what happened in the outer Core Zone in late Medio times was driven by Casas Grandes. We sum up our observations on this point under three headings: economics, ritual, and demography.

### Economic Indicators

We recently have asserted that some of the Core Zone's agricultural productivity was controlled by the primate center (Minnis, Whalen, and Howell 2006). This argument is based upon the sizes and distributions of systems of trincheras, or low terraces used for soil and water control in the uplands. Most of these systems are small and clearly were built by individual communities. A few are much larger, however, and these are believed to have been constructed and operated under the authority of Casas Grandes and for its benefit. The implication of this argument is that the primate center had the ability to organize labor to construct and operate the terrace systems, as well as to move the produce. The distribution of these large field systems thus is a partial measure of the center's economic reach. Previous discussion showed that the systems are found in the inner and outer parts of the Core Zone. Few small terrace systems and no large ones presently are known outside of the Core. It is clear that this aspect of the economic reach of Casas Grandes extended all through the Core Zone, but not beyond it.

### Ritual Indicators

Ball courts and ritual paraphernalia are the most conspicuous indicators of ceremonial activities in the Casas Grandes area. We begin with the observation that Casas Grandes seems to have been the focus of ball-court activity in the region, as it is the only community with more than one court. Outside of the primate center are found courts of I, T, and open shapes. The last is the simplest, consisting only of two parallel rows of stones set in the ground. These simple, open courts are the most widely scattered, with examples occurring from the Casas Grandes region to southwestern New Mexico. Courts of the I and T shapes have more restricted distributions. The T-shaped courts are rarer than their I-shaped counterparts (Whalen and Minnis 1996b:736). Interestingly, 9 of the 10 reported courts of I or T shape are located in the Casas Grandes Core Zone. The tenth court, an I-shaped one, is at the Río Gavilán site in the nearby mountains. Of the 9 courts of I and T shapes in the Core Zone, three are at Casas Grandes, and the remaining 6 are all in the outer Core Zone, some 15 to 30 km from the primate center. Most of them are attached to pueblo residential sites, but there are several isolated courts that have a number of small communities in their vicinities.

There are two major and interrelated questions about these courts: their ages and their implications for regional organization. Two somewhat different answers have been proposed. The earliest of these is our ball-court study (Whalen and Minnis 1996b). None of the region's ball courts have been directly dated, but we cited data from northern to southern Mesoamerica to show that open courts appeared early in local sequences, and they continued in use through late times. At the same time, however, there was a steady increase over time in the frequency of I-shaped courts. It is tempting to imagine a progression from the simpler open courts to the more complex I-shaped ones. The Mesoamerican data, however, indicate that the situation was more complicated. It appears to have been so in Chihuahua and vicinity as well. The open court at the Joyce Well site in New Mexico is associated with a late Animas phase pueblo where Ramos Polychrome is present. In chapter 4 we showed that the presence of this pottery places the site in the late part of the Medio period. Another open court in the Casas Grandes area is beside the Casa de Fuego site, a pueblo whose occupation has been dated primarily to the late part of the Medio period (Harmon 2005:161). The chronological position of open courts thus remains incompletely understood. They could have been present all through the Medio, or they could all belong to the late part of the period.

Beyond these chronological considerations, our original study largely ignored the question of why courts of different shapes existed. Instead, we focused on ball-court locations. We took the concentration of courts in the outer Core Zone to reflect the limit of Casas Grandes' strict monopoly over ritual activities. Furthermore, the large number of outer Core Zone courts was taken to indicate a significant degree of competition among those populations. This argument was based on Mesoamerican data, where ball courts often served as stages upon which elite factions played out their rivalries. Increases in ball-court frequency in Mesoamerica coincided with periods of weakened regional centralization, and this interpretation was extended to Casas Grandes' outer Core Zone. That is, these communities were seen as under the influence of the primate center but also as under less strict centralized control than those of the inner Core.

A different interpretation of these ball courts recently has been made by Harmon (2005, 2006), who sees the ball courts of the region as reflecting unity rather than disunity. He uses phylogenetic analysis to form a seriation of the region's ball courts. His contention is that the simple, open courts appeared in the 1200s, or early in the Medio period. The courts of I and T shapes were dated to the 1300s, or later in the Medio period. Harmon attaches significance to ball-court shape, seeing the simple, open courts as the settings for an older version of the ball game that was played all over the region before the ascendancy of Casas Grandes. These open courts were built by individual communities for their own integrative purposes. In contrast, the courts of I and T shapes represent a new and more strongly Mesoamerican version of the ball game that was introduced and promoted by the rising elites of Casas Grandes. This elite-sponsored ball-game cult thus became a vehicle for and a marker of the transmission of a Casas Grandes–dominated ritual system among its neighbors. Ball courts of I and T shapes, and the version of the game associated with them, represent yet another aspect of the foreign-derived ritual and symbolism that was used so heavily by the primate center's political entrepreneurs to strengthen and legitimize their positions (Harmon 2005:273).

We are intrigued by Harmon's idea that the several shapes of courts represent different versions of the ball game, and we believe that it is not necessary to argue for a simple replacement of open courts by I-shaped ones. Instead, as in Harmon's model, the open courts could represent an original version of the ball game that was played widely among Medio communities. As Casas Grandes rose to its apogee, the new version of the ball game that was marked by I-shaped courts was projected into the countryside. In this scenario, the new ball game overlies the older tradition without completely replacing it. This would explain the apparent late Medio contemporaneity of open and I-shaped courts. An analogous situation is the simultaneous presence in Mexico from colonial times to the present of shrines to prehispanic gods and to the Virgin of Guadalupe.

It is most interesting that in chapter 4 of this volume we described a similar situation with ceramic design motifs. In that discussion, we asserted that the original Chihuahuan style of ceramic painting used broad, coarse lines to form simple, geometric designs. The opening of the late Medio saw the introduction of a new style of Polychrome painting using fine lines and combinations of local and Mesoamerican motifs that were more complex than ever before. Significantly, this new style of painting existed beside the original style throughout the Medio period. The new overlies the old without completely supplanting it. In short, we see the same process at work in late Medio contexts as disparate as design motifs and ball courts. Discussion in chapter 8 of this volume also indicated that ritual paraphernalia of the types that are plentiful at Casas Grandes largely were absent at early Medio site 204. They increased considerably in frequency in the late Medio occupation. Significantly, all of the items just mentioned functioned in symbolic and ceremonial contexts. We may suggest, therefore, that ritual and ritually sanctioned authority were important—perhaps central—components of the power of the primate center. The ritual authority that was projected outward from Casas Grandes clearly reached into the outer Core Zone. This is the location of site 204, with its I-shaped ball court and Casas Grandes–style ritual paraphernalia. The same is true for site 242. This interpretation of ball courts and ritual activity does not indicate a reduction of the authority of the primate center in the outer Core Zone.

## Demographic Indicators

Earlier in this chapter we linked the reduction in population at site 204 after 1300 to the growth of Casas Grandes. The implication was that the growing primate center absorbed at least some of the regional population. Site 204 lies in the outer part of the Core Zone, some 25 km from Casas Grandes. This indicates that absorption of population was not confined to the nearest neighbors of the primate center. There are a few large Medio period sites in the inner Core Zone, within ca. 15 km of Casas Grandes, and there is one more besides 204 in the outer Core. Unfortunately, none of these have been excavated, and we do not know whether their occupational histories parallel that of site 204. It may be, of course, that the extent of population absorption was not determined solely by proximity to the primate center but by other factors of which we remain ignorant.

Concentration of population in the rising center of Casas Grandes would have changed regional demography in the late part of the Medio period. In our original interpretation (Whalen and Minnis 2001a), the hinterland of Casas Grandes had a distinctly hierarchical structure. This model is reviewed in chapter 1. It was based on the questionable but necessary assumption that Medio period communities of all sizes were contemporaneous. The new work described in the present volume, however, shows the inaccuracy of this characterization in the case of at least one of the large neighbors of Casas Grandes. The 204 community, postulated head of the Tinaja cluster, is now known to have declined substantially in size as the primate center reached its peak. By the mid-1300s, the once-large 204 community began to contract considerably. This new realization removes much of the perceived hierarchical structure of the Tinaja cluster. Instead of a much larger community surrounded by smaller neighbors, we are left with only a cluster of small and medium-sized sites by late Medio times. This is not to assert that no local organization existed in the Tinaja area in the late Medio. In fact, the ball courts suggest otherwise, as was discussed earlier in this chapter. The situation does not now seem to have been as conspicuously hierarchical as originally supposed, however.

This observation has interesting implications for settlement system interpretation. If other large Medio communities have histories like 204's, the structure of the Core Zone settlement system at the apogee of Casas Grandes would be somewhat different than we originally thought. The direction of this difference is toward a reduction in hierarchical structure in Casas Grandes' near-hinterland. Less Core Zone hierarchy in the late Medio could, in turn, argue for an increase in the control exerted by the primate center. This line of thought has another, complementary implication as well. A reduction of large Core Zone communities after the middle 1300s would make the settlement pattern look somewhat more like that of the Middle Zone. The characteristic that they would share is a scatter of small and medium-sized communities without much access to large nearby settlements. In this scenario, the burden of administration would be on the primate center. In such a situation, the primate pattern would have been even more extreme than it was in our original interpretation. Likewise, the area under the strong control of the primate center would have extended farther than we originally envisioned.

## Concluding Thoughts and Future Directions

As we made clear in chapter 1, we see Casas Grandes as a chiefdom-level society, and this interpretation implies characteristic levels and kinds of local and regional organization.

In particular, we do not expect to see a simple, uniform hegemony over a large area around the primate center. States are capable of exerting this level of control, but chiefdoms characteristically are not. Instead of a uniform hegemony, we expect a situation in which the central place projects its authority outward through a complex, negotiated set of relationships in fragmented political contexts. Furthermore, we presume that the center's control should become more discontinuous and less comprehensive with movement away from it. In any specific case, the relevant question is how far from the center it is necessary to go before finding the limit of strong control.

In the Casas Grandes case, we envision a low level of regional organization among the pueblos of the early part of the Medio period, before 1300. This situation remains poorly understood, however. About 1300 is the beginning of our late Medio interval, when we see the rise and spread of a system of organization that focused on the community of Casas Grandes. A number of methods of regional integration were used to form this polity, and some of these are visible in the Core Zone communities studied in this volume. The entire Core Zone appears to have been tightly tied to Casas Grandes, and we envision the primate center's hegemony there. It is clear, however, that several different control strategies were employed.

One of these is monopoly of organizational and integrative activity, especially ritual, by the primate center. This occurred within the limit of daily interaction, or a radius of about 15 km. We presume that there was equally powerful economic and political control over these nearest neighbors of Casas Grandes. Beyond this small area of monopolistic control, the primate center projected its authority into the countryside in at least two ways. One of these was the establishment of new, special-purpose settlements that served the needs of the central place. Site 242 has been interpreted in this volume as a specialized control node that functioned to organize agricultural productivity in its part of the uplands. This alone was not sufficient to organize the entire Core Zone, however. The second control strategy was the absorption of existing, once-autonomous communities into the Casas Grandes–centered polity. Late Medio site 204 exemplifies this process, of which ritual and public ceremony appear to have been powerful parts. Economic control likely was equally important, although the details are less clear in our present state of ignorance. We do not know what other kinds of links might have been formed between prominent people in the 204 community and those of Casas Grandes. It is plausible that linkages of kinship or alliance might have existed, as such connections commonly form networks for a variety of social, political, and economic actions. We envision a combination of ritual, economics, kinship, and alliances as closely tying communities such as 204 to Casas Grandes. Indeed, the strength of that tie eventually resulted in absorption of people from the 204 community into Casas Grandes. The previously cited distribution of the regional signifiers of power argues that this level of organization of the hinterland extended only about 30 km from the primate center. We do not, of course, see this as the limit of the power of Casas Grandes, but only as the extent of its area of *maximum* control. In this volume, we have attempted to use our Core Zone excavation data to clarify some of the organizational strategies in use there. It is clear, however, that the nature and extent of Casas Grandes' control over its neighbors was a complex and multifaceted situation about which the last words have not yet been written.

# REFERENCES CITED

Adams, E. Charles
   1983    The Architectural Analog to Hopi Social Organization and Room Use, and Implications
           for Prehistoric Northern Southwestern Culture. *American Antiquity* 48(1): 44–61.
   2002    *Homol'ovi: An Ancient Hopi Settlement Cluster.* Tucson: University of Arizona Press.
Adams, E. Charles, and Andrew I. Duff
   2004    Settlement Clusters in the Pueblo IV Period. In *The Protohistoric Pueblo World, A.D.
           1275–1600,* edited by E. C. Adams and A. I. Duff, pp. 3–16. Tucson: University of Arizona
           Press.
Adams, Karen R.
   2004    Anthropogenic Ecology of the North American Southwest. In *People and Plants in Ancient
           Western North America,* edited by P. E. Minnis, pp. 167–204. Washington, D.C.: Smithson-
           ian Books.
Aitken, M. J.
   1990    *Science-Based Dating in Archaeology.* London: Longman.
Amick, Daniel S., and Raymond Mauldin
   1997    Effects of Raw Material on Flake Breakage Patterns. *Lithic Technology* 22: 18–32.
Amsden, Monroe
   1928    *Archaeological Reconnaissance in Sonora.* Paper No. 1. Los Angeles: Southwest Museum.
Anderson, David G.
   1994    *The Savannah River Chiefdoms: Political Change in the Late Prehistoric Southeast.* Tusca-
           loosa: University of Alabama Press.
Andrefsky, William, Jr.
   1998    *Lithics: Macroscopic Approaches to Analysis.* Cambridge: Cambridge University Press.
Anscombe F. J.
   1960    Rejection of Outliers. *Technometrics* 2(2): 123–48.
Arthur, John W.
   2003    Brewing Beer: Status, Wealth, and Ceramic Use Alteration among the Gamo of Southwest
           Ethiopia. *World Archaeology* 34(3): 516–28.
Ash, David L., and James A. Brown
   1990    Stratigraphy and Site Chronology. In *At the Edge of Prehistory: Huber Phase Archaeology in
           the Chicago Area,* edited by J. Brown and P. O'Brien, pp. 174–85. Kampsville, Ill.: Center for
           American Archaeology.
Bandelier, Adolph F.
   1890    The Ruins of Casas Grandes. *The Nation* 51: 185–87.
Bayham, Frank, and Pamela Hatch
   1985    Archaeofaunal Remains from the New River Area. In *Hohokam Settlement and Economic
           Systems in the Central New River Drainage, Arizona,* edited by D. E. Doyel and M. D. Elison,
           pp. 405–33. Publication in Archaeology No 4. Phoenix: Soil Systems.
Beck, Margaret
   2001    Archaeological Signatures of Corn Preparation in the U.S. Southwest. *Kiva* 67(2): 187–218.
Beck, Robin A., Jr.
   2003    Consolidation and Hierarchy: Chiefdom Variability in the Mississippian Southeast. *Amer-
           ican Antiquity* 68(4): 641–61.
Berry, Michael S.
   1982    *Time, Space, and Tradition in Anasazi Prehistory.* Salt Lake City: University of Utah Press.
Blackiston, A. Hooton
   1906    Ruins of the Tenaja and the Rio San Pedro. *Records of the Past* 7: 282–90.

Blanton, Richard E., Stephen A. Kowalewski, Gary M. Feinman, and Peter N. Peregrine
    1996    A Dual-Process Theory for the Evolution of Mesoamerican Civilization. *Current Anthropology* 37(1): 1–14.

Bluhm, Elaine A.
    1957    *The Sawmill Site: A Reserve Phase Village in the Pine Lawn Valley of Western New Mexico.* Fieldiana: Anthropology, Vol. 47, No. 1. Chicago: Natural History Museum.

Bradley, Ronna J.
    1999    Shell Exchange within the Southwest: The Casas Grandes Interaction Sphere. In *The Casas Grandes World,* edited by C. Schaafsma and C. Riley, pp. 213–28. Salt Lake City: University of Utah Press.

Brand, Donald D.
    1933    *The Historical Geography of Northwestern Chihuahua.* Ph.D. diss., Department of Geography, University of California, Berkeley.
    1935    The Distribution of Pottery Types in Northwest Mexico. *American Anthropologist* 37(2): 287–305.
    1943    The Chihuahua Culture Area. *New Mexico Anthropologist* 6–7(3): 115–58.

Braniff Conejo, Beatriz
    1986    Ojo de Agua, Sonora, and Casas Grandes, Chihuahua: A Suggested Chronology. In *Ripples in the Chichimec Sea: New Considerations of Southwestern-Mesoamerican Interactions,* edited by F. J. Mathien and R. H. McGuire, pp. 70–80. Center for Archaeological Investigations. Carbondale: Southern Illinois University Press.

Bronk Ramsey, Christopher
    2000    *OXCAL Program, V3.4.* Oxford: University of Oxford Radiocarbon Acceleration Unit. www.rlha.ox.ac.uk/oxcal/oxcal.htm#author.

Bruman, Henry J.
    2000    *Alcohol in Ancient Mexico.* Salt Lake City: University of Utah Press.

Burd, Karen, Jane Kelley, and Mitchel Hendrickson
    2004    Ceramics as Temporal and Spatial Indicators in Chihuahua Cultures. In *Surveying the Archaeology of Northwest Mexico,* edited by G. Newell and E. Gallaga, pp. 177–204. Salt Lake City: University of Utah Press.

Bustard, Wendy
    2003    Pueblo Bonito: When a House Is Not a Home. In *Pueblo Bonito: Center of the Chacoan World,* edited by J. Neitzel, pp. 80–93. Washington, D.C.: Smithsonian Books.

Camacho Uribe, Daniel
    1988    *La Madera: Estudio anatómico catálogo de especies mexicanas.* Colección Científica. Mexico City: Instituto Nacional de Antropología e Historia.

Cameron, Catherine M., ed.
    1995    Migration and the Movement of Southwestern Peoples. Special issue, *Journal of Anthropological Archaeology* 14(2): 99–250.

Cameron, Catherine M.
    1999    Room Size, Organization of Construction, and Archaeological Interpretation in the Puebloan Southwest. *Journal of Anthropological Archaeology* 18(2): 201–39.

Cannon, Michael D., and Michael A. Etnier
    1997    Report on the Analysis of Faunal Materials from the Reconocimiento Regional Paquimé, 1996. Report on file at the Department of Anthropology, University of Tulsa, Okla.

Carey, Henry A.
    1931    An Analysis of the Northwestern Chihuahua Culture. *American Anthropologist* 33(3):325–74.

Carlson, Roy L.
    1982    The Polychrome Complexes. In *Southwestern Ceramics: A Comparative Review,* edited by A. H. Schroeder, pp. 201–34. Arizona Archaeologist no. 15. Phoenix: Arizona Archaeological Society.

Castetter, Edward F., Willis Bell, and A. R. Grove
    1938    *Ethnobiological Studies of the American Southwest IV: The Early Utilization and Distribution of Agave in the American Southwest.* Bulletin No. 335. Albuquerque: University of New Mexico.

Chapman, Kenneth M.
    1923    Casas Grandes Pottery. *Art and Archaeology* 16(1–2): 25–50.

Ciolek-Torrello, Richard, and J. Jefferson Reid
    1974    Change in Household Size at Grasshopper Pueblo. *Kiva* 40(1–2): 39–48.

Clark, J. J.
    2001    *Tracking Prehistoric Migrations: Pueblo Settlers among the Tonto Basin Hohokam.* Anthropological Papers 65. Tucson: University of Arizona Press.

Cordell, Linda S.
    1995    Tracing Migration Pathways from the Receiving End. *Journal of Anthropological Archaeology* 14(2): 203–11.

Cotterell, Brian, and Johan Kamminga
    1990    *The Mechanics of Pre-Industrial Technology.* Cambridge: Cambridge University Press.

Crabtree, Don E.
    1972    *An Introduction to Flintworking.* Occasional Papers No. 28. Pocatello: Idaho University Museum.

Crown, Patricia L.
    1994    *Ceramics and Ideology: Salado Polychrome Pottery.* Albuquerque: University of New Mexico Press.

Cruz Antillón, Rafael, Robert D. Leonard, Timothy D. Maxwell, Todd L. VanPool, Marcel J. Harmon, Christine S. VanPool, David A. Hyndman, and Sidney S. Brandwein.
    2004    Galeana, Villa Ahumada, and Casa Chica: Diverse Sites in the Casas Grandes Region. In *Surveying the Archaeology of Northwest Mexico,* edited by G. E. Newell and E. Gallaga, pp. 149–75. Salt Lake City: University of Utah Press.

Curet, L. Antonio
    2003    Issues on the Diversity and Emergence of Middle Range Societies of the Ancient Caribbean: A Critique. *Journal of Archaeological Research* 11(1): 1–42.

Dean, Jeffrey S., and John C. Ravesloot
    1993    The Chronology of Cultural Interaction in the Gran Chichimeca. In *Culture and Contact: Charles C. Di Peso's Gran Chichimeca,* edited by A. I. Woosley and J. C. Ravesloot, pp. 83–104. Dragoon, Ariz.: Amerind Foundation; Albuquerque: University of New Mexico Press.

Deaver, William L., and Robert A. Heckman
    2005    Archaeomagnetic Dating in Chihuahua. Poster presentation at the Archaeological Sciences of the Americas Conference, Tucson. www.sricrm.com/amag/images/Chihuahua.jpg.

Dering, Phil
    1999    Earth Oven Plant Processing in Archaic Period Economies: An Example from a Semi-Arid Savannah in South-Central North America. *American Antiquity* 64(4): 659–74.

Dietler, Michael, and Brian Hayden
    2001    *Feasts: Archaeological and Ethnographic Perspectives on Food, Politics, and Power.* Washington, D.C.: Smithsonian Institution Press.

Di Peso, Charles C.
    1974    *Casas Grandes: A Fallen Trading Center of the Gran Chichimeca.* Vols. 1–3. Dragoon, Ariz.: Amerind Foundation; Flagstaff, Ariz.: Northland Press.

Di Peso, Charles C., John B. Rinaldo, and Gloria J. Fenner
    1974    *Casas Grandes: A Fallen Trading Center of the Gran Chichimeca.* Vols. 4–8. Dragoon, Ariz.: Amerind Foundation; Flagstaff, Ariz.: Northland Press.

Doolittle, William E.

1993    Canal Irrigation at Casas Grandes: A Technological and Developmental Assessment of Its Origins. In *Culture and Contact: Charles C. Di Peso's Gran Chichimeca,* edited by A. I. Woosley and J. C. Ravesloot, pp. 133–52. Dragoon, Ariz. and Albuquerque: Amerind Foundation and University of New Mexico Press.

Doyel, David E.

1976    Salado Cultural Development in the Tonto Basin and Globe-Miami Areas, Central Arizona. *Kiva* 42(1): 5–16.

Drennan, Robert D.

1995    Chiefdoms in Northern South America. *Journal of World Prehistory* 9(3): 301–40.

1996    *Statistics for Archaeologists: A Commonsense Approach.* New York: Plenum Press.

Earle, Timothy

1997    *How Chiefs Come to Power: Political Economy in Prehistory.* Palo Alto: Stanford University Press.

Emerson, Thomas E.

1997    *Cahokia and the Archaeology of Power.* Tuscaloosa: University of Alabama Press.

Feinman, Gary M., and Jill Neitzel

1984    Too Many Types: An Overview of Sedentary Prestate Societies in the Americas. In *Advances in Archaeological Method and Theory.* Vol. 7, edited by M. B. Schiffer, pp. 39–102. New York: Academic Press.

Fish, Paul R., and Suzanne K. Fish

1999    Reflections on the Casas Grandes Regional System from the Northwestern Periphery. In *The Casas Grandes World,* edited by C. Schaafsma and C. Riley, pp. 27–42. Salt Lake City: University of Utah Press.

Fish, Suzanne K., Paul R. Fish, and John Madsen

1992    *The Marana Community in the Hohokam World.* Anthropological Papers of The University of Arizona No. 56. Tucson: University of Arizona Press.

Flannery, Kent V.

1966    The Postglacial "Readaptation" as Viewed from Mesoamerica. *American Antiquity* 31(6): 800–5.

Frost, Dawn A.

2000    Architecture as Chronological Marker: Testing Di Peso's Assumptions at Paquimé, Chihuahua, Mexico. Master's thesis, Department of Anthropology, University of Tulsa, Okla.

Garraty, Christopher P.

2000    Ceramic Indices of Aztec Eliteness. *Ancient Mesoamerica* 11(2): 323–40.

Gasser, Robert E., and Scott M. Kwiatkowski

1991    Food for Thought: Recognizing Patterns in Hohokam Subsistence. In *Exploring the Hohokam,* edited by G. G. Gumerman, pp. 417–60. Dragoon, Ariz. and Albuquerque: Amerind Foundation and University of New Mexico Press.

Gentry, Howard S.

1982    *Agaves of Continental North America.* Tucson: University of Arizona Press.

Gladwin, Harold S.

1936    Discussion. In *An Archaeological Survey of Chihuahua,* by E. B. Sayles, pp. 89–108. Medallion Papers No. 22. Globe, Ariz.: Gila Pueblo.

Gladwin, Winifred, and Harold S. Gladwin

1934    *A Method for the Designation of Cultures and Their Variations,* Medallion Papers No. 15. Globe, Ariz.: Gila Pueblo.

Guevara Sánchez, Arturo

1986    *Arqueología del área de las cuarentas casas, Chihuahua.* Colección Científica. Mexico City: Instituto Nacional de Antropología e Historia.

Hair, Joseph F., R. E. Anderson, and R. L. Tatham
  1987     *Multivariate Data Analysis.* New York: Macmillan.
Hammond, George P., and Agapito Rey
  1928     *Obregón's History of the Sixteenth Century Explorations in Western North America Entitled: Chronicle, Commentary, or Relations of the Ancient and Modern Discoveries in New Spain, New Mexico, and Mexico, 1584.* Los Angeles: Wetzel.
Harmon, Marcel J.
  2005     Centralization, Cultural Transmission, and "the Game of Life and Death" in Northern Mexico. Ph.D. diss., Department of Anthropology, University of New Mexico, Albuquerque.
  2006     Religion and the Mesoamerican Ball Game in the Casas Grandes Region of Northern Mexico. In *Religion in the Prehispanic Southwest,* edited by T. L. VanPool, C. S. VanPool, and D. A. Phillips, pp. 185–218. Walnut Creek, Calif.: AltaMira Press.
Hassan, F. A., and S. W. Robinson
  1987     High-Precision Radiocarbon Chronometry of Ancient Egypt. *Antiquity* 61(1): 119–35.
Haury, Emil W.
  1976     *The Hohokam: Desert Farmers and Craftsmen.* Tucson: University of Arizona Press.
Hendrickson, Mitchel J.
  2000     Design Analysis of Chihuahuan Polychrome Jars from North American Museum Collections. Master's thesis, Department of Archaeology, University of Calgary, Alberta, Canada.
  2003     *Design Analysis of Chihuahuan Polychrome Jars from North American Museum Collections.* BAR International Series 1125. Oxford: Archaeopress.
Hill, James N.
  1970     *Broken K Pueblo: Prehistoric Social Organization in the American Southwest.* Anthropological Papers 18. Tucson: University of Arizona Press.
Huckell, Lisa W., and Mollie S. Toll
  2004     Wild Plant Use in the North American Southwest. In *People and Plants in Ancient Western North America,* edited by P. E. Minnis, pp. 37–114. Washington, D.C.: Smithsonian Books.
Humphrey, Robert R.
  1987     *90 Years and 535 Miles: Vegetation Changes along the Mexican Border.* Albuquerque: University of New Mexico Press.
James, Steven R.
  1995     Change and Continuity in Western Pueblo Households during the Historic Period in the American Southwest. *World Archaeology* 28(3): 429–56.
Jeske, Robert J., and Rochelle Lurie
  1997     The Archaeological Visibility of Bipolar Technology: An Example from the Koster Site. *Midcontinental Journal of Archaeology* 18(2): 131–60.
Johnson, Allen W., and Timothy Earle
  2000     *The Evolution of Human Societies: From Foraging Group to Agrarian State.* Palo Alto: Stanford University Press.
Jones, Jenna F.
  2002     Ceramics and Feasting in the Casas Grandes Area, Chihuahua, Mexico. Master's thesis. Department of Anthropology, University of Tulsa, Okla.
Judd, Neil M.
  1964     *The Architecture of Pueblo Bonito.* Miscellaneous Collections 147, No. 1. Washington, D.C.: Smithsonian Institution.
Kantner, John W., and Keith W. Kintigh
  2006     The Chaco World. In *The Archaeology of Chaco Canyon: An Eleventh-Century Pueblo Regional Center,* edited by S. H. Lekson, pp. 153–88. Santa Fe: School of American Research Press.
Kantner, John W., and N. M. Mahoney
  2000     *Great House Communities across the Chacoan Landscape.* Anthropological Papers 64. Tucson: University of Arizona Press.

Kelley, Jane H., Joe D. Stewart, A. C. MacWilliams, and Loy C. Neff
    1999    A West Central Chihuahuan Perspective on Chihuahuan Culture. In *The Casas Grandes World,* edited by C. Schaafsma and C. Riley, pp. 63–77. Salt Lake City: University of Utah Press.
Kidder, Alfred V.
    1916    The Pottery of the Casas Grandes District, Chihuahua. In *The Holmes Anniversary Volume: Anthropological Essays,* pp. 253–68. Washington, D.C.: Privately printed.
    1924    *An Introduction to the Study of Southwestern Archaeology.* New Haven: Yale University Press.
Kintigh, Keith W.
    2002    *Tools for Quantitative Archaeology: Programs for Quantitative Analysis in Archaeology.* Tempe: K. W. Kintigh.
Knight, Vernon J., Jr.
    1989    Symbolism of Mississippian Mounds. In *Powhatan's Mantle,* edited by P. Wood, G. Waselkov, and M. T. Hatley, pp. 279–91. Lincoln: University of Nebraska Press.
    2004    Characterizing Elite Midden Deposits at Moundville. *American Antiquity* 69(2): 301–21.
Kobayashi, Hiroaki
    1975    The Experimental Study of Bipolar Flakes. In *Lithic Technology: Making and Using Stone Tools,* edited by E. Swanson, pp. 115–27. The Hague: Mouton.
Kohler, Timothy A., and Meredith H. Matthews
    1988    Long-Term Anasazi Land Use and Forest Reduction: A Case Study from Southwestern Colorado. *American Antiquity* 53(3): 537–64.
Kooyman, Brian P.
    2000    *Understanding Stone Tools and Archaeological Sites.* Calgary: University of Calgary Press.
LeBlanc, Steven A.
    1980    The Dating of Casas Grandes. *American Antiquity* 45(4): 799–806.
Lekson, Stephen H.
    1984    Dating Casas Grandes. *Kiva* 50(1): 55–60.
    1986    *Great Pueblo Architecture of Chaco Canyon, New Mexico.* Albuquerque: University of New Mexico Press.
    1999    *The Chaco Meridian: Centers of Political Power in the Ancient Southwest.* Walnut Creek, Calif.: AltaMira Press.
    2000    Salado in Chihuahua. In *Salado,* edited by J. S. Dean, pp. 275–94. Dragoon, Ariz.: Amerind Foundation; Albuquerque: University of New Mexico Press.
    2002    *Salado Archaeology of the Upper Gila, New Mexico.* Anthropological Papers 67. Tucson: University of Arizona Press.
Lekson, Stephen H., ed.
    2006    *The Archaeology of Chaco Canyon: An Eleventh-Century Pueblo Regional Center.* Santa Fe, N.M.: School of American Research Press.
Lepofsky, Dana
    2004    Paleoethnobotany in the Northwest. In *People and Plants in Ancient Western North America,* edited by P. E. Minnis, pp. 367–464. Washington, D.C.: Smithsonian Books.
Lesure, Richard G., and Michael Blake
    2002    Interpretive Challenges in the Study of Early Complexity: Economy, Ritual, and Architecture at Paso de la Amada, Mexico. *Journal of Anthropological Archaeology* 21(1): 1–24.
Lewis-Beck, Michael S.
    1980    *Applied Regression: An Introduction.* Quantitative Applications in the Social Sciences Series 22. Beverly Hills, Calif.: Sage Publications.
Lightfoot, Kent G.
    1984    *Prehistoric Political Dynamics: A Case Study from the American Southwest.* DeKalb: Northern Illinois University Press.

Lister, Robert H.
1946    Survey of Archaeological Remains in Northwestern Chihuahua. *Southwestern Journal of Anthropology* 2(4): 443–52.

Long, Austin, and Bruce Rippeteau
1974    Testing Contemporaneity and Averaging Radiocarbon Dates. *American Antiquity* 39(2): 205–15.

Lowell, Julia C.
1991    *Prehistoric Households at Turkey Creek Pueblo, Arizona.* Anthropological Papers 54. Tucson: University of Arizona Press.
1999    The Fires of Grasshopper: Enlightening Transformations in Subsistence Practices through Fire-feature Analysis. *Journal of Anthropological Archaeology* 18(4): 441–70.

Lyons, Patrick D.
2003    *Ancestral Hopi Migrations.* Anthropological Papers 68. Tucson: University of Arizona Press.

Martin, Paul S., J. B. Rinaldo, and W. A. Longacre
1961    *Mineral Creek Site and Hooper Ranch Pueblo, Eastern Arizona.* Fieldiana: Anthropology, Vol. 52. Chicago: Natural History Museum.

Martin, William C., and Charles R. Hutchins
1981    *A Flora of New Mexico.* Vaduz, Liechtenstein: J. Cramer.

Mauldin, Raymond P., and Daniel S. Amick
1989    Investigation Patterning in Debitage from Experimental Bifacial Core Reduction. In *Experiments in Lithic Technology,* edited by D. Amick and R. Mauldin, pp. 67–88. BAR International Series 528. Oxford: British Archaeological Reports.

McCluney, Eugene B.
2002    The 1963 Excavation. In *The Joyce Well Site: On the Frontier of the Casas Grandes World,* by J. M. Skibo, E. B. McCluney, and W. H. Walker, pp. 11–96. Salt Lake City: University of Utah Press.

McKay, Michael W.
2005    Observing Social Complexity within the Paquimé Polity: A Comparison of Ground Stone Implements from the La Tinaja Site and the Site of Casas Grandes, Chihuahua, Mexico. Master's thesis, Department of Anthropology, University of Oklahoma, Norman.

McKusick, Charmion R.
2001    *Southwest Birds of Sacrifice.* Phoenix: Arizona Archaeological Society.

Miller, Christopher L.
1995    Chipped Stone Analyses from Northwestern Chihuahua, Mexico. Master's thesis, Department of Anthropology, University of Tulsa, Okla.

Mills, Barbara J., ed.
2004    *Identity, Feasting, and the Archaeology of the Greater Southwest.* Boulder: University Press of Colorado.

Mindeleff, Victor
1891    A Study of Pueblo Architecture: Tusayan and Cibola. In *Annual Report of the Bureau of American Ethnology* 8, pp. 3–288. Washington, D.C.: Smithsonian Institution.

Minnis, Paul E.
1985    *Social Adaptation to Food Stress: A Prehistoric Southwestern Example.* Chicago: University of Chicago Press.
1987    Identification of Wood from Archaeological Sites in the American Southwest I. Keys or Gymnosperms. *Journal of Archaeological Science* 14(1): 121–31.
1988    Four Examples of Specialized Production at Casas Grandes, Northwestern Chihuahua. *Kiva* 53(2): 181–93.
1989    The Casas Grandes Polity in the International Four Corners. In *The Sociopolitical Structure of Prehistoric Southwestern Societies,* edited by S. Upham, K. Lightfoot, and R. Jewett, pp. 269–305. Boulder, Colo.: Westview Press.

Minnis, Paul E., and Steven A. LeBlanc

    1976    An Efficient, Inexpensive Arid Lands Flotation System. *American Antiquity* 41(4): 491–93.

Minnis, Paul E., and Michael E. Whalen

    2005    At the Other End of the Puebloan World: Feasting at Casas Grandes, Chihuahua, Mexico. In *Engaged Anthropology: Research Essays on North American Archaeology, Ethnobotany, and Museology,* edited by M. Hegmon and B. Eiselt, pp. 114–28. Anthropological Papers No. 94. Ann Arbor: University of Michigan Museum of Anthropology.

Minnis, Paul E., Michael E. Whalen, and R. Emerson Howell

    2006    Fields of Power: Upland Farming in the Prehispanic Casas Grandes Polity, Chihuahua, Mexico. *American Antiquity* 71(4): 707–22.

Minnis, Paul E., Michael E. Whalen, Jane H. Kelley, and Joe D. Stewart

    1993    Prehistoric Macaw Breeding in the North American Southwest. *American Antiquity* 57(3): 270–76.

Montúfar López, Aurora, and Luisa Reyes Landa

    1995    Estudio de los Restos Botánicos de la Cueva de la Olla, Chihuahua. In *Investigaciones Recientes en Paleobotánica y Palinología.* Mexico City: Instituto Nacional de Antropología e Historia.

Moulard, Barbara L.

    2005    Archaism and Emulation in Casas Grandes Painted Pottery. In *Casas Grandes and the Ceramic Art of the Ancient Southwest,* edited by R. F. Townsend, pp. 66–97. Chicago: Art Institute of Chicago.

Muller, J., and D. R. Wilcox

    1999    Powhatan's Mantle as Metaphor: Comparing Macroregional Integration in the Southwest and Southeast. In *Great Towns and Regional Polities in the Prehistoric American Southwest and Southeast,* edited by J. E. Neitzel, pp. 159–64. Dragoon, Ariz.: Amerind Foundation; Albuquerque: University of New Mexico Press.

Nelson, Margaret C.

    1999    *Mimbres During the Twelfth Century: Abandonment, Continuity, and Reorganization.* Tucson: University of Arizona Press.

Odell, George H.

    2004    Lithic Analysis. New York: Kluwer Academic/Plenum Publishers.

Ottaway, B. S.

    1987    Radiocarbon: Where We Are and Where We Need to Be. *Antiquity* 61(1): 136–38.

Parry, William J., and Robert L. Kelly

    1987    Expedient Core Technology and Sedentism. In *The Organization of Core Technology,* edited by J. Johnson and C. Morrow, pp. 285–304. Boulder, Colo.: Westview Press.

Pauketat, Timothy R.

    2003    Resettled Farmers and the Making of a Mississippian Polity. *American Antiquity* 68(1): 39–66.

Pendergast, David M.

    1962    Metal Artifacts in Prehispanic Mesoamerica. *American Antiquity* 27(4): 520–45.

Pepper, G. R.

    1920    *Pueblo Bonito.* Anthropological Papers 27. New York: American Museum of Natural History.

Pitezel, Todd

    2000    Typological and Temporal Definition in the Casas Grandes Ceramics: A Study from the Casas Grandes Volumes. Master's thesis, Department of Anthropology, University of Tulsa, Okla.

    2003    The Hilltop Site of El Pueblito. *Archaeology Southwest* 17(2): 10.

    2007    Surveying Cerro de Moctezuma, Chihuahua, Mexico. *Kiva* 72(3): 353–69.

Plog, Stephen

    1997    *Ancient Peoples of the American Southwest.* London: Thames and Hudson.

Prentiss, William C., and Eugene J. Romanski
 1989   Experimental Evaluation of Sullivan and Rozen's Debitage Typology. In *Experiments in Lithic Technology,* edited by D. Amick and R. Mauldin, pp. 89–99. BAR International Series 528. Oxford: British Archaeological Reports.
Rakita, Gordon F. M.
 2001   Social Complexity, Religious Organization, and Mortuary Ritual in the Casas Grandes Region of Chihuahua, Mexico. Ph.D. diss., Department of Anthropology, University of New Mexico, Albuquerque.
Rakita, Gordon F. M., and Gerry R. Raymond
 2003   The Temporal Sensitivity of Casas Grandes Polychrome Ceramics. *Kiva* 68(3): 153–84.
Ravesloot, John C.
 1984   Social Differentiation at Casas Grandes, Chihuahua, Mexico: An Archaeological Analysis of Mortuary Practices. Ph.D. diss., Department of Anthropology, Southern Illinois University, Carbondale.
Ravesloot, John C., Jeffrey S. Dean, and Michael S. Foster
 1995   A New Perspective on the Casas Grandes Tree-Ring Dates. In *The Gran Chichimeca: Essays on the Archaeology and Ethnohistory of Northern Mesoamerica,* edited by J. Reyman, pp. 240–51. Aldershot, UK: Ashgate Publishing.
Rebnegger, Karen J.
 2001   Lithic Technology, Craft Production, and Site Variation in the Casas Grandes Region. Master's thesis, Department of Anthropology, University of Oklahoma, Norman.
Reid, J. Jefferson, and Stephanie M. Whittlesey
 1982   Households at Grasshopper Pueblo. *American Behavioral Scientist* 25(6): 687–703.
 1990   The Complicated and the Complex: Observations on the Archaeological Record of Large Pueblos. In *Perspectives on Southwestern Prehistory,* edited by P. Minnis and C. Redman, pp. 184–95. Boulder, Colo.: Westview Press.
Renfrew, Colin
 2000   Production and Consumption in a Sacred Economy: The Material Correlates of High Devotional Expression at Chaco Canyon. *American Antiquity* 66(1): 14–25.
Rick, John W.
 1987   Dates as Data: An Examination of the Peruvian Preceramic Radiocarbon Record. *American Antiquity* 51(1): 55–73.
Riggs, Charles R.
 2001   *The Architecture of Grasshopper Pueblo.* Salt Lake City: University of Utah Press.
Riley, Carroll L.
 2005   *Becoming Aztlan: Mesoamerican Influence in the Greater Southwest, A.D. 1220–1500.* Salt Lake City: University of Utah Press.
Rissman, Paul
 1988   Public Displays and Private Values: A Guide to Buried Wealth in Harappan Archaeology. *World Archaeology* 20(2): 209–28.
Rowles, Ryan A.
 2004   Stone Tool Manufacture, Craft Specialization, and Intrasite Variation at the Arroyo La Tinaja Site (204) in the Casas Grandes Region, Chihuahua, Mexico. Master's thesis, Department of Anthropology, University of Oklahoma, Norman.
Santley, Robert S., Michael J. Berman, and Rani T. Alexander
 1991   The Politicization of the Mesoamerican Ballgame and Its Implications for the Interpretation of the Distribution of Ball Courts in Central Mexico. In *The Mesoamerican Ballgame,* edited by V. Scarborough and D. Wilcox, pp. 3–24. Tucson: University of Arizona Press.
Sayles, E. B.
 1936a  *Some Southwestern Pottery Types, Series V.* Medallion Papers No. 21. Globe, Ariz.: Gila Pueblo.

Sayles, E. B.

    1936b   *An Archaeological Survey of Chihuahua, Mexico.* Medallion Papers No. 22. Globe, Ariz.: Gila Pueblo.

Schaafsma, Curtis F., and Carroll L. Riley

    1999   Introduction to *The Casas Grandes World,* edited by C. F. Schaafsma and C. L. Riley, pp. 3–11. Salt Lake City: University of Utah Press.

Schmidt, Kari

    2005   Faunal Remains for Sites 204 and 242, Chihuahua, Mexico. Manuscript on file at the Department of Anthropology, University of Tulsa, Okla.

Shackley, M. Steven

    2005   *Obsidian: Geology and Archaeology in the North American Southwest.* Tucson: University of Arizona Press.

Shafer, Harry J.

    2003   *Mimbres Archaeology at the NAN Ranch Ruin.* Albuquerque: University of New Mexico Press.

Shott, Michael J.

    1986   Technological Organization and Settlement Mobility: An Ethnographic Examination. *Journal of Anthropological Research* 42(1): 15–51.

    1992   Radiocarbon Dating as a Probabilistic Technique. *American Antiquity* 57(2): 202–30.

Silva, R. Jane

    1997   *Introduction to the Study and Analysis of Flaked Stone Artifacts and Lithic Technology.* Tucson: Center for Desert Archaeology.

Skibo, James B.

    1992   *Pottery Function: A Use-Alteration Perspective.* New York: Plenum Press.

Skibo, James B., Eugene B. McCluney, and William Walker

    2002   *The Joyce Well Site on the Frontier of the Casas Grandes World.* Salt Lake City: University of Utah Press.

Smith, Carol A.

    1977   Regional Economic Systems: Linking Geographical Models and Socioeconomic Problems. In *Regional Analysis.* Vol. 1, *Social and Economic Systems,* edited by C. A. Smith, pp. 3–68. New York: Academic Press.

Sobolik, Kristin D., Laurie S. Zimmerman, and Brooke M. Guilfoyl

    1997   Indoor Versus Outdoor Firepit Usage: A Case Study from the Mimbres. *Kiva* 62(3): 283–300.

Sphren, Maria S.

    2003   Social Complexity and the Specialist Potters of Casas Grandes in Northern Mexico. Ph.D. diss., Department of Anthropology, University of New Mexico, Albuquerque.

Spielmann, Katherine A., ed.

    1998   *Migration and Reorganization: The Pueblo IV Period in the American Southwest.* Anthropological Research Papers 51. Tempe: Arizona State University.

Stewart, Joe D., Jane H. Kelley, A. C. MacWilliams, and Paula J. Reimer

    2005   The Viejo Period of Chihuahua Culture in Northwestern Mexico. *Latin American Antiquity* 16(2): 169–92.

Stewart, Joe D., A. C. MacWilliams, and Jane H. Kelley

    2004   Archaeological Chronology of West Central Chihuahua. In *Surveying the Archaeology of Northwest Mexico,* edited by G. E. Newell and E. Gallaga, pp. 205–45. Salt Lake City: University of Utah Press.

Stuiver, M., P. J. Reimer, E. Bard, J. W. Beck, G. S. Burr, K. A. Hughen, B. Kromer, G. McCormac, J. Van der Plicht, and M. Spurk

    1998   INTCAL98 Radiocarbon Age Calibration, 24,000–0 cal B.P. *Radiocarbon* 40(3): 1041–83.

Swanson, Steven J.

    2003   Documenting Prehistoric Communication Networks: A Case Study in the Paquimé Polity. *American Antiquity* 68(4): 753–67.

Szarka, Heather J.
2006    Exotica and Ritual Power at Casas Grandes and La Tinaja: Two Contemporary Sites in Northwest Chihuahua, Mexico. Master's thesis, Department of Anthropology, University of Oklahoma, Norman.

Szuter, Christine R.
1991a   Hunting by Hohokam Desert Farmers. *Kiva* 56(3): 277–92.
1991b   *Hunting by Prehistoric Horticulturalists in the American Southwest.* New York: Garland.

Szuter, Christine R., and Frank E. Bayham
1989    Sedentism and Prehistoric Animal Procurement among Desert Horticulturalists of the North American Southwest. In *Farmers as Hunters: The Implications of Sedentism,* edited by Susan Kent, pp. 80–95. Cambridge: Cambridge University Press.

Taylor, R. E.
1987    *Radiocarbon Dating: An Archaeological Perspective.* New York: Academic Press.
1997    Radiocarbon Dating. In *Chronometric Dating in Archaeology,* edited by R. E. Taylor and M. J. Aitken, pp. 65–96. New York: Plenum Press.

Townsend, Richard F.
2005    Casas Grandes in the Art of the Ancient Southwest. In *Casas Grandes and the Ceramic Art of the Ancient Southwest,* edited by R. F. Townsend, pp. 1–28. Chicago: Art Institute of Chicago.

Turner, Raymond, Robert H. Webb, Janice E. Bowers, and James Rodney Hastings
2003    *The Changing Mile Revisited.* Tucson: University of Arizona Press.

Van Dyke, Ruth
2004    Memory, Meaning, and Masonry: The Late Bonito Chacoan Landscape. *American Antiquity* 69(3): 413–31.

VanPool, Christine S.
2003a   *The Symbolism of Casas Grandes.* Ph.D. diss., Department of Anthropology, University of New Mexico, Albuquerque.
2003b   The Shaman-Priests of the Casas Grandes Region, Chihuahua, Mexico. *American Antiquity* 68(4): 696–718.

VanPool, Christine S., and Todd L. VanPool
2007    *Signs of the Casas Grandes Shamans.* Salt Lake City: University of Utah Press.

VanPool, Todd, and Robert D. Leonard
2002    Specialized Ground Stone Production in the Casas Grandes Region of Northern Chihuahua, Mexico. *American Antiquity* 67(4): 710–30.

VanPool, Todd, Christine VanPool, R. Cruz, R. Leonard, and M. Harmon
2000    Flaked Stone and Social Interaction in the Casas Grandes Region, Chihuahua, Mexico. *Latin American Antiquity* 11(2): 163–74.

Vargas, Victoria D.
1995    *Copper Bell Trade Patterns in the Prehispanic U.S. Southwest and Northern Mexico.* Archaeological Series 187. Tucson: Arizona State Museum.
2004    Shell Identifications from Surveyed and Excavated Sites in the Casas Grandes Area, Chihuahua, Mexico. Manuscript on file at the Department of Anthropology, University of Tulsa, Okla.

Ward, G. K., and S. R. Wilson
1978    Procedures for Comparing and Combining Radiocarbon Age Determinations: A Critique. *Archaeometry* 20(1): 19–31.

Webster, Grady L., and Conrad J. Bahre
2001    *Changing Plant Life of La Frontera: Observations on Vegetation in the U.S./Mexico Borderlands.* Albuquerque: University of New Mexico Press.

Whalen, Michael E.
1981    The Origin and Evolution of Ceramics in Western Texas. *Bulletin of the Texas Archaeological Society* 52: 215–29.

Whalen, Michael E.
1998    Ceramic Vessel Size Estimation from Sherds: An Experiment and a Case Study. *Journal of Field Archaeology* 25(2): 219–27.

Whalen, Michael E., and Paul E. Minnis
1996a    Studying Complexity in Northern Mexico: The Paquimé Regional System. In *Debating Complexity: Proceedings of the 26th Chacmool Conference,* edited by D. A. Meyer, P. C. Dawson, and D. T. Hanna, pp. 161–68. Calgary: Archaeological Association and Department of Archaeology, University of Calgary.

1996b    Ball Courts and Political Centralization in the Casas Grandes Region. *American Antiquity* 61(4): 732–46.

1997    Investigaciones especializas sobre el sistema regional de Paquimé, Chihuahua, México. Report to the Consejo de Arqueología, INAH.

2001a    *Casas Grandes and Its Hinterland: Prehistoric Regional Organization in Northwest Mexico.* Tucson: University of Arizona Press.

2001b    Architecture and Authority in the Casas Grandes Region, Chihuahua, Mexico. *American Antiquity* 66(4): 651–99.

2003    The Local and the Distant in the Origin of Casas Grandes, Chihuahua, Mexico. *American Antiquity* 68(2): 314–32.

Wheat, Joe Ben
1967    A Paleo-Indian Bison Kill. *Scientific American* 2161: 44–52.

Wilcox, David
1986    A Historical Analysis of the Problem of Southwestern-Mesoamerican Connections. In *Ripples in the Chichimec Sea: New Considerations of Southwestern-Mesoamerican Interactions,* edited by F. J. Mathien and R. H. McGuire, pp. 9–44. Center for Archaeological Investigations. Carbondale: Southern Illinois University Press.

1999    A Peregrine View of Macroregional Systems in the North American Southwest, A.D. 750–1250. In *Great Towns and Regional Polities in the Prehistoric American Southwest and Southeast,* edited by J. E. Neitzel, pp. 115–42. Dragoon, Ariz.: Amerind Foundation; Albuquerque: University of New Mexico Press.

Wilcox, David R., and L. O. Shenk
1977    *The Architecture of the Casa Grande and Its Interpretation.* Archaeological Series 115. Tucson: Arizona State Museum.

Wilshusen, Richard H., and Ruth M. Van Dyke
2006    Chaco's Beginnings. In *The Archaeology of Chaco Canyon: An Eleventh-Century Pueblo Regional Center,* edited by S. H. Lekson, pp. 211–60. Santa Fe, N.M.: School of American Research Press.

Wilson, S. R., and G. K. Ward
1981    Evaluation and Clustering of Radiocarbon Age Determinations: Procedures and Paradigms. *Archaeometry* 23(1): 19–39.

Windes, Thomas C.
2003    This Old House: Construction and Abandonment at Pueblo Bonito. In *Pueblo Bonito, Center of the Chacoan World,* edited by Jill E. Neitzel, pp. 14–32. Washington, D.C.: Smithsonian Books.

Wiseman, Regge N.
1986    *An Initial Study of the Origins of Chupadero Black-on-White.* Albuquerque: Albuquerque Archaeological Society.

# INDEX

# ABOUT THE AUTHORS

**Michael E. Whalen** received his Ph.D. in anthropology and archaeology from the University of Michigan in 1976. He currently holds the rank of professor in the Department of Anthropology at the University of Tulsa. His research interests include complex societies, processes of sociocultural evolution, and prehistoric social structure. His technical interest is ceramic analysis. He began his career in Mesoamerica, where his dissertation excavation was at a Formative period community occupied between ca. 1600 and 500 B.C. The work was done under the auspices of Dr. Kent V. Flannery's Oaxaca Human Ecology Project. Between 1975 and 1986, he conducted large-scale surveys and excavations in the southern deserts of the U.S. Southwest, around El Paso, Texas. This area is only about 200 km from Casas Grandes, and imported Chihuahuan pottery is found on its prehistoric Pueblo period sites. It was while working here that he became interested in Casas Grandes. Since 1989, he has been investigating the Casas Grandes regional system through a program of large-scale surveys and excavations in northwestern Chihuahua.

His publications include *Excavations at Santo Domingo Tomaltepec: Evolution of a Formative Community in the Valley of Oaxaca, Mexico* (Memoir No. 12 of the University of Michigan Museum of Anthropology, 1981), *Turquoise Ridge and Late Prehistoric Residential Mobility in the Desert Mogollon Region* (University of Utah Press, 1994), and *Casas Grandes and Its Hinterland: Prehistoric Regional Organization in Northwest Chihuahua, Mexico* (University of Arizona Press, 2001). He also has written a series of monographs, journal articles, and book chapters on Oaxaca, western Texas, and northwestern Chihuahua. His research has been supported by the National Science Foundation and the National Geographic Society.

**Paul E. Minnis** received his Ph.D. in anthropology and archaeology from the University of Michigan in 1981. He is professor of anthropology at the University of Oklahoma. His research interests include paleoethnobiology, human ecology, and the prehistory of the U.S. Southwest and northern Mexico. His early work was done in the Mimbres area of southwestern New Mexico, where his dissertation, done as a part of the long-term work of the Mimbres Foundation, focused on social adaptations to food stress among the prehistoric populations. Since then, he has carried out other survey and excavation work in those parts of New Mexico and Arizona that border on the Republic of Mexico and that formed the outer edges of the interaction sphere that focused on Casas Grandes. His most recent work includes investigation through survey and excavation of the Casas Grandes regional system in northwestern Chihuahua.

His publications include *Social Adaptation to Food Stress* (University of Chicago Press, 1985), *Perspectives on Southwestern Prehistory* (Westview Press, 1990), *Biodiversity and Native America* (University of Oklahoma Press, 2000), *Ethnobotany: A Reader* (University of Oklahoma Press, 2000), *Casas Grandes and Its Hinterland* (University of Arizona Press, 2001), *People and Plants in Ancient Eastern North America* (Smithsonian Books, 2003), *People and Plants in Ancient Western North America* (Smithsonian Books, 2004), and a series of journal articles and book chapters on the U.S. Southwest and on northern Mexico. His research has been supported by the National Science Foundation, the National Geographic Society, and the Kaplan Foundation for Latin American Research.